Women Strike for Peace

Women Strike for Peace

TRADITIONAL MOTHERHOOD
AND RADICAL POLITICS
IN THE 1960s

AMY SWERDLOW

THE UNIVERSITY OF CHICAGO PRESS
CHICAGO AND LONDON

AMY SWERDLOW is professor of history at
Sarah Lawrence College.

The University of Chicago Press, Chicago 60637
The University of Chicago Press, Ltd., London
© 1993 by The University of Chicago
All rights reserved. Published 1993
Printed in the United States of America

02 01 00 99 98 97 96 95 94 93   5 4 3 2 1

ISBN (cloth): 0-226-78635-8
ISBN (paper): 0-226-78636-6

Library of Congress Cataloging-in-Publication Data

Swerdlow, Amy.
    Women strike for peace : traditional motherhood and
radical politics in the 1960s / Amy Swerdlow.
        p.   cm. — (Women in culture and society)
    Includes bibliographical references and index.
    ISBN 0-226-78635-8. — ISBN 0-226-78636-6 (pbk.)
    1. Women Stike for Peace—History.   2. Women and peace—
History.   3. Peace movements—United States—History.   4.
Women in politics—United States—History.   5. Vietnamese
Conflict, 1961–1975—Protest movements—United States.
I. Title.   II. Series.
JX1965.S94   1993
327.1'72'082—dc20   93-16801
                                                               CIP

∞ The paper used in this publication meets the minimum re-
quirements of the American National Standard for Information
Sciences—Permanence of Paper for Printed Library Materials,
ANSI-Z39.48-1994.

For
STANLEY SWERDLOW AND JOAN KELLY

Contents

Photo galleries follow pages 48, 96, and 158.

Foreword

On 1 November 1961, a year after John F. Kennedy was elected president of the United States, thousands of American housewives did something absurd. They went on strike in 60 communities. Their goal was nothing less than peace on earth and the control of nuclear weapons. On their picket signs they printed the slogan, "End the Arms Race, Not the Human Race." Women Strike for Peace (WSP), a movement as vivid as America, had given birth to itself.

In 1961, Amy Swerdlow was a housewife on Long Island, the mother of three children. She was one of the thousands. Within a few months, she was happily planning strategy, editing newsletters, and, pregnant with a fourth child, flying to Geneva with a WSP delegation to plead with a Soviet diplomat to make the world safe for her child. In 1972, after a decade of activity, she returned to gradutate school to earn a Ph.D. and to become a professor of history who applied her skills to the study of women in peace movements.

Amy Swerdlow is also my friend. For years, I have watched her live, research, and write *Women Strike for Peace*. She was drafting her last chapters as the Cold War ended and the number of "regional conflicts" increased. She had resolved that the record of WSP would not disappear as flagrantly as that of previous women's peace movements. Indeed, she writes ruefully of how little WSP knew of these mothering movements—of Julia Ward Howe's appeal for peace in 1870, or the Women's Peace Party in 1915, or the Women's International League for Peace and Freedom. Her book is an immense and necessary labor of love, a testimony to both the movement in which Swerdlow came of political age and the imperfect people who, beyond all expediency and often beyond common sense, yearn for social justice. Unlike some labors of love, *Women Strike for Peace* is direct, honest, and mindful of the claims of evidence. Swerdlow is a dreamer and a historian. The dreamer believes in social justice and peace. The historian refuses to permit the dreamer to romanticize the past; the investigator tempers the dreamer's Utopianism with skepticism.

In 1961, Swerdlow was like most of the women who started WSP. She was affluent, white, educated, and optimistic. Embracing post-1945

ix

culture, she believed that she best served her community, family, and herself by being an enthusiastic wife and mother. As a child, she had grown up in Left and liberal circles. She had been a "red diaper baby," born into a quarrelsome, poor family that then had Communist and Socialist sympathies. Although she built a life of marriage and motherhood that hid her political identity, it persisted—like a foundation. Significantly, that submerged identity did not include the women's movement. Although WSP was a beneficiary of the First Wave feminism that struggled for women's education and suffrage, WSP's self-image was feminine, not feminist.

By 1961, the founders of WSP were angry, passionately and rightly so. They were mothers whose sanctioned task was to nurture children and human life. Yet, the nuclear arms race threatened to annihilate their children and all human life in a man-made apocalypse. Stronium 90 was detected in babies' milk. WSP implored both the Soviet Union and the United States, the nuclear combatants of the Cold War, to change.

Other peace groups were issuing the same urgent plea, but WSP, Swerdlow shows, was different. First, it refused to be a conventional, hierarchical organization. It prided itself on spontaneity, lack of structure, the autonomy of local groups. Next, the members of WSP appealed to the public, with canny skill, *as* housewives and mothers. Consciously or unconsciously, their rhetoric was maternalist. One of Swerdlow's most vital stories is what happens when women simultaneously run a public, political movement and define themselves as domestic, apolitical beings. Although people often compared the activities of WSP to the classical Greek comedy *Lysistrata,* Swerdlow finds the analogy inadequate. For Lysistrata and her companions, a band of sisters, berate and revile war-mongering men. The members of WSP, though they gained strength and took pleasure from being in a band of women, cast themselves as wives and mothers who loved the men in their lives and wanted to save them. This motive was so compelling that women would go public, demonstrate while they pushed baby carriages, speak, march, picket, petition, write research reports and press releases. Some husbands were more supportive than others of the consequences of this devotion for the dinner table and laundry pile.

By 1963, WSP had amazing successes, beyond all its dreams and prophecies. Making both dissent against the superpowers and superpower cooperation more respectable, WSP had helped to change the discourse of the Cold War. Making nuclear war less respectable, WSP had aided in the ratification of a treaty that banned atmospheric nuclear testing. It had also created a debacle for the House Un-American Activities Committee, that perversion of democracy. Under FBI surveillance since the beginning, members of WSP were subpoenaed by the Committee in 1962. Their appearance, shrewdly planned and bravely executed, was a comic masterpiece. Women jammed the committee room, rose in support when witnesses were called, applauded the performances of these witnesses, wore flowers and gave out bouquets, and dandled babies. "Peace Gals," read one headline, in the rhetoric of the day, "Make Red Hunters Look Silly."

Given their successes, given the exhilaration that success breeds, WSP wanted to go on after 1963. It shifted its focus from the Cold War to the Vietnamese War, a focus that endured until the end of the war in 1973. I remember being a part of one activity that WSP helped to organize, the Jeannette Rankin Brigade (or Rank and File), named after the first woman to serve in Congress, who voted against the entry of the United States into World War I and World War II. A coalition of women from the black civil rights movement, peace movement, and feminism, we took a train to Washington, D.C., on 15 January 1969. There, on a cold and snowy day, we marched through the streets of our capital, stamping our booted feet and exercising our First Amendment rights, calling on our country to stop the killing.

Mobilizing against the Vietnamese War, WSP embarked upon three activities that Swerdlow analyzes lucidly. First, led by the redoubtable Bella Abzug, it entered, despite misgivings, the domain of electoral politics. Next, it organized and supported resistance to the draft. Confronting the *machismo* of the New Left, WSP took on the supple role of the self-sacrificing, protective mother of young men. Finally, again with some strong misgivings, especially about cooperation with official Soviet women's groups, WSP became a part of international women's coalitions designed to end war and violence. Their only weapons were the empowering quality of these coalitions, the passion of their convictions, rhetoric, and, in one demonstration against NATO in the Netherlands, some tulips.

These activities irrevocably altered WSP. Electoral politics entailed the abandonment of a purely moral, apolitical standpoint for the impurities of party politics. Antidraft counseling meant leaving a separatist, middle-class women's group to work with male-dominated organizations and, more fortunately, across class lines. The consequences of international coalitions were perhaps even more complex. One was the encounter between WSP and feminism. Young radical American feminists often lashed out against WSP's gender politics like belligerent daughters with a laggard Mom. Bit by bit, the Moms of WSP became feminists. Swerdlow notes an irony of this evolution. As members of

WSP became "re-entry women," returning to school and the work force, they began to devalue the volunteerism that had made WSP possible.

Another result of internationalism was the friendships between WSP members and Vietnamese women, from both South and North. WSP people visited North Vietnam and the organization served as a liaison between American prisoners of war and their families. Swerdlow is too scrupulous not to ask if WSP was too gullible, too uncritical of Vietnamese Communism. In the early 1960s, conservatives had accused WSP of being a "dupe" of Soviet Communism. Although WSP probably had few Communist members, and although Swerdlow was not alone in having a Communist or Socialist background, she argues convincingly that this accusation was false and malicious. Sorting through WSP's relations with Vietnam, she presents a more difficult history. She tenderly remembers the friendships between American and Vietnamese women. She also states that postwar Vietnamese politics might have been far less repressive if women had continued to be a powerful part of the government and if America had not waged such a long, destructive war in the first place. Yet, she suggests, WSP had its blindnesses, for example, to the realities of the prisoner-of-war camps in North Vietnam. Here, and elsewhere, WSP reflected the fractures of modern politics and some of the problems of American radicalism.

I am proud of my friend's book, of the historian who has listened to and judged her younger self. Without *Women Strike for Peace,* women's history, indeed contemporary history, would be the poorer. Those thousands of women in November 1961, despite their frailties, were witnesses in a tradition as necessary as food and shelter. Unless men and women do strike for peace, "ethnic cleansers" and barbarians with missiles will bring us to our knees and our children to their doom.

Catharine R. Stimpson
Rutgers University

Acknowledgments

Both activists and scholars have inspired and informed this book. My thanks go first to my sisters in Women Strike for Peace, whose words and deeds, hopes, and demands animate every page. I am indebted to Dagmar Wilson, WSP's founder and spokesperson in the 1960s, for her support and cooperation in the preparation of this study, and for being the perceptive, spontaneous, and reflective leader and friend she was then and is now.

I have benefited enormously from the generosity and the insights of Bella Abzug, Barbara Bick, Mary Clarke, Madeline Duckles, Mickey Flacks, Folly Fodor, the late Ruth Gage-Colby, the late Eleanor Garst, Lorraine Gordon, Hazel Grossman, Frances Herring, Lyla Hoffman, Judy Lerner, Ethel Taylor, and Cora Weiss. All of these friends and colleagues gave hours to interviews, questions, discussions, and debates about our days in WSP. They also contributed flyers, photos, letters, scrapbooks, and clippings. Thanks also go to Dorothy Marder for being WSP's brilliant photographic eye in the 1970s, and to Jeanne Shulman, the coordinator of the New York City office, for providing a number of the photos I have used.

Joan Kelly (1928–82) and Gerda Lerner, my teachers in the M.A. program in women's history at Sarah Lawrence College, set me on the path that led to this book. Kelly's talent for history, theory, and friendship, her clarity of vision, her generous spirit, and her commitment to woman's cause are a never-ending source of inspiration. I owe much to Gerda Lerner's creativity and energy as a teacher and to her audacious scholarship. Lerner's analysis of female culture and women's movements for social transformation has helped to shape my analysis of WSP.

My mentors and friends at Rutgers University, Judith Walkowitz and the late Warren Susman, were generous with their time and advice. Walkowitz, particularly, made important contributions to the conceptualization of this history of WSP at the dissertation stage. A Woodrow Wilson National Fellowship Foundation Women's Studies Dissertation Grant in 1980 and support from the Rutgers University History Department helped me to complete the research on WSP and the test-ban treaty.

The loving friendship of Alice Kessler Harris, Blanche Cook, Grace Paley, Eva Kollisch, Phyllis Kriegel, Jane Gould, Judith Papachristou, and Sandi Cooper, as well as their own dedication to a world of peace and social justice, has kept this project fresh for me over the many years it gestated. Marilyn Young read this book at various stages, much to my benefit. I have been instructed and delighted by her witty and frequently brilliant comments. Florence Howe, with her unfailing eye and ear, read an early version of the book. She prodded, and urged me on when I most needed it. Martin Fleisher read every version. His expertise in political theory and his loving support were crucial in the final stage. Jean Bethke Elshtain's interest in WSP and her understanding of its transformative impact on traditional notions of motherhood and peace politics gladdened my heart, as did the encouragement of Sheila Tobias.

The stimulating circle of writers, teachers, and activists, including Lourdes Beneria, Carol Cohn, Dorothy Dinnerstein, Adrienne Harris, Ynestra King, Rhoda Linton, Phyllis Mack, Sara Ruddick, and Anne Snitow, that met regularly in a feminist peace study group in 1983 and 1984, and the subsequent "motherist" study group organized by Temma Kaplan, in which Dana Frank, Meredith Tax, and Marjorie Agosin participated, were vital to the formulation of many of the theoretical and tactical questions I have addressed. Sara Ruddick's comments and encouragement helped to convince me that the story of WSP was not only an important part of peace history but also a building block in the construction of a theory of feminism and the struggle for peace.

It was Catharine Stimpson's editorial presence that actually brought this project to publication. Her discernment, coupled with patience and confidence, were what I needed. The fact that so many scholars have read this book, or discussed its thesis with me, makes it imperative that I declare myself solely responsible for any errors in judgment or failures of imagination.

I am indebted to the archivists at the Swarthmore College Peace Collection, Jean Soderlund and Wendy Chmielewski, for their cooperation in creating the WSP document collection and for their enthusiastic help with all research questions and problems. My thanks go also to Roseanne Berstein, Charling Fagan, Judy Kicinski, and Stephanie Pfaff at the Sarah Lawrence College Library for their patience and their aid in locating and securing hard-to-find books, articles, and manuscripts. Special thanks go to Melanie Gustafson, Anette Igra, Maureen McCarthy, Margaret Haas, Kathy Sarno, and Elizabeth McCall for their enthusiastic help in research as they pursued their own graduate studies. Karen Wilson at the University of Chicago Press was generous with her editorial guidance, as was Candace Rossin with advice and help. I am particularly grateful to Joann Hoy for her careful and patient copy editing.

I want to recognize my children, Joan, Ezra, Lisa, and Tommy, for providing the motivation for my own participation in WSP. I am profoundly grateful for their faith in my efforts, even when they were too young to understand them fully. It was for them, and for my grandchildren, Jessica, Alexis, and Nick, and the world they inherit, that Women Strike for Peace was founded and this book was written. Finally, I want to thank my husband and friend, Stanley Swerdlow, for his support and his belief in me, and "the cause," from the day WSP was born until his death in 1991.

Introduction

My goals in this narrative history and organizational study of Women Strike for Peace (WSP) are threefold: to restore a significant women's movement of the 1960s to the historical record from which it has all but disappeared; to probe the political, social, and gender consciousness that moved "ordinary housewives" to militant political action in the name of motherhood; and to examine the seeming contradiction between the traditionalist rhetoric of WSP and its radical political stand in the context of debates among scholars and activists regarding the relationship of female culture to the political empowerment of women.

WSP was born on 1 November 1961, when thousands of mainly white, middle-class women staged a one-day national peace protest. At a time when the public image of women was domestic and maternal rather than political, and passive rather than active, an estimated fifty thousand women in over sixty communities came out of their kitchens and off their jobs to demand that President Kennedy "End the Arms Race—Not the Human Race." The call to strike came from a small group of women in Washington, D.C., who identified themselves only as "concerned housewives." They were moved to drastic action, they declared, by the Soviet resumption of atmospheric nuclear tests, after a three-year moratorium, and by the United States' declaration that it would hold its own tests in retaliation. According to WSP founder Dagmar Wilson, the women were also alarmed by the Soviet-American confrontation over the Berlin Wall, which raised the specter of a nuclear war between the United States and the USSR, either by accident or design.

Most of the women who joined the strike, and the movement that grew out of it, were in their midthirties to late forties. They came from liberal to left political backgrounds, having been pacifists, Quakers, New Deal Democrats, socialists, anarchists, Communist sympathizers, or Communist party members in the years before and during World War II. By 1961 those who had been Communists seemed to be disillusioned with Soviet policies and with the CPUSA, but many still believed that the United States posed the greatest threat to world peace. (A more detailed profile of the WSP activists appears in chapter 3.) The majority

1

were college-educated women who had participated in the work force in the war years, many finding more interesting and satisfying employment than their older sisters and mothers had, because of the shortage of men. At the war's end most of the future WSP women left the work force, sometimes reluctantly, to contribute to the baby boom and to practice full-time live-in motherhood while populating the suburbs, along with millions of their white, middle-class cohorts.[1]

Many of the leading WSP women had prepared for careers, and a number had pursued them throughout the 1950s, but most who could afford to do so acceded to the pressure on educated women to use their talents where they were told that it counted most, in full-time parenting.[2] They took to heart the warnings, not of those extreme antifeminists who, like Marynia Farnham and Ferdinand Lundberg, authors of *Modern Woman: The Lost Sex*, scorned and denigrated female intellectuals and professionals as "masculine women," but of such liberal social critics as journalist and *Washington Post* publisher Agnes Meyer. During the war Meyer had called for support services for women workers, but in 1952 she was asserting that women could have many careers but "only one vocation—motherhood." Meyer urged fifties women to "boldly announce that no job is more exacting, more necessary, or more rewarding than that of housewife and mother."[3] In 1961 Meyer was still held in high regard by the WSP founders. They invited her to speak at the first strike meeting in Washington, D.C., but she apparently refused. The future WSPers were swayed also by comments like those of presidential candidate Adlai Stevenson, baby doctor Benjamin Spock, and the celebrated anthropologist Ashley Montagu. Montagu declared in an article in the liberal and antinuclear *Saturday Review* "that the making of human beings is far more important than the making of anything else, and that in the formative years of a child's life the mother is best equipped to provide those firm foundations upon which one can subsequently build."[4]

The women who joined the peace strike lived in a world where they seemed to have more options than the women of earlier generations to work outside the home and live independent lives. Yet they made the choice to devote themselves to live-in motherhood. They did this not only because the experts told them to do so, but also because their socialization, their role models, and family expectations called for and valued self-sacrifice. However, the future WSPers never became completely domesticated or privatized. They were the kind of women, judging by the concerns they expressed in WSP, whose devotion to children extended far beyond their own.

The women of WSP were beneficiaries of the first wave of feminism, which gave them a sense of entitlement to education and meaningful paid employment. They had lived through the Great Depression, the rise of fascism in Europe and Asia, World War II, the Holocaust, and Hiroshima. Like hundreds of thousands of their generation who had been involved in liberal or left politics prior to World War II, they were an optimistic group, believers in individual responsibility coupled with collective action for social betterment. In the period of Cold War consensus, when political, cultural and gender-role dissent was deemed deviant and dangerous, most of these women had withdrawn from the larger political arena into the Parent-Teacher Association (PTA), the League of Women Voters, church or temple social action groups, volunteer social services, local arts centers, or music societies. Some of the women had worked with the Democratic party, particularly in the Adlai Stevenson presidential campaign, but few had done more than clerical work, fund-raising, or local canvassing. Judging by the political agendas they brought to WSP in 1961, they had maintained a social conscience throughout the 1950s, reflected and refracted through the prism of motherhood, but they had found it difficult to find a significant place for themselves in the political spectrum.

These women rallied to WSP the moment they heard of it, because they were searching for a space in which their moral, political, and maternal stance could be translated into actions that they could initiate without interference by higher, usually male, authorities. In the process of transforming their successful one-day peace strike into a national movement with over one hundred locals, ten regional offices, and contacts all over the world, the organizers of WSP devised an innovative political style. The WSP method was characterized by a nonhierarchical, loosely structured "unorganizational" format that allowed autonomy to each chapter. Without a paid staff, designated organizers, or spokespersons, WSP developed a simple maternal rhetoric, spontaneous direct action on the local level, relentless political lobbying in Washington, and an instantly effective national telephone chain. At a time when politicians solemnly declared, "Better Dead than Red," and when the press and the public tended to dismiss peace advocates as either "commies" or "kooks," the image projected by WSP of respectable middle-class, middle-aged ladies, wearing white gloves and flowered hats, picketing the White House and protesting to the Kremlin to save their children and the planet, helped to legitimize a radical critique of the Cold War and U.S. militarism. By exposing the contradictions between mothers' responsibility for preserving life and the state's nuclear recklessness, WSP was able to gain public support for its attacks on such sacrosanct military and political institutions as the Pentagon, NATO, and the House Un-American Activities Committee (HUAC).

In its struggle for a nuclear test ban treaty and later against the war in Vietnam, WSP tapped a reservoir of dormant political outrage, organizational talent, political inventiveness, and a hunger for sisterly collaboration. Through participation in the WSP movement thousands of women who had identified themselves only as housewives found to their surprise that they could do serious research, write convincing flyers and pamphlets, speak eloquently in public, plan effective political strategies, organize successful long-range campaigns, and challenge male political leaders of the Left as well as the Right, to whom they had previously deferred. In a decade of struggle WSP moved from seeking to *influence* the men in Congress to do the right thing to electing one of its key women, Bella Abzug, to the U.S. House of Representatives, where she became a recognized leader.

WSP appeared on the horizon at a time when the regressive political and cultural consensus of the 1950s was giving way to a rising wave of dissent. The women of WSP helped to swell that wave and to create the climate of opinion that led to the partial test ban treaty of 1963. The movement continued to work against nuclear proliferation until 1965, when it found itself facing another pressing emergency—the escalation of U.S. military intervention in Vietnam. Again moral outrage and concern for the preservation of life moved the women to protest. WSP undertook a campaign to end the war, first demanding a negotiated settlement, then total U.S. withdrawal from Southeast Asia. Using legal pressure tactics such as petitions, demonstrations, letter writing, mass lobbies, and lawsuits, as well as illegal, nonviolent direct actions such as sit-ins in congressional offices, "die-ins" on the streets of major cities, and statements of complicity with draft resisters aimed at tying up the courts, WSP played an active and important role in the antiwar movement.

Yet the WSPers seemed to experience no sense of triumph as their stated political goals were achieved. The test ban treaty, they pointed out, was only partial, and nuclear arms continued to proliferate. WSP called for the seating of the People's Republic of China in the United Nations and the resumption of normal U.S. relations with China, but when that goal was achieved, it seemed relevant only to the Nixon administration's geopolitical goals. The war in Vietnam was winding down, but the policy of Cold War containment was escalating in Latin and Central America, and the ever-rising military budget made peace and economic justice at home seem more and more utopian.

Moreover, in the late 1960s and early 1970s the women of WSP were bewildered to find that their middle-class, middle-aged status and their political stance based on traditional notions of mothers' rights and responsibilities were dismissed and denigrated by the new Left, the counterculture, and the rising women's liberation movement. The WSP cadre were often confounded, and sometimes put off, by the disdain leveled at them by the radical young feminists who saw WSP as an example of their own mothers' "false consciousness." But their message was not lost on WSP. A decade of political struggle against the gendered uses of power, and a sense of personal efficacy and female solidarity based on working in a separatist movement, propelled the women to question and reexamine their assumptions regarding the female role in the family as well as in national and international politics. By 1970 WSP was marching in the first Women's Equality Day March, carrying a banner that read, "The Women of Vietnam Are Our Sisters."

In telling this story of the militant middle-aged, middle-class white mothers of WSP, I am also writing about myself. I was one of the thousands of women who struck for peace on 1 November 1961. I marched with hundreds of other New York women outside the U.S. Mission to the United Nations, carrying a placard that read, "No Tests, East or West." A few days prior to 1 November, a Great Neck, Long Island, neighbor, Lyla Hoffman, had called me to join the strike, which, she explained, was being organized by a Washington, D.C., woman named Dagmar Wilson. Wilson's call came at a critical moment for me, as it did for thousands of other women. I was indignant over the Russian resumption of testing and even more outraged by the fallout-shelter program that was being promoted vigorously in New York State by Governor Nelson Rockefeller. I had just been involved in an effort organized by a few woman in my community of Great Neck Estates to defeat a proposal for a community fallout shelter in our village hall. Having succeeded so easily in my first political effort in almost twenty years, I was ready to do more. I was particularly enthusiastic about the strike call from Washington because it charged *both* superpowers with nuclear irresponsibility and posed women as a moral third force. When I called Dagmar Wilson to offer my support, I was able to reach her. This I felt was a triumph because I did not know her husband's name, and in 1961 most women were not listed in the telephone directory under their given names. Wilson welcomed me into her ad hoc campaign and referred my name to Valerie Delacorte, who invited me to the first organizing meeting in New York City. Thus I became a WSP founder.

Like many of the other women I met in the movement, I was not a newcomer to peace activism or left politics. I had been a first-generation Red-diaper baby. My father, who was a Communist party member when I was a young child in the 1920s, and a party functionary as I was growing up in the 1930s, became rabidly anti-Soviet in the 1950s. My mother was an idealistic and romantic anarchist whose vision was so morally pure and utopian it could never encompass communism or even liberal party politics. She died in 1950, so I was never able to discuss WSP with her, but I know she would have approved of its nonideological moral stance and its international outlook. As a growing child I lived through the Depression among unemployed garment workers in the Workers Cooperative Colony, a housing development overlooking Bronx Park. My father explained to me that our apartment's large windows facing the park were designed especially to capture the sun for workers' children and for their fathers and mothers who never saw the light in the windowless factories in which they labored. My father, however, was not one of those laborers. He was a full-time paid official of his trade union.

The cooperative colony lost its building after the stock market crash of 1929, my father was blacklisted by his union for Communist activities, and we were threatened with eviction. My parents were in constant conflict with each other, a situation my father attributed to the miseries of the capitalist system. He explained to me that in Russia, a workers' paradise, there were no such things as unemployment, injustice, or deprivation—thus no fighting parents. Life was, indeed, difficult for us. There was never enough money for food, for doctor bills for my chronically ill mother, for toys, or for just plain fun. I did have books, however, many of which contained stories of class struggle written for "workers'" children. Two that stand out in my memory are *The Red Corner Book* and *Our Lenin*.

As a child, I often resented my father's stern political lectures because I experienced them as dismissive of my feelings and needs, but I never questioned his fanatical hatred of capitalism and his belief in a proletarian utopia. His vision of a socialist world without conflict or war promised the harmony I yearned for within my own home. I recognize now that I owe to my parents' belief in peace and justice the impulse to join WSP and my faith in collective action for the cause of humanity. I also owe to my mother's distrust of the ideological rigidity of the Communist party and her suspicion of political leaders lacking in humor, compassion, and humility my own utopian, and romantic, political dreams.

What I found particularly appealing about WSP as a political movement was its refusal to exclude Communists or former Communists from its ranks, while it resisted the dictates of any ideology or party. This was especially clear in the original and independent tactics WSP developed in 1962 to face its investigation by HUAC (discussed in chapter 5) and in its decision to protest the Soviet intervention in Czechoslovakia in 1968 (described in chapter 9).

As a teenager I was involved in popular front peace politics. I believed passionately in the Loyalist cause in Spain. Trembling with shyness and fear I would stand in subway cars at the age of fourteen, pleading for contributions to medical aid for republican Spain. I also recall picketing at dawn on Forty-second Street in support of "collective security" as the lights atop the New York Times Building flashed the news that Neville Chamberlain had signed the Munich pact. I was only fifteen years old, but I remember that I wept because I understood that fascism and war had prevailed. Once each year, in my high school days, I left my classroom for a one-hour strike in support of the Oxford Oath, which pledged me never to participate in any war my government might conduct. Striking for peace was not condoned in my high school, and the strikers were threatened with suspension. I was called to the office of the dean of girls, an intimidating experience in those days, and told that I would never be admitted to college because of my "record." I was frightened by the threat, which I hoped would be forgotten, but as a member of the American Student Union (ASU), a coalition of socialist and Communist youth opposed to militarism, I stood firm.[5] I was afraid for my future, but I knew that my parents would have been devastated if I had succumbed to pressure and played it safe.

Even while striking for peace, I admired and supported the young men who joined the Lincoln Brigade to fight against the Fascists in Spain. I believed in "collective security," which I interpreted as the military cooperation of the good people to isolate and defeat the bad. Being my father's daughter, I had no trouble including the Soviet Union among the good people and was neither alarmed nor put off by the influence of young Communists in the leadership of the ASU. I perceived them as brilliant and persuasive fighters for peace and justice.[6]

In 1940 I served as national high school secretary, a staff position in ASU. This was the period when ASU declared that the war in Europe was a phony war and that "The Yanks Are Not Coming over There." We campaigned actively against the Selective Training and Service Act of 1940 and continued through 1941 to oppose American involvement in the European war. Eileen Eagan reports that after the Germans invaded the Soviet Union, ASU's "Yanks Are Not Coming" poster was put aside for "All Out Aid to the Allies."[7] I don't remember the posters being changed, but I do recall that I was confused and demoralized as ASU voted in December 1941, immediately after the Japanese attack on Pearl Harbor, to disband itself. I wanted desperately to see Germany and Japan defeated, but at the same time I felt that we had been inconsistent and had betrayed our principles.

By the late 1940s I had lost all interest in politics, in part because I could not express my deepening doubts about Russian domestic and foreign policies for fear it would place me on the side of the Red baiters and Cold Warriors who seemed determined to overturn progressive public policy gains and repress all radical dissent. I turned away from

politics to the traditional female pursuits of child rearing and nest building because I found both the politics of the mainstream and the old Left
lacking in simple humanity and morality. By the mid-1950s I had married, given birth to three children—two girls and a boy—and was living
the life of a suburban mother and housewife. I supported the causes of
civil liberties and civil rights, but I gave most of my energy to the local
community arts center, where my children took music and dance lessons and I studied painting. Although I was a driving force in the North
Shore Community Arts Center and my husband was an occasional master of ceremonies at center events, it was he who was elected president.
I thought that was as it should be, because I and the other women involved in the day-to-day leadership did not want the center to look like
a ladies' club.

A fourth child, a son, was born in August 1962, when I was already
active in WSP. In March of that year I carried him, in utero, to Geneva
to the Seventeen-Nation Disarmament Conference, to participate in the
WSP lobby for a test ban treaty described in chapter 9. In Geneva I
demanded from Valerian Zorin and Arthur Dean, the Russian and U.S.
chief negotiators, that they act immediately to protect my unborn child
from the nuclear contamination of the atmosphere that we in WSP already perceived as dangerous to health and life. As I pointed to my own
abdomen, I was careful to explain that my concern was not private, that
I was pleading for all the world's children, born and yet unborn.

For the rest of the decade I functioned as a "key woman" in WSP, a
term used for those who took part in local and national planning meetings or acted as links in the communications chain. I attended the first
national conference, which drafted the WSP policy statement, and because I was one of the key activists in New York who was not subpoenaed by HUAC, I helped to plan the strategy and the rhetoric for WSP's
confrontation with the committee. I also helped to draft the WSP statement of complicity with draft resisters and served as editor of the WSP
national publication, *MEMO*, from 1970 to 1973.

WSP helped me to find my own political voice and to act in my own
name. It took me out of the suburbs to many parts of the world, including embattled Laos and Vietnam, without feeling guilty about leaving
my children. My justification for what some of us self-deprecatingly
called "movement jet-setting" was that WSPers had to leave the home
to save it. I did not know then that this was an argument used by
women abolitionists, moral reformers, and peace activists since the
early nineteenth century.

My work with WSP was joyful and empowering. I was enchanted by
Dagmar Wilson's wit, sense of irony, British accent, and firm moral
stance. I was captivated by the Washington founders' simple, nonide-

ological rhetoric and disdain for hierarchical structure. I sensed that this was a new political mode, a woman's style, one with which I could be comfortable. I still consider my years in WSP as the happiest and most exhilarating of my life. Making political decisions that I believed mattered, issuing calls that invoked a response, confronting male authority both on the Right and the Left were heady experiences. I felt that I was free, at last, of my father's ideological politics, and of all the fathers who had led all the failed political movements of the past.

WSP gave me, a suburban housewife-mother, the opportunity to engage in challenging intellectual and political work, to interact collectively and noncompetitively with women I respected, and to take personal risks. WSP not only enhanced my sense of political and personal worth, it eventually sparked my interest in feminism, particularly women's efforts to achieve political power and affect social change.

In 1961 I knew nothing of women's history. One evidence of my ignorance still causes me shame and pain. It is my meeting with Gertrude Baer in Geneva in 1962. I encountered Baer, who was then the international secretary of the Women's International League for Peace and Freedom (WILPF), while I was serving as advance party for a WSP mission to the Seventeen-Nation Disarmament Conference. I asked her for help in finding my way through the maze of international organizations, agencies, embassies, and missions in Geneva. At that time I viewed Baer as a well-informed, opinionated old woman, possessing far too much knowledge about the status of diplomatic negotiations and protocol for WSP purposes. The fact that Baer was a professional peace bureaucrat in Geneva concerned with laws, conventions, and resolutions gave her less value in my eyes than the housewives with whom I was engaged in dramatic and militant direct action. I also faulted her generation for failing to prevent World War II and the Holocaust, and I was convinced, at that time, that we in WSP would do better, because global survival was at stake. I demanded a good deal of service from Baer for our delegation, but I took little advice. In no way did I give her the deep respect and admiration I have since come to feel for her important role in women's peace history; for her courage in coming to the International Congress of Women at the Hague in 1915 while her country, Germany, was at war; and for her outstanding leadership in organizing women's opposition to the Versailles Treaty. Baer, a founder of WILPF, was also one of the first to point out how few women were represented among the top leadership and bureaucrats at the United Nations.[8]

We WSPers in Geneva never asked Gertrude Baer to address us, not only because we did not know her history but also because in 1962, like others in the radical movements of our time, we regarded history as irrelevant. We saw ourselves as new, bold, and potentially successful. We believed we would accomplish what the WILPF women had failed to do. We chose to use the rhetoric of motherhood even in Geneva because it was clear to us that the language of diplomacy and pacifism had failed. As for feminist discourse, most of us had never heard of the first wave, and the second wave was only in formation.

In 1972, when the Vietnam War was winding down and the feminist movement was on the rise, I decided to enter the M.A. program in women's history at Sarah Lawrence College. Having been exposed to feminist thinking while working as one of the planners of the Jeannette Rankin Brigade, a woman's antiwar demonstration that took place on 15 January 1969, I was determined to learn more about the historical forces that had shaped my life and dictated the choices I had made as a woman. My M.A. essay was on the New York Ladies' Anti-slavery Society, a women's political movement of the 1830s that based its radical politics on traditional female culture very much as WSP did, with the same kind of problems and deficits.[9] As I studied abolitionist women, I was often saddened or enraged by the knowledge that my generation had been robbed of the history of our radical foremothers. I decided to write the story of WSP to pass on the history of its accomplishments and its unresolved political and gender problems to future generations of women who will be carrying on the fight for world peace. Noting that the first wave of historians of the 1960s was continuing to ignore women in the peace struggle, I determined to make WSP's campaign for the test ban treaty of 1963 the subject of my doctoral dissertation at Rutgers University.[10] But the history of the WSP campaign for the partial test ban treaty of 1963 is not the whole story. It does not deal with the campaign to end the Vietnam War, WSP's contribution to ending the draft, and the way in which the middle-aged women of WSP were overshadowed by the youth movement and the counterculture and jolted by the women's rights movement. These are the themes of this book.

When I turned to the systematic study of WSP, investigating the goals, program, tactics, internal debates, and public rhetoric of the movement as well as the political and gender consciousness of its key women, I made scrupulous efforts to apply to it the same kinds of political and social analysis I would give to any other movement for social change. I have included my own political history to make clear my background and biases. I share Sara Evans's concern in writing *Personal Politics* that she might substitute autobiography for the history of women's civil rights activism in the 1960s and fail to ask questions and hear answers that challenged her assumptions.[11] This is always a danger for any historian. I also want to make clear that this study is not the work of a participant observer. It is true that in the 1960s and early 1970s I was an active participant in WSP, but I was not a conscious or systematic observer. My research and analysis for this book were undertaken twenty years later.

Writing about a movement in which one has participated has obvious advantages and serious problems. I have tried to make the most of the insights that derive from having been there and to avoid the blindness and selective vision that result from preconceived interpretations and selective memory. I use my own voice in this book infrequently, only when I want to make it clear that I was present at an event and thus am offering my own observation and reaction in addition to drawing upon those of others.

For evidence of WSP's program, goals, tactics, and rhetoric, I have used the printed record instead of my own impressions and recollections. This includes newspaper and magazine articles as well as WSP newsletters, flyers, advertisements, internal memoranda, minutes of meetings, and correspondence. But these have their problems in terms of bias, narrowness of vision, regional chauvinism, racism, and intentional misrepresentation. For information on the background and motivation of the important founders of WSP I have relied on personal interviews. I am fully aware that these oral histories reflect the limitations of memory and the effect of the new feminist consciousness on the perceptions of the founders and prime movers of WSP as well as on my own.

I have relied heavily on the rhetoric of the movement for my analysis and evaluation of WSP because I believe that it reveals the self-image and the political and gender consciousness of the women who created it, as well as the image they wished to convey to the "ordinary housewives" they hoped to recruit and to the politicians they were determined to sway. Unfortunately the lack of formal structure in WSP has resulted in large gaps in the movement's records. The archivist of the State Historical Society of Wisconsin pointed out, in a description of its holdings on WSP, that functional records such as annual reports, proceedings, directories, and rolls are missing, largely because decisions within the various branches of the movement were made primarily by telephone and not by correspondence. And, as I know by experience and discussions with former activists, many chapters intentionally kept no records or lists, and the WSPers never had the historical consciousness to create an official archive in one repository.[12]

Due to the ad hoc, temporary, "just for the emergency" nature of the WSP movement, each campaign, demonstration, flyer, or petition was considered unique and never to be repeated; because they were unaware that anything they did was of historical significance, WSPers almost never dated their flyers or other printed material, except for news-letters. I have often had to make judgments as to the dates of flyers and other communications, based on my personal knowledge of the event or of the chronology and program of WSP, but errors are possible. One serious lack in the record is financial information. Budgets and ledgers are missing from the records of the national office, and because each chapter and each region made its own financial arrangements I found it impossible to estimate how much money WSP raised and spent on a national basis.

The influence of WSP on the political events of the early 1960s has been recognized by a number of influential journalists, historians, and political leaders. I. F. Stone, the independent radical journalist, pro-claimed in 1970 that he knew of no other antiwar or radical organiza-tion of any kind that had been "as flexible and intelligent in its tactics, and as free from stereotypes and sectarianism in its strategy."[13] (Stone was referring to political stereotypes. This brilliant political analyst was apparently as blind as the WSP leadership to the ways in which the movement was reenforcing sex-role stereotypes.) Jerome Weisner, science advisor to President John F. Kennedy, who exerted a strong in-fluence for ending atmospheric nuclear testing, credits WSP, along with SANE and antinuclear Nobel laureate Linus Pauling, with having more influence on the president regarding the test ban treaty than the profes-sional arms controllers in the government had.[14] A number of histori-ans of HUAC have credited WSP with striking a crucial blow in what Eric Bentley has called "the fall of HUAC's Bastille."[15]

Despite this recognition, the movement is fast disappearing from the history of the 1960s and from the memory of a new generation of young women concerned with peace and disarmament. WSP has been ignored or misrepresented in the reminiscences of male movement leaders and historians of the social movements of the 1960s. The his-torical amnesia that has enveloped WSP is strikingly reminiscent of the fate of Julia Ward Howe's Women's Peace Festival of 1873, the Commit-tee on the Causes and Cure of War supported by millions of women in the period between the two world wars, and the Congress of American Women, which was forced to disband by the order of the Department of Justice in 1950.[16]

As I conclude this book, I recognize that my purpose was not only to add the story of WSP to the historical record, but also to make certain that the middle-aged women of WSP are recognized as significant actors and movers in the antiwar movement and the radical ferment of the 1960s. The struggle WSP conducted to forward ordinary housewives into the political arena, as well as the nonhierarchical, participatory for-mat that it created, was a harbinger of the second wave of the women's liberation movement. By stressing global issues rather than private family interests, WSP challenged the key element of the feminine mystique: the domestication and privatization of the middle-class white woman. By making a recognized contribution to the test ban treaty of 1963, WSP raised women's sense of political efficacy at a time when women were expected to exert their influence, not their power. The struggle WSP conducted in the name of motherhood to rein in the power of the Pentagon demonstrated to its participants, even if they did not yet have the vocabulary to make the point themselves, that the familial and personal are political and that the public and private spheres are one.

1

"Raising a Hue and Cry"

> You know how men are. They talk in abstractions
> and prestige and the technicalities of the bomb, al-
> most as if this were all a game of chess. Well, it
> isn't. There are times, it seems to me, when the
> only thing to do is let out a loud scream. . . . Just
> women raising a hue and cry against nuclear
> weapons for all of them to cut it out.
> —Dagmar Wilson, 26 October 1961

*O*n 1 November 1961 an estimated fifty thousand women walked out of their kitchens and off their jobs, in an unprecedented nationwide strike for peace.[1] As a radioactive cloud from a series of Russian atom bomb tests passed over American cities and the United States threatened to retaliate with its own cycle of nuclear explosions, the striking women sent delegations to their elected officials—governors, mayors, congressional representatives, school board members—to express their deep anxiety and indignation concerning the pollution of the atmosphere by radioactive isotopes released by nuclear explosions. They demanded that their local officials pressure President John Kennedy on behalf of all the world's children, to end nuclear testing at once and begin negotiations for nuclear disarmament.

The strike took many forms and included a variety of antimilitarist demands, but banning nuclear testing was the dominant theme. Maternal indignation was manifested by the number of women pushing baby carriages, holding aloft placards that read, "Save the Children," "Testing Damages the Unborn," and "Let's Live in Peace Not Pieces." In a Detroit public square women held up enlarged photographs of their own children. In Washington, D.C., 750 to 800 women, a few youngsters, and a collie dog marched in front of the White House, carrying signs urging peace and disarmament. The collie wore a bib inscribed with the slogan "Please No More Strontium 90"—a reference to one of the most dangerous components of nuclear fallout.[2] To demonstrate their impartial anger toward the leaders of both the United States and the USSR and their belief in women's civilizing influence, the women sent identical

15

letters to Jacqueline Kennedy and Nina Khrushchev, urging them to press their husbands to act for peace.

In Los Angeles four thousand women assembled on the steps of the State Building, demanding an end to the stockpiling and testing of nuclear weapons. Attorney General Stanley Mosk, addressing the women, complimented them for their "sincerity and their efforts."[3] This was a gratifying moment, because critics of U.S. nuclear policies had been dismissed or excoriated by most public officials since the first nuclear explosion over Japan. Leaving the State Building the women marched silently to City Hall and then to the Federal Building, carrying their messages, "The Soviet 50-Megaton Bomb Is an Outrage against Humanity" and "Ban All Atomic Weapons."[4] In New York City concurrent marches took place at the Russian embassy, the Atomic Energy Commission, and the U.S. Mission to the United Nations. At AEC the director of the New York office expressed his sympathy with the "worried mothers," and outside the Soviet embassy passersby joined the march. Even a New York "cop" told one striker, "We certainly sympathize with you, ma'am."[5] Six hundred marchers from the Cambridge area, including students from Harvard and Brandeis universities, picketed the Watertown arsenal. Their slogan was "Ban the Bomb, Let's Not Imitate the Russians." Illustrating the conventional sex-role agenda that motivated many of the women to join the strike was a placard hung around the neck of a little girl in Cambridge, asserting, "I want to be a mommy someday." Similar demonstrations took place in Philadelphia, Cleveland, Cincinnati, St. Louis, Baltimore, Denver, San Francisco, and Newark.

The women's strike for peace was an instant success in that it drew attention to women's profound fear of the dangers posed to health and life by nuclear testing, and at the same time restored women's voice to foreign policy discourse for the first time since the interwar period (see chapter 2). The size of the turnout, its national scope, the traditional and respectable yet militant image projected by the women astonished government officials as well as the media. Sophia Wyatt, from London, who marched with the Los Angeles women, tried to determine who and what had brought them out. She asked a woman walking beside her what organization she belonged to. Wyatt reported in the *Manchester Guardian* that the Los Angeles woman replied with a laugh, "I don't belong to any organization. I've got a child of ten."[6]

The U.S. press and public officials were equally puzzled regarding the origins of the strike. Because the marchers seemed to belong to no unifying organizations and because their language was so maternal and nonideological, their sudden appearance on the political stage seemed to be totally apolitical and spontaneous.

But this was not the case. The strikers were responding to a call issued five weeks earlier by a handful of women in Washington, D.C., who had identified themselves primarily as "housewives and mothers." The Washington initiators had been brought together by Dagmar Wilson, a children's book illustrator, mother, and wife who was distressed not only by the resumption of nuclear testing after a three-year hiatus but also by the Berlin Wall crisis, which, she feared, could escalate into a push-button nuclear holocaust. Wilson has since stated that she was motivated to action not so much by fear as by frustration. She was outraged by the failure of the men in government and in the established peace organizations to respond with sufficient urgency to what she perceived as a full-blown planetary emergency.

At a cocktail party in her Georgetown garden, Wilson tried to share her concern with a mixed group of friends who seemed indifferent. Her husband suggested that she turn to women, "because," he argued, "once women become determined they usually get their way."[7] This Georgetown garden party, and Christopher Wilson's comment, was embraced enthusiastically by the media and became the founding legend of WSP. The strike was actually conceived and initiated a few days later, on 21 September 1961, in the Wilson's living room. This is the way Dagmar Wilson remembers the meeting.

> It was a warm September night in 1961. Six women sat in a
> Georgetown living room. We were worried. We were indignant.
> We were angry. The Soviet Union and the U.S.A. were accusing
> each other of having broken a moratorium on nuclear testing.
> What matter who broke it when everyone's children would fall
> victim to radioactive Strontium 90? . . . Perhaps, we told our-
> selves that night, in the face of male "logic," which seemed to us
> utterly illogical, it was time for women to speak out.[8]

The record reveals that those present at the 21 September meeting were a small group of women and two men, all of whom Wilson had met in the Washington chapter of the Committee for a Sane Nuclear Policy (SANE). Among those present, in addition to Dagmar Wilson, who were to become organizers of the strike and key women of WSP were Jeanne Bagby, Folly Fodor, Eleanor Garst, and Margaret Russell.[9] The subject under discussion was what women could do, *as women*, to reverse the nuclear arms race. The "exploratory meeting," as Wilson called it, enthusiastically adopted the suggestion of Lawrence Scott, a pacifist activist who had already played a key role in the founding of SANE and the Committee for Nonviolent Action (CNVA), that women stage a one-day peace strike. It seemed to the women present that a strike was the most militant and dramatic way to manifest their desperation and attract media attention. "At once we recognised an idea whose time was come," Wilson recalled.[10] It should be noted that, while men were present at the first meeting and the strike idea was generated by a man, this was the last time the Washington women included men in their planning meetings or looked to them for leadership.

On 22 September a call was issued from Washington to women across the nation, urging them to suspend their regular routine of home, family, and jobs for one day, in order to "Appeal to All Governments to End the Arms Race—Not the Human Race." The organizational call declared: "We strike against death, desolation, destruction and on behalf of life and liberty. . . . Husbands or babysitters take over the home front. Bosses or substitutes take over our jobs!" It was circulated rapidly through informal female networks, by word of mouth and chain-letter fashion from woman to woman, from coast to coast and brought forth an instant response. Using personal phone books, Christmas-card lists, and contacts in PTAs, church and temple groups, women's clubs, and old-line peace organizations, the founders and those who joined them managed in only five weeks to reach thousands of women who were able to organize sixty-eight local actions that brought thousands of women into the streets or to protest rallies.[11]

Sophia Wyatt, the British visitor in Los Angeles, heard of the strike in much the same way as the U.S. women did: "An old friend rang me up and said she was sending me some literature which was the most exciting thing she had ever heard, and would I pass it on to the neighbors, talk to my friends, and be a darling and give her a lift on November 1st. When I started to ask who and what, she cut me short. There were no names; it was not an organization; would I just read it and come."[12] There were, indeed, no names on the first call to strike. In fact, the names of the founders would have meant little, as they were unknown as public figures.[13] But there were other, more critical reasons for the founders' reticence. At a time when the names of those who signed peace petitions were being subpoenaed by congressional committees, when the FBI was compiling lists of subversives, and when even foreign policy dissent groups were choosing to exclude those suspected of Communist affiliations, the Washington women wanted no lists open to scrutiny. They made it clear that they were "not asking anyone to sign anything, join anything, or to support any political ideology, or tactic."[14]

It was not only fear of Red baiting that prompted this open political style. The women were tired of top-down organizational structures with fixed ideologies that inhibited spontaneous direct action and withheld decision-making power from the grass roots. They had experienced frustrations working with the hierarchical structures of SANE and WILPF, organizations made cautious by Cold War repression. "In these days of super-organizations," the founders explained, "we feel the individual has virtually ceased to participate directly in support of his [sic] views." "We don't want chairmen, boards, committees, long series of meetings. We just want to speak out loudly, to tell our elected representatives that they are not properly representing us by continuing the arms race and increasing the threat of total destruction." By rejecting hierarchy and boring meetings, the Washington organizers encouraged the strikers to speak out in their own voices and political styles. The loosely structured participatory format initiated by the Washington group set the tone not only for the strike but also for the national movement that emerged afterward. Although the question of organizational structure was hotly debated in the early years, "structurelessness" came to be the movement's hallmark and its most important legacy to the feminist peace groups that followed. The women of WSP, socialized for powerlessness and humility, referred apologetically to their innovative format as our "unorganization," never recognizing that it foreshadowed new left political culture.

In the weeks before the strike, the Washington organizers were barraged with questions about their backgrounds and their goals. To identify themselves more fully to their new contacts, they dispatched a second communication, titled "Who Are These Women?—You Ask." This letter listed Dagmar Wilson of Georgetown as coordinator of the strike and twelve other women as the organizers.[15] In this second communication the organizers no longer referred to themselves merely as housewives, but as "teachers, writers, social workers, artists, secretaries, executives, saleswomen." "Most of us are also wives and mothers," they explained, adding, "We are Quakers, Unitarians, Methodists, and Presbyterians, Jews and Catholics and many ethnic origins. First of all we are human beings." Despite this new explanation, the housewife identification clung to the WSP movement throughout the 1960s and early 1970s.

The differences in language between the first and second communications demonstrates that in only two weeks the strike organizers had moved from uncertainty and coyness to conviction. In the original call the founders stated that they were "appalled at our own audacity, for we're just ordinary people, not experts." In the second communication they declared, without apology: "We're not politicians—we're housewives and working women. . . . We don't make foreign policy—but we know to what end we want it made: toward preservation of life on earth." The model for their bold action, they explained, was the civil rights movement—particularly the sit-ins in the South, and the "suffragettes of long ago who reminded us of the power for good in each person."[16] While this statement attempted to associate WSP with the woman's rights movement, it made no feminist demands. The suffragists had "reminded" the founders, not of women's militant struggle for political power, but of their power to advance the good of others.

The only piece of political or social philosophy expressed in the Washington call identified the organizers more closely with the nineteenth-century peace movement's invocation of traditional female culture than with the ideological politics of the Left. "Nations disagree as families disagree," the call stated. "Women believe that nations can solve differences as families do without killing each other." This notion of women's special talent for life preservation and for "social housekeeping" had been a theme in female moral and social reform since the early nineteenth century. It would be used frequently by WSP in the years to come, although the women had no historical memory of the tactics or rhetoric of their political foremothers. Disclaiming any platform beyond the slogan "End the Arms Race—Not the Human Race," the founders nevertheless listed six demands: (1) a ban on all atomic weapons testing; (2) negotiations to put all atomic weapons under international control; (3) concrete steps to be taken at once toward worldwide disarmament; (4) immediate allocation of as much of the national budget to preparation for peace as was being spent in preparation for war; (5) an immediate moratorium on name-calling on both sides; and (6) the strengthening of the United Nations.

Although the strike organizers did not seek official sponsorship from established organizations, they did contact a number of prominent women whose support, they hoped, would give the movement political legitimacy and media attention. Letters asking for participation or endorsement were sent to Agnes Meyer, Marian Anderson, Margaret Mead, Judy Holliday, Jean Kerr, Pearl Buck, Katharine Hepburn, and Faye Emerson, among others. On 13 October Dagmar Wilson wrote to Eleanor Roosevelt, who was a member of the National Board of SANE, asking her to speak at a prestrike rally: "Your presence and voice would give incalculable inspiration to women strange to the ways of political activity, but brought together to ask the leaders of the world and the lawmakers of our nation for a peaceful and uncontaminated present and future for us all."[17] Roosevelt's reply indicates how deeply Cold War suspicion of foreign policy dissent and fear of Communist infiltration had penetrated the liberal establishment. "I am sorry to say that I cannot be with you on October 25th, and I do not plan to do anything to help unless you have consulted the President and the Secretary of State and have their consent." Roosevelt also commented in her column on 5 November, a few days after the strike, that she had been deluged with requests to join a women's peace strike movement and to speak to the United Nations regarding the women's demands. "This I will not do," she wrote, "because I do not approve of this kind of action. It seems meaningless to me." There is no evidence in the WSP files to indicate that any of the women solicited, other than the actress Faye Emerson, agreed to support the strike, so the Washington "housewives" had to make their way alone.[18] Their concern that they would be ignored because they were only housewives was misplaced. What attracted the media was the notion that the "lady next door," who had been living in her kitchen in domestic bliss for over a decade, was moving into public spaces and occupying them with militancy and determination. Instead of listening demurely, she was lecturing and demanding, and she could not be ignored or attacked because she was doing it all in the name of a hallowed institution—motherhood.

The extensive press coverage WSP received was due not only to the novelty of a middle-class women's strike but also to the founders' talent for public relations. They understood, from the first exploratory meeting, that to reach and sway the average woman and her representatives in Congress they would have to reach and sway the media.[19] They knew that their protest actions had to be both photogenic political "events" and human-interest stories. An example of WSP's sense of what might attract the press was the decision to deliver identical letters to Jacqueline Kennedy and Nina Khrushchev, asking them to exert their influence with their husbands to halt nuclear testing. This wifely appeal developed into an ongoing story for many weeks after the strike, as the replies to the WSP letters from Kennedy and Khrushchev were published in newspapers across the country, along with a response by Dagmar Wilson.[20] The fact that the WSP story continued to be reported in the press after the strike brought it to the attention of those who missed the story when it happened, extended the interest of the participants beyond one day, and helped create the pressure to continue the initiative.

The organizers also had a talent for staying just within the bounds of political credibility in the anti-Communist climate of the early 1960s. Understanding that even impartial criticism of both nuclear powers could be interpreted as anti-American and pro-Soviet, they always maintained in their speeches and media interviews that they were supporting their own president, John Kennedy, in his proclaimed "peace race." In fact, the theme of the entire strike, Dagmar Wilson explained to the *Washington Post,* came from the president's own words, "Mankind must put an end to war, or war will put an end to mankind."

Wilson caught the fancy of the press from the start. It was apparently her ladylike articulation of radical ideas, her cheerful "good breeding" manifested by an upper-class British accent, that appealed to the reporters who interviewed her after the first announcement of the forthcoming strike. The press chose to identify Wilson primarily as a mother, despite the fact that she had made it clear in the first strike press release that she was a "well-known children's book illustrator."[21] The *Baltimore Sun* described Wilson as a "small elfin woman who has three daughters and whose usual spare-time occupation is illustrating children's books."[22] Mary McGrory, then a staff writer for the *Washington Evening Star,* referred to Wilson as "the trim, brown-haired mother of three teen-age daughters, who is a children's book illustrator" and "who did not talk like a feminist."[23]

If sex-role stereotyping in the media involves what sociologist Gaye Tuchman has described as "set portrayals of sex-appropriate appearance, interests, skills, behaviors, and self-perceptions," Wilson was stereotyped as a gracious leader of traditional ladies from the start.[24] The media need not take all the responsibility, however, as Wilson herself and many of the other women of WSP assisted in typecasting the movement. A few days before the strike Wilson explained to the *Baltimore Sun,* "Our organization has no resemblance to the Lysistrata theme, or even the suffragettes. We are not striking against our husbands. It is my guess that we will make the soup that they will ladle out to the children on Wednesday [1 November]."[25] Although she justified the strike idea to the *Washington Evening Star* by stressing traditional gender roles and characteristics, she also offered a powerful, if soft-spoken, critique of male responsibility for global violence. "You know how men are," she said with a sigh. "They talk in abstractions and prestige and the technicalities of the bomb, almost as if this were all a game of chess. Well, it isn't. There are times, it seems to me, when the only thing to do is let out a loud scream. . . . Just women raising a hue and cry against nuclear weapons for all of them to cut it out."[26] Thirty years ago, without any knowledge of women's history or feminist theory, Wilson un-self-consciously presented an insightful critique of the power assumptions in male technocratic language, posing female concern for life as an antidote to male abstraction and detachment.[27] Psychologist Carol Cohn, in a brilliant study of the language of "nuclear defense intellectuals," proposed in 1989 what Wilson attempted in 1961: "If we could expose and unravel this discourse that justifies the unjustifiable, the political barriers to nuclear disarmament would start to crumble."[28]

Wilson's words and those of the other Washington founders were echoed by women all over the country who had no difficulty claiming them as their own. Gladys Farber assured the *Los Angeles Mirror* that the strike "is not necessarily hostile to men," and Patricia Kempler told the *Los Angeles Times* that "the sit-in strikers have reminded us, as the suffragettes did long ago, of the tremendous power for good in each single person."[29] These statements came directly from the Washington call.

The quantity and quality of media attention received by the strike amazed even its organizers. In most communities where demonstrations occurred on 1 November, local newspapers ran front-page stories featuring the women, their children, and their demands. Network television showed their faces and slogans to millions of Americans, and their voices were heard on radio nationwide. Most media reports conveyed amazement, amusement, and condescension, accompanied by sympathy for a mother's plight in the nuclear age along with admiration for women who fought like lions for their children's welfare.

The *Los Angeles Times* (2 November 1961) emphasized the affluent, traditionally feminine, and amateurish quality of the peace demonstrators. Self-deprecating remarks by the women were quoted with relish. An explanation of how the strike was organized, offered by "Mrs. Gerry Dreyfuss of Beverly Hills," was printed verbatim. "You know the saying—'telephone, television, tella-woman,'" Dreyfuss quipped, "well that's what we did and this is the result." Another striker's remark that funds were raised for publicity through "a sort of martinis-for-peace approach," along with the rueful comment, "my husband only gave me ten dollars for stamps," marked WSP as a proper middle-class women's group.

The *Washington Post*, which relegated the strike story to the "For and About Women" page, emphasized the women's down-to-earth, even-handed common sense. It quoted WSP founder Margaret Russell as she emerged from the Russian embassy, "We gave them our propaganda, and they gave us theirs," and Dagmar Wilson's follow-up, "A funny thing, it sounded very much the same."[30] An Associated Press dispatch, reprinted in hundreds of newspapers across the nation, made much of the folksy female quality of the peace strike. The fact that the women were pushing baby buggies was noted, and a picture of a group of the Washington picketers tailed by the collie dog Candy was captioned "Picketing Pooch." The tone of the caption confirmed the old adage, when women and dogs step out of their space and place, they make good copy.[31]

A few press reports and responses by public officials were serious and respectful. In San Francisco the mayor agreed to dispatch a telegram to the president, expressing the fears and demands of the strikers. A *San Francisco Chronicle* editorial praised the mayor for "a courteous, civilized performance of duty by a city official—duly according consideration to a petition from a group of citizens on a matter of extreme gravity."[32] The fact that the citizens were women was not even mentioned. Governor Edmund G. Brown of California told sixty-five Sacramento peace strikers that he hoped their plea for peace would be heard around the world: "I wish you could go to Moscow and let them know how the American people feel about this. I wish we could let them know we don't want an inch of their territory, that if they want to be Communists that is all right, and that all we want is to be left alone."[33] Governor Brown's response was just what the Washington founders had hoped for. They had propelled Brown into speaking out for international peace, something governors rarely did. Brown's words, they believed, along with similar statements by other public officials, would help to bring about the ground swell needed to end nuclear testing.

Not all of the press and politicians were sympathetic. Cold War fears loomed large for those who were concerned that emotional and impetuous women would undermine the U.S. bargaining position with the Russians either through foolishness or by design. Chief William H. Parker of the Los Angeles Police Department attacked the strikers: "There undoubtedly were many fine people duped into thinking they were doing something constructive, but this type of revolution against constituted authority serve[s] the Soviet well. I'm sure this 'demonstration for peace' has been well noted in the Kremlin and that they are happy about the whole movement."[34] Mayor Sam Yorty of Los Angeles, along with the mayor of Oakland, refused to see the women, telling them to take their appeal to Moscow. Senator Hugh Scott of Pennsylvania scolded the four hundred strikers who met with him in Philadelphia: "I urge that you restate your allegiance to your country and acknowledge that government must be supported in whatever it must do to deal with international events."[35] Robert H. Austin, chairman of the National Committee for a Representative Congress, attacked the strikers for exercising "do-it-yourself power" in foreign relations. Austin charged that by writing to Nina Khrushchev the women had given the Kremlin a million dollars' worth of worldwide anti-U.S. propaganda. He also suggested that the women were guilty of violating the Logan Act, which prohibits private citizens from "attempting foreign relations negotiations."[36]

The "club editor" of the Los Angeles Herald Express was one of those who were suspicious of the Washington organizers' claim that they were acting independently of any established political group. He attacked the strikers as "a mob of women" who, while they claimed to be "just housewives," carried prepared and matching banners. The implication was that they were under orders from a higher source, undoubtedly in Moscow.

It is true that women in different cities carried banners with slogans similar or identical to those used in Washington. There is no evidence, however, that these slogans were dictated. The explanation is that the women at the local level adopted the arguments and the language of the strike organizers as their own because they expressed, with eloquence and feeling, the political opinions, and gender assumptions identical to the strikers' own. The WSP women not only sounded alike, they looked alike. They came, for the most part, from the same class, race, and age group. They wore their status of middle-class wifehood and motherhood proudly, while asserting their responsibility for nurturance, moral guardianship, and life preservation.

The sudden and unprecedented female outcry manifested by the peace strike puzzled a number of peace activists and social scientists, as well as the media and the FBI. It was difficult for them to comprehend how, in only five weeks, a small group of unknown and unaffiliated women could develop a common program, an effective "unorganizational" format, and the unifying rhetoric needed to create an instant movement of national scope and international impact. Was it the dangerous resumption of atmospheric nuclear testing that produced this spontaneous reaction? Was it the immediate threat to the health of their children, or long-held political beliefs in international cooperation, or even socialism that brought thousands of women into the streets? Or was it the influence of an articulate young president, who spoke of a nuclear sword of Damocles hanging over humanity and of the need to conclude a test ban treaty with the Russians, that created the sense of possibility and hope that encourages political protest?[37] Why did the women of WSP take to the streets in 1961 and not in 1959 when SANE and CNVA were organized? Were the Washington organizers simply fed up, or were they part of the new wave of protest from unrecognized and powerless segments of society that was beginning to sweep the country and would come to characterize the politics of the 1960s?

To understand the WSP phenomenon, it is not enough to look at the nuclear crisis that terrified the women into action. We must look at the women themselves, who chose to act rather than to cower. We must explore their political and gender consciousness, as well as their economic and educational status. We must place them in the context of the politics of the 1930s and 1940s, the years in which they were socialized, educated, and assumed adulthood. We must place them in the culture of the postwar period, the years in which they made their life choices regarding marriage, motherhood, and vocation. While WSP was something new on the American scene in 1961, it carried with it an ambiguous legacy: 1930s liberalism and radicalism as well as 1950s political repression, middle-class affluence, which provided a certain degree of freedom and power, along with gender constraints that limited mobility and even personal ambition. WSP came out of a century-long tradition of female peace activism of which it was largely unconscious. We must examine this tradition to determine the ways in which

WSP mirrors and departs from its rhetoric, tactics, and gender assumptions.

The following chapters explore the history of women's peace protest inherited by WSP, the social and gender issues, and the domestic politics and world events that influenced WSP programs, goals, and rhetoric. They examine the lives of its key women and the movement they shaped, and focus on the way a group of unaffiliated women developed a movement that met their own political and psychological needs, while making an impact on world affairs. Subsequent chapters also illuminate the process by which a group of women, engaged in a political movement based on traditional female culture, transformed themselves and their understanding of social reality to join the second wave of feminism in its struggle for female empowerment. As one of the peace strikers remarked on 1 November 1961: "For a lot of women this is the first time on a picket line. Women are naturally conservative. But once they take the step they become stronger and much more radical."[38]

2

Prelude to a Peace Strike

As women we feel a peculiar moral passion of revolt against both the cruelty and waste of war. As
women, we are especially the custodian of life of
the ages. We will no longer consent to its reckless
destruction.
—Women's Peace Party, "Preamble and Platform
   Adopted at Washington, January 10, 1915"

Women spend years of their lives bringing up children to be healthy individuals and good citizens.
Now, in the nuclear age all women—not only
mothers—have an . . . urgent duty to work for
peace in order that our children may have a future.
—Women Strike for Peace, October 1961

In the first poststrike communication to their organizational contacts, the Washington organizers expressed amazement
at their success. "There is no doubt about it," they declared, "the
Women's Strike for Peace movement . . . promises to be the biggest
thing of its kind that has occurred in the USA since our mothers and
grandmothers claimed their right to vote 41 years ago."[1] Judging from
the rhetoric of the new movement and its internal communications,
none of the strike organizers and very few of the women who joined
them were aware that they were writing a new chapter in the long, if
discontinuous, history of women's peace activism in the United States.
The WSPers would have been astounded to learn that they were following in the steps of millions of their foremothers who had, for over a
century, petitioned, lobbied, and demonstrated against America's major
wars and military interventions. They seemed to be totally unaware
that organized women, as far back as the early nineteenth century, were
persistent advocates of national laws and international treaties to limit
arms and prohibit war.[2]

Although the women who marched for peace in 1961 were for the
most part ignorant of women's peace history, their arguments regarding

27

women's special right and responsibility to oppose militarism were almost identical to those made by female pacifists in the early nineteenth century. The WSPers would have understood and sympathized with the 1836 call to Republican mothers issued by William Ladd, leader of the American Peace Society. Ladd declared that it was the duty of women to persuade both sons and statesmen to apply the familial values of nurturance, conciliation, and harmony to affairs of state.[3] What would have jolted the WSPers, however, had they known it, is that, even before the Civil War, women in the Garrisonian wing of the abolitionist movement connected women's work for peace with demands for their own political rights as citizens.[4] The women who banded together in WSP would have been in total sympathy with an 1870 appeal by Julia Ward Howe to the mothers of the world to unite across national boundaries "to prevent the waste of human life which they alone bear and know the cost." Howe, author of "Battle Hymn of the Republic," the rousing Civil War song that sent tens of thousands of men into battle, found herself so distressed by the human cost of that war and the Franco-Prussian War that she sailed for Europe to organize an international women's peace congress.[5] Failing in her attempt because the British peace societies were unwilling to deal seriously with a female peace leader, Howe returned home to organize a Mothers' Peace Day that was celebrated in 1873 in several U.S. cities, including New York, Philadelphia, Chicago, St. Louis, Wilmington (Delaware), New Haven, New Bedford, and Lowell (Massachusetts), and abroad in Rome, London, Manchester, Geneva, and Constantinople. The women of WSP, who asked only for nuclear disarmament, would have been inspired and perhaps radicalized had they read the "Exposition of Sentiments" issued by the Philadelphia organizers of Mothers' Peace Day ninety years earlier. After stating that "women, as mothers of the race, have the right to be heard," the Philadelphia women protested the "economic and social injustice that feed the war system" and demanded "from those in power . . . that no invidious oppressive distinctions be made politically, religiously or socially because of *sex, color, or race*" (emphasis in original).[6]

From the late nineteenth century until World War I, the promotion of world peace was an important cause with hundreds of thousands of traditional middle-class American women, organized in women's clubs, benevolent societies, and social reform groups. These organizations, while overwhelmingly white and Protestant, also included the National Council of Negro Women and the National Council of Jewish Women. What united these groups in support of peace was their belief that war was a gender-linked social evil, caused by male competitiveness, materialism, and violence. Women, they were convinced, would play a decisive role in ending war because world peace could be achieved only if men behaved more like women.[7] Lillie Devereux Blake spoke for thousands of peace-minded women in an 1896 address to the National American Woman Suffrage Association when she deplored men's inability to settle conflict without violence and their willingness to "deluge the world in blood for a strip of land in Venezuela or a gold mine in South Africa."[8]

Blake was not the only suffragist to advocate peace. The strong ideological and organizational connection between feminism and peace during the suffrage struggle is exemplified by women like Hannah Bailey, founder of the peace department of the National Woman's Christian Temperance Union (WCTU), Lucia Ames Mead of the American Peace Society, and May Wright Sewall of the International Council of Women, all of whom were presidents of state suffrage societies.

Motivated by religious and political perspectives ranging from moral reform to conscious anti-imperialism, female peace advocates at the turn of the century undertook a number of campaigns to prevent war. In 1891, for instance, the National Council of Women (NCW) and the WCTU conducted a petition drive calling on the U.S. government to avoid war with Chile. Women's groups also issued a call for arbitration during the Venezuelan border controversy with England in 1895. They pressured President McKinley to reject war with Spain in 1898 and opposed the annexation of the Philippines on moral and political grounds. One of the most widespread women's peace campaigns was waged in support of the 1899 Hague Conference on international disarmament and arbitration. To bolster support for the Hague Conference, women initiated a Peace Day that was celebrated nationally. In 1903 NCW, with fifteen member organizations comprising hundreds of thousands of women, reported that women working to publicize Peace Day had distributed literature to clergymen, boards of education, teachers, newspaper publishers, and editors, and had presented programs on peace issues in churches, synagogues, public and Sunday schools, and lyceums and on university campuses. NCW called for the revision of textbooks to include more examples of the accomplishments of conciliators and peacemakers than those of military heroes. In 1905 the National Women's Relief Society and the Young Ladies' Mutual Improvement Society sponsored fifty-six Peace Day meetings in Utah, Idaho, Washington, and Montana, indicating the scope of women's peace activities at the turn of the century.[9]

Under the leadership of Hannah Bailey the WCTU developed a peace department, which functioned in twenty-eight states. It published the *Banner of Peace* and circulated hundreds of thousands of "children's leaflets" in Sunday schools all over the country. According to peace historian Merle Curti, the peace department of the WCTU trained women to lecture on peace at their literary clubs, and persuaded ministers to preach against war and teachers to present the idea of international goodwill to their classes. "From time to time Frances Willard [president of the WCTU] herself spoke out against war to the half million women enlisted in the WCTU, and one may be sure that her words carried weight."[10]

In 1914, prior to the outbreak of World War I, the General Federation of Women's Clubs with 800,000 members, the Council of Mothers with 100,000, the Women's Relief Corps with 161,000, the WCTU with 325,000, and NCW with about fifteen national organizations all contained planks in their programs committing their members to the promotion of peace. It was not until 1915, however, that the first autonomous women's peace organization, the Women's Peace Party (WPP), was established. What moved women to found a separatist organization was the outbreak of the war in Europe. Women who had already identified themselves with the cause of peace were appalled to find that the traditional, male-led pacifist groups, with which they were affiliated, were silent and immobile, unwilling or unable to make any effort to stop the war. A group of prominent women reformers, including settlement-house leaders Jane Addams and Lillian Wald, suffrage leader Carrie Chapman Catt, labor advocate Crystal Eastman, and peace advocates Fannie Fern Andrews and Fanny Garrison Villard, decided that it was up to the women to restore peace and moral order. Catt put it this way: "When the great war came, and the women waited for the pacifists to move, and they heard nothing from them, they decided all too late to get together themselves and try to do something at this eleventh hour."[11] This explanation for the organization of WPP is similar to Dagmar Wilson's statement that one of the reasons she turned to women to organize a peace protest in 1961 was that the leadership of SANE, of which she was a member, did not respond with a sufficient sense of urgency to the testing crisis and the contamination of milk by radioactive isotopes.[12]

The platform of WPP was more radical than that of any of the traditional peace groups, and, indeed, more radical than that of WSP almost half a century later. It called for democratic control of foreign policy, the limitation of armaments, and the nationalization of their manufacture. It was committed to the education of youth in the ideals of peace, and the removal of the economic causes of war. In 1960, after a decade of governmental and public intolerance of foreign policy dissent, the women of WSP did not feel free to raise issues regarding ultimate foreign policy goals, social injustice, or class conflict. They understood that raising such issues would have marked the movement as political rather than maternal, subversive rather than traditional.

The preamble to the WPP platform of 1915 declared:

As women we are particularly charged with the future of childhood and with the care of the helpless and unfortunate. We will
no longer endure the added burden of maimed and invalid men
and poverty-stricken widows and orphans which war places
upon us. . . . Therefore as human beings and the mother half of
humanity, we demand our right to be consulted in the settlement of questions concerning not alone the life of individuals
but of nations be recognized and respected.[13]

Connecting the responsibilities of motherhood to political rights, WPP
demanded that "women must be given a share in deciding between war
and peace in all courts of high debate—within the home, the school, the
church, the industrial order, and the state." This was an outlook also
shared by African-American women leaders. In the 1915 "Symposium
by Leading Thinkers of Colored America," Coralie Franklin Cook, a
black member of the Washington, D.C., Board of Education, stated that
women generate responsibility for all humanity, and therefore should
help both to make and to administer the laws under which they live.[14]
So successfully had feminist demands been banished from the liberal
and radical political agenda in the 1940s and 1950s, that by 1961 it
seemed inappropriately self-serving for the women of WSP to make a
forthright demand for political power; all they could demand was maternal influence over the men who made nuclear decisions.[15]

Maternal interest and influence for peace is obviously not a notion
WSP invented. Crystal Eastman, one of the most radical of the founders
of WPP, wrote to Jane Addams that there would be "more meaning and
passion" in a separate organization of women to end war than in an
organization of both sexes because women are mothers, or potential
mothers, and "therefore have a more intimate sense of the value of
human life."[16] WPP did bring more passion, determination, and drama
into the peace movement than it had seen during a century of male
leadership. Peace historian C. Roland Marchand suggests that it was
their experience in the suffrage struggle that had radicalized the leaders
of the WPP to the point where they "did not share the distrust of demonstrations and the fear of indiscreet actions that inhibited leaders of
older peace organizations."[17]

The first dramatic action undertaken by WPP was to help organize
and send forty-seven U.S. women to the International Congress of
Women at the Hague in 1915. The goals of this unprecedented international meeting of women, including those from nations at war with
each other, was to negotiate a just and lasting end to the war and to
encourage the struggle for female enfranchisement. The congress,

noting that male political leaders were doing nothing to end the war, sent two delegations, including the Americans Jane Addams, Emily Balch, and Alice Hamilton, to the capitals of Europe to meet with heads of government to urge adoption of a plan devised by Julia Grace Wales of Wisconsin for continuous mediation until cessation of the war.[18] They also visited battlefields to view and assess the human cost of the war. This informal direct action by women during a time of war was immediately attacked by male politicians as female meddling in affairs beyond their competency.[19] The damage it did to Addams's national reputation as America's saintly reformer and "maiden aunt" was a stern warning to feminist pacifists that the foreign policy establishment would brook no interference from ordinary citizens, especially women. Nevertheless, WPP together with the American Union against Militarism (AUAM) played an important role in avoiding war with Mexico. In 1916 WPP and AUAM publicized an eyewitness report by an American officer charging that American troops had been the aggressor in a skirmish with the Mexican army, an incident that prompted President Woodrow Wilson to seek congressional approval for the occupation of northern Mexico. A series of public meetings and letter writing and telegram campaigns organized by WPP influenced public sentiment to the point where President Wilson reversed himself.[20] As historian William O'Neill points out, this incident was one of the very few times in American history when an administration preparing for war was deterred by the peace movement. "Female pacifists," he asserts, "could rightly draw comfort from such a remarkable accomplishment."[21]

Despite the valiant and persistent efforts of the pacifist feminists, they did not stop World War I or prevent the United States from entering the conflict. Jeannette Rankin, the first woman elected to the U.S. House of Representatives, cast her ballot against the war, stating, "I want to stand by my country, but I cannot vote for war."[22] While she was deliberating her daring action, she was advised by suffrage militant Alice Paul, "It would be a tragedy for the first woman ever in Congress to vote for war." Paul recalled in a 1972 interview: "The one thing that seemed to us so clear was that women were the peace-loving half of the world and that by giving power to women we would diminish the possibilities of war."[23] However, not all suffragists and peace advocates took Rankin's principled position. Carrie Chapman Catt, president of the National American Woman Suffrage Association (NAWSA), pledged the support of the suffrage movement to the war effort in the hope that such a display of patriotism would bring women the vote.

When women did achieve the vote in 1920, thousands of newly enfranchised women, including those who had been torn between loyalties to pacifism, patriotism, and suffrage during the war, turned their attention to antimilitarism. Only one week after the armistice was signed, suffrage leaders urged President Wilson to appoint a woman to the peace treaty delegation, but he ignored their plea.[24] The 1920s saw the birth of four autonomous women's peace groups: the Women's International League for Peace and Freedom (WILPF), the Women's Peace Society (WPS), the Women's Peace Union (WPU), and the National Committee on the Causes and Cure of War (NCCCW).

WILPF, founded in 1919 and still functioning today, grew out of WPP and the International Congress of Women at the Hague. It was an internationalist organization dedicated to strengthening cooperation among women on all continents on behalf of peace based on economic and social justice. From its founding WILPF supported the League of Nations, which had been conceptualized and recommended by the women at the Hague congress of 1915. Confident that educated, elite, and enfranchised women, armed with the facts, would be able to influence foreign policy decisions in the United States and Europe, WILPF in its early years was noted for sending teams of women to "danger spots" to make firsthand studies of situations threatening world peace.[25]

WPS was also founded in 1919, by Fanny Garrison Villard, daughter of the nineteenth-century abolitionist William Lloyd Garrison. WPS advocated total nonresistance; thus it attracted a constituency of absolute pacifists who could not accept WILPF's support of the League of Nations because the League included a military peace-keeping force. WPS did, however, cooperate with WILPF on occasion. One such event was a public hearing before the House Military Affairs Committee in 1921 in which both groups expressed the opposition of the "newly enfranchised women" to military training in the public schools and to the presence of U.S. military troops in other countries.[26] The fact that WPS could arrange an official hearing in the House of Representatives attests to its leaders' elite status and their knowledge of the legislative process, learned in the years of suffrage lobbying.

WPU was organized by Caroline Lenox Babcock and Elinor Byrns in 1921 to work within the U.S. political system to outlaw war. WPU campaigned steadily and single-mindedly from 1923 to 1939, along with Senator Lynn Joseph Frazier of North Dakota, for a constitutional amendment that would outlaw war and the preparation for war in the United States and all its territories.[27]

The largest of the women's peace groupings was established in 1924 by Carrie Chapman Catt. Catt, who had supported U.S. military efforts in World War I, decided at the conclusion of the war that peace was the most important item on women's political agenda. Building on her national reputation and connections as the triumphant president of NAWSA, she brought together a coalition of eleven national women's organizations, representing millions of women, to form an entity she named the National Committee on the Causes and Cure of War (NCCCW). Merle Curti estimated that in 1936 the organization included, by affiliation, one-fifth of the adult women in the United States.[28] The fact that so many women were, even nominally, in the peace camp in 1924 would have astounded the WSP leadership, who seem to have known nothing of NCCCW or of the fact that there was a time when propeace sentiment was widespread among traditional middle-class women.[29]

Brenda Marston, in a study of women's peace activism in the state of Wisconsin from 1914 to 1934, argues that NCCCW was not only the most broadly based but also the most conservative of the women's peace groups, in that it never placed itself squarely in opposition to government policies. It refused to ally itself with WILPF when that organization conducted campaigns against the military budget or protested against the sending of U.S. Marines to Central and Latin America.[30] Its significance in terms of women's foreign policy dissent is that it involved hundreds of thousands of women in peace education activities and petitioning in support of such legal peace reform measures as U.S. membership in the World Court and the ratification of the Kellogg-Briand Pact. The WSPers would also have been delighted to know that the PTA, which during the 1950s prided itself on its nonpartisanship, refusing to take a stand on such "controversial" issues as the contamination of children's milk by nuclear fallout, had in the interwar period made the campaign for world peace its first priority. The PTA had even attempted to influence curriculum by urging that the nation's public schools take on the responsibility for educating the next generation to prevent war.[31]

As the women's peace constituency grew in numbers, the U.S. War Department launched an all-out attack on the major mass organizations of women, accusing them of internationalism, socialism, and subversion. This attack was a part of the general "Red scare" that followed the Bolshevik revolution, but its focus on women's groups stemmed from a fear that the newly enfranchised organization woman not only would vote against war, as Jeannette Rankin had done, but would raise sons who would refuse to fight.

The historian Joan Jensen suggests that the specific inspiration for labeling pacifist women's groups as subversive may have come from a successful campaign by the former suffragists to defeat Secretary of War John D. Weeks in his bid for the Senate. Weeks, who had denounced "silly pacifists" for circulating "insidious propaganda," encouraged General Amos A. Fries, chief of the Chemical Warfare Service, to assign to Lucia Maxwell, librarian of the Chemical Warfare Service, the task of drawing up and distributing a so-called Spider Web Chart. The chart professed to diagram the ways in which women's organizations and individual women leaders had spun a web of international Communist conspiracy to enmesh ordinary women and undermine national security.[32] Among the groups identified by the Spider Web Chart were WILPF, the General Federation of Women's Clubs, the League of Women Voters, the WCTU, the Young Women's Christian Association (YWCA), the American Association of University Women, and the PTA. The effect of the chart was to sow suspicion and distrust among women who had previously worked together, to isolate the woman's peace movement from so-called patriotic groups such as the Daughters of the American Revolution, and to move the entire female peace constituency to the right.

Charges of Bolshevik influence on peace proponents continued throughout the 1920s and were particularly virulent from 1924 to 1928 as the women's peace movement grew. Carrie Chapman Catt, no radical, was often labeled subversive. She defended herself against these attacks in a number of speeches delivered in 1923, pointing out that the enemies of peace were also the enemies of women's rights. "The little group who seem to have got this entire country hoodooed on the question of peace . . . is almost the same group that held woman suffrage back in Washington for ten or fifteen years, and the very man who is preparing the publicity calling everybody Red who does anything for Peace is the very man who called all the suffragists Reds."[33] But attacks did not abate, and several new lists of feminist subversives were developed, including one produced in Boston in 1928, which listed not only Addams and Catt, but also Zona Gale, Charlotte Perkins Gilman, Julia Lathrop, Lucia Ames Mead, Margaret Sanger, and Mary E. Wooley.[34] The only two American women to have won the Nobel Peace Prize, Jane Addams and Emily Balch, were prominently featured in the Spider Web Chart, and both stood firm in their antimilitarism.

The creativity and energy of the women's peace movement in the late 1920s and early 1930s are astounding to those of us who have read only conventional histories that view this period as a time of stagnation for political women. In 1928 the member organizations of NCCCW sponsored fourteen thousand meetings at which resolutions were adopted calling for ratification of the Kellogg-Briand Pact. And in 1932 NCCCW and WILPF, in cooperation with the League of International Women's Organizations, collected over 600,000 signatures in the United States and 8 million around the world for presentation to the 1932 Geneva Conference for the Reduction and Limitations of Armaments. A cross-country peace motorcade of 150 vehicles, cheered on its way from Hollywood by a crowd of five thousand, carried the petitions to Washington, stopping in 125 cities to stage mass rallies and secure the endorsement of fifty-six mayors. The signatures for peace were presented to President Herbert Hoover before being sent to Geneva.[35] WILPF, which in 1961 was perceived by WSP as a staid and tactically conservative group, was apparently much bolder in its early years. In 1931 it engaged one of the first women aviators, Ruth Nichols, to drop peace flyers over the Democratic party convention in Chicago.[36] WILPF was also the major force behind the 1933 investigation of the arms industry by Senator Gerald P. Nye of North Dakota, chairman of the Senate Munitions Committee.[37] The Nye committee hearings caused a national sensation by documenting the extraordinary profits made by arms manufacturers during World War I and the industry's role in bribing public officials to vote for higher military budgets and to collude in price fixing.

Woman's special interest in peace and her capacity for peace activism and leadership was a widely held assumption of both men and women in the 1930s. Judging by the proliferation of antiwar dramas, women were seen not only as auxiliary peace activists but as the very embodiment of pacifism. Historian Barbara Melosh, in an insightful overview of antiwar drama in the 1930s, reports that antimilitarist plays figured prominently in the presentations of the Federal Theater Project, and that over two hundred plays with an antiwar theme were listed and summarized by the National Play Bureau. She attributes this unprecedented phenomenon to the influence of a vigorous peace movement, which, she asserts, "was the largest political movement, and the most active, with the possible exception of the labor movement."[38] What is of particular interest to us is that in the antiwar plays of the 1930s, written by women as well as men, women are rarely shown outside the family. Even in the one play in which a woman becomes president, she leaves her public duties when her grandchild becomes ill. However, when women are presented as a moral force, the message projected is that men should learn from female examples of conflict resolution, and that women should renounce passivity for peace activism.

The massive women's peace movement of the interwar period could not survive the onslaught of fascism in Europe and the Japanese attack on Pearl Harbor, which was followed by fervent public support for U.S. entry into the war. WILPF was the only feminist pacifist group that survived the war despite the fact that it opposed U.S. military involvement in World War II even after the attack on Pearl Harbor. During the war WILPF concentrated on issues of justice and democracy at home, and unlike most other liberal organizations in the country, it protested the internment of Japanese-Americans as a violation of civil liberties and a manifestation of racial discrimination. By the end of the war WILPF's membership had fallen to approximately thirty-eight hundred, and for almost a decade it had been unable to replace its old members of the suffrage generation with young women.

The end of World War II brought a revival of peace sentiment and a determination that the tragedy of modern warfare, with its millions of deaths, and the Nazi holocaust would never be repeated. Among those who raised the call for peace, international law, and nuclear restraint were the traditional anti-Communist pacifist groups, such as the War Resisters League, the Fellowship of Reconciliation, and WILPF. The old Communist left, concerned for the survival of the Soviet Union and for the protection of revolutionary movements throughout the world, also initiated a series of popular front peace organizations calling for friendly relations between the East and West.[39] Among those popular front peace groups was a short-lived national women's organization, the Congress of American Women (CAW), that connected the issue of peace to women's rights and social justice. CAW was founded in 1946, cited as subversive in 1948 by HUAC, and disbanded in 1950 when the Justice Department ordered it to register as an enemy agent.[40] CAW was the U.S. branch of the Women's International Democratic Federation (WIDF), an organization of 81 million women in forty-one countries, founded in 1945 by an international coalition of women of the anti-Fascist, pro-Communist left. While the CAW program was similar to that of other popular front coalitions, heavily influenced by the Communists and their allies but also including liberals who were willing to work with the party on a minimum coalition platform, it was distinct in its dedication to women's rights. In fact, a number of its leaders had been active in the suffrage struggle, and two were the offspring of its most prominent nineteenth-century leaders—Susan B. Anthony and Elizabeth Cady Stanton. At the time of its founding, CAW seemed destined to be the postwar, left-wing successor to the feminist peace movement of the interwar period. With a sense of women's history rare for its time, CAW identified itself with women's democratic struggles in America. This can be attributed, in part, to the influence of the Communist party's attempts during World War II to identify itself with indigenous American struggles for democracy and social justice. Under the slogan "Communism Is Twentieth Century Americanism," the Communist party encouraged research, writing, and rhetoric by its followers on the democratic tradition in the United States. It is not surprising, then, that in the postwar period, when the call for peace was being labeled as Communist and un-American, the CAW would proclaim: "In the past the fight for women's rights was part of the fight against slavery and economic exploitation, today it is also part of the fight for peace and security everywhere."[41] The preamble to the CAW constitution invoked the memory of historic women such as Anne Hutchinson, "pioneer in the fight for the Free Will of Man"; Betsy Ross, "whose needle sewed the stars into our flag"; and Harriet Tubman and Sojourner Truth, "who wrote a page in the history of freedom." The preamble also praised Harriet Beecher Stowe, Susan B. Anthony, Elizabeth Cady Stanton, and Lucretia Mott for launching "the long battle for Women's Rights." Recognizing working-class women as well as middle-class reformers, CAW recalled the Lowell Mill girls and the women garment workers of the early twentieth century "who struck for economic justice."[42]

As the Cold War accelerated, the peace issue became the central focus of CAW. The movement, along with its mother organization, WIDF, opposed the Truman Doctrine, the Marshall Plan, and "the presence of American troops in Greece, China, Vietnam, Indonesia, Malaya, Burma, and South Korea in support of anti-communist regimes."[43] The continued participation of CAW leaders in WIDF conferences behind the iron curtain provoked anger and ridicule in the U.S. press. The Paris edition of the *Herald Tribune* reported that some thirty American women at a WIDF conference in Budapest supported resolutions that made the Soviet Union "seem pure as the driven snow," while America "was depicted as simply dreadful."[44] The *Christian Science Monitor* stated flatly that CAW was part of the Kremlin's front against American democracy. It quoted Eleanor Roosevelt, who was a little more tolerant. "I wouldn't say they're all Communists or pro-Communists," Roosevelt stated, "but they are somewhat foolish, if they don't know they're playing a dangerous game for themselves and their country."[45] CAW's support of "coexistence" with the Soviet Union, its opposition to the Truman Doctrine, and its militant fight to maintain New Deal policies led to an investigation by HUAC. HUAC's purpose, it stated, was to warn naïve women who might be attracted to CAW because of its prowoman line that the goal of the organization was simply "to disarm and demobilize the U.S."[46] To sever the connection between CAW and women's rights, the committee singled out for attack two women who in their persons connected the organization directly to the suffragists: Susan B. Anthony II, the grandniece of Susan B. Anthony, and Nora Stanton Blatch Barney, granddaughter of Elizabeth Cady Stanton and daughter of Harriet Stanton Blatch. Using information provided by paid informers, HUAC charged Anthony with wide-ranging associations with left causes, including Writers for Wallace, and the Progressive party. Particularly damaging was the unsubstantiated accusation by an FBI informer that he had seen a picture of Lenin in Anthony's apartment.[47] Much was made by HUAC of an article on CAW Anthony had written for the Communist party newspaper, *Daily Worker*. In it she charged that the suffragists had been diverted by reactionary and misguided women leaders into study groups and women's clubs instead of militant political organizations.[48] HUAC did not mention that Anthony had also written an article on women's rights for the respectable *Women's Home Companion* in June 1945, in which she declared that the working woman was here to stay but that she is "almost the same old gal that grandma was if you go by our state laws."[49]

To undermine Nora Barney's credentials as a patriotic American, descended from a long line of upper-class abolitionist and women's rights activists, HUAC reprinted a *Daily Worker* news story that placed Barney at a CAW celebration of the centennial of Seneca Falls. Quoting the Communist press was a standard HUAC tactic for the incrimination of witnesses. In this case the *Daily Worker* report stated:

> The granddaughter of Elizabeth Cady Stanton placed a large floral wreath on the grave of her famous grandmother for the Congress of American Women . . . centennial commemorative ceremony. . . . Present also at the services was the nephew of Frederick Douglass. . . . It was Frederick Douglass who seconded Elizabeth Cady Stanton's first resolution in 1848 declaring it was the duty of all women to secure the franchise. Susan B. Anthony II, grandniece of Susan B. Anthony, a pioneer along with Elizabeth Cady Stanton [was] present at the ceremonies. [A] message was received from Alice Stone Blackwell, daughter of Lucy Stone.[50]

A comment, made by Nora Barney in Hungary while attending a WIDF conference, that she had met non-Communists in Hungary who seemed to have more freedom than Communists in her own country, was cited by HUAC as further proof that she was un-American.

CAW was cited as subversive by the attorney general in 1948 and began to lose its liberal members out of fear of persecution and disapproval of Soviet policies in Eastern Europe. But CAW continued to function, with less emphasis on women's rights than on peace, until it was required by the Justice Department in 1950 to register as an enemy agent. Although the CAW leadership decided to disaffiliate from WIDF and denied the accusation of working for the enemy, the Justice Department would not rescind its order. CAW disbanded by 1950 when its leadership was forced to recognize that there was no way to continue the organization without a legal battle that would have required more resources than were available and would probably have been doomed to failure in the political climate of the day. Thus a connection between women's rights and female peace protest was lost.

The fact that most of the women who joined WSP, eleven years after the demise of CAW, had never heard of it, is hard to believe. Yet there

are no references to CAW in any WSP literature or internal memoranda, and it was never mentioned at any of the dozens of local and
international meetings I attended. I remember occasional veiled references to a women's peace group that had been driven out of the United
Nations nongovernmental organizations because of its connection to a
pro-Soviet international group. Those who mentioned it never called it
by name and made it clear that the only thing WSP could learn from
that unnamed group was to be wary of international ties, especially
with WIDF.

The answer to the puzzling question of why most WSPers had been
unaware of the CAW in the late 1940s lies in the privatization and de-
politicization that pushed former liberals and radicals like the WSPers
out of national politics in the late 1940s. Many of those who had been
part of the old Left, and this included men as well, were disillusioned
with Stalinism and traumatized by McCarthyism. They were fearful and
suspicious of anything that could lead to Red baiting, with its disastrous
economic, political, and social consequences. And for women there was
yet another inhibition to political activism. Educated white women
with political ambitions were driven out of politics by the ridicule and
calumny heaped upon so-called masculine women by the promoters of
the new family ideology. Historian Elaine Tyler May in her brilliant examination of women's role in Cold War culture, *Homeward Bound*, ob-
serves that many educated women who accepted the new family ideology and its regressive notions of femininity, professionalized
homemaking and made it their career, investing it with skills, prestige,
and importance. "Thus women whose aspirations for personal achievement had little chance of realization in the wider world put their energies into full-time motherhood."[51] Thoughtful observers, according to
May, have suggested that the baby boom was a response to feelings of
impotence in the wider world, which fostered the greater privatization
and isolation of the family. One team of scholars argues that "if [men
and women] lacked the hope to affect congressional decisions, they
could still hope to influence their children and the local school board."[52]

It is no personal whim that prompted Dagmar Wilson, the organizer
of WSP, to work from a studio in her home. She had followed the advice
of baby experts such as Dr. Benjamin Spock, who counseled mothers of
young children to forgo full-time employment outside the home, and
Dr. Lawrence Frank, who advised that no matter how proficient hired
help might be "they cannot replace a mother in a child's life." Frank's
suggested alternative solutions to those women who wanted or needed
full-time jobs included "a secretarial typing service conducted from the
home, or the development of a latent skill such as painting tiles or
hooking rugs, which will help keep you alert and active without dis-

rupting your entire home."[53] Wilson's volunteer work as well as her professional work took place in an arena in which she, as a woman and artist, could be effective without transgressing gender boundaries. Like thousands of other women in WSP, Wilson became active in the PTA when her children entered elementary school. She was also a member of a Washington, D.C., committee to improve school libraries, and gave illustrated talks to children to foster their interest in reading.

According to statistics compiled by the Woman's Bureau in 1958, the average American woman could be expected to work a year or two after leaving school, marry at age twenty, and withdraw from the labor force after the birth of her first child. The bureau suggested that "she will likely devote ten to fifteen years exclusively to the important functions of childbearing and childcare."[54] Many of the key women of WSP had followed this pattern. By 1961 their children had outgrown the need for full-time mothering, and the women were becoming restless at home, ready for work of their own that would offer a greater sense of personal and social accomplishment than domesticity provided. Those I worked with during the 1960s and have interviewed since then recall that they were not quite sure what they wanted to do with the rest of their lives, and not being pressed financially, they were considering their options carefully when the nuclear emergency turned their attention from family matters, community service, and personal introspection to political activism. Less than half of those who participated in WSP had already joined a peace or civil rights group, but none had taken active leadership in any organization save WILPF. WSP offered an opportunity to express frustration and anger at the male policymakers, East and West, in one's own words. It was an opportunity to plan strategies in the name of women, write flyers, speak in public, meet with important political leaders, and, above all, save the children. For the WSP activists it was an opportunity for public service and personal expression that came at the right moment, both historically and personally, and the women welcomed it with energy and passion.

The women who joined the national peace strike on 1 November 1961 had been concerned about the bomb for many years. Some may not have given it much thought when the atom bombs were dropped on Hiroshima and Nagasaki. Most U.S. citizens were overjoyed that World War II was over and that "the boys" would be coming home. There were many with pacifist leanings, or a greater sensitivity to the costs of war, who would have agreed heartily with Norman Cousins's declaration a week after Japan surrendered that "Modern Man Is Obsolete" and doomed to live with a primitive fear of the forces he can neither channel nor comprehend.[55] Yet the earliest post-Hiroshima polls reveal what historian Paul Boyer describes as "a considerable will to think positively about the bomb."[56] Fear of the consequences of the bomb for Americans did not enter public consciousness on a discernible level until 1954, when U.S. atomic tests in the Pacific Ocean spread radioactive ash over seven thousand square miles and caused radiation poisoning to twenty-three Japanese fishermen on a vessel called, ironically, *Lucky Dragon*. When the Japanese government found it necessary to destroy the *Lucky Dragon*'s entire catch of eight hundred pounds of tuna because of contamination, the Japanese people panicked, creating an international furor. World indignation over the fate of the Japanese fishermen was so great that Chairman W. Sterling Cole of the Joint Committee on Atomic Energy wrote to President Eisenhower: "The American people, and more particularly other people throughout the world, have been struck with terror by the horrible implications of nuclear weapon development—and I think with much justification." Cole urged Eisenhower to announce that the United States would neither build nor test any weapons larger than those it now possessed.[57] The Soviet Union was also testing hydrogen bombs, which added to world levels of radiation in 1954 and 1955. In 1955 radioactive rain fell on Chicago, but the majority of the American people remained unconcerned and uninformed. In 1955 only 17 percent of the American people knew what the word *fallout* meant, according to a Gallup poll. However, in July of that year Nobel laureate Linus Pauling and British philosopher Bertrand Russell issued an appeal to world public opinion, declaring that *men* had to "learn to think in a new way. . . . we have to learn to ask ourselves, not what steps can be taken to give military victory to whatever group we prefer," but "what steps can be taken to prevent a military contest of which the issue must be disastrous to all parties."[58] Although the Pauling-Russell appeal was addressed to men, there were many women listening and worrying.

In 1956 Adlai Stevenson, the Democratic presidential candidate, increased public awareness of the nuclear danger by proposing a multilateral halt to atomic testing. The future WSPers applauded him for that, and many said later that they worked for his election because of his courage in raising the nuclear issue. But Stevenson's proposal brought forth denunciations from Eisenhower and Vice President Richard Nixon, who labeled it "not only naïve, but dangerous," and from conservative senator Karl Mundt, who pointed out that the Communist *Daily Worker* endorsed the proposal.[59]

The testing debate did not end with Stevenson's defeat. By 1957 the number of U.S. citizens who recognized the word *fallout* had grown to 28 percent because of a marked upsurge in antinuclear protests by religious leaders, atomic scientists, and pacifist groups, who were alarmed by the fact that the United States, the USSR, and Great Britain had all tested nuclear weapons during the year. In June 1957 Linus Pauling released a petition signed by eleven thousand scientists, including almost three thousand Americans, calling for immediate action toward an international agreement to stop the testing of all nuclear weapons. The petition proclaimed that scientists had special knowledge of the dangers involved in testing and therefore felt a special responsibility to make them known. Media coverage of the petition plus the testimony of several scientists at a March 1957 hearing on radiation by the Joint Committee on Atomic Energy served to increase public concern. During the hearings strontium 90, a component of radioactive fallout from nuclear tests, was described in alarming detail, including the ways in which it entered the atmosphere, fell to the ground, mixed with rain and snow, was ingested by cows, and entered the food cycle of humans through the milk they drank. One witness explained how small amounts build up in the human skeleton, particularly in growing children. This served to undermine confidence in government assurances that radiation poses no physical dangers to human beings. "Not since Hiroshima," commented *Newsweek*, "had such a bitter and fateful debate raged over the building, testing, and ultimate use of the A-bomb and its vastly more destructive offspring, the H-bomb. Governments, scientists, military men, just plain ordinary citizens were caught up in the controversy."[60]

On 6 August 1957, the twelfth anniversary of the atom bombing of Hiroshima, the newly formed CNVA demonstrated outside the gates of the AEC proving grounds in Nevada, creating a model for direct action by ordinary citizens in opposition to nuclear testing that would be followed by WSP.

By the end of 1958 the world had experienced at least 190 atom and hydrogen bomb tests: 125 by the United States, 44 by the Soviet Union, and 21 by Great Britain. In 1959 radiation levels increased sharply due to the large number of nuclear blasts in the previous year. The sharp rise in the strontium 90 levels in milk prompted *Consumer Reports* to warn: "The fact is that fresh milk, which looks and tastes just as it always did, nevertheless contains . . . an unseen contaminant, a toxic substance known to accumulate in human bone."[61] The fallout scare had apparently spread beyond the informed, health-conscious, and antinuclear community, judging by the fact that the conservative *Saturday Evening Post* published a two-part article in 1959 describing fallout as "a silent killer" that would "extort a heavy toll in disease, deformity and early death for many yet unborn."[62]

Historian Paul Boyer, who has tracked and analyzed political and cultural reaction in the United States to the atom bomb, asserts that, in the years immediately prior to the test ban treaty, "nuclear fear was a shaping cultural force."[63] Books, essays, and symposia exposed the medical, psychological, and moral consequences of the atomic arms race. The films *On the Beach, Fail Safe,* and *Dr. Strangelove* delivered a powerful message to millions of viewers that nuclear war was possible, if not probable. The number of science fiction stories dealing with nuclear issues increased, and Boyer, along with other cultural historians and critics, contends that the spate of mutant movies in the 1950s had clear psychological roots in fears of genetic damage from radioactive fallout. Worried mothers, some future WSPers, wrote thousands of letters to Congress and local newspapers, expressing their fears regarding contaminated milk, but widespread criticism of the nuclear arms race was inhibited by fear of communism and concepts of national loyalty. "The American people worried even more about national security than the humanitarian concerns stressed by test ban advocates. They placed their trust in the wisdom and judgement of President Eisenhower," according to Eugene Rosi, who conducted an analysis of American public opinion in relation to nuclear weapons tests.[64]

Shortly before he died Albert Einstein analyzed the dilemma the world faced in regard to the greatest threat to its survival: "In essence the conflict that exists today is no more than the old-style struggle for power. . . . The difference is that this time the development of atomic power has imbued the struggle with a ghostly character; for both parties know and admit that should the quarrel deteriorate into actual war, mankind is doomed."[65] These words had a profound impact on the emerging peace constituency. They enabled those who supported one side or another in the Cold War to identify the bomb as a greater enemy to humanity than either the USSR or the United States. The articulation of a "third-camp" position by pacifist leader A. J. Muste, psychoanalyst Erich Fromm, and sociologist C. Wright Mills also provided the rhetoric and political space for a new type of peace activism, devoid of Cold War or class war implications. Muste, like Einstein, called for a new way of thinking and new political behavior as the only route to salvation. Muste's words were particularly appealing to the women who founded WSP, because they were convinced that traditional ideological politics with its abstractions and absolutes led nowhere but to nuclear holocaust.

It was the growing public awareness of the radiation menace, a new understanding that Russians could kill Americans as many times over as Americans could kill Russians, and the articulation of the third-camp position that led a group of liberal political, intellectual, and religious leaders to found SANE, the first mass organization in opposition to the nuclear arms race. Lawrence Scott, later a founder of WSP, then peace education secretary of the American Friends Service Committee (AFSC), called the meeting that led to the organization of SANE in the summer of 1957. Robert A. Divine in his book *Blowing on the Wind: The Nuclear Test Ban Debate, 1954–1960* credits a woman, Catherine Cory, an organizer for the Friend's Committee on National Legislation, for the suggestion that SANE make the ending of bomb tests its primary demand. But Cory did not see atomic testing as a women's issue. "By calling for an end to bomb tests," she wrote to Norman Cousins and Clarence Pickett, "at least we have an issue that the average *Joe* understands" (emphasis added).[66]

On 15 November 1957 the founders of SANE advertised in the *New York Times* that the American people were "Facing a Danger Unlike Any Danger That Has Ever Existed." The big challenge of the age, SANE proposed, "is to develop the concept of a higher loyalty, the loyalty by man to the human community." The SANE ad was signed by forty-six respected liberal peace and public affairs leaders, three of whom were women: Eleanor Roosevelt, novelist and poet Lenore G. Marshall, and lay disarmament expert Josephine Pomerance.[67] The response to the SANE ad was overwhelming. By the summer of 1958 SANE had approximately 130 chapters.[68] Peace was beginning to seem like a respectable cause and a possible goal, as Eisenhower and Khrushchev met at Camp David in a prelude to a summit meeting in Berlin, and the United States and the Soviet Union agreed to a moratorium on nuclear testing. In 1960 SANE seemed destined to become an effective massive movement for peace when it was assailed by Red-baiting attacks from Congress and by the inability of its leaders to deal with the very Cold War assumptions the organization had pledged itself to transcend. In May 1960 Senator Thomas J. Dodd, temporary chairman of the Senate Internal Security Subcommittee, an outspoken foe of arms control, charged that SANE was infiltrated and ordered it to clean house. The Dodd attack came a few days before SANE's most ambitious public effort: a Madison Square Garden rally that attracted a packed house of twenty thousand people, and a roster of speakers such as Eleanor Roosevelt, Governor G. Mennon Williams of Michigan, Walter Reuther of the United Auto Workers, Norman Thomas, and A. Philip Randolph, president of the Brotherhood of Sleeping Car Workers. Following the rally Reuther, Thomas, and Harry Belafonte led a march of five thousand people to the United Nations for a midnight prayer. In Hollywood hundreds of film personalities participated in a parallel event led by Steve Allen and Robert Ryan, cochairmen of Hollywood for SANE. A few days before the rally Senator Dodd had subpoenaed Henry Abrams of New York SANE, the organizer of the mass meeting. Norman Cousins then requested the resignation of Abrams, who was known to have been a member of the left-of-center American Labor party and an activist in the Henry Wallace campaign in 1948. The ostensible reason for forcing Abrams's resignation was that he had resorted to the Fifth Amendment at the Senate Internal Security Subcommittee hearing in order to avoid answering questions about his political affiliations, and also had refused to divulge to Cousins, in private, whether or not he was or had been a member of the Communist party. Abrams did, however, assure Cousins and the SANE board "that he was not under the orders or instructions of any outside agent or organization, and that his sole concern was to make SANE a success."[69]

Reports in the press, later denied by Cousins, hinted that the Senate investigation had been instigated by Cousins himself. After heated discussions the SANE board voted to issue guidelines to its chapters excluding from membership those with present or past Communist associations. Pacifist leader A. J. Muste resigned as sponsor of the greater New York SANE committee, and Stewart Meacham and Robert Gilmore resigned from the SANE board in protest.[70] Linus Pauling and Bertrand Russell withdrew their sponsorship from SANE.

Erich Fromm criticized the exclusionary policy but did not withdraw from SANE. Socialist pacifist Norman Thomas, on the other hand, declared himself to be in support of the SANE board on the grounds that "one has to deal with those Americans, whose name is legion, who connect peace and communism."[71] Muste's condemnation of SANE's capitulation to Dodd influenced the WSP response to HUAC when it was the women's turn to confront congressional Red hunters. Muste wrote: "The Committees are instruments of the Cold War. They stand for the policy of nuclear deterrence. They aim to discredit and weaken the peace movement. No peace organization pressured by such agencies or which has commerce with them can maintain its integrity or develop drive and power."[72] In the weeks and months after the decision to exclude alleged Communists from membership, many individuals and whole chapters were either expelled or withdrew from SANE. The Washington, D.C., chapter opposed the national board's decision but did not withdraw. The Washington chapter wrote to the national board: "The greatest internal dangers of the last years have been the activities of investigating committees like the Internal Security Subcommittee. Their goal is nothing less than thought control."[73] This was the SANE chapter from which WSP arose.

In view of their deep concern about the health and welfare of their children, and their political orientation toward world peace, it is not surprising that the Washington women who founded WSP were all members of SANE. Dagmar Wilson recalls that she, Margaret Russell, Folly Fodor, and Miriam Levin, all organizers of WSP in 1962, opposed the national board's action as a capitulation to Cold War thinking.[74] Based on their experience in SANE they decided, from the outset of their movement, that they would have no formal requirements for membership or even membership lists. Their fierce dedication, as their movement grew, to the autonomy of each chapter and their rejection of the notion of a national policy-making board were a reaction not only to governmental repression of foreign policy dissent, but also to "the crisis in SANE."

The inauguration of John Kennedy in 1960 brought new energy and hope to peace advocates. To the peace constituency Kennedy promised a continuation of the testing moratorium, new initiatives in disarmament, and new overtures to the Soviet Union. The peace people were not unaware that he also promised Cold War supporters an increased military budget and a tough stand against communism, but his mention of the word *disarmament* was interpreted by the hopeful as a promise and a legitimation of what had formerly been unmentionable. President Kennedy fulfilled his Cold War promises sooner than the disarmament pledge. After an unsuccessful meeting with Khrushchev in Vienna in June 1961, he returned home to push through Congress a $3.2 billion supplemental military appropriation and $207 million for an accelerated fallout-shelter program. He tripled draft calls, mobilized 158,000 reservists and National Guardsmen, increased the armed forces by 300,000 men, and shipped 400,000 to Europe, to the dismay of the women who struck for peace five months later. Khrushchev countered what he saw as a U.S. military buildup by erecting the Berlin Wall to cut off West Berlin from East Germany. As tensions mounted between the two powers, Khrushchev announced on 30 October 1961 that the Soviet Union would resume atmospheric testing after a four-year moratorium. The moratorium had been broken by France in the Sahara in 1960, but it continued to be observed by the United States, the USSR, and Great Britain. Kennedy responded to the Soviet move by ordering a resumption of underground testing and suggested that full-scale atmospheric tests would follow. The threat to world peace and human survival seemed grave and palpable. A. J. Muste expressed the fears of thousands of women like Dagmar Wilson, Folly Fodor, Eleanor Garst, Jeanne Bagby, and Margaret Russell, the WSP founders: "I am worried about the international situation," he stated, "more so than at any time since World War II. . . . Practically nobody talks anymore about the *abstract* possibility of nuclear war 'in our time.' Now the discussions all have to do with the concrete possibility or probability of nuclear war today or the day after tomorrow."[75]

Peace protest in England, which had accelerated in response to the world crisis, was being watched by many Americans for confirmation, inspiration, and legitimation. In September 1961 Bertrand Russell was jailed for an act of civil disobedience calculated to draw world attention to what he believed to be the very imminent danger of thermonuclear war. As the eighty-nine-year-old philosopher prepared to serve his seven-day sentence, he issued an apocalyptic message, which was reprinted by Cold War critic I. F. Stone in his "Weekly." "You, your families, your friends and your countries are to be exterminated, by the common decision of a few brutal, but powerful men," Russell declared. "To please these men, all the private affections, all the public hopes, all that has been achieved in art and knowledge and thought, and all that might be achieved hereafter, is to be wiped out forever. . . . It is for seeking to prevent this that we are in prison."[76]

The Berlin Wall crisis, the Russian atomic tests, and the jailing of Bertrand Russell had a profound effect on Dagmar Wilson and the thousands of women who rallied in only six weeks to stage a nationwide strike for peace. Russell's example called for action. Wilson recalls that she felt like hiring a plane, filling it with friends, and descending on the London jail where he was being held.

The top leadership of SANE, all men, were less agitated, more deliberate, and more slowly moved to action. Wilson and her friends concluded that if the men in the peace movement, as well as those in the State Department, were paralyzed by Cold War attitudes, the women would have to act to fulfill their prescribed responsibility. Had not the leading scholars, educators, psychologists, and theologians been pointing out for centuries that it was women's task to civilize man? Only a few months before WSP was founded, the *Ladies' Home Journal* had reprinted the baccalaureate address of the headmistress at Concord Academy, who advised women, "It is woman's business to clinch civilization. Freed of the necessity of competing in the economic struggle, woman, far better than man, can define the idealistic goals for which we strive."[77]

The women who struck for peace in November 1961 were ready to accept the challenge to save the world. Free for the most part from paid employment outside the home and from childcare, deeply angered by the nuclear recklessness of the superpowers, and frustrated by what they perceived as the timidity of the traditional peace movement, they made a conscious choice to step forward to save their children and the planet. On a less conscious level they perceived an opportunity to do something important, useful, and rewarding. Building on their moral, political, and social concerns, and operating within the parameters of traditional female culture and the political conservatism of the time, the women of WSP stepped onto the political stage to wage a struggle for an end to the nuclear testing, the arms race, and the Cold War. In the course of that struggle, they transformed themselves and the image of traditional motherhood.

WSP fills both sides of Pennsylvania Avenue in front of the White House on 15 January 1962. Marching in the rain, carrying balloons decorated with the slogan, "Pure Milk—Not Poison," and placards demanding, "No Tests—East or West," the women stage the largest White House Peace protest since the 1940s. UPI/Bettmann

WSP women attempt to enter the Nevada test site in July 1962 to prevent a scheduled atmospheric explosion. Records of Women Strike for Peace, Swarthmore College Peace Collection

Los Angeles WSP, 1962.

Congressional space becomes women's and babies' space at the Old House Office Building, Washington, D.C., on 11 December 1962, as WSP prepares to challenge the HUAC Hearings on Communist Infiltration into the Peace Movement. Standing at left is Blanche Posner, of Scarsdale, N.Y., the first WSP witness. UPI/Bettmann

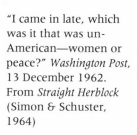

"I came in late, which was it that was un-American—women or peace?" *Washington Post*, 13 December 1962. From *Straight Herblock* (Simon & Schuster, 1964)

WSP founders Dagmar Wilson (left), Eleanor Garst (next to her) and Margaret Russell (far right) with Linus Pauling and Ava Helen Pauling lobbying the State Department, Washington D.C., May 1963. Photo by Olga Diamond

Linus Pauling with actress Julie Harris (left) and East Side N.Y. WSP, Chris Dubusky at the United Nations, Spring 1963. Records of Women Strike for Peace, Swarthmore College Peace Collection

"Thank You for the First Step." WSP celebrates its second anniversary, 1 November 1963. Dagmar Wilson and Coretta Scott King (front row) lead a march at the United Nations Headquarters to give thanks for the achievement of the August 1963 treaty banning nuclear tests in the atmosphere.

Michigan Women for Peace (WFP) present antiwar petition to Lieuenant Governor John Lesinski. Representatives from Ann Arbor, Detroit, Lansing, and Kalamazoo visited their state legislators on 24 April 1964 to demand pressure on Congress to divert funds from the military budget to the war on poverty. The woman on the right of the Lieutenant Governor is Mickey Flacks of Ann Arbor WSP and SDS. From Alice Herz's scrapbook, Records of Women Strike for Peace, Swarthmore College Peace Collection

Philadelphia WSP women and their children bid farewell to Ethel Taylor (holding flowers) as she departs for the Women's NATO Peace Force meeting at The Hague in May 1964. Taylor carried with her a box containing thousands of petitions protesting the MLF, a proposed NATO nuclear fleet. Records of Women Strike for Peace, Swarthmore College Peace Collection

Barbara Bick editing MEMO in Washington, D.C., WSP office, June 1964.

Holding paper doves, WSP women from the northeastern seaboard gather at
Pennsylvania Station for a Mothers' March on Capitol Hill to Stop the War in
Vietnam. UPI/Bettmann

WSP March on the Pentagon, 15 February 1967. Pentagon doors were slammed shut
as the women attempted to gain entrance. Some removed their shoes to bang them at
the doors until Secretary of Defense Robert McNamara agreed to see a delegation.
UPI/Bettmann

Ruth Krause of New Jersey WSP and Dagmar Wilson present a shopping bag, typical of those WSP women carried to antiwar marches in the 1960s to Premier Pham Van Dong of North Vietnam. Hanoi, 1967. Records of Women Strike for Peace, Swarthmore College Peace Collection

Mary Clark (left) and Dagmar Wilson (right) visit an underground school in a Vietnamese village north of Hanoi in September 1967. Photo courtesy of Cora Weiss

3

Who Are These Women?

Who are these women? Are they really young
mothers with small children at their skirts, and no
previous experience in community affairs . . . or
are they "old pros" with a well-defined idea of
some kind of world social order?
—Elise Boulding, "Who Are These Women?"

*P*lanning only a one-day protest, the organizers of the 1 November peace strike were astonished and overwhelmed by the hundreds of communications from women "around the country and all over the world" that inundated Dagmar Wilson's home immediately after the strike. Almost all the letters to the founders expressed a strong desire to keep the women's peace strike idea going, but also a reluctance to establish a formal organization. What most of the letters suggested was that the women who had demonstrated on 1 November stay in touch, but "unorganized." The Washington initiators responded favorably to the notion of a loose communications network. They made it clear to their growing list of contacts not only that they were eager to share leadership, but that they claimed little authority or credit for themselves.[1] This does not mean that the founders were ready to abandon or relinquish the political initiative they had seized so dramatically, but rather that they were reluctant to build yet another top-down bureaucratic peace organization similiar to those they had fled.

An evaluation meeting, held one week after the strike, was attended by approximately seventy-five women from the Capitol district, plus a handful of visitors from Baltimore, Philadelphia, San Francisco, and New York. The meeting decided to continue the pressure on elected officials to end the nuclear arms race in the name of an entity to be called Women Strike for Peace. The follow-up meeting rejected any notion of repeating the strike, sensing that it would be difficult to replicate the initial success and that large-scale national mobilizations should be reserved for the grave crises that were still to come. The organizers proposed, instead, that the existing local strike groups set aside the first day of each month as a "women's strike for peace day." Each local group was free to observe the first-of-the-month strike day in any way it

49

chose. The only requirement was that the groups call attention to the need to end the nuclear arms race. Thus local autonomy was built into the WSP movement from the start.[2]

By projecting a monthly event, the Washington organizers insured that local groups would continue to meet and to develop a leadership cadre capable of planning local actions, recruiting new participants, and maintaining a communications network locally and to and from Washington. Whether or not the founders had foreseen it or even approved of the notion, they had set up a structure that required an enormous investment of time and effort on the part of hundreds of women across the country who began to develop a passionate interest in perpetuating their new movement and in influencing its tactics and goals.

The desire for minimal structure and the demand for local autonomy came mainly from women who were already members of established peace organizations in which they had found themselves powerless to influence policies and programs. Stymied by top-down rules and restrictions, they were frustrated not only by the male-led SANE but also by the feminist-founded WILPF, which they perceived as paralyzed by Cold War fears and an unresponsive hierarchical structure. Those who turned from WILPF to WSP did so because the new movement afforded them the space to initiate and engage in spontaneous direct actions in response to what they perceived as a planetary crisis, without interference from a national office. Among those active WILPF members who became WSP leaders were Ethel Taylor and Evelyn Alloy of Philadelphia, Frances Herring of Berkeley, Janet Neuman and Donna Allen of Washington, D.C., Charlotte Keyes of Urbana, Illinois, and Alice Herz of Detroit. Recognized WILPF leaders such as Elise Boulding of Ann Arbor, Ava Helen Pauling of Palo Alto, California, and Ruth Gage-Colby of New York City, who were drawn to WSP by the new energy and militancy it brought to peace protest, found a way to function as leaders of both groups. Ethel Taylor, and Hazel Grossman, who had been active in San Francisco WILPF, recalled that when they received the Washington call to strike they were feeling hamstrung by the top-down leadership of WILPF and were ready to move on.[3] Taylor has stated several times that "if WILPF had been dynamic, WSP would probably never have been born."[4] A letter from Evelyn Alloy, written in March 1962 to the WILPF executive committee, indicates the kinds of constraints that led some WILPF members to turn toward WSP. Alloy demanded to know "what degree of autonomy does a state branch have? I would hope that the state Board does not become so timid that it wants all PAC projects to be submitting flyers, etc. to Mrs. Olmstead and Mrs. Hutchinson [executive director and president] for approval."[5] Apparently so much interest in WSP's new freewheeling activism was expressed by members of WILPF that in March 1962, four months after the birth of WSP, the WILPF National Executive Committee advised the Denver branch to remain officially separate from WSP.[6] The WILPF board declared that groups like WSP were not organizations "and therefore do not necessarily have a common philosophy or a common politics." It was suggested that WILPF cooperate with WSP as individuals, not as an organization. Members were warned that they could not work on WSP projects as WILPF members, unless the project was specifically endorsed by a local, state, or national body of WILPF. WILPF members were advised that in case of doubt regarding the guidelines they should consult the national office.[7] Despite some tensions between national WILPF and WSP, the women in both groups worked together on the local level and were cordial and respectful to one another. Ruth Gage-Colby, a WILPF board member who became a WSP spokesperson, stated in an interview almost twenty years after the founding of WSP that she remembered a long session at WILPF headquarters, where "we really tried to persuade this younger group, this Women Strike for Peace, to merge with us in a united movement, and I felt a little sad that the younger women were not quite ready to do this, but we remained good friends."[8] New York WSP attributed the difference between the two groups to the fact that WILPF was a "structured membership organization that emphasized long-range educational projects rather than spontaneous direct-action." But Gage-Colby attributed the differences between the two groups to the fact that WILPF "could be called a bit more conservative."

What WSP brought to the 1960s peace movement was a new mode of operation, sometimes referred to as "the new WSP way." The WSP way was intentionally simple, pragmatic, nonideological, moralistic, and emotional. It was nonexclusionary in that it refused to bar any woman, regardless of her past political affiliations, from membership, and reached out to the apolitical woman in a language that was accessible, free of jargon either political, ideological, or scientific. The constituency to be reached by WSP flyers, posters, pamphlets, and advertisements was always visualized as the neighbor next door, the woman one met in the doctor's office, stood next to at the supermarket checkout counter, or worked with in the PTA or the League of Women Voters. WSP made a conscious effort to demystify the political process, to close the barrier between thinkers and doers, leaders and rank-and-file followers. The school car pool organizational chart and class mother's telephone tree were models for a national decision-making and communications network that substituted for a designated leadership core and a paid staff.

From its first day the movement tapped a vast reservoir of moral outrage, organizational talent, and playful irreverence for male political culture that gave its pressure tactics, such as lobbying, petitioning, and demonstrating, a joyful and human face. WSP was one of the biggest stories of 1961 in terms of newspaper and television coverage. And in its first two years WSP was able to make an impact on nuclear policy in a way that few citizens' groups had since World War II.

Although the words "group process" had not yet entered the vocabulary, WSP placed its faith in group interaction as a source of creativity and power. WSP meetings, national and local, rejected polarizing votes that could lead to majority rule, trying unceasingly to arrive at consensus. Mickey Flacks, a twenty-one-year-old member of Students for a Democratic Society (SDS), living in Ann Arbor in the early 1960s, recalls that she joined WSP because the women offered "a new vision of how to operate politically" and did not seem to be talking in old political terms. In 1980 Flacks still thought of WSP as "the most participatory organization of its time."[9]

Two radical youth organizations, SDS and the Student Nonviolent Coordinating Committee (SNCC), founded at the same time as WSP, were also antihierarchical, but they made much of their named and acclaimed leaders. WSP women, on the other hand, insisted that every participant was equally qualified to speak for the movement. In fact, the WSP women seem to have had an almost pathological antipathy to selecting leaders who might usurp their newfound privilege of thinking, talking, and planning for themselves and their movement. The media, however, found it difficult to accept a leaderless movement and chose to see Dagmar Wilson as the head of WSP. Wilson was uncomfortable with the designation. Only three weeks after the 1 November strike she told the *New York Times* that "it's about time I stop being head of this. We have many excellent volunteers, I just happened to be the starter."[10]

This was not altogether true. Wilson was much more than the starter. She was the only one of the founders that the majority of the WSP women were able to identify with and accept completely. And it was her diffidence, a deeply internalized humility, and her gentle force that the women found most appealing. Also important was her nondoctrinaire, "common-sense" approach to world affairs. A thoughtful person with a finely honed sense of justice and decency, she possessed the charisma of those who reflect the feelings and perceptions of their constituents, and who add to that their original perceptions and special passion. Despite her own judgment that she was not a public orator, Wilson was an eloquent speaker with a clear eye for the ridiculous and meretricious in political dogma.

Possessing a beautiful speaking voice, a crisp manner, and the kind of British accent that Americans identify with good breeding, Wilson was an ideal spokesperson for a group of women who insisted that they were only housewives, but who wanted to be heard, heeded, and respected. North Shore Chicago Women for Peace, a WSP chapter, announced Wilson's forthcoming visit with this tribute: "As the founder and inspiration of Women for Peace, Dagmar Wilson has called attention to peace as no other individual today. . . . Wherever she goes she radiates charm and dignity and gives voice to the convictions which we hold dear and for which we work."[11] Kay Hardman, a Los Angeles key woman, wrote to Wilson after she had heard her speak at a WSP luncheon: "I was moved to tears, as were others seated near me. . . . One of the reasons, of course, is that we have become unaccustomed to that deep level of honesty, and another is that many of us are attempting to look within ourselves for those sources of womanliness you limned so beautifully."[12]

Valerie Delacorte, a former Hungarian film star and wife of the influential publisher George T. Delacorte of Dell Press, attributed her own involvement in peace protest directly to the influence of Wilson. A devout Catholic, deeply concerned with Christian morality, Delacorte was appalled by the campaign to build fallout shelters. When she discovered that a shelter being built on her Connecticut estate could not accommodate her gardener and his six children, she was deeply troubled. She regarded it as highly un-Christian for her family to be sheltered while others were not. "I felt the only thing we could do was die with the others." On deeper reflection she decided that the "truly moral thing was to work for an end to the possibility of nuclear war."[13] Delacorte contacted Wilson after reading about the strike and was so taken with Wilson's sincerity and conviction that she became a WSP sponsor immediately. She brought together in her Fifth Avenue apartment 110 women, whose names were provided by Wilson from a list she had compiled of those who had supported the strike, to found New York WSP. After the founding meeting, at which Wilson was the chief speaker, Delacorte wrote to her: "Every word of your speech went through my heart—because it came from your heart and because you are a true person. And in a way, you are my mother, and the mother of all of us—you are the Mother Superior of our Lysistrata convent."[14]

A measure of WSP consciousness of itself and its concept of leadership is the contrast in the treatment of Dagmar Wilson and Bella Abzug by the WSP women in the 1960s. Wilson was the acknowledged spokesperson and sought-after speaker, while Bella Abzug was an active member of the New York group and the chairperson of WSP's national legislative committee, which she had launched. Abzug's expertise and tactical brilliance on legislative matters was highly respected within the movement, but she was never a spokesperson for the national group because she did not fit the WSP "mother and housewife" image. It was not until the second wave of feminism legitimized self-assertive professional women with political ambitions that Abzug was recognized and admired for her oratory and the leadership she had given WSP from its earliest days.

Dagmar Wilson was a self-proclaimed political neophyte at the time she called the small meeting that led to the founding of WSP. She was the mother of three daughters, aged twenty, sixteen, and thirteen, and a successful illustrator of children's books. She practiced her art from a studio in her Georgetown home, which she occupied with her daughters and her husband, Christopher. Wilson was born in New York City on 25 January 1916 but had been reared and educated in Germany and England. Her father, Caesar Searchinger, was a music critic and journalist who took up residence in Europe in 1919. He was subsequently appointed European director of CBS and later European news analyst for NBC. Wilson spent most of her childhood in a political home where influential American journalists and news commentators, notably Raymond Gram Swing, Dorothy Thompson, and John Gunther, were frequent visitors. These people wrote about world affairs, Wilson recollected in 1976, "but they did precious little to influence their course." She recalled her feeling at the time, the period of the rise of nazism and fascism, that her parents and their friends should *act* on their political convictions, not just talk and write about them.[15] However, she herself did not become involved in any form of organized social protest while growing up in prewar England. It would have been easy for her to do so, she pointed out, as she attended a progressive school where her classmates were "dissenters—not quite the average type—sons and daughters of psychiatrists, writers, vegetarians." Wilson devoted her young adult years in England to the study of art. She attended the Slade School of Art from 1933 to 1937, winning prizes in all the major areas of study and a scholarship for a postgraduate year. While teaching art in a London elementary school, she met her future husband, an Englishman who was supporting himself in medical school by teaching. In 1939, shortly before the outbreak of World War II, Dagmar and Christopher left England for the United States, where they were married. In her first year back in her native land Wilson lived on a farm near St. Louis. There she cooked for the farmer and his son and painted rural landscapes while her husband attended medical school. The Wilsons then moved on to New York City, where Christopher, who had given up his medical studies, went to work for the British government as a commercial attaché. In New York City, Dagmar taught art at the Lincoln School of Teachers' College, Columbia University.

In 1942 the Wilsons moved to Washington, D.C. There Dagmar spent the remaining years of World War II working as a graphic artist for the U.S. government. She left full-time employment after the war, as many other women did, to rear her children.

Becoming a resident mother did not prevent Wilson from practicing her profession. She continued painting, became a fellow of the Phillips Gallery, and exhibited her work from time to time. She also became a free-lance illustrator to supplement the family income. In 1946 Wilson illustrated her first children's book, *While Susie Sleeps,* which became a best-seller. By the time she initiated WSP, Wilson had illustrated approximately twenty other children's books.

Like thousands of other women in WSP, Wilson became active in the PTA when her children entered elementary school. In 1959 she was instrumental in founding the Action Committee for School Libraries in the District of Columbia and was a leading force in the Children's Book Guild. With the cooperation of the *Washington Post,* Wilson ran a children's book fair each year. In her pre-WSP days Wilson was in great demand as a presenter of illustrated talks on children's books. She was adept at drawing while speaking but insists that political speeches were never her style. She explained to an interviewer from the *Washington Post:* "I am not a speech maker. It takes a tremendous lot out of me. . . . It's no accident that I took to art, a visual form of expression. I find it the most difficult thing in the world to discuss self-evident matters."[16]

In view of her professional accomplishments, her community activism, and her economic role in her family, one might wonder why the founder of WSP identified herself primarily as a housewife.[17] Reflecting on this issue fifteen years later, Wilson maintained that she called herself a housewife because she thought of herself that way. The proof, she claimed, was that she did her professional work at home. After some prodding to explain why the other Washington founders also chose to stress their domestic role, Wilson offered an additional reason that may have been influenced by her more feminist consciousness of 1976: "My idea in emphasizing the housewife, rather than the professional, was that I thought the housewife was a downgraded person and that housewives had as much right to opinions . . . and that we deserved as much consideration as anyone else. I wanted to emphasize that this was an important role and that it was time we were heard."[18] Wilson's claim to the title of housewife fitted comfortably with her stand as a political amateur. She made it clear in all interviews that she had never belonged to any political group but SANE, which she had joined because of her fear and loathing of the atom bomb. Fifteen years after the founding of WSP, Wilson still insisted, "I am not at all a political animal. . . . I have no interest in the political game, which for many is a real hobby." She insisted that she "never bought the Cold War" but was not moved to active opposition until she began to feel a growing sense of doom. "The State Department line . . . was being repeated without challenge or question by the press, . . . and accepted by intelligent, educated, intellectual, liberal Americans. . . . It had the effect on me of being in prison without access to the outdoors—no change of weather, no sun, no clouds, no stirring breezes."[19] Wilson believes that if she had perceived any effective political challenge to Cold War militarism anywhere in the country she would not have started WSP. "I was not only disturbed by our policies, but angered by the gutlessness of the professional men who were part of the social circle to which my husband and I belonged. Who, if not they," she asked herself, "should respond to the warnings of intellectual leaders such as Linus Pauling, Bertrand Russell, and Albert Einstein?"[20] Despite her disagreements with the "State Department line," Wilson was not a follower of the Soviet line or an advocate of Marxism. "I never was enough of a scholar to study Marxist theory," she reflected, "but I always had a hunch that there was some truth in it. If only I had the wit to settle down and analyze it."[21]

Wilson says that it was a sense of imminent catastrophe that finally moved her to action. A speech by Jerome Frank, a psychiatrist, prompted her to take a personal role in the struggle for the survival of the planet. Frank, like Albert Einstein, Albert Schweitzer, and Erich Fromm, argued that the human mind, which was capable of splitting the atom and putting satellites into space, was forced, in the nuclear age, to construct alternatives to war.[22] After hearing Frank, Wilson joined SANE to learn how a citizen could function effectively in opposition to national policy. She recalled: "That was really my first political activity, but very quickly I became the secretary of the local chapter. I couldn't type, I wasn't very good . . . but I undertook the job because I had joined to learn." At first, Wilson was very much impressed with SANE's program and its Washington coordinator, Sanford Gottlieb. But she soon became impatient with SANE's professional brand of peace politics. She tried to join in SANE's lobbying on the Hill but never was sufficiently knowledgeable on legislative issues to feel effective. She recalls that she was troubled by SANE's exclusionary guidelines, which barred Communists and former Communists from membership, but she did not make her objections known because she sensed that "you had to either get out or shut up."[23] The immediate impulse to start a women's peace action, however, was precipitated by her dissatisfaction with SANE on another count.

Wilson was returning with her family from summer holiday when she heard on the car radio the news of the Berlin Wall crisis and talk of a possible confrontation between the nuclear superpowers. When she entered her home, she found a pile of mail topped by *I. F. Stone's Weekly.*

Its front page carried a dramatic and ominous statement by Bertrand Russell, delivered on his way to jail for an act of antinuclear civil disobedience.[24] The jailing of Lord Russell, whom Wilson had admired in her youth, was the final blow. She decided that, "when a man like Russell, who has the ear of anyone in the world, has to have a public temper tantrum to demonstrate the gravity of the nuclear threat, the time had come for extraordinary action." She thought of chartering a plane and heading for London to picket the jail, but that was beyond her resources. Later that day, when friends arrived for drinks in the Wilsons' garden, Dagmar attempted to share her distress. But her sense of outrage met with little response. "All my questions were turned off with jokes as though the topic was unimportant," she recalled with as much indignation, fifteen years after the incident, as she had felt then. "We were calmly sipping gin and tonics as though nothing was the matter, but I was deadly serious."

The next morning Dagmar called the SANE office to inquire what the organization was going to do about Russell's arrest. When she learned that SANE planned no active response, she was stunned. Wilson remembers that she just sat there at the phone, numb. After ten or fifteen minutes she began to call all the women she knew, using her personal phone book and not caring whether the she was reaching Chicago, Philadelphia, or Los Angeles. She was encouraged by the fact that all her women friends were as worried as she was, and that their responses to the idea of a women's action was almost unanimously positive.

Three nights later, Wilson and a group of Washington women, all of whom had met each other through SANE, were sitting in the Wilson living room planning the first massive national women's peace demonstration since the onset of the Cold War. Among those present were Eleanor Garst, Folly Fodor, and Margaret Russell. They, together with Wilson and Jeanne Bagby, who some believe was present at the meeting but who is not listed in the minutes, became known as the five founders of WSP.

Dagmar Wilson contends that she had no female role models and that her only inspiration for the WSP action was the civil rights movement in the South. She was aware of the suffrage struggle, which was referred to in the official call to strike, but it had little relevance for her at the moment, because she was convinced that women's battle for equality had been won. "My mother belonged to that generation," she told me. "Although she was not a member, both my parents were strongly behind suffrage." Wilson recalled that as a child she was aware that one of her mother's friends wore a prison badge signifying that she had been jailed for suffrage. In fact, Wilson believes that the course of her life was strongly affected by the suffrage movement. Her parents' feminist consciousness prompted them to give her every educational advantage a son could have. She was made to feel that she had to take herself seriously professionally, but she found this to be a great burden because "I was a sweet little girl, and still am shy."

Wilson's mother, a capable and ambitious woman, did not have a profession or work of her own while Wilson was growing up. She invested all her intelligence and energies in her husband's career, serving as a helper in business, as well as taking care of domestic matters. Later she served as business manager for such distinguished musicians as the Budapest String Quartet and Dame Myra Hess. The double message Wilson received from her parents regarding professional goals and domestic obligations was later to resonate in the unbearable conflict she experienced between her political work, her art, and her family obligations. The message of self-sacrifice learned from her mother contributed to Wilson's reluctance to accept the "star status" conferred upon her by the international peace movement. Wilson's sense of virtue permitted dedication only to a moral cause, not to self-promotion.

Christopher Wilson had supported the 1 November peace strike wholeheartedly, according to his own account fifteen years later.[25] He even coined the principal slogan of the day, "End the Arms Race—Not the Human Race." But as the movement continued after 1 November, he grew impatient with the way it upset family life. From then on, Christopher admits, he "sabotaged Dagmar's work with WSP."[26] She, on the other hand, continued to rely on his judgment. Attached to the draft of a 1963 letter to Linus Pauling is Dagmar's note, which reads, "I want to get Christopher's OK on this before we send it."[27]

What Dagmar told few people at the time was that her outspoken opposition to Anglo-American military policies placed Christopher in a vulnerable position as an employee of the British embassy. But he maintains that this was not the major source of conflict between them. He approved of his wife's antinuclear commitment and was willing to stand with her on that. What was most distressing to him was that Dagmar's interest was focused away from home and family, and that her production of saleable drawings had dwindled in direct proportion to the expansion of her political celebrity. As her drawing board began to gather dust, the family income dropped, and the three-times-a-week domestic worker had to go. "We used to have a very smoothly running household," Wilson told a WSP steering committee; "now it's hit or miss all the time. Our standard of living has gone down."[28] A few weeks earlier, Wilson had written to her friend Peggy Darnell:

> Thank you for your contribution, it brought tears to my eyes. I
> did use it to pay my fare and part of my telephone bill; not that

I intended to, but it was, at one moment, the only cash I had in my hand. Thank goodness my visit to New York, following the Philadelphia party, resulted in a long-delayed check which will ensure my staying out of jail until I decide to go there for a good cause.[29]

Pressure on Wilson was so severe that in July 1963 she and her volunteer secretary, Belle Schultz, wrote a joint letter to the Washington steering committee, confessing they had been harboring a secret desire to turn the tables and "go on strike" themselves. "What we had not recognized," Wilson and Schultz explained, was "that by selling the piano and replacing it with a desk, file cabinet and shelves of WISP [Women's International Strike for Peace] literature, we had established a full blown national office. What other members of the Wilson household have realized, but are not inclined to accept, is that this office is in their dining room."[30] The letter concluded gloomily, "Dagmar will have to return to her much neglected drawing board in the fall, and things are bound to get worse, not better."

Although reluctant at first to be designated official leader of WSP, Wilson realized that if she were to fulfill the many requests for talks, attendance at conferences, and participation in demonstrations, WSP would have to raise money for her travel, telephone bills, and other movement-connected expenses. She also would need some income to contribute to the family budget. Dagmar found it difficult and demeaning to make it clear that she needed financial support, and the informal movement was not forthcoming with a salary or stipend because the WSP women were not accustomed, in the early 1960s, to taking financial responsibility for their own political cause. In addition, they were reluctant to give up their commitment to a structureless movement without an official leader and a paid staff.

Wilson was forced to return to her work as an illustrator. While she had not asked for financial support from WSP, she was saddened and depressed that it was not made available. By 1968 she had withdrawn from the front ranks of WSP, never to return except as an inspirational guest speaker on anniversaries or other special events. She is still a community activist on peace and ecology issues, but on a local scale.

Dagmar Wilson could not have launched WSP without the help of Eleanor Garst. Garst attended the first meeting, eager to discuss the possibility of a women's action against the bomb. She stayed on to write the call to strike and to become one of the national leaders of WSP. It was Garst's simple, direct, moralistic, but nonideological prose that played a crucial role in mobilizing and unifying WSP in its first five years. Garst's opposition to any form of bureaucratic structure, her faith in the grass roots, and her almost mystical belief that consensus could always be achieved, struck a responsive chord in the key women across the country, most of whom had not previously encountered the Quaker process embodied in "the sense of the meeting."

Unlike Wilson, Garst came from a conservative, small-town, Baptist background. She recalls that everything in her upbringing told her that the only thing a woman should do is marry, have babies, care for her husband, and "never mind her own needs."[31] Yet in 1961 Garst was the only founder who was a self-supporting professional woman, living alone after two divorces. When in 1976 I asked Garst about what she thought were the origins of her commitment to pacifism and radical activism, she thought back to her conservative Baptist upbringing and responded that she was "just a rebel." On further reflection, she offered this explanation: "Well, my mother always wanted me to be a missionary."

Eleanor Garst was born in 1915 in what she calls a "tiny town" in Nebraska. Her family moved to Montana when she was six years old and later to Spokane, Washington, where she grew up. Garst's father owned a pharmacy, and her mother was a housewife who had taught school in her youth while her family was homesteading in Nebraska. Garst's mother had also worked as a legal secretary before her marriage and continued to do so from time to time when Garst was very young. Garst remembers that her mother's work outside the home was always considered temporary because "her life was housewife," and "her main interest was the Baptist church," into which Garst was baptized at the age of eight. Garst insists that she became a dissenter at the age of ten and that she acquired her radical notions from history books. It was then that she began writing peace poems. She left the church in her early adolescence after encountering Darwin. She recalled that the only way she could read *The Origin of the Species* was on the front doorstep, as her mother would not allow the book to enter her home.

Garst was largely a self-educated woman, although she did attend the University of Missouri for a short time. She dropped out to marry a man about whom she would say very little and to spend several years as a housewife and mother. She loved her baby boy, she says, but hated every minute of domestic life. "All I wanted to do was to get away, to read, to think, and to experience everything." She later worked in a bookstore in Spokane, which was run by a woman rumored to be a Communist. "This didn't bother me at all," Garst recalled. "She had interesting ideas, and we had good discussions. That's all that mattered." This was stated with a good deal of emphasis, perhaps as an explanation of her opposition to SANE's exclusionary policy toward Communists

and her later stand in support of the WSP women who were subpoenaed by HUAC in an investigation of Communist influence in the
women's peace movement.

By 1940 Garst was divorced from her husband and had moved to
Bethlehem, Pennsylvania, where she worked in a bookstore once
again. When the war broke out in Europe, Garst was horrified, but in-
capable of taking any action because it seemed to her that the only
people who opposed the war were "those isolationist Senators," with
whom she disagreed profoundly on most social issues. She explained
that she was very much opposed to the rise of fascism, but at the time
she believed that Hitler could be stopped without U.S. military intervention. Shortly before the United States entered World War II, Eleanor
married Merritt Eugene Garst, a merchant seaman who shared her
pacifist philosophy. Together they decided that he would refuse to be
drafted into military service. On their own, without any contacts in the
peace movement or any political, moral, or financial support, Garst and
her husband spent their honeymoon writing an eighty-page brief op-
posing peacetime conscription. They did all the research themselves,
spending days at the local public library, where they "learned the whole
past history of conscription."[32] Garst was fired from her job after her
husband refused to be drafted. As she sat around waiting for him to be
jailed, "the Quakers arrived to offer their support." This was Garst's first
encounter with Quakers. She remembered that she "loved them on
sight" and that "they changed her life" by inviting her to come to Philadelphia to live and work with them. From then on, Quaker teachings
on peace and social justice were part of Garst's thinking and living. In
the early 1960s Garst taught the WSPers how to run a Quaker-style
meeting in which polarizing votes were replaced by frequent pauses or
long, sometimes very long, moments of silence and contemplation."
Under Garst's leadership quiet reflection and introspection usually led
to real consensus.

During World War II Garst worked first as a publicist for WILPF, a
movement she encountered for the first time when she moved to Philadelphia. She then became assistant director and lobbyist for the
Women's Committee to Oppose Conscription, an ad hoc national committee of church and labor groups established to defeat a pending bill
that would have conscripted women for wartime nonmilitary service.[33]
She interviewed congressional representatives, sent news releases to
supporting groups, and made a nationwide speaking tour on behalf of
the campaign against female conscription.

At the war's end Garst and her husband returned to Spokane, where
she gave birth to a daughter, Jeannie, who was later to be an active par-

ticipant in WSP. The Garsts were divorced a few years later, but Eleanor stayed on in Spokane where she became a professional organizer for social change, as the executive secretary of the International Center, an umbrella group for the World Affairs Council, the Race Relations Council, and the local chapter of the National Conference of Christians and Jews. According to Garst, all interfaith, interracial, and international efforts in the Spokane area were channeled through her office.

In addition to her professional work for peace, Garst served as a volunteer secretary and program chairperson of the first regional branch of the American Association for the United Nations, which she had helped to organize. She was also regional vice president of the United World Federalists, and what she calls "a political force" in the Democratic party. Garst admitted with embarrassment that she helped to get Henry B. "Scoop" Jackson elected to the Senate. In 1975 she found an old letter from the senator in which he had written, "Dear Eleanor, I have just decided to run for the Senate and can't wait to get your advice." Garst never forgave Jackson for his "hawkish" support for U.S. intervention in Vietnam.

Having become a pacifist at the age of ten and an active opponent of World War II when still in her twenties, it is not surprising that Garst was opposed to the atom bomb from the moment she heard of it. In the late 1950s, while living in Los Angeles where she was working as assistant to the director of the Los Angeles County Conference on Community Relations, Garst became a founder of the Los Angeles chapter of SANE. When she went to Washington, D.C., in 1958 to work as a specialist in community organizing for the Adams-Morgan Demonstration Project, she promptly joined Washington SANE. Garst's work for the Adams-Morgan project, which was an attempt to keep an area of Washington racially integrated, put her in touch with many politically conscious women who were later to join her in WSP. During the late summer of 1961 Garst was experiencing the same kind of nuclear anxiety Wilson had felt, including alienation from the traditional groups with which she had worked in the past. She began to correspond "frantically" with friends and political contacts all over the country, communicating her fear of impending disaster and asking her contacts to report what they were doing in their own communities. Carol Urner wrote from Portland, Oregon, that she had started a women's group and was visiting state officials. Urner, who was to become a key woman in Portland WSP, sent Garst a copy of a letter she had written on 29 August to columnist Seymour Friedan in response to his complaint that the general public was not exhibiting sufficient support for the allied governments in the Berlin Wall crisis. Urner's statement of maternal concern had a WSP ring. She wrote:

I watch my small son at play—sturdy, bright, and filled with
promise. I think how we have raised him in love and gentle-
ness, protected him from accident and disease, prayed that he
might grow into a useful vocation . . . and I think . . . how helpless we are to protect him from this greatest danger . . . how . . .
our dreams and hopes for him will suddenly end, and with
them the dreams of millions of parents for their young.[34]

Although Garst claims that she herself would not have chosen to found
a separatist organization, Urner had sparked her interest in such an
idea. It had one great advantage, Garst believed, which was that women
were more free than men to oppose entrenched national policies.[35]
When Margaret Russell, who was a friend and colleague in community
organizing, invited Garst to the exploratory meeting at Dagmar Wilson's
home, Garst was ready and eager to participate. Recognized as a professional writer who had been published in the *Saturday Evening Post*, the
Reporter, and the *Ladies' Home Journal*, Garst was the logical choice to
draft the "Dear Friend" letter that became the call for the women's
strike for peace.

Folly Fodor, also one of the founding group, was to become WSP's
designated national lobbyist on Capitol Hill. Like Garst, Fodor was a
longtime peace activist and a recent arrival in Washington. She had
come to the nation's capital to follow her husband's job in the U.S.
Labor Department. She joined Washington SANE almost immediately
upon her arrival and was elected to its local board shortly thereafter.
Thirty-seven years old at the time of the founding of WSP, Fodor lived
in suburban Maryland with two young children and her husband.
Fodor was the daughter and the daughter-in-law of people who had
been involved in liberal and radical politics, and had been a political
organizer since her youth. "Politics was talked about, social causes were
talked about a lot at home."[36] Fodor described her mother as "an early
'woman's libber'" who had at one time attempted to join the Communist party but had been rejected because she was too young. Fodor's
husband also came from people close to the Communist party, according to Folly, and they also "talked it a lot." Her mother-in-law had run
afoul of a congressional Red-hunting committee and had been forced to
resign her job with the public health service. "So I come from people
who generally mix in that kind of thing," she explained.

As an undergraduate at Antioch College, Fodor had become active in
the Young People's Socialist League (YPSL), eventually becoming "the
head of it." In retrospect she believes that she spent too much time
fighting Communists on campus and "never did a goddamn thing." In
1946, at the time of her marriage, Fodor became active in the Democ-

ratic party and was elected chairperson of Young Democrats of Claremont, California. Most of her activities in electoral politics, she explained, involved trying to get liberals into Jerry Vorhis's and Richard
Nixon's old congressional seats. Thinking back, she pointed out that not
one of the candidates for whom she had worked was elected. An off-
hand shrug and smile indicated that she was stating the obvious, and
wouldn't have it any other way. In 1948, while holding office in the
local Democratic party, Fodor worked for the election of Henry Wallace
on the Progressive party ticket. "We had to be a little careful how we did
it, because it really was not quite the thing to do." During the 1950s,
years known for political apathy, Fodor organized an antinuclear mothers' group. "That was the year Becky was born," she recalled in the way
mothers count the years, "so that was 1956."

After the birth of her daughter, Fodor found herself fearful, upset,
and subject to "awful dreams" about nuclear holocaust.[37] She contacted some women friends, including the woman who had been her
hospital roommate when Becky was born. Fodor, her hospital roommate, and other friends began to contact every newspaper, organization, and service club in their area to publicize peace meetings and
other antinuclear activities they organized. She recalled a public forum
featuring a Nobel Prize–winning nuclear scientist, which drew the
largest turnout in the history of the Claremont church in which it was
held. A sympathetic and cooperative minister smoothed the way for
the dissenting women by offering his name as sponsor of their invitations and statements. "He gave us respectability, otherwise we would
have looked like far out kooks," Fodor explained. By the time Fodor
became a founder of WSP, she had a good deal of experience in community organizing and public relations. She also knew the power of
the mimeograph machine. She remembered that she had offered to be
the press relations chairperson of the Claremont League of Women
Voters because that group owned a mimeograph machine that could
be used by her mothers' peace group.

When asked about role models and influences, Fodor stated that she,
too, had no historical models for WSP. She knew nothing about Nobel
Peace Prize winners Jane Addams and Emily Balch; nor had she heard
of Crystal Eastman or WPP. In the early 1960s when Fodor began to
lobby on the Hill, she knew neither the name nor the reputation of
Dorothy Detzer, the influential WILPF lobbyist. The fact that Addams,
Balch, Detzer, and Eastman were female peace leaders would have
meant nothing to her, Fodor asserts, because her mother had made too
much of the "woman issue." Women's rights and women's achievements were drummed into her head until she was sick of it. "My mother
would always tell me," she reminisced, "this is a woman who did this."

Her own response, she said, was "big deal!" "I heard it all the time." Fodor recalled that her father shared her mother's feminist outlook. Both parents advised her never to get married. "Don't ever wash dishes, or you will be doing it all your life. Be free, stay loose, have a good life and have it be your own," her parents had counseled.

Although at the time of the WSP founding, Folly Fodor was washing dishes and caring for children, her parents' message had stayed with her. When being interviewed by newspaper and television reporters during WSP demonstrations, Fodor always objected to being asked her husband's name for purposes of identification. When told that the appellation *Mrs.* followed by the husband's first name was the only form of identification employed by the *Washington Post* for married women, Fodor, unlike most other WSPers, objected vociferously. "That's just too bad," she would say, refusing to give her husband's name, "because it's me doing it, not my husband."[38] Fodor, like Dagmar Wilson, obviously felt burdened by her parents' feminist message but, unlike Wilson, chose to identify herself as a painter, not as a housewife. She did this as a step toward self-definition, and as a way of showing that she took her work seriously, even if it was earning no money.

Fodor believes that most of the women who became WSP leaders were people who thought of themselves, "as sort of special in some way." "As kids we were let know, even if there were a lot of conflicting messages, that there was something about us that had a kind of importance, and that we were destined to do something." When asked if she had any sense in the early 1960s that she, as an individual, could do something to stop nuclear testing and the arms race, Fodor replied: "Oh, absolutely. There was never any question in my mind. I remember saying at a meeting, 'I figure that what I do may just be a drop in the bucket, but maybe that will be the drop that makes the difference. So I have to do it.' And I always had the feeling that it would make a great difference. I really believed that." "I guess that's where I am no longer at," she added fifteen years after the founding of WSP. "What a shame!"

Margaret Russell, who declined to be interviewed for reasons that were unexplained at the time but may now be attributed to the onset of Alzheimer's disease, and Jeanne Bagby, who was to lead the radiation action committee of WSP and whose background and contributions are discussed in chapter 4, also were active in foreign policy dissent and other social justice causes prior to their involvement in WSP. In fact, the Washington founders of WSP were hardly the politically inexperienced housewives they claimed to be in their early communications.

But what about the thousands of women who joined the WSP founders on 1 November and afterward? What brought them into the streets, what kept them there, and why? This was a question often

asked by journalists and political observers in the first year of the movement. They wondered whether the strikers were simply concerned
mothers with little experience in political affairs or they were old political "pros," masking deeply held leftist ideologies. Elise Boulding, active
both in WILPF and WSP, decided to find out by conducting a survey of
the WSP constituency.[39] Believing that answers to the questions she
wanted to ask about the motivation and background of the women
would have to be obtained very quickly out of the freshness and spontaneity of the original experience, she enlisted the aid of the Ann Arbor
chapter of WSP and the cooperation of a number of social scientists
associated with the Survey Research Center in Ann Arbor to design a
questionnaire for WSP participants.[40]

Seven months after the founding of WSP the survey was mailed to
forty-five local groups with a total list of fourteen thousand participants.
Each group was instructed to mail questionnaires to every eighth name
on its list in envelopes that were sealed, stamped, and ready for addressing. Boulding asked of each group that the random sampling of their
locality be done on the basis of the total mailing list so that "inactives"
would be picked up. A total of 1,770 questionnaires were distributed by
the end of June 1962, and by the fall of that year a total of 279 questionnaires had been returned from thirty-seven localities in twenty-two
states. This represents a 16 percent return.[41] Boulding admitted that she
had hoped for a better return, as she had counted on a high motivation
level from the recipients of the questionnaire based on their eagerness
to learn about their movement so that they might improve it. One must
bear in mind, therefore, that the results of this survey shed light only
on those of the WSP women who chose to respond, not necessarily on
all of WSP, as it did not come from a true random sample, which would
have had to include all the groups and the thousands of women who
joined local actions, whose names were not on mailing lists. Those who
did respond were a self-selected group, as Boulding points out, because
one needs a college education, or a very high level of motivation, to be
able to, or want to, fill out a seven-page questionnaire.[42]

It turned out that 65 percent of the respondents did have a B.A. degree or higher, and only 9 percent of those who answered had no college education at all. This reflected a much higher percentage of college
graduates among WSPers than in the general female population, as in
1962 only 6.8 percent of the female population twenty-five years of age
and over had achieved a B.A. degree or more.[43] Boulding had sought to
discover if the respondents to her survey had been "organization
women" before they joined WSP. The survey revealed that less than half
(41 percent) were active at the time in civic, race relations, civil liber-

ties, peace groups, or political parties. Only 11 percent of the women were active in church work, 7 percent in hobbies, and 4 percent in professional organizations.[44]

Thirty-eight percent of the women rated themselves as "very active" in WSP, and 10 percent only as "active." Eight percent said they were not members of WSP but of WILPF, and 42 percent said they were "not active." Seventeen percent of the respondents worked from six to fifteen hours per week for WSP, 29 percent worked from one to six hours, and 22 percent worked one hour or less per week. Six percent put in no time at all. The age of the WSP women was of great interest to Boulding, but she found that exact figures were hard to come by even in an anonymous questionnaire. "These enlightened, seemingly non-conformist women protected the secret of their years with remarks like 'now really,' or a coy 'let's just say over forty.'"[45] The survey revealed that, while 66 percent of the WSP women were concentrated in the twenty-five to forty-four age bracket, the ages of WSPers ranged from eighteen to over ninety.[46] The majority of those who responded to the survey were married, middle-class mothers who did not work outside the home. Only 5 percent of the group were "never marrieds." Of the married women 43 percent had from one to four children under six; 49 percent had from one to four or more children between the ages of six and eighteen; and 20 percent had children over eighteen. Sixty-one percent were not employed outside the home. Nearly 70 percent were the wives of professionals. The majority of their husbands, 62 percent, were active in the peace movement.[47]

As WSP was born of a demonstration and devoted much of its activity to peace marches, Boulding was interested to learn how women ranked "marching" in a list of WSP actions, and how much they enjoyed it. The answers were surprising. Only 66 percent of the women who considered themselves part of WSP had ever participated in a demonstration. Of those who had, only 19 percent said they had enjoyed it. Seventeen percent stated that they had not. "We do it because it must be done," was a typical answer. Despite mixed feelings in the movement about demonstrations, it was the only activity to which most of the respondents gave high marks for effectiveness.

The experience reported by nine WSP women in Cedar Rapids, Iowa, seems to confirm Boulding's findings regarding the importance of demonstrations in politicizing women. The Cedar Rapids women, accompanied by four youngsters, conducted a four-mile peace walk, which they found to be an important personal experience. One of the marchers reported: "Two years ago, had anyone told me I would some day be walking through the shopping district carrying a banner and handing out leaflets I would have thought that person was crazy. When I found myself doing it, it was not nearly so difficult as I had expected." Another women said, "It wasn't as difficult to force myself to walk in the demonstration as I thought it would be. . . . And I am glad that I did it." Still another commented, "When one sacrifices something of time, energy, or that symbol of both—money and reputation—for the sake of an idea, then that idea is given life."[48]

The activity that attracted the largest number of WSP women was letter writing to politicians and editors. Next came the distribution of literature. Visits to public officials, in which the key women were frequently engaged, were not a high priority for the respondents; only 30 percent took part. This is probably because some women were not sufficiently confident that they could face up to the entrenched male politicians who tended to patronize them. Self-education attracted 40 percent, and peace research 21 percent. It is interesting to note that civil disobedience, which became a staple of anti–Vietnam War activity later in the decade, was engaged in by only 2 percent of the women. This was consistent with the early image of the movement, which was law-abiding and ladylike.[49]

Those who identified themselves as "committed" worked from six hours weekly "to all the hours there are." The survey also revealed that WSP was changing the daily lives of its participants. Forty-nine percent of the women who responded were working more hours for peace than ever before and were consequently doing less of the things they used to do.

Boulding concluded that the WSP women were more reflective and philosophical about political issues than their "concerned mommy" image indicated. To the question "How would you state the fundamental purpose of your group?" only 10 percent replied "to stop testing," although this was the immediate goal of the movement. Twenty-three percent answered in general terms of educating the community, and 21 percent in specific terms of developing a mechanism for conflict resolution. As for political affiliations, 53 percent of the women called themselves Democrats, but according to Boulding's report, many wrote in parentheses, "an unhappy Democrat" or an "unsatisfied Democrat" or "used to vote Democratic." Thirty-five percent of the women called themselves independents. The gender gap, which came to public attention in the 1980s, was already discernible in the mothers of the WSP women. Boulding pointed out that women have traditionally voted with their husbands, "not only in the United States but the world over," yet only 26 percent of the WSPers' mothers were Republicans, while 35 percent of their fathers were Republicans.[50]

Boulding concluded that the WSP women had been aroused to such a keen sense of urgency about the state of the world that they were willing to break out of usual behavior patterns and do odd things like demonstrating in public. She ended her report on a note of optimism, predicting that this new group of angry women, possessed of education and leisure time, would make an impact on national and world affairs. "This," she declared, "is something new under the sun."

4

Organizing a "Nonorganization"

We are a do-it-yourself movement, depending on
individual women who move *freely* in and out of
our activities as their interest, concerns, energies,
time, permit. . . . We are unique in our non-structured, chosen, fiercely-guarded lack of organization—and yet we accomplish a great deal, learn
even more, inspire each other.
—"What Is an Ann Arbor W.F.P. Anyhow?"

The ability of the WSP movement to involve tens
of thousands of women in direct action at short notice was due to its
excellent, if expensive, communications network. An important component of this network that helped, in the first year, to transform WSP
from a one-day strike to a national movement was the monthly
Women's Peace Movement Bulletin (WPMB). It was initiated, not by the
Washington women, but by Elise Boulding of Ann Arbor, Frances Herring of Berkeley, and Ruth Gage-Colby of New York City.[1] They were
able to reach Dagmar Wilson's ear to suggest a format for ongoing communications with all the women who had participated in the 1 November strike because all three were recognized, experienced leaders of
WILPF, charismatic and articulate people, and experienced organizers
with national visibility and contacts. They were part of the "old girl"
peace network, but all three were eager to support and work with the
"new girls." As envisioned by Boulding, Gage-Colby, Herring, and Wilson, the function of the bulletin, to be edited by Elise Boulding, would
be to transmit information and proposals for action arising in local WSP
groups to women peace activists across the country, without editorial
comment. In the first year *WPMB* played a key role in keeping the original strikers, and those who joined them later, "loosely" in touch.[2] When
it became clear, in the first weeks, that a monthly bulletin could not
handle the vast amount of information produced by the rapid growth
of WSP and that day-to-day tactical decisions needed to be made with

the input of women from different parts of the country, a telephone chain for quick contact was also established. It was made up of a list of "key women," appointed by their local groups, who were responsible for communicating information to and from the de facto national headquarters in Washington to regional, state, and local contacts. The calls for "instant" demonstrations in response to emergencies, such as the October 1962 Cuban missile crisis, a confrontation between the United States and the USSR over Russian nuclear weapons on Cuban soil that could have led to worldwide nuclear war, and the resumption of atmospheric nuclear tests by the United States and the USSR, were all handled by phone. Some WSPers and their husbands joked that WSP was a not a Communist conspiracy, as the extreme Right suggested, but a plot by AT&T to increase its revenue by tens of thousands of dollars each month.

By the end of 1962, when WSP was little over one year old, it had involved thousands of women in approximately one hundred different communities in mass demonstrations, peace walks, vigils, petition drives, lobbies, forums, and rallies for nuclear disarmament. Women new to peace protest found themselves staffing literature tables in shopping centers and at county fairs, educating themselves on radiation hazards and the history of disarmament negotiations, writing letters to local editors in opposition to the fallout-shelter program, or wiring President Kennedy and Premier Khrushchev to demand serious negotiations for a test ban treaty. A number of WSP women became early peace-token purveyors, designing and selling such items as peace emblems, seals, car stickers, umbrellas with the message "Peace Is the Only Shelter," and matchbooks with the slogan "We Don't Want to Set the World on Fire."

It took less than a year for WSP chapters to develop informed local leaders who could speak cogently and passionately to the public, the media, and the government on the need for a test ban treaty. A letter to *WPMB* from the Bergen County, New Jersey, chapter of WSP described a first year typical of the experience of many other suburban groups.

> Our first year saw us going in a carload to all the big demonstrations in New York City. . . . Hundreds of leaflets have been distributed warning against fallout contamination in our children's food and milk, and strongly protesting the high altitude tests last summer. We have kept up a steady flow of letters to the editors . . . and have made trips to DC on our own to speak with our congressmen and senators about disarmament and strengthening the UN. We collected 700 signatures for our political repre-

sentatives in November, and attempted to meet with candidates
to engage them in debate on the issues raised in our petition.[3]

The greatest satisfaction of the first year, according to the Bergen
County women, was having discovered one another—"a devoted band
of 50." While WSP never used the words "beloved community," as
SNCC did, there was an implicit understanding that the most exciting
ingredient in WSP, and a constant source of energy and empowerment,
was the community of women working together, receiving and giving
the kind of support and respect they had not experienced in male-led
organizations for social change.

Another source of pride, in fact an obsessive goal for all WSP chapters, was media coverage. How to get publicity was a constant topic of
discussion among WSP organizers. Choosing the kind of action that
would receive the most sympathetic media attention was a major consideration of the founders of WSP when they chose to organize a peace
strike. The WSP participants valued media coverage because it was the
only way a group with no funding and no institutional or political base
could reach the "average woman" the movement was seeking to influence. After years of feeling themselves and their concerns ignored, coverage of a WSP action by the *New York Times* or the *Washington Post*
brought a sense of power and influence to those who had participated,
and spurred them on. A media blackout was viewed by the women as
a failed action, even if thousands had participated and public officials
heard their demands. The *New York Times* reported on Easter Sunday of
1962, "Women Strike for Peace has called on its followers to mass in
front of St. Patrick's Cathedral today in full view of TV cameras."[4] Dagmar Wilson, speaking in Chicago shortly after WSP's first anniversary,
noted that WSP was the first women's effort since the "suffragettes" to
make the headlines. "Women should continue to use their unique gifts
to get the message across," she declared. "It doesn't matter what you do
so long as you keep making the headlines."[5]

WSP was seeking more than a moment of fame, or even the opportunity to spread its message. Aware of the 1950s cultural proscriptions
against social or gender deviance, the WSPers believed that their political credibility depended on projecting a ladylike, ordinary image. The
New York Times relayed their message: "For the most part they [WSP]
stress femininity rather than feminism. They are amateurs, women
who, in less urgent times, would never have put down the mop to write
a Congressman, much less demonstrate with their children in the
street."[6] Although many of the women rarely touched a mop, as they
were sufficiently affluent to employ cleaning help, the media were in-

trigued with the contradiction between domesticity and political activism. The WSP women were delighted to be described as amateurs. "It's a lovely word, 'amateur,'" Ruth Rosenwald, a New York founder, told a *New York Times* reporter. "It means love of something. What else would we be in this for?"[7]

La Wisp, the influential Los Angeles WSP monthly newsletter, advised its readers to get out their flowered bonnets and white gloves when they distributed flyers at conferences of groups such as the American Pediatrics Association, the national PTA, the California Democratic Council, or the General Federation of Women's Clubs. The following item in *La Wisp*, though it seems superficial and frivolous, is a highly political statement in that it seeks to assure those who were fearful of Red baiting or social disapproval that WSP could be both militant and lovable.

> Our public image is good, if the April 26th vigil is a criterion. We made a distinctly good impression on all those who saw us walking, and received several fine compliments For instance: one of the reporters who interviewed us went out of his way to tell us that back at the Press Club the guys had decided that we were the prettiest picket line they had ever seen. A lieutenant of police who was most helpful and courteous from early morning on, commented favorably on our appearance—and our decorum.[8]

A number of WSPers with whom I have discussed the way we dressed for demonstrations, vigils, and lobbies recall that they made special efforts to dress and behave in a stereotypical fashion on these occasions, more than in ordinary circumstances. Wilson expressed it this way: "We wanted to look nice, to emphasize the fact that this was who we were, college graduates, mostly, middle-aged women and some younger ones too, that did not usually resort to this kind of activity. We felt that [looking nice] in itself expressed the urgency of our concern."[9] Appearance was deemed important not only by WSPers but also by those who observed them. An editorial in *Labor News*, the organ of the AFL-CIO in Monroe County, New York, reported: "Because quite an attractive young Rochester matron, in the name of Rochester's Women's Strike for Peace, appeared personally before the recent session of the Rochester AFL-CIO Council to urge that unions go to hear a fellow unionist Sidney Lens . . . we went and we were not sorry that we did." The article did go on to something more substantive than the looks of the WSP representative and dealt with Lens's argument that the United States should not aid "dictators and butchers in Latin America merely because they were anti-Communist."[10] But one had to wonder if this subject would have reached the ears of the Rochester labor leaders had "the Rochester matron" not been young and attractive.

Art Hoppe, columnist for the *San Francisco Chronicle*, was totally captivated by the WSP image, describing the movement as "the only organization I'd join." "Some are old, some are young. A few are nuts, a few are university professors. Most are housewives, most are mothers. Some are confused, some are militant, some glow with self-deprecatory good humor." What Hoppe liked most about the WSPers, he told his readers, was that they were desperately afraid of the impending incineration of their husbands and children and that they marched with placards, "which confess they are afraid."[11]

Appearance was not the only aspect of their image that concerned the WSPers. The word *strike* presented a problem to a number of chapters because the women did not want to be identified with class struggle—a word associated with the Communist left. Mickey Flacks of Ann Arbor, a political radical herself, recalled that the word *strike* sounded either "too labor movement to fly in Ann Arbor, or too strident, which also wouldn't fly."[12] The Ann Arbor group was one of those that called itself Women for Peace (WFP). Dagmar Wilson acknowledged that criticism of the word *strike* had cropped up in certain sections of the country, but that the general consensus had been that "strike is a dynamic word denoting the need for quick, intelligent, persistent, and courageous action in a world posed precariously on the brink of disaster."[13] Not only did Wilson insist on using the word *strike,* but she maintained that persistent and courageous strike action should come only from individual initiative, not from programming by a national board.

While most of the women agreed with Wilson, some doubted that a movement could succeed without a designated structure.[14] The monthly bulletin of Ann Arbor WFP attempted to explain the phenomenon of effective "unorganization" to its readers: "We are a do-it-yourself movement, depending on individual women who move *freely* in and out of our activities as their interest, concerns, energies, time, permit. . . . We are unique in our non-structured, chosen, fiercely-guarded lack of organization—and yet we accomplish a great deal, learn even more, inspire each other."[15] Eleanor Garst attributed the movement's success precisely to its lack of formal structure. "No one must wait for orders from headquarters—there aren't any headquarters," Garst proclaimed in an article published in *Fellowship,* the journal of the Fellowship of Reconciliation (FOR), an old-line pacifist organization. "Any woman who has an idea can propose it through an informal memo system. If enough women think it's good, it's done. Sounds crazy? It is—but it utilizes the creativity of thousands of women who

would never be heard from through ordinary channels."[16] Midge Decter, a neoconservative Cold Warrior who was critical of WSP, also observed that the movement's greatest advantage was its informality. "If
there was nothing to join and nothing to sign, there were no official
policies to approve or disapprove, and therefore no internal dissension."[17]

WSP's unorganization amused the press and troubled representatives
of more structured peace groups. A reporter for a White Plains, New
York, newspaper, reporting on a WSP conference, wondered: "Where
was Madam Chairman, where the firm hand of the Organization
Woman in the workshops, where the mimeographed 'Conference
Agenda and Aims,' and where was lunch? . . . There was apparently no
printed program, and if one didn't get the word via the 'telephone tree'
to bring your own sandwich, one just went hungry."[18]

Of course, nobody went hungry, as each WSPer brought enough to
share. Nina Jones, the reporter for the *White Plains Reporter Dispatch*,
noted with amusement that 75 percent of the women talked at the
meeting, "sometimes a lot of them together," and that unshackled ideas
popped all over, "free as the moppet who curled up with a bottle and
went to sleep in a folding chair." When Jones asked the women how
they came to any decisions if they worked with such a lack of organization and without any votes, Blanche Posner, one of the local founders,
replied, "They aren't necessary because we believe in the same thing—
peace."[19] Emily Greenblatt of Washington, D.C., disagreed. She complained that an informal, invisible secret leadership made secret decisions. She was particularly dismayed because the argument in defense
of WSP's "invisible process" was that times were critical. She and many
others suggested that the urgency of the situation required more planning, not less.[20]

Most of the key women believed, with Garst and Wilson, that when
there is no official hierarchy in a movement, power struggles vanish.
And on the surface this seemed to be true. What was not so apparent,
however, was that an informal but entrenched leadership clique did
develop in WSP. As Jo Freeman proposed in her analysis of the tyranny
of structurelessness in the early stages of the second wave of the feminist movement, the informal leadership was made up of women who
knew the unspoken rules and possessed the resources and the networks
to make a bid for decision making.[21] Recognized standing in WILPF or
other peace groups, personal friendships with the Washington founders
or other national leaders, professional standing or media recognition,
powerful husbands, and personal economic resources for travel and
communication—all played a role in the empowerment of WSP leaders.
Mickey Flacks recalls that the women in the Midwest, who thought of

themselves as "more grass roots," resented the fact that women in the big cities on the East and West coasts seemed to run the organization.[22] Los Angeles always felt that the Northeast was favored in decision making because of its proximity to Washington, just as the other boroughs in New York City resented the power of the Manhattan group.

The most important requirements for leadership in WSP were the middle-class privileges of discretionary time and money. Few women in the work force could be active in WSP because the majority of WSP locals met on weekday mornings to allow mothers of school-aged children to return home before 3:00 P.M. The Chicago area steering committee met on Saturdays to enable women in the paid labor force to take leadership roles, perhaps because this group, unlike most others, had a working woman, high school teacher Shirley Lens, as its most outspoken leader. In Marin County, California, the women alternated between night and morning gatherings to accommodate both the mothers of small children and those in paid employment. Women with full-time jobs found it difficult to attend the New York Steering Committee meetings, and most dropped out. Bella Abzug had to curtail her law practice as she assumed leadership of the WSP legislative and political action task forces, because all WSP meetings in the New York area took place during the day.

To play a role in WSP's informal leadership required the funds to pay for hundreds of phone calls, endless hours of childcare, restaurant meals or other substitutes for mothers' home cooking, and the plane and train fares to regional, national, and international meetings. As no dues were collected, most of the women who represented WSP at national and international meetings could afford to pay their own way. Virginia Naeve of Vermont criticized the New York metropolitan area groups for classism in their selection of delegates to an international women's conference in Moscow in the summer of 1962. She wrote to Wilson that there was a feeling by some she had spoken with on the lower East Side of New York City "that uptown women will just have the means, and just go ahead and go."[23]

I recall that there was a good deal of insensitivity to class differences and to economic inequalities among the white women, including me, whereas there seemed to be a greater moral and political awareness that WSP had to make special efforts to recruit women of color and to pay their way to international meetings. It seems that WSPers were aware of racism because it was at the top of the liberal and left agenda in the early 1960s due to the rising level of African-American protests, but class was totally overlooked by all of us, as the Cold War consensus had declared class struggle either obsolete or unmentionable. The middle-class image consciously promoted by WSP was resented by women who perceived its bias against working-class women or felt themselves excluded. From time to time attempts were made to counter the power of the purse, but they did not take hold. A demand was raised that delegates to all meetings, domestic and foreign, be chosen by vote instead of being selected on the basis of ability to pay. This would have required that the delegates have their childcare and fare paid for by a local group or the national movement, which rarely happened.

The issue of who represented WSP to the media or at international meetings was constantly debated because the women were concerned more with political image than with racial or class imbalance. Control of any kind was impossible, however, as WSP rejected the concept of clearance by any authority or the inhibition of individual initiative by a central office. The New York metropolitan area was typical in its decision that its city office function "solely as a source of information with no authority to restrict individuals or groups acting under the name of Women Strike for Peace."[24]

Discomfort with the absence of clear and democratically established lines of responsibility led to some disputes and resignations within WSP, but these never caused visible disruptions, as there were no formal votes, membership lists, or institutional bodies to resign from or disband. A letter from Anne Cochran, dated 5 March 1962 reflected the malaise felt by those who chose to leave because of the lack of formal structure and democratic representation. "Is it possible to resign from a committee that has not functioned since early December?" Cochran asked. She complained of indecisiveness and arbitrary decisions, an aura of mystery about finances, leadership, program, and platform. "As long as WSP refuses to consider itself an organization, I don't think there is much room for improvement," Cochran concluded.[25] Dagmar Wilson's reply was characteristic of the way complaints were handled within WSP. "Before cutting yourself away from the movement, why don't you join a Steering Committee meeting and see whether you can help us to be more consistent and efficient?"[26] There were many who agreed with Cochran, but there were no mass defections.

Jeanne Bagby, a WSP founder and a self-identified former hippie, recognized the difficulties some women were having in "our haphazard, intuitive, and unparliamentary way of proceeding." She suggested that this was only natural in a "machine culture which places high values on technological efficiency, on objective, scientific procedures—to the point of making them rituals." Defending WSP process, Bagby declared: "We should all realize by this time that our impulsive, flitter-headed way has become fantastically effective and is the lifeblood of the movement."[27]

Not only did some women complain about the lack of structure, but government officials in the United States and the Soviet Union also found the WSP format perplexing. A public information officer at the U.S. Mission to the United Nations told Helen Frumin of Scarsdale, New York, who was attempting to secure nongovernmental observer status at the United Nations for WSP, "Why can't you girls get organized? You should have recognized leaders rather than the amoeba-like form you now have. How can you accomplish anything that way?" Frumin noted in a letter to Wilson that the U.S. government official's complaint about WSP's unorganization was similar to those of Madame Khimatch, the Soviet cultural attaché for women in Washington, D.C. Frumin suggested facetiously: "If they put enough pressure on us, we will succumb." "Imagine the headlines," she mused, "Russians and Americans urge women to organize."[28]

One of the contradictions within WSP was that the demands of disseminating information and organizing women to take part in demonstrations required effective organization. As the movement entered its second year, most of the local groups found it necessary to devise some sort of structural format, usually based on thematic or action-oriented committees. The Los Angeles chapter established eight committees: Billboards for Peace, Peace Lobby, Monitoring Mass Media, Peace Demonstrations, Women's Peace Plane to the Soviet Union, Public Health and Survival, Peace Education, and Peace Bulletin.[29] Berkeley WFP rejected committees, encouraging its participants to undertake a series of activities similar to those of Los Angeles, but on an individual basis. The women were urged to "carry a white sash in one's purse at all times ready to unfurl when necessary to become a member of a silent public demonstration for peace."[30]

In the New York metropolitan area the women who had worked in highly structured organizations in the past, such as trade unions or political parties from the Democratic party to the Communist party, insisted on structure. The structure proposed in New York in the name of democratic representation required that each local send two delegates to a county group and that county groups, such as Bronx, Westchester, and Nassau, send two delegates to the Central Coordinating Committee (CCC) in New York City. According to the proposal, the CCC would be composed of local representatives plus women working on issue-oriented committees or task forces. Even those who proposed a tight structure made it clear that local groups need not abide by the decisions of the CCC.[31] The proposed structure seemed to meet with general approval in New York when it was discussed, mainly because it promised democratic representation. But it was never carried out, and New York WSP remained as loosely coordinated, spontaneous, and sometimes chaotic as Washington, D.C. Any woman working on a project or ready to propose a new one was encouraged to attend meetings of the CCC, and anyone who just wanted to attend to participate in the discussion was also welcome. Thus decisions were made by those who happened to be present at a particular moment. If one was absent, one lost one's influence that week. In effect, anyone highly motivated could help to shape WSP program and tactics.[32] This was not viewed with alarm by most WSPers, because any individual or group that disapproved of a decision could choose to ignore it. If it was a proposal for a demonstration, a petition campaign, or attendance at an international conference, they could just sit it out.

The most innovative, organic format was developed by the women of Ann Arbor, Michigan, a university town. The WFP participants in Ann Arbor were an intellectual, introspective group, protofeminist in their process but careful not to appear too radical in their politics. Ann Arbor worked out a circular structure, a time and work continuum, new to political movements but consistent with women's activities in the home, where work is continuous and repetitive. The Ann Arbor group conceived of itself as a circle with a nucleus made up of the steering committee and the phone chain. Decision making moved both inward and outward, from the periphery to the center, and around the periphery of the circle, but never top-down, as there was no top.[33]

The lack of structure and the absence of paid office staff produced the greatest strains in Washington, D.C., where the local WSP chapter and the national office were deeply and hopelessly intertwined. The Washington women often complained that there were no boundaries between national and local assignments and that national matters diverted energy from local organizing projects. The Washington WSPers were a unique and talented band, skillful writers and experts in public relations, politically perceptive and well informed, as well as brave, daring, and selfless. They had undertaken to run a communications committee and issue a memo composed of all intramovement information. But they found that keeping the office going as the movement expanded its contacts and activities was impossible. They apologized and complained in one issue of the *MEMO* that "kids get the mumps, cars break down, husbands have to be fed." There were, apparently, thousands of letters from all over the world awaiting answers, petitions needing to be tabulated and distributed to appropriate members of Congress, and literature from local groups ready to be sent out to other groups, but lacking staff and money the *MEMO* committee was stymied and frustrated. This was an ongoing problem through all the most active years of WSP, as erratic monthly donations from local groups were the only means of supporting the national office. In addition, the WSP women's reluctance to hire a staff of paid organizers meant that the major portion of WSP work, particularly its special organizing drives, fell upon the shoulders of volunteers, who were frequently overwhelmed by the double day of political and family work.

Recognizing that they would have to be very well informed on the issues with which they were concerned if they were to make an impact on government officials and the media, almost all the WSP groups undertook study programs. They studied the history of the Cold War and disarmament negotiations, the economics of disarmament, and radiation hazards at a time when those were a well-kept government secret. The many hundreds of pieces of literature issued by WSP from 1961 to 1973 included bibliographies, study guides, and *The Story of Disarmament*, written by Miriam Levin and Janice Holland of Washington, D.C. These study groups helped hundreds of women to overcome shyness and feelings of intellectual inadequacy. Frances Herring of Berkeley recalled that "the women found that they could write flyers and press releases, and talk sense to millions of TV viewers and radio listeners. It was a heady experience."[34] It did not take long for the WSP women to learn that the talents they had exhibited in their school days or in the jobs they held before retiring into motherhood were still available to them. They soon began to suspect, and later to be convinced, that they had become more knowledgeable about the scientific and diplomatic issues involved in nuclear disarmament than most of the men in Congress. They also sensed that they possessed more common sense, more feeling, and more courage than most of the men in the peace movement to whom they had once looked for inspiration and leadership.[35]

The most intensive, extended, consistent, and broad-based campaign, one in which WSP played a leading role in shaping public opinion, was the campaign to halt nuclear testing in the atmosphere. This goal was achieved in 1962 when the U.S. Senate ratified the American-Soviet Treaty Banning Nuclear Weapons Tests in the Atmosphere, in Outer Space, and Underwater.[36] Although the key women understood that their victory was only partial, as the treaty permitted underground testing to continue along with the proliferation of nuclear arms, they were nevertheless proud of their contribution to what they called "the first step." Ethel Taylor, coordinator of Philadelphia WSP, expressed the jubilation of tens or thousands of WSP women in a letter to the *Philadelphia Inquirer.*

> We feel that self-congratulations are in order for everyone who
> worked to build up the climate of opinion that helped to make

the Nuclear Test Ban possible. We of Women Strike For Peace, have in our short, full life, given much time and energy to the struggle for a Treaty. Many Senators, have, in fact, referred to the influence of the "Mother's Vote" as a factor in shaping their decision to vote for the treaty.

Taylor concluded her letter with a promise that the women would continue to march in the name of motherhood. "Our motivation," she declared proudly, "is purely and simply our desire to make this a better world for our children."[37] Jerome Weisner, President Kennedy's science advisor during the years the test ban treaty was under discussion and negotiation, agreed with Taylor's estimate of the WSP contribution. The journal *Science* reported in 1970 that Weisner gave the major credit for moving Kennedy toward negotiating the limited test ban treaty, not to the arms controllers inside the government, but to WSP, SANE, and Linus Pauling.[38]

The organization of the antitesting campaign used the talents of women of many different political perspectives. Some were interested only in pure milk for their children, others saw a test ban treaty as a way of lessening Cold War tensions, and still others saw it as a step in the long journey toward total disarmament and world government.

From November 1961 to September 1963, WSP organized an uninterrupted stream of visits to congressional representatives, to public officials such as Kennedy advisors Arthur Schlesinger, Jr., and Jerome Weisner, and to the directors of government agencies such as the Department of Health, Education, and Welfare; the Federal Drug Administration; the Arms Control and Disarmament Agency; and the Joint Committee on Atomic Energy. In the two years in which WSP campaigned for the test ban treaty the women displayed a high level of political acumen, a sense of the strategic moment for pressure, and a talent for research, education, and public relations. The women of WSP also exhibited a constancy and drive in their political activities that was unusual, at the time, for "ordinary housewives."

In the early months of WSP, immediately after the strike, the Washington women organized a radiation committee to deal with the problem of milk that had been contaminated by nuclear fallout from the Russian tests. This Committee on Radiation Problems was headed by Jeanne Bagby, a WSP founder. Throughout the campaign for the test ban treaty Bagby played a key role as an organizer, researcher, writer, typist, and sometimes mailer of radiation facts, bibliographies, and action sheets. The key women across the country depended on her for the background data for their flyers, newspaper advertisements, speeches, and lobbying campaigns. Bagby's work was so important to WSP that, when she was introduced at the first national conference in Ann Arbor in June 1962, she was greeted with a standing ovation, something even Dagmar Wilson did not receive until the last moment.

Jeanne Bagby was the mother of three small children when she began her work with WSP. She was already involved in pacifist direct action projects and a member of SANE. The *Washington Evening Star,* in a story about the 1 November strike, referred to Bagby as an "experienced hand at this sort of thing," because she had been on a daily White House vigil for weeks before the strike. An able, dedicated, determined, highly intelligent, and energetic person, Bagby was culturally less traditional than the average WSPer. Eleanor Garst referred to her as "our own beatnik," noting that Bagby had introduced the WSP women to the dress style of the later sixties.[39] In the May 1959 issue of the radical pacifist journal *Liberation,* Bagby wrote a well-received analysis of the beat phenomenon, in which she revealed that five years earlier she had been part of the "beat scene in New Orleans." She recalled the times she had enjoyed when some "famed beat character rolled into town to hold court at a favorite cafe, bringing news of other swinging centers." "We were awed by those really crazy ones," Bagby wrote, "but the fact that they usually flipped out, and wound up in jail, or in mental institutions, prevented us from too literal emulation." Bagby revealed her own difficult times in the 1950 New Orleans beat scene, her unutterable misery, self-torture, and doubt, accompanied at times by ecstatic mystical visions. It had taken four years of intense introspection and self-therapy, she reported, for her to break through the beat viewpoint and to learn that the hated word *responsibility* was the key to the true path that all must follow. "Beatism," Bagby argued, was a political response to pressure toward standardization, a turning inward due to the difficulty of making change in the political world.[40] According to a *Liberation* poll, Bagby's article won more votes as the kind of material its readers wanted than did articles by A. J. Muste or Dave Dellinger, two of the most influential pacifist leaders.[41]

A month after WSP was born, the Committee on Radiation Problems sent a memorandum to the president and to Secretary of Health, Education, and Welfare Abraham Ribicoff, expressing profound concern about radiation hazards and demanding that radiological monitoring be improved. Failing in their attempt to extract radiation information from the president, the Congress, and the AEC, the Washington radiation committee took on the job of disseminating the most accurate information it could find from dissenting scientists. But definitive information was hard to come by in 1962. The radiation committee confessed that it was able to report only that most experts agreed that any amount of radiation could be harmful. "As mothers whose children may become expendable through a statistical approach," the committee stated, "we feel that current protective measures may not be adequate, especially in consideration of the overall cumulative effect."[42] Today new evidence and mortality figures are revealing that the women's fears and warnings were valid. In only one of a number of civil damages trials in which 1,192 plaintiffs accused the U.S. government of negligence while conducting atmospheric nuclear tests, physicist Karl Z. Morgan argued that minimal protective measures taken as radioactive fallout drifted from atmospheric atomic tests in the Nevada desert were substandard. Morgan charged that they were not in the spirit of what was known as early as 1940 about the health hazards of radiation.[43]

Traditional peace groups tended to concentrate on foreign policy and disarmament issues, while the WSPers, as mothers, knew that milk was a critical issue for women responsible for their family's daily intake of food. Recognition on the part of WSP women all over the country that "Pure Milk Not Poison" was their most effective peace slogan did much to swell the ranks of WSP in 1962 and 1963. Mothers had to decide whether to let their children drink any milk at all during testing periods, and worried whether milk products used later had been made from contaminated milk, which could cause childhood leukemia and other cancers. Unlike male radicals, and more like later feminists, the WSP women were not content to wait for the "revolution," in this case the test ban. They distributed warnings and information as fast as they could get it, along with household hints on how to make emergency alternatives such as powdered milk palatable to children. They also made certain that the powdered milk came only from areas where there had been no known radiation contamination.[44]

The WSP antiradiation campaign had a simple "do-it-yourself because nobody else will" quality. As radiation hazards persisted, Bagby and her committee came to be recognized, by default, as experts in the field. They were invited to speak at PTAs and other community meetings, to write for various peace publications, and to appear as panelists on radio broadcasts. Bagby claimed that it was the government's inaction regarding safety standards and decontamination that forced the women to educate themselves on the issue and spread the information.

Consumer pressure also became a WSP antitesting tactic. In 1962 home delivery of glass-bottled milk was still standard for middle-class families. The WSP radiation fact sheets urged women to leave notes in their empty bottles threatening cancellation unless decontamination of milk was undertaken immediately. A "Dear Neighbor" letter circulated by WSP urged women to boycott milk in times of testing. It included a fact sheet on strontium 90 that assured those who read it that "it is not something to get panicky about. But it is something we must understand clearly for it is of vital importance to the health of our children." Attempting a reasonable, nonstrident tone, the "Dear Neighbor" letter assured the community that WSP's primary sources of information were the AEC, the U.S. Public Health Service, and the Federal Radiation Council.

So effective were the WSP education campaign on the dangers of nuclear fallout hazards and WSP's threat of a milk boycott should atmospheric testing be resumed that on 26 April 1962 the U.S. Public Health Service issued a warning to mothers not to curtail their children's milk in protests against the resumption of U.S. atomic testing. According to the *Washington Post,* this warning came "after the Radiation Committee of the Women's Strike for Peace announced that its supporters would boycott fresh milk for one week as a protest to the resumption of nuclear testing in the atmosphere."[45] More evidence that the WSP campaign made an impact is contained in a *New York Times* report that, despite government reassurances, pediatricians were finding that many mothers were stockpiling powdered milk in fear of the expected spring rise in fallout. If this was so, it attests to the influence of WSP and the other citizens' peace and antinuclear groups, because there was little information on radiation dangers that the average citizen could gather from the mainstream press.

By April 1962 WSP women had created forty radiation committees around the nation and were pressuring dairies, milk processors, the Department of Agriculture, and Congress for counterradiation measures to purify milk. The most effective measure was, of course, an end to atmospheric tests.

Just six weeks after the first strike, on 15 January 1962 WSP chapters on the eastern seaboard picketed the White House and conducted a massive lobby in Congress, in what the media described as the largest protest rally since the beginning of the Cold War. Marching in a downpour that did not deter them, the WSP spokespersons confidently declared that they were marching to raise the consciousness of the nation regarding the use of science, technology, and national resources for death instead of life. The *New York Herald Tribune* report of the 15 January march was typical of many others in that it expressed both sympathy and condescension to the marchers:

Twenty railroad coaches filled with women—tweedy, well-shod matrons for the most part—arrived here [Washington, D.C.] yesterday in a driving rain. . . . Ink ran down their placards, their fur hats collapsed and hung limp over their ears, tweeds constricted and steamed. . . . A majority of the women were thirty to fifty years old, almost all of them mothers, with a middle and upper-class background. But the rich were also represented and some humble homes in Brooklyn.[46]

The mass-circulation New York daily, the *New York Post,* offered the following editorial comment:

In a day when vast impersonal forces appear to be automatically moving East and West on a collision course, it is difficult for the private citizen not to shrug his shoulders and abandon himself to a "what-can-I-do-about-it" feeling. But the stakes are too high. Travelling hundreds of miles, sloshing through puddles, the women demonstrated their unwillingness to surrender themselves to events. Their example may encourage statesmen to make the most effort when all appears lost.[47]

The most gratifying aspect of the march on Washington, for the women of WSP, was the approval and encouragement it received from the Kennedy administration. Responding to a question from reporter Milton Viorst about the WSP presence outside his door, Kennedy stated that he had seen the women, believed them to be sincere, and had received their message.[48] At a time when most women felt powerless to affect the course of government, recognition of their presence and their message was viewed by the WSPers as a triumph.[49] What was most encouraging to the women was the fact that at the same press conference in which he acknowledged the WSP protest, President Kennedy stated that the greatest disappointment of his first year in office was his failure to get an agreement on a nuclear test ban treaty. This statement by the president, in addition to the favorable press comment, was interpreted by the determined women as a sign to escalate their pressure.

While the women from the eastern seaboard marched in the rain in Washington, the WSP women in other cities held their own demonstrations. The Los Angeles group conducted a massive balloon-letting and sent delegations to the City Council and the Board of Supervisors to demand that those civic bodies adopt resolutions calling for an end to testing and in support of world disarmament. Mary Clarke of Los Angeles presented Mayor Sam Yorty with a disarmament petition and informed him that women in fifty-nine cities in the United States and in thirty-one foreign countries were simultaneously calling on their national leaders to take steps toward disarmament. She made it clear to Yorty that this included women in Russia.[50]

As soon as WSP had mastered the legislative process and developed its own understanding of which bills before Congress it should support, the movement created an entity called Lobby by Proxy. Through it WSP women all over the country were represented on the Hill by a Washington, D.C., sister who spoke their language, stated their demands, and carried a photo of their children, so the representative or senator knew it was a particular family he was dealing with. It was understood by most WSPers that the Friends' Committee on National Legislation and WILPF could do a more professional job of lobbying Congress than WSP could. WSP looked to these organizations for information on legislative issues but insisted that what it brought to the Hill—a nonprofessional, human, emotional, militant style—was essential to create a much-needed sense of urgency in Congress. By 1964 the Lobby by Proxy had represented over five thousand women. According to Fodor, the "proxies varied from a hurried 'speak for me' on a post card to a thoughtful and comprehensive statement typed on the best bond stationary." Fodor reported at the third national conference that "a whole fist-full of fluttering papers with women's names, names, names could not be underestimated in lobbying for or against specific legislation."[51]

Lobbying demonstrations and other protest actions against civil defense programs, particularly fallout shelters, also occupied WSP in 1962. In fact, opposition to civil defense programs was second only to protests against nuclear testing. In January 1962, when WSP was only in its third month, Berkeley WFP mobilized one thousand women to attend the budget session of the California state legislature to demonstrate their opposition to civil defense legislation. When 25 million booklets promoting domestic fallout shelters were distributed by the federal Office of Emergency Planning, *Newsweek* commented that "the ultimate public protest" was registered on the West Coast by Berkeley WFP, which urged citizens to mail the pamphlets back to President Kennedy with a note asking for a more positive approach.[52] The Los Angeles group helped to curtail its city's civil defense budget through persistent lobbying, and WFP in Portland, Oregon, played a key role in the abolition of civil defense in that city.[53] In some areas the campaign against civil defense centered on school air-raid drills. As mothers and as teachers, many WSPers were involved on a daily basis with the educational system. It was not difficult, therefore, for WSPers to meet with school superintendents and prominent educators, to speak at PTA meetings, and to hold public discussions with psychologists in an attempt to expose the dangers of pretending to school-age children that "duck and cover" was an adequate solution to the threat of nuclear war.

As the WSP women petitioned and lobbied for disarmament, exchanging ideas and debating with government officials and neighbors, it became clear to them that the average American believed that economic prosperity depended on defense spending. The WSP leaders became convinced that the question of economic conversion was an issue they could not ignore. But the WSPers soon discovered that economic conversion was not as "natural" a woman's issue as "pure milk." While the WSPers' expertise on radiation hazards was tolerated by politicians, the public, and the media because protection of children was women's job, the women were characterized as arrogant and meddlesome when they aspired to expertise on industrial or economic policies. Although male politicians insisted on telling them that business was not their business, WSP was not deterred. Donna Allen, a professional economist and one of the Washington leaders, testified at the Second International Arms Control and Disarmament Symposium that defense spending was bad, not good, for the economy. This was a relatively new idea at the time and commanded a great deal of interest. New York representative William Fitts Ryan inserted Allen's speech into the *Congressional Record,* noting that it was an important and provocative view of the relationship between our economic situation and military spending.[54]

WSP established a Clearing House on the Economics of Disarmament in 1963 and began to publish a bulletin "edited by novices as a help to other novices." The word *novice* was used with pride by WSPers because the women had little confidence in the experts, who had led the world to what they perceived as the brink of disaster. This did not keep them from consulting and quoting dissenting experts such as economist Seymour Melman.[55]

During the first formative months of WSP's existence, the communications network not only spread the WSP message across the country but also turned some of the key women, who came from diverse backgrounds and different regions, into colleagues and close acquaintances. But the majority continued to know very little about each other's lives, political ideology, or long-range goals. The need to establish greater trust and to resolve such controversial issues as who was entitled to speak for WSP, whether anyone should be censored, whether WSP representatives should travel to conferences in the Eastern bloc countries, whether WSP should endorse specific political candidates, whether civil disobedience was an appropriate tactic for a mothers' organization, and even whether the WSP political program should be radical or "middle of the road" convinced many of the key women that the time had come for a national conference.

The call to hold a conference came from a regional meeting in the Midwest, which set the date of 9–10 June 1962 and proposed Ann Arbor as the site. Although the Midwest group hoped for a structured, representative assembly, the Washington women rejected such a formal approach. Instead they issued an informal invitation to a gathering they called a "Wispuree," the meaning of which was sufficiently unclear and ambiguous to indicate that anyone who called herself a WSPer was welcome.

One hundred and five women from sixteen states plus the District of Columbia attended the first WSP conference in Ann Arbor. Two and one-half days of almost continuous meetings produced a unifying policy statement, affirmed the goals and methods projected by the founders, and consolidated the communications network that was to serve the movement for the decade to come. The Ann Arbor policy statement, which was agreed upon by consensus, proved to be so appropriate for WSP that it was in use without revision throughout the 1970s and 1980s. The WSP policy statement declared:

> We present a resolute stand of women in the United States against the unprecedented threat to life from nuclear holocaust.
>
> We are women of all races, creeds, and political persuasions who are dedicated to the achievement of general and complete disarmament under effective international control.
>
> We cherish the right and respect the responsibility of the individual in a democratic society to act to influence the course of government.
>
> We join with women throughout the world to challenge the right of any nation or group of nations to hold the power of life or death over the world.[56]

The decision by the Washington organizers to open the conference to all WSPers served to keep the movement unstructured. A detailed proposal from the Midwest for an elected national steering or coordinating committee was rejected because most of those present had not been empowered by their local groups to make decisions on their behalf. As was pointed out frequently during the conference, when there are no official delegates there can be no official decisions. This did not foreclose heated discussions regarding structure, but the conference ended in unanimous agreement that national policy would be decided only at annual conferences and that local policy would remain the responsibility of each area.

To improve communications, it was agreed to establish an official national office in Washington, with the proviso that it be distinct from the local chapter. This office, to be called the National Information Clearing House, was assigned the task of issuing a *National Information Memo* containing all proposals for national actions without any screening or selection by the national office. This replaced *WPMB*. The national memos were intended for key women in every community, who were to be designated by their local steering committee. Other women could also subscribe to the *MEMO*, but they were not assigned the responsibility for transmitting information to their groups. "Clearing houses," or task forces, were also established for the dissemination of information and action proposals on specific issues such as radiation, the economics of disarmament, and international outreach.[57] These clearing houses remained the key component of WSP's modus operandi into the 1970s.

Except for their efforts to keep the conference unstructured, the Washington founders made no attempts to control the first national meeting. As Elsa Knight Thompson of Berkeley, a founder of the independent radio station KPFK, reported: "The 'founding Mothers' . . . made no efforts to take over. Dagmar Wilson could be singled out especially—her grace and tact and good humor were faultless—and when she left on Sunday afternoon and the women gave her a standing ovation it was the only time during the conference that an outsider could have identified her among the other delegates."[58]

Although there was unanimity on the major issue of nuclear disarmament, and a determination among those present not to be divided by ideological struggles, there were four major unresolved political and tactical disputes that caused internal debate and dissension: (1) whether WSP should take a position on "hot spot" issues such as the sending of American advisors to Vietnam; (2) whether WSP should call for unilateral steps to disarmament or continue to call for internationally negotiated peace initiatives; (3) whether WSP, as a movement, should become involved in the civil rights struggle; and (4) whether WSP should endorse civil disobedience. Disputes over these issues continued for many years, but they never evolved into a major factional struggle because there were no polarizing votes and no official leaders to dictate program or tactics.

The Cuban missile crisis in October 1962 was typical of the foreign policy issues that seemed to fall outside WSP's stated purpose of ending the nuclear arms race. Cuba was what the WSPers chose to call a "hot spot," a contested area that could lead the United States and the USSR into a nuclear confrontation. Most of the women who stated their positions regarding "hot spots" in the various internal memoranda believed that WSP could not respond to all the small fires in the world, while still working effectively against the greatest planetary crisis, the nuclear arms race. Another argument offered by a number of women for ignoring the dangerous missile crisis was that it would lead to direct confrontation with the president to whom the women had pledged their support in his "peace race." It was this support for the president, some argued, that had attracted liberal followers, who would be alienated by an anti-Kennedy posture. Others, who were furious with a president who spoke for peace but seemed, in his confrontation with Khrushchev, to be bringing the entire world to the brink of nuclear war, argued that WSP should protest every use of violence in the international arena. After a day of cross-continental telephoning on the WSP "crisis hot-line," most of the WSP groups in the major cities issued statements condemning both President Kennedy's unilateral quarantine of Cuba and Premier Khrushchev's provocation.[59] After Kennedy's announcement of the Cuban quarantine, the New York women took to the streets to protest, in even-handed fashion, the existence of all missile bases all over the world. They could not conceal, however, that their greatest anger was directed to their own country for the way it had managed to hold the whole world hostage with its threat to use the atom bomb. In the days after the crisis, New York WSP argued that it had been hampered by the lack of a national policy on "hot spots" and urged that the national statement of purpose be amended to include a statement that would affirm the responsibility of WSP women to alert the nation to any international crisis that could threaten the world with nuclear war.[60] No action was taken on this proposal or any other recommendation for dealing with world crises. However, a resolution adopted by consensus at the second national conference called on the United States to seek solutions, wherever international tension or conflict existed, within the framework of the United Nations and other international agreements.[61]

The issue of racism, WSP's role in the civil rights struggle, and how WSP should deal with black women within its own movement surfaced on the first day of the first national conference. A debate at the opening session foreshadowed hundreds of others in the ensuing years, as African-American women defined their own needs and demands within the peace movement. At the opening session of the Ann Arbor conference it was announced from the floor that a group of four Detroit women, representing a committee to "ban the bomb and end segregation," had been refused admittance. This was strange indeed, as the premise of the conference was that all women who identified with the WSP movement were welcome. It turned out that the black women from Detroit were in conflict with the group that considered itself Detroit WSP. The group of African-American women had insisted upon carrying placards to WSP actions bearing the slogan "Desegregation Not Disintegration." The white women in Detroit had made it clear that they opposed the mingling of issues, had banned the desegregation placards, and had refused to allow the black women to be part of their delegation at Ann Arbor. A bitter and painful discussion followed. WSP's commitment to inclusion rather than exclusion, its concern that it not act in a racist fashion, and its compassion for those excluded created sympathy and support for the black Detroiters, and they were seated immediately. Barbara Bick of Washington, D.C., recalled in a radio commentary several years later, "The tension was terrific; everyone felt very deeply about civil rights but, I think, most women there also felt deeply that WSP should be a peace-issue movement only."[62] The four black women, on the other hand, made it clear that for them social justice would have to come first, and that participation in any movement that refused to make a primary commitment against segregation would have no appeal to the majority of African-American women.

Elsa Knight Thompson reflected the conflict many of the white women experienced. She was repelled by one white women who insisted that WSP goals did not preclude accepting segregationists, but she was also shaken when a member of the black group declared on the floor, "If the next hundred years are going to be like the last, we don't care whether there is peace or not." "It hit me like a physical blow," Thompson declared.[63] Tension around racism also arose over an all-white delegation WSP had selected to send to Ghana in June 1962. Clarie Harvey, a black WSP activist from Mississippi, and Eunice Armstrong, who had funded the black WSPers who went to Geneva as part of the WSP delegation earlier in the year, insisted from the floor that "to send only white women to Ghana, a country in Africa, seems seriously bad judgment."[64] But others were not so sure. Eleanor Garst apparently disagreed. Having been nominated herself, she declined in favor of either Nancy Mamis, a white woman, or Clarie Harvey, a black, without expressing a preference.

The question of racism had been forced on the conference in its first hours by the situation in Detroit, but a discussion of WSP's relationship to the civil rights movement had been planned in advance. Because no agreement could be reached on the floor whether WSP should include civil rights as one of its demands or remain a single-focus antinuclear movement, the question was sent to committee. What emerged instead of a policy decision, and what can be interpreted as an attempt to avoid polarization on the issue, was a letter addressed to Coretta Scott King, who had joined WSP in lobbying the Geneva disarmament conference. The letter stated:

> As women dedicated to bringing about a world where every child may live and grow in dignity, we identify ourselves with the heroic effort of Negro citizens to achieve this goal. As a movement working for an atmosphere of peaceful cooperation

among nations, we support the movement for peaceful integration in our nation. Our goals are inseparable, the movement for
civil rights is part of the movement for a world of peace, freedom, and justice to which we have dedicated ourselves.[65]

Local groups were instructed to use this letter in place of a policy statement on civil rights, especially in communication with civil rights
groups. In May 1963 the Los Angeles women, dissatisfied with the national policy statement, issued their own declaration on women and
civil rights, stating: "We feel that the time has come for all women to
stand up and be counted on this matter of grave concern. We feel that
the time has come for us to match the thought with the deed. We call
upon all women working for peace to dedicate themselves to the struggle of the Negro people for freedom."[66] Los Angeles was responding to
a great moral pressure on the WSP women to work for civil rights because the need for action was clear and success seemed possible. Dagmar Wilson was one of those WSPers who, despite qualms, felt that
WSP had a unique task and that it should not abandon its campaign for
disarmament in favor of civil rights. When Barbara Deming, who served
as a prod to the WSP conscience on moral issues such as unilateralism,
civil disobedience, and civil rights, suggested that WSP find in its ranks
a replacement for a civil rights worker in the South who had to leave
for personal reasons, Wilson explained that most of the WSP "girls" are
mothers and it would be hard to find one who could leave home for
such a mission. "WSP is in a constant state of conflict over Civil Rights
vs. Peace," she added:

> The civil rights movement has a tremendous emotional appeal—
> as it naturally would do to the kind of women who are moti-
> vated by a sense of indignation at the disregard for human
> rights which the arms race represents. It has been very tempting
> at times to drop everything and work for civil rights, except for
> the fact that we all realize that civil rights without nuclear disar-
> mament won't do any of us any good. We realize that the two
> movements are different aspects of the same problem and that
> eventually the two will meet and merge.[67]

Despite Wilson's insistence that WSP remain a single-issue movement,
Washington WSP was working officially with Washington Congress of
Racial Equality (CORE).

On 7 May 1963 Coretta King wired her support to a WSP mass mothers' lobby for a test ban treaty, which she could not attend, assuring
WSP that it had her full support. "Peace among nations and peace in

Birmingham, Alabama, cannot be separated," she stated.[68] It was not until 1968, however, that WSP joined the welfare rights movement and civil rights organizations to protest the war abroad and racism and poverty at home.[69]

The United States resumed atmospheric atomic testing in April 1963, to the dismay of all peace advocates. However, President Kennedy continued to state that he hoped a testing ban could be negotiated and to express concern over the proliferation of nuclear weapons. But the standoff between the United States and Great Britain on one side and the USSR on the other continued until mid-1963.

In December 1962, shortly after the Cuban missile crisis had been resolved, Khrushchev wrote to Kennedy that he believed the time had come to "draw a line" through all nuclear tests. Khrushchev expressed an understanding of Kennedy's need for a minimum number of inspections in order to secure Senate ratification, and informed the U.S. negotiators that he was ready to meet Kennedy halfway. But when negotiations resumed in January, strong pressure for strict and numerous inspections was asserted by Governor Nelson Rockefeller, Senator Everett Dirksen, Senator Thomas J. Dodd, Admiral Lewis Strauss, the Joint Chiefs of Staff, and others who opposed the treaty as a "giveaway to the Russians." Khrushchev felt betrayed, the negotiations fizzled, and the WSP women despaired. According to Arthur Schlesinger, Jr., Kennedy continued to press for the treaty. Chester Bowles, who was close to the president at this time, attributes his persistence to parental concern. According to Bowles, Kennedy explained his continuing efforts to conclude a test ban, in the following manner: "It may sound corny, but I am thinking not so much of our world but of the world that Caroline will live in."[70] In April and May 1963 new approaches were made to the Soviet Union by the United States, and strong public pressure continued from nuclear scientists and from WSP and other peace groups. On 27 May, two weeks after a massive WSP-sponsored Mothers' Lobby for a Test Ban Treaty, thirty-three senators introduced a resolution declaring it to be the sense of the Senate that the United States undertake unilateral efforts to secure a test ban. Even if the Russians rejected the plan, the Senate resolution declared, the United States should nevertheless pursue it with vigor.[71]

This encouraged WSPers to keep up their pressure on Congress. Even more encouraging was the president's American University address, which echoed Pope John XXIII's *Pacem in Terris* encyclical, in its insistence that peace was not only a political issue, but a human and moral one. In this major speech Kennedy expressed the conviction that the United States had to reexamine its attitudes in the Cold War and not just blame the Russians. "Our problems are man made, " he said, "and therefore can be solved by man."[72] WSP would have added, "With the influence and determination of women!"

When the treaty was agreed upon. U Thant, secretary general of the United Nations, paid tribute to WSP's role by receiving three WSP representatives, Dagmar Wilson, Lorraine Gordon, and Helen Frumin, for a short meeting before he left for Moscow to witness the signing of the Treaty Banning Nuclear Weapons Tests in the Atmosphere, in Outer Space, and Underwater, on 5 August 1963.

Aileen Hutchinson of Washington, D.C., testified at the Senate Foreign Relations Committee hearings on the ratification of the test ban on behalf of the "health, safety, and survival of the world's children." "To women sharing the common longing to see the future approach with ever greater fulfillment through the constructive lives of the children, it is unthinkable that there may be no future for all of mankind."[73] Phyllis Schlafly of Illinois, known today for her active opposition to the Equal Rights Amendment, reproductive and gay rights, also testified against the test ban treaty on behalf of children. Schlafly stated: "I appear here as a mother who is eager that her five small children have the opportunity to grow up in a free and independent America, and because I do not want my children to suffer the fate of children in Cuba, China and the 20 captive nations."[74] Senator Maurine Neuberger of Oregon, arguing on the floor of the Senate in favor of ratification, spoke in language similar to that of WSP. "We have been told that Senate ratification of the test ban treaty will be more a tribute to the political potency of the 'mother's vote,'" Neuberger stated, "than a rational reflection of our national self interest." "There is, indeed, a mother's vote," she told her fellow senators, "but it is not a sentimental vote. It is a vote that flows from the rational concern of any mother for the welfare of her children, and her natural and acute sensitivity to the survival of future generations in recognizable form. It is a vote cast for the genetic future of mankind."[75]

On 24 September 1963 scores of WSP women were present in the Senate gallery to witness the ratification of the treaty between the United States, Great Britain, and the USSR. They distributed carnations to every senator who had voted yes, and one of the first went to Senator George McGovern. Folly Fodor, the Lobby by Proxy chairperson, told the *Washington Post* that the women had chosen McGovern as a symbol because "he's so sweet, and he has been a leader in the fight for disarmament."[76] Later that day, a fifty-car WSP motorcade toured the city for an hour, stopping to allow the women to chat with and congratulate two men the WSP women had lobbied and badgered regularly for almost two years. They were William Foster and Adrian Fischer of the Arms Control Agency.

Across the nation the WSP women were jubilant but aware of the limitations of the treaty, which allowed underground tests to continue. In Chicago the women staged a celebratory march through the Loop. In Los Angeles they gathered at the Federal Building. In Brooklyn WSPers distributed "Hooray for the Test Ban" balloons to neighborhood children. In Manhattan WSPers visited the U.S. Mission to the United Nations, the scene of their very first picket line, to leave flowers and thank-you notes for Secretary of State Dean Rusk and Ambassador Adlai Stevenson. Although they did not meet with Stevenson, he responded to the WSP tribute with gratitude. "Dear Ladies," he wrote, "Your flowers on the day of ratification of the Test Ban Treaty pleased me immensely. It is comforting to know that some people remember the history of this issue. I shall always be proud of my connection with it, and your flattering recollection."[77]

By the second anniversary of WSP, November 1963, the media had brought WSP's antinuclear message to the attention of millions of women the peace movement could never have reached through its own channels. President Kennedy, recognizing the growing concern among mothers of young children about the nuclear threat and estimating the importance of mothers' pressure in getting the nuclear test ban treaty of 1963 ratified, agreed to an interview with the editors of seven leading women's magazines, in which he exhorted women to play a role in foreign policy debate. The editors of *Cosmopolitan, Family Circle, Good Housekeeping, McCall's, Parent's Magazine, Redbook,* and *Woman's Day* had become aware through their incoming mail that women were concerned about nuclear dangers to the lives of their children but were fearful of speaking out because foreign policy dissent was deemed unpatriotic. The editors called upon the president to "clarify the confusion and allay the concerns" of their readers regarding "the issues involved in the nation's effort toward . . . control of nuclear weapons." The president's response was to encourage women to engage in the widest possible discussion of arms control and disarmament questions in their church groups, PTAs, and women's organizations of all kinds. Kennedy urged women to write to their congressional representatives when a specific issue bearing on peace and the safety and survival of the world's children arose: "I have said that control of arms is a mission that we undertake particularly for our children and our grandchildren, and that they have no lobby in Washington. No one is better qualified to represent their interests than the mothers and grandmothers of America."[78] When asked if protest actions were a source of embarrassment of any kind and if they had any political value, Kennedy replied that some groups were more controversial than others but he thought they probably were "very good too." He explained that there was a great deal of pressure against peace efforts and that without women's groups helping to balance that pressure he, as a president working toward peaceful solutions, "would be very isolated. . . . So I would urge women to get into whatever groups they feel reflects their judgment as to how things ought to be done. . . . it is very helpful to have a significant group of women working for peace in their communities."[79]

"He has not exactly told them to join WSP," Dagmar Wilson noted at WSP's second anniversary celebration, "but he has told them to join something, to inform themselves, to make each vote count for more by writing letters to their congressmen. . . . I am not suggesting that he would not have said the same two years ago had he been asked. The point is that the questions are being asked, and we can take some credit for that."[80]

Interlandi From *The Los Angeles Times*.

BELOW OLYMPUS   By Interlandi

Interlandi From The Los Angeles Times

"You'll never abolish war as long as men are running the world. Now, if you want to do something about that, I'll march with you!"

"What's Bugging Those 'Strike for Peace' Women . . . Why Aren't They Home Looking After Their Children's Welfare!"

Cartoon by Parker, *Washington Post,* 11 May 1963. Reprinted with permission

WSP-sponsored Paris Conference of Women of the Belligerent Nations in Vietnam, April 1968. Left to Right: Ethel Taylor, Philadelphia, WSP coordinator, Stana Buzatu, Women's International Committee for Solidarity with Vietnam, Althea Alexander, Los Angeles social worker and community leader representing Black Resistance Against the War, and Mothers of Watts, Mary Clarke, Los Angeles WSP coordinator, and Mme. Nguyen Thi Binh, Chief Negotiator for the National Liberation Front at the Paris Peace Talks with the United States. Photo courtesy of Cora Weiss

Evelyn Whitehorn and son Erik at Palo Alto, California, press conference in April 1969. Ms. Whitehorn announced that she was taking legal action to prevent her son, a minor, from being inducted into the armed forces. The Whitehorns eventually lost their case, and Erik was inducted into the U.S. Army. Records of Women Strike for Peace, Swarthmore College Peace Collection

Cora Weiss pins "Not Our Sons, Not Their Sons, Not Your Sons" sash on Vietnamese women in Hanoi, December 1969. Photo courtesy of Cora Weiss

WSP at the Women's Equality March, New York City, August 1970. Woman at right is Lyla Hoffman. UPI/Bettmann

WSP children at a Boston peace march. Records of Women Strike for Peace,
Swarthmore College Peace Collection

Five hundred WSP women take over the U.S. Capitol steps on January 20, 1971 to inaugurate Bella Abzug into the 92d Congress, and launch a national "set-the-date" campaign for total withdrawal of all U.S. forces from Indochina. Representative Bella Abzug is in the center. Directly on her right is Congresswoman Shirley Chisholm of New York. To the right of Chisholm is Congressman Ed Koch, also of New York. Left (behind Abzug's hat) is Amy Swerdlow, editor of MEMO, and above her is Judy Lerner, WSP political action organizer in Westchester County, N.Y. To the left of Lerner, wearing a hat, is Jeanne Shulman, coordinator of the New York WSP office, and at the extreme left is Shirley Margolin, WSP's political spokesperson and coordinator in Queens County, N.Y. UPI photo

Another view of WSP Inauguration of Bella Abzug into the 92d Congress. Photo by Dorothy Marder

WSP Billboard at busy intersection in Los Angeles, Easter 1971.

UN Secretary General U Thant honors Women Strike for Peace on its tenth anniversary. Left to right are Shirley Margolin, U Thant, Congresswoman Bella Abzug, and Amy Swerdlow. Photo by Dorothy Marder

Elizabeth Moos pickets at the Forty-second Street Library in New York City on the occasion of WSP's tenth anniversary, 1 November 1972. Photo Dorothy Marder

Die-In: One hundred WSP women hit the sidewalk on 12 April 1972 in a "die-in" at the national headquarters of ITT in New York City to protest ITT's manufacture of military parts for the bombing of Cambodia. WSP also called for a boycott of Wonder Bread, manufactured by an ITT subsidiary. Photo by Dorothy Marder

Fathers and children march with WSP in the Mobilization Against the Vietnam War, 22 April 1972. Photo by Dorothy Marder

Two thousand women form a "Ring Around the Congress" in June 1972 demanding that Congress vote to cut off funds for the Vietnam War. Photo by Dorothy Marder

5

Ladies' Day at the Capitol

Communism? A stuffy old doctrine. It's a pity we
have such a blind terror of it, because Communism is out of date. "East" and "West"? It's where
you happen to live.
—Dagmar Wilson

If the House Un-American Activities Committee
knew its Greek as well as it knows its Lenin, it
would have left the women peace strikers alone.
. . . Instead, with typical male arrogance, it has subpoenaed 15 of the ladies, . . . spent several days trying to show them that woman's place is not on the
peace march route, and has come out of it covered
with foolishness. The lesson is as old as Aristophanes, who lived 400 years before Christ: Men
confronted by women peace strikers should either
make peace or leave the ladies alone.
—Russell Baker

As WSP was beginning its second year, with a
strong sense of mission and pride in its political effectiveness, the movement suddenly faced a chilling threat to its survival. In November 1962
The House Un-American Activities Comittee (HUAC) served subpoenas
on fourteen WSP women in the New York metropolitan area, com-
manding them to appear at an investigation into Communist infiltration
into the American peace movement. The hearing was scheduled for
11–13 December 1962.[1]

As might be expected from the previous history of the movement,
the tactics invented by WSP to face this awesome challenge were nonideological, pragmatic, feminine, yet combative, far different from those
of any other radical or liberal group that had faced the dreaded committee. The WSP response to the HUAC summons was so ingenious in its
exploitation of traditional domestic culture in the service of radical politics that it succeeded in doing permanent damage to the committee's

97

image. Eric Bentley, in his book *Thirty Years of Treason*, gives WSP the credit for striking the crucial blow in "the fall of HUAC's Bastille."[2]

In the first days after the subpoenas were received there was some uncertainty within WSP regarding HUAC's specific goals and intentions. Because three of the women summoned by the committee were not active in WSP, while dozens of others who were well-known leaders were ignored, there was some hope that it was not the movement but only its far left New Yorkers that HUAC sought to expose and condemn. The fact that two of the New York women subpoenaed had already been accused of Communist party membership by FBI informers and that one, Elizabeth Moos, had been identified by convicted Russian spy William Remington both as his mother-in-law and as a Communist party member, prompted Eleanor Garst to write to the New Yorkers that "we shouldn't assume that it is WSP being attacked." Garst believed, or hoped, that it was much more likely that there had been a decision "to discredit WSP by knocking over those they consider easiest for any number of reasons."[3]

Given the confusion and fear the subpoenas engendered among the women across the country, the New York and Washington leadership moved quickly to protect those under attack and to unite the movement in its own defense. At an emergency meeting of approximately fifty key women from the New York area, plus a handful from Washington, including Dagmar Wilson, it was agreed unanimously that WSP would embrace, as its own, every woman summoned before HUAC, regardless of her past or present political affiliations, even if she had not been a WSP activist. The only requirement for inclusion was that she oppose both Russian and U.S. nuclear testing and support a program for general and complete disarmament under United Nations control. It was thus understood that the three women not previously connected with WSP would also come under WSP protection. They would be given access to the same lawyers as the WSP women and would not be isolated or attacked either for their past associations or for the ways in which they might choose to defend themselves against the committee. This WSP decision was different from that of SANE, which had in 1960 expelled Henry Abrams of New York because he invoked the Fifth Amendment at a Senate Internal Security Subcommittee hearing and had refused to disclose to Norman Cousins, the national chairperson of SANE, whether he had ever been a Communist. WSP, in sharp contrast, asked no questions about the political affiliations of the subpoenaed women prior, during, or after the HUAC hearings.[4]

The decision made by the New York and Washington women not "to cower" before the committee, to conduct no purges, and to acknowledge each woman's right to work for peace in her own way and according to the dictates of her conscience was bold for its day. It was arrived at within the movement without consultation with the leaders of traditional peace or civil liberties groups or of the old Left, who had a great deal of experience with HUAC. Credit for WSP unity in the face of a situation calculated to produce internal Red baiting and hysteria should go to the Los Angeles chapter. The Los Angeles women who participated in the first national convention in June 1961 brought a resolution to the floor that called upon WSP to reject political screening of its members as a manifestation of outdated Cold War thinking. After a long debate initiated by Mary Clarke and Kay Hardman, a plank inserted in the national policy statement read: "We are women of all races, creeds, and political persuasions." The Los Angeles women, who were experiencing intense movement dissension in California over the issue of Communist exclusion, argued that, "unlike Turn toward Peace and SANE, WISP must not make the error of initiating its own purges." "We must ask ourselves this question: If there are Communists or former Communists working in WISP, what difference does that make? We do not question one another about our religious beliefs or other matters of personal conscience. How can we justify political interrogation?"[5] The Los Angeles group won the day when they argued, "If fear, distrust and hatred are ever to be lessened, courageous individuals will have to come forward who do not hate and fear and can get together to work out tolerable compromises." "This," they insisted, "is a role women should be particularly equipped to play."

The decision not to allow the committee to isolate or intimidate any woman was based not only on the political considerations debated in Ann Arbor. Feelings of empathy and compassion also played a role; particularly strong was the desire on the part of the key women to see that not one of the subpoenaed women was isolated or humiliated. Working together at a feverish pace, night and day for three weeks, writing, phoning, speaking at rallies, the WSP leadership seemed to be acting like a family under attack for which all personal resources, passion, and energy had to be marshaled. This time, the family was "the movement" and it was the sisters, not the fathers, who were in charge.

An anti-HUAC declaration was drafted by the New York and Washington groups to be used for education within the movement and as a basis for press releases, statements by local groups, flyers, and advertisements. "With the fate of humanity resting on a push button," WSP proclaimed, "the quest for peace has become the highest form of patriotism." In this first sentence, the New York and Washington leadership set the ground rules for their confrontation with the committee and for their appeal to the public. It was to be a contest, they decided, between masculine and feminine notions of patriotism. The test of patriotism for

WSP was commitment to the survival of the planet and its children. "Differences of politics, economics, or social belief disappear when we recognize man's [sic] common peril. We do not ask an oath of loyalty to any set of beliefs. Instead we ask loyalty to the race of man. The time is long past when a small group of censors can silence the voice of peace."[6] WSP was saying, as it had since its inception, that traditional male-defined politics, either of the Right or the Left, were obsolete in the nuclear age, as was the Cold War and hence the committee itself. The WSP statement served notice on the committee that a new day had arrived and that the prospect of nuclear holocaust was more threatening than anything the committee could inflict. This is the spirit Eric Bentley caught when he wrote, "In the 1960s a new generation came to life. As far as HUAC is concerned, it began with Women Strike for Peace."[7]

The WSP policy statement on HUAC was dispatched across the country to the key women, who activated their "hot lines" immediately and stayed on the phone for days and as late into the night as possible. My children remember that they found me in the same position when they came from school as when had they left: sitting in the kitchen on my 1950s freezer chest, with one hand holding the phone to my ear and the other holding on to four-month-old Tommy's baby seat, which sat next to me on the freezer. It was my job to call the media, which I did all day long, stopping only to feed my family, sleep, attend meetings, or consult with the Washington women on revisions of our daily press releases.

WSP scooped HUAC by announcing the hearings before the committee did. When Chairman Francis E. Walter issued a press release on 6 December announcing that HUAC would investigate "the Communist Party tactics of infiltration of non-Communist organizations, with special reference to the Women Strike for Peace," the news media already had on hand the WSP attack on HUAC, which reporters and editorial writers juxtaposed with the committee's press release. The *New York Times* followed the HUAC press release with Dagmar Wilson's statement: "We recognize this investigation as an attempt to divert our attention from the most important issue women have ever faced, the preservation of our families in a world armed with nuclear bombs." The *Times* also gave space to Wilson's contention that nobody, meaning not even Communists, could take over WSP because "we are the movement. We decide everything by group decision, nothing is dictated."[8]

The women of WSP were familiar with HUAC's reputation for misusing its constitutional mandate to conduct hearings for legislative purposes. Knowing that HUAC's intention was not legislative but punitive, that the committee sought to create sensational headlines to discredit organizations and individuals who could not defend themselves because the hearings did not allow for cross-examination of accusers, WSP decided it had to discredit the committee by getting its own story to the American public. Any media coverage of the WSP point of view was seen by the women as their only legal and political defense. A *Washington Post* editorial bolstered WSP morale by declaring: "What they have to say . . . should be heard for what it is worth as part of the running debate on public policy which is the essence of the democratic process." The *Post's* charge—"The Un-American Activities Committee imperils democracy itself. For democracy can function only where protest can find free expression"—helped to convince many individuals and organizations who had remained silent in the face of HUAC's abuses that the time had come to stand up to the committee.[9]

There was much speculation in the peace movement and among liberals regarding the committee's motivations for staging an investigation of WSP. Some of the women who had little political experience were surprised that their movement, which supported President Kennedy's "peace race," could be Red baited. Others had suspected all along that WSP would not get away with its challenge to the Pentagon. They were also aware that WSP's potential power to bring the "average" woman out of her kitchen and into the political arena was becoming a source of concern to conservatives in the media and the surveillance establishment.

Committed Cold Warriors were suspicious of WSP. Hearst columnist Jack Lotto denounced WSP for describing itself as a "group of unsophisticated wives and mothers who were loosely organized in a spontaneous movement for peace." "There is nothing spontaneous about the way the pro-Reds have moved in on our mothers and are using them for their own purposes," Lotto sneered.[10] In an article published in *Harper's* after the HUAC investigation, but written earlier, Midge Decter aired her suspicion of WSP motives: "They march (and weep and picket) for Peace with the noblest of emotions—but it isn't quite clear who they are trying to persuade to do what . . . or how they picked up some rather curious company."[11] On the West Coast the *San Francisco Examiner* claimed to have actual proof that "scores of well-intentioned, dedicated women . . . were being made dupes of by known Communists . . . operating openly in the much publicized Women for Peace demonstrations." Drawing on information either from the FBI or the Police Department Red Squad, the *Examiner* reported that at the very first WSP action in Oakland, thirty-two of the ninety women present were recognized as actual Communist party members or as members of various "pro-Communist organizations."[12] Evidence that WSP was under surveillance from its first planning meeting in Washington is to be found in the forty-nine volumes of FBI records on WSP which were made available to the movement's attorneys under the provisions of the

Freedom of Information Act. These memos show that FBI offices in major cities, such as New York, Washington, Los Angeles, San Francisco, Boston, Philadelphia, Detroit, Chicago, Baltimore, Portland, Seattle, Milwaukee, Cleveland, St. Louis, Norfolk, Indianapolis, Jacksonville, Kansas City, Mobile, Phoenix, Pittsburgh, San Antonio, and Atlanta, were sending and receiving reports from national FBI headquarters, often prepared in cooperation with the Red squads of local police departments.

As early as 23 October 1961, a week before the strike, the Cleveland office of the FBI identified a member of the WSP planning group in that city as a known Communist.[13] A radio message to FBI director J. Edgar Hoover, dated 1 November 1961, reported that at the Los Angeles strike "eight security index subjects were observed marching."[14] The FBI report did not mention the fact that the "eight security index subjects" were part of a group of two to four thousand women, according to varying estimates by the Los Angeles newspapers.[15] When WSP sent a delegation to the Geneva disarmament conference in the spring of 1962, the FBI enlisted the Swiss federal police and covert CIA agents in the American embassy to spy on the women.[16]

As late as 1965 the FBI was still unable to find evidence to connect the Washington, D.C., WSP leadership to the Communist party. In fact, the Washington field office advised J. Edgar Hoover that there was no record of Communist activity, past or present, among the visible leadership of WSP, and that there had been no instructions by Washington or Maryland Communist groups to their members to work within WSP. Even informers planted in the Communist party reported that the party was not directing its members to infiltrate WSP.[17]

Why, then, did the committee feel the need to "investigate" WSP? There are several plausible reasons. HUAC lived on media coverage of its hearings, which it perceived as a vote-getter for its members and as the source of public support for its budget. Thus it needed to find new subjects for investigation to insure new headlines and new victims. The committee members were also zealous supporters of the Cold War, who viewed peace dissenters as threats to the military budget and the national security. Thus HUAC seized on any opportunity to isolate and smear the peace movement as un-American and subversive. HUAC was undoubtedly aware that the peace movement was growing after a hiatus of two decades. The Rand Corporation, a conservative think tank, had begun to alert its staff and its clients to the fact that in 1960 there had been only one peace candidate running for Congress, in Massachusetts, and that in 1962 at least twenty were campaigning across the country. A Rand Corporation report published in December 1962 warned that the peace movement was a "growing cause" with "scores of organizations" and that it had the potential to make an important political impact on military affairs. The new peace groups of particular concern to the Rand Corporation were identified as Women Strike for Peace, Political Action for Peace, and Leo Szilard's Council for Abolishing War.[18] The Rand Corporation's research, the reams of material on peace activities that the FBI was amassing, and the publicity WSP was receiving in the mainstream media must have played a role in HUAC's decision to "investigate" WSP.

The question remains, however, why, if HUAC wished to discredit the entire peace movement with charges of subversion and un-Americanism, did it single out a loosely structured, one-year-old women's group? The Washington Committee for the Abolition of HUAC offered one explanation: "Since its birth last year, WSP has been the main force in American life to give voice to women's desire for an end to nuclear testing. . . . WSP has supported the President's Peace Race, the Peace Corps and the United Nations Bond issue."[19] The *Washington Post* pointed out that it was inevitable that WSP would be investigated as soon as it won any degree of notoriety or public recognition.[20] SANE described the HUAC inquisition as "another example of the committee's affront to the President of the United States and our international prestige."[21]

Those sympathetic to HUAC's purpose gave specific reasons for the committee's interest in WSP. Midge Decter attributed it to WSP's "anti-U.S." position during the Cuban missile crisis, and the committee's chief counsel, Alfred M. Nittle, implied during the hearings that WSP's "spectacular" demonstration at the Geneva disarmament conference had attracted HUAC's attention.[22]

Even if one can make the case that HUAC's motive was to discredit the peace movement through its most active, and potentially its most influential, force, one further question remains unanswered. Why were the WSP women subpoenaed in mid-December, just two weeks before Christmas? Surely the committee was aware that this was a time when proper American women were shopping and making other domestic preparations for the holidays, and a time when Christian sentiment for "peace on earth" runs high. Walter Goodman in *The Committee: The Extraordinary Career of the House Committee on Un-American Activities* has suggested that HUAC desperately needed favorable publicity before the next session of Congress, which would be reviewing its financial commitment to the committee. As HUAC's record for the greater part of 1961 and 1962 was "like summer television, heavily dependent on cheap packages and reruns," Goodman argues that the HUAC strategists counted on a woman's group that had already attracted media attention to bring in headlines.[23]

The proceedings reveal that the committee thought it had persuasive evidence that New York WSP was dominated by Communists and that the New York women controlled the Washington founders. In the McCarthyite atmosphere of the late 1950s and the early 1960s, such a charge, even if unproved, could be sufficient to damage the credibility of an entire national movement. To prove that Communists in New York dominated the naïve Washington founders, Dagmar Wilson was called to testify. This was the committee's greatest mistake. On hearing the news, Frances Herring of Berkeley, one of the movement's most astute leaders, wired Wilson: "Congratulations to us that you will carry banner—Committee couldn't have made a worse choice from their view point or a better one from ours—This may be the beginning of their last days."[24] Once Wilson was called before the committee, there was no danger the movement would fracture, as each WSP woman felt that an attack on Wilson was a personal affront. I remember a letter from Jeanne Bagby, the Washington founder who led the task force on the hazards of nuclear fallout. Bagby wrote on the day she heard the news of the subpoenas, "Don't panic! Let's investigate *them*." WSP did, and found that every one of the HUAC members had voted against all peace and civil rights legislation.[25]

A communication from the national office reported that women from all over the country were calling to communicate their indignation that they had not been summoned to the hearing and to express their desire to stand with Wilson before HUAC.[26] Proposals to offer voluntary testimony came simultaneously from so many groups that no one can remember where it arose. Washington decided to promote the action, and a telegram was dispatched to all key women suggesting that they, too, contact HUAC to request they be subpoenaed so that they could tell the committee all about the wonderful work they were doing for peace.[27]

Although voluntary testimony was something new in the annals of HUAC, it was not as naïve as it may seem. Its effect and consequences were weighed carefully by the New York and Washington leadership and explained in detail through the internal communications network. A letter from Washington suggested four advantages: (1) It would dramatize the fact that "we are open and above-board and eager to state what we stand for." (2) It would provide a national platform for WSP to explain its program. (3) A HUAC refusal of the WSP offer would demonstrate to the press and the public that the committee was not honestly seeking information but rather hoping to intimidate the peace activists. (4) A large enough number of women offering to testify might result in the cancellation of the hearings, as processing the requests could overload the committee's staff.[28] As was usual with WSP, there were differences of opinion regarding voluntary testimony. Berkeley and El Cerrito, California, women wired their objections, as did the Champaign/Urbana women, who pointed out that, although they admired the courage and "imaginativeness" of the plan, they found an irreconcilable contradiction in denying the right of HUAC to exist "and at the same time offering to testify freely in an investigation of us."[29] The Champaign/Urbana group also expressed concern that, by volunteering to testify, those who had nothing to hide might jeopardize the chances of the subpoenaed women who might want to remain silent. The Champaign/Urbana women made it clear, however, that although they disagreed with voluntary testimony, they would continue to solicit funds for WSP and to circulate the national anti-HUAC statement.

Approximately one hundred women volunteered to testify before HUAC and were refused. Carol Urner of Portland, Oregon, spoke for many of those who volunteered. She made it clear that she would not "name names." "I think each woman should be—and probably is—proud of her own participation," Urner asserted, "but some might not trust the Committee's intent or use of the names." "Each woman's name is her own, and each woman, regardless of her views, her goodness or her badness, is too precious to be violated for an abstraction like the state. I suppose, such a refusal could lead one to contempt and prison, and things like that . . . and no mother can accept lightly even the remote possibility of separation from the family which needs her. But mankind needs us too."[30]

It is difficult today to comprehend the emotions that a summons from HUAC could evoke in the repressive political atmosphere of the 1950s and early 1960s. Victor Navasky describes eloquently in *Naming Names* the pressure, dread, and sense of isolation a HUAC summons could evoke. "Guilt was in the air," Navasky contends, "and in the absence of community support, many of the victims internalized the larger society's verdict."[31] The WSP leaders, familiar with the terrors of the 1950s, were determined that their sisters would not experience isolation or abandonment. Trying to keep spirits and energy high, the Washington office reminded the key women that WSP was not alone. Sixty national organizations, including the American Jewish Congress, Americans for Democratic Action, the Unitarian Fellowship for Social Justice, the Rabbinical Assembly, and the United Auto Workers were already on record in opposition to HUAC. Using this list it was not difficult for the women to enlist the local chapters of these organizations to support WSP. Every letter or statement of support that was secured on the local or national level and every newspaper editorial published was immediately dispatched to local groups to generate further support. Chicago WFP, a WSP chapter, reported that it had succeeded in getting fifty-six prominent members of the community to protest the investigation on the grounds that HUAC lacked legitimate legislative purpose, and that the hearings would inhibit free discussion of paths toward world peace. Among the signers were the president of Roosevelt University, the chief psychologist of the Children's Memorial Hospital, the dean of the School of Social Service Administration at the University of Chicago, dozens of ministers, one rabbi, and several businessmen and academics, including several professors of history at Roosevelt University, Northwestern University, and the University of Chicago.[32]

The Southern Conference Educational Fund (SCEF), a civil rights organization very much in the public eye because of the growing celebrity of one of its leaders, Martin Luther King, Jr., identified itself strongly with WSP in its fight against HUAC. SCEF declared: "This attempt to harass the peace movement, like the efforts to intimidate southern integration workers, underscores once more the need to abolish the Committee before it destroys us all." Among those who came to the defense of WSP were known anti-Communist intellectuals such as Lewis Mumford, Alfred Kazin, and Matthew Josephson. Also included in the list of supporters was the distinguished feminist doctor Alice Hamilton, Harvard Medical School emeritus, who had been a founder of WPP and a participant in the international women's peace congress at the Hague in 1915. Lacking any knowledge of women's peace history, WSP never contacted Hamilton or used her name to connect itself with the suffragist-feminist peace movement.

The WSP records show that HUAC did not demoralize the movement. In fact, it strengthened WSP, and increased the number of its adherents and financial supporters. As one of the organizers of the New York area defense against HUAC, I remember that I never worked harder in my life, that I was energized by anger and hope and a feeling that we were "living on the edge" of either victory or disaster. We were empowered by our sense that we women were on our own, and by our conviction that all our decisions and actions were of enormous planetary significance. A letter from the Denver group indicates that WSPers in other parts of the country were experiencing the same sense of urgency and potential power: "Since receipt of your wire this morning, Denver WFP has contacted about 300 members of various peace organizations, asking support by groups and individuals. We have already received word of actions taken in behalf of WSP by the Denver branches of WILPF, SANE, Alliance of Unitarian Women, ACLU, CNVA, AFSC, and the Denver Peace Center."[33] The Los Angeles area WSP groups were particularly active in opposition to the House committee's attack. They prepared their own anti-HUAC statement, which they published as an advertisement in the 4 December 1962 California edition of the

New York Times under the headline "Gentlemen What Are You Afraid Of?" In a sermonlike query and response, the ad asked:

Are they afraid the women are planning acts of sabotage, poisoning the water supply, perhaps?
Hardly likely, especially from a group that first met to protest the poisoning of the earth's atmosphere by the Soviet Union, France, Britain, and the United States. . . .
Are they afraid that the women will talk too much?
Yes, very likely! They are afraid of women who are not afraid to express unpopular views.

Kay Hardman, who wrote the Los Angeles anti-HUAC statement and who came to WSP from the Unitarian Church peace movement, seems to have had a greater knowledge of women's history and far more of a feminist consciousness than the average WSP activist. Using this knowledge and awareness in a way that the WSPers admired and appreciated, she identified WSP with its radical foremothers in the antislavery movement: "We have not progressed very far in 128 years since groups of American men mobbed the meeting in Philadelphia where the leaders of the Women's Antislavery Society were speaking, stoned the building, and subsequently burned it to the ground." "We are the new abolitionists," WSP proclaimed.

As the subpoenaed women made their own preparations for the hearings, they drew together like any group of people about to share an ordeal. They met frequently to exchange information on their legal rights and strategies and to give each other support and assurance. Ruth Meyers recalled that, "in the twelve days between the time we received the subpoenas and the date we had to appear, WSP became one large, hardworking legal committee to find out all we could about our rights and the committee's rights. We read the constitution, law books, case histories, everything."[34]

For Lyla Hoffman the subpoena precipitated a frantic study of the Bill of Rights, with special concentration on the First Amendment. Hoffman, who had been a Communist party member in her youth but had left the party because of its lack of internal democracy and its unquestioning support of all Soviet policies, felt it was high time to say, "What difference does it make what anyone did or believed many years ago? That's not the problem facing humanity today." "But," she explained, "I had to say this in legal terms."[35]

Elizabeth Moos, one of the non-WSPers subpoenaed, carried a heavy burden of guilt toward WSP because she had been identified as a Communist and feared that her personal record would tarnish the image of a new movement with enormous potential for reaching nonpolitical women. When asked about her feelings at the first emergency meeting in New York where decisions were being made regarding the WSP stance in relation to the investigation, she replied: "I remember that meeting with great pain. I was very much afraid that I might be harmful to Women Strike for Peace. I thought I was chosen because my past might be used to smear the others . . . because I was the most vulnerable."[36] Moos was surprised and moved, she told me, that despite the political climate of the timles WSP did not reject her. Sylvia Contente, another witness, was "beset by fear and trepidation," but these feelings were soon dispelled by the supportive response of friends and associates in her community: "Most pleasing and gratifying were the many offers of legal assistance. We were particularly heartened by the fact that Mr. Thurman Arnold and General Telford Taylor agreed to represent us before the Committee."[37] Thurman Arnold had been the assistant attorney general under Franklin D. Roosevelt, and General Taylor had made his reputation as the U.S. prosecutor at the Nuremberg Trials; the WSPers felt fortunate to have such respectable mainstream lawyers on their team.

On 11 December 1962 at 10:00 A.M., the HUAC hearings, "relating to the Communist Party's united front tactics of infiltrating peace organizations, with particular reference to Women Strike for Peace and its Metropolitan New York, New Jersey, and Connecticut section" opened in the Caucus Room of the Old House Office Building of the U.S. Congress with Representative Clyde Doyle presiding.

Earlier that morning a group of thirty-five WSPers from Washington, D.C., and New York attempted to lay a wreath at the statues of the women's rights leaders Susan B. Anthony, Elizabeth Cady Stanton, and Lucretia Mott that stand in the basement below the Rotunda in the Capitol.[38] The wreath bore the inscription "To the brave women who made America listen. We too shall be heard." The wreath laying was conceived by Janet Neuman, a long-time WILPF activist who was of the generation that remembered the suffrage struggle and the interwar feminist peace movement. Her goal was to identify WSP symbolically with the women in America's past who had been persecuted and reviled for their political militancy and who had triumphed. Others saw it as a way of proving that not all dissenters were "un-American."[39] But WSP's attempt to identify with the women's rights movement was never consummated, because the Capitol police interceded, claiming that WSP had no permit for wreath laying. As the women attempted to argue with the police, using the smiles and wiles that had been effective in the past, they were jostled and shoved up against the stony bodies of their militant foremothers.[40] Accustomed to the courtesy, if not the sympathy, of police and government officials, the WSPers were shocked to find that their image was changing. The summons from HUAC seemed already to have transformed them from respectable peace ladies to dangerous "Reds."[41]

Upstairs in the Old House Office Building every one of the five hundred seats was occupied by WSPers who had come from eleven states, some from as far as California. They were colorfully dressed in their best "go-to-demonstration" attire, but they seemed tense and solemn. They had come to share with each witness whatever punishment the committee would hand out, and were ready to give back better than they received in what the movement's publicity called "the good new WISP way."

I was one of the women who surveyed the room with pride, but deep apprehension. Like many others, I did not understand why I had not been subpoenaed and feared that the committee would correct its error at any moment and demand that I march forward for my share of humiliation, if not imprisonment. My response, like that of most of the women present, was to pay close attention and use every effort to support those who had to face the committee.

Chairman Clyde Doyle of California opened with a statement of the committee's purpose and assumptions. Quoting from Lenin, Stalin, and Khrushchev, he declared: "Communists believe that there can be no real peace until they have conquered the world, eliminating all other systems. . . . The initiated Communist, understanding his Marxist-Leninist doctrine, knows that a Moscow call to intensify the fight for peace means that he should intensify his fight to destroy capitalism and its major bastion, the United States of America."[42] He concluded, "Peace propaganda and agitation have a disarming, mollifying, confusing, and weakening effect on those nations which are the intended victims of Communism."[43] The WSP audience remained silent through most of the introductory statement but broke into applause when Doyle stated, "The fact that Communists have infiltrated peace organizations does not mean that all members of them, or even a majority of them, are Communists, or Communist sympathizers, or fellow travelers."[44] This spontaneous outburst cheered the women and set the tone for their active, good-humored participation throughout the hearings. It also demonstrated from the outset the unorganized, spontaneous way in which the WSP women would respond. The WSP applause took Congressman Doyle by surprise. He hesitated, looked pleased and baffled, then continued. At the end of his opening statement, he commented, "It was very pleasant to hear that applause; of course we must ask there be no applause for, or demonstration against, anything that is said in this room today."[45] That was a warning he was to repeat many times throughout the three days of the hearings, with less and less effect.

The committee called as its first friendly witness Richard A. Flink, whose role was to establish a connection between WSP and Russia. Flink, an attorney, testified that he had been in contact with Russian agents while acting as an informer for the FBI. He claimed that the Russians had offered him $3,000 in 1962 when he was a candidate for the New York State Assembly from the Twelfth District. The money was allegedly offered as an inducement to "relate whatever I was discussing to the general subjects of armaments, nuclear testing and the like." Mr. Flink, to whom the *New York Times* referred as "Mr. Slink" in a Freudian typographical error, was asked by committee counsel Alfred M. Nittle to describe his connection with WSP. Flink explained that during the month of October he had received an invitation to be interviewed by local representatives of WSP. "Would you tell us what was said in the course of that interview?" Nittle asked. Flink replied that the WSP women had presented him with literature on disarmament and talked to him about the "conversion of presently operated military plants to peacetime use." According to Flink, they had also mentioned a proposal for the introduction of legislation to set up an economic committee in the state legislature to study questions of disarmament.[46] Flink had not even tried to make a direct connection between WSP and Russia, but the women were very much concerned about his insinuations.

Some of them rushed up to the witness as he left the stand to try to convince him that he was being used by the committee and that what he had done was morally wrong. They invited him to lunch for a friendly chat, and they were apparently effective. On 13 December the New York WSP office received a copy of a notarized statement by Flink, in which he amended his testimony to include the statement "At no time did I express or imply that WSP is in any way equated with the world-wide Communist conspiracy." He also made it clear in the amended statement that WSP had held routine interviews with all candidates. The committee added Flink's corrected statement to the record of the hearings with a footnote indicating that it had received and approved a request from Flink to supplement his testimony. But the committee printed a different version of Flink's last sentence than the one received by WSP. The WSP version read: "I have absolutely no knowledge or any opinion with regard to this group either favorable or unfavorable, nor do I know of any of the activities or affiliations of this group or its members."[47] Thus the first and only hostile witness summoned by the committee was neutralized largely because of the women's confidence in their cause, and their conviction that most people, if reached in a nonthreatening, personal, and friendly way, will act in kind.

The WSP women in the audience rose as one when the committee called its first WSP witness, Blanche Posner, a retired teacher who was serving as the volunteer office manager of New York WSP. The decision to rise with the first witness, to stand with her as if all the women present had also been called, was spontaneous. It was suggested only a few moments earlier in an unsigned note that circulated through the room. Posner took matters into her own hands, lecturing the committee members as if they were recalcitrant boys at De Witt Clinton High School in the Bronx, where she had taught. Talking right through the interruptions and objections raised by the chairman and the committee counsel, Posner declared:

> I don't know, sir, why I am here, but I do know why you are here, because you don't quite understand the nature of this movement. This movement was inspired and motivated by mothers' love for children. . . . When they were putting their breakfast on the table, they saw not only the Wheaties and milk, but they also saw strontium 90 and iodine 131. . . . They feared for the health and life of their children. This is the only motivation.[48]

Doyle warned, "Now, witness, witness, just a minute. . . . If you insist on interrupting the hearing, we will have to ask that you be removed from the hearing room." The committee counsel then introduced a series of exhibits, including a document titled "Structure for Women Strike for Peace, Metropolitan N.Y., New Jersey, Conn." The presentation of this document, labeled Exhibit 1, was calculated to prove that, despite its assertions to the contrary, WSP had a highly organized hierarchical structure, conceived and controlled by the Communist party. At the sight of Exhibit 1 the WSP audience burst into laughter, relieved to know that the committee was hopelessly and haplessly on the wrong track.[49] Posner refused to answer any questions about the structure or personnel of WSP, resorting to the Fifth Amendment forty-four times. Each time Posner invoked the Fifth Amendment she offered a pointed criticism of the committee or a quip that endeared her to her sisters, who needed to keep up their spirits in the face of charges that Posner had been identified by an FBI informer as a Communist party member.[50] One exchange between Nittle and Posner led to particularly enthusiastic applause and laughter: "Nittle: Did you wear a colored paper daisy to identify yourself as a member of the Women Strike for Peace? Posner: It sounds like such a far cry from communism it is impossible not to be amused. I still invoke the Fifth Amendment."[51] In a telephone interview with the author in May 1981, Posner explained, almost nineteen years later, that she had invoked the Fifth Amendment even though she herself had not been a member of the party because she understood that, according to the committee's rules, once one answered a question about oneself, one could be cited for contempt if one refused to answer questions about others. Posner, like the others, stated that she wanted to avoid being forced to discuss other people who could be hurt.

Heartened by the large friendly audience and feeling that she had to do her best for the cause, Posner was forceful, impertinent, and disdainful of the committee's power and purpose. She set the tone for the day and for the rest of the hearings. She embodied the WSP image of outraged moral motherhood.

Posner had less to fear from the committee's smears, innuendo, and publicity than most of the witnesses in the past, as neither her career nor her livelihood was in danger. She had retired from school teaching and was married to an independent, successful lawyer who also had nothing to fear in terms of his practice. She was, however, vulnerable on one count. Her son, who had recently graduated from Harvard Law School, was serving as a clerk in the office of Supreme Court Justice William Brennan. Blanche Posner had no way of knowing whether her notoriety would affect her son, but she believes, on reflection, that she had no choice but to testify as she did. The possibility of nuclear holocaust was, in her view, a more important consideration than a small setback in her son's career. There were, in fact, no repercussions.

Before Posner left the stand, Chairman Doyle attempted to discredit her and divide the WSPers. "I think that the women who are not Communists . . . are entitled to know who in the organization is a Communist and whether or not it has been infiltrated. . . . We happen to know from experience that Communists can dupe most anyone they set about duping." Posner retorted, "We are too bright for that." As Posner left the stand, Doyle thanked her. She replied, in her best schoolteacher manner, "You are welcome, Mr. Doyle. And thank you. You have been very, very cooperative."[52] The audience roared, and Posner was greeted with prolonged applause. Women rushed to hug her. Shouts of "You were wonderful" enveloped Posner as she took her seat. The WSPers ignored the fact that she was accused of having been a member of a Communist cell and had refused to answer any questions regarding her possible involvement in the Communist party under the protection of the Fifth Amendment of the U.S. Constitution. The fact that Posner had spoken for WSP in the language and ideas that the women recognized as their own was sufficient.

In the first round, Posner had acquitted herself gallantly, whereas Doyle had made a serious error for which he was forced to apologize. He had stated: "So far as we know she [Posner] is a Communist now because there is no evidence that she is not." This violation of the American principle of law that one is innocent until proven guilty was picked up by the press. At first Doyle denied to a news reporter that he had made a statement to the effect that the burden of proof was on the witness, but on the following morning, in open session, he was forced to admit that upon examination of the transcript, he found that he had indeed been recorded as making such a statement, for which he apologized.

Ruth Meyers of Roslyn, Long Island, was the next witness. She stepped forward "swathed in red and brown jersey, topped by a steeple crowned red velvet hat," and according to the *Washington Post*, "was just as much of a headache to the committee as Posner had been." "Are you a member of Women Strike for Peace?" Nittle asked. "No sir, Women Strike for Peace has no members," Meyers answered, as she began her tussle with the committee. Nittle then asked, "You are familiar, I understand, with the structural organization of Women Strike for Peace as evidenced by this plan?" Meyers replied: "I am familiar to the extent of the role that I play in it. I must say that I was not particularly interested in the structure of Women Strike for Peace. I was more involved in my own community activities. . . . I felt that structure, other than the old telephone, was not much of what I was interested in."[53] Nittle continued in his attempt to prove that Meyers was involved in the top leadership of WSP, pointing out that she had been in charge of congressional appointments at the first Washington demonstration, and the organizer of a send-off for the fifty-one WSP women who flew to Geneva to lobby and demonstrate at the Seventeen-Nation Disarmament Conference. He proceeded to deliver what he believed to be the coup de grace for Meyers. "Mrs. Meyers," he intoned ominously, "it appears from the public records that a Ruth Meyers, residing at 175 East 10th Street, Brooklyn, New York, on July 27, 1948, signed a Communist Party nominating petition. . . . Are you the Ruth Meyers who executed that petition?" Meyers shot back, "No, sir!" She examined the petition carefully and then declared, "I never resided at that address, and it is not my signature."[54] Although the official transcript does not contain the following statement, many, including me, heard Meyers add, "My husband could never get me to move to Brooklyn." This female remark brought an explosion of laughter and applause, which Meyers topped with "Perhaps, sir, I should not have accepted the subpoena, if there are so many people named Ruth Meyers." As she left the witness stand, Meyers received a one-minute ovation for courage, humor, and mistaken identity. In the corridor outside the Caucus Room, before the television cameras, she told reporters that she had never been a Communist. "But I will never acknowledge the Committee's right to ask me that question."[55]

Lyla Hoffman, the next witness, took a far different approach from that of the preceding two. Hoffman had made the decision to acknowledge her past membership in the Communist party to the committee but to invoke the First Amendment to defend her right not to answer questions that would infringe on her freedom of thought or that would implicate others. Columnist Mary McGrory of the *Washington Evening Star* depicted Hoffman as "a modish, mascaraed, self-described housewife and peace worker, who said she had left the Communist party, but, standing on her first amendment rights, stubbornly refused to tell Representative Doyle whether she had become an anti-Communist."[56] Hoffman had taken a courageous position. In revealing her own past but refusing to testify about others, she had removed herself from the privileges of the Fifth Amendment to the Constitution and was subject to prosecution. She did this, she explained, to make the point that the ideologies people embraced before the nuclear emergency were no longer relevant, and that what mattered in the nuclear age was whether or not people understood the dangers emanating from both superpowers, one avowedly Communist, the other capitalist. Hoffman explained in a memo to the national WSP office why she did not resort to the Fifth Amendment, a strategy used by most of the other women to avoid incriminating themselves and others. "While I admired the Fifth as a highly principled position," she stated, "I personally felt that it did not offer sufficient challenge to the committee's authority and power, whereas the First Amendment did."[57]

The committee did not appreciate Hoffman's frankness or her defense of the rights of former Communists to continue to work for political change. She was pressed to explain why she left the party and to convince the committee that she had really turned against communism. Hoffman then resorted to the First Amendment, insisting gallantly on her right to political freedom.[58]

On the second day of the HUAC hearings, the witness who attracted the most press attention was Anna MacKenzie of Westport, Connecticut, a professional journalist who, like the other WSP witnesses, identified herself as a housewife. Her accusation that HUAC was "throwing stones, not questions" was much quoted in newspaper, television, and magazine accounts of the second day of the hearings.[59] To a question about the structure of WSP, MacKenzie replied: "The Central Coordinating Committee is something that you have given great stature to and made it sound almost as a Congressional Committee. In Connecticut, we don't take it very seriously. Perhaps we should, but we don't."[60] MacKenzie insisted on her right to prepare petitions and sign petitions whether they be nominating petitions or petitions for general and universal disarmament. She also resorted to the First Amendment, refusing to answer any questions about her activities in 1937 as editor of the *Vassar Miscellany News* or whether she was involved with the American

Student Union, an organization Nittle labeled a Communist front. "It is irrelevant," she replied; "that was back in the 1930s. It is irrelevant because I have a right to become an editor or a writer of any publication I see fit."[61] As she left the witness stand, also to great applause, MacKenzie broke into tears, for she felt certain that she would suffer economic consequence or even might be jailed for refusing to answer questions. Huddling with friends who gathered around to comfort her, she confessed that she "felt bad" about crying, especially because one of her children had told her before she left home, "Mommy, you know you cry so easily. Don't . . . cry in front of those men."[62]

At the end of the second day the WSP leadership was confident that it was winning its battle with the committee. But they were worried that they might lose the support of those women who might be confused or put off by the witnesses' reliance on the Fifth and First Amendments, and by one confession of a Communist past. In response to this concern, the national office issued a press statement reaffirming WSP unity: "At the close of the second day of this ordeal, Women Strike for Peace remains more than ever a movement of dedicated, undivided, and unintimidated individuals. Each woman who has so far testified has, according to her own conscience, upheld the heritage of our Constitution and reaffirmed her right and responsibility to work for peace despite the disruptive nature of these investigations."[63]

The third day of the hearings was clearly a special, almost celebratory day for the women. Each WSPer in the audience wore a white rose tied with ribbon bearing the inscription "Women Strike for Peace." A cheer arose as Dagmar Wilson was called to the stand. A young woman with a baby on her hip stepped forward to hand Wilson, not one rose, but a bouquet. Nittle and Doyle treated Wilson with more deference than they had shown to any of the previous witnesses. It was clear that Wilson had been called not to be reviled as a Communist, but rather to be exposed as a well-intentioned dupe. "The Committee has no evidence of Communist Party membership or activity in support of front groups, or of pro-Communist sympathies on your part, and this we wish to emphasize," Nittle stated. He charged that the New York witnesses had been uncooperative, and expressed the hope that Wilson, as a leader of the movement and a patriotic American citizen, would do better.[64]

Wilson had engaged in a great deal of solitary reflection before the hearing. In the end she relied on her own unfettered brand of radical individualism. Her decision to answer freely all questions about the movement was her own, although she consulted with her husband and with close friends, lawyers, and leaders of other peace groups, some of whom disapproved of the decision. In addition to being concerned for the fate of WSP, Wilson had to deal with her ongoing worry that her political activism might lead to her husband's dismissal from his position as cultural attaché at the British embassy. Wilson recalled in a 1981 letter to me that soon after the 1 November 1961 strike, the commercial counselor at the British embassy called Christopher Wilson into his office to inform him that his wife's activities were ill-advised and played into Communist hands. Christopher, according to Dagmar, told the counselor that his wife was a U.S. citizen and quite within her rights according to U.S. law and that, furthermore, he agreed with her views on disarmament. The counselor's retort was that Christopher would have a hard time finding another job at his age.

To add to the Wilsons' anxiety around the hearings, Christopher, who had worked for the British government since 1941 and who had held a responsible job as the secretary of the Combined Raw Materials Board, had never been subjected to a security check during World War II. It was not until Dagmar made a trip to the USSR as a guest of the Soviet Women's Committee that he was asked to submit to a security investigation.

"On the eve of the hearings," Dagmar recalled, "not knowing how they would go" and having decided to answer questions about herself but not about anyone else, "I was quite prepared for a jail sentence. It had happened to others." "C. and I agreed rightly or wrongly, that this could lead to his dismissal and were prepared to accept this outcome without any ideas for another occupation. C's unflappable attitude was very reassuring to me, enabling me to respond unguardedly to the inquisitors."[65]

As two of the previous witnesses had refused to give their ages, Nittle began, "As to the date of your birth, you may simply state that you are over 21 years of age." "I don t mind telling you," Wilson replied instantly, in a most pleasant and cooperative manner, "I was born in 1916 in New York City." When asked if she was the leader of WSP, Wilson answered, "People like to call me leader, I regard it more a term of endearment, or shall we say, an honorary title." In a gracious, witty, and occasionally condescending style, Wilson demolished the charge that a small core of well-organized New York Communists were in control of WSP and of Wilson herself. One exchange among committee counsel Nittle, Wilson, and chairman Doyle illustrates the way in which Wilson tried in every instance to appeal to the humanity of the committee members, to touch whatever positive feelings they may have had toward women and children. Nittle asked Wilson if she had coordinated the 1 November 1961 demonstrations in fifty-eight cities. Wilson replied: "I find it very hard to explain to the masculine mind. I can't answer yes or no. It was my initiative that resulted in, yes, all of these demonstrations that took place on that day. By the way, there were 60 not just 58." Doyle then interceded, "I think the masculine mind can understand that." Wilson then looked squarely and kindly at the HUAC subcommittee chairman and said, "I thought you would be able to, Mr. Doyle, because I have been watching your face." Finally, the committee counsel arrived at what he was sure would be the question that would make headlines for the committee. "Would you permit Communist Party members to occupy leading posts in Women Strike for Peace?" he asked, and Wilson replied without hesitation: "Well, my dear sir, I have absolutely no way of controlling, do not desire to control, who wishes to join the demonstrations and the efforts that the women strikers have made for peace. In fact, I would also like to go even further. I would like to say that unless everybody in the whole world joins us in this fight, then God help us." Nittle asked, "Would you knowingly permit or welcome Nazis or Fascists?" Wilson answered, "If we could only get them on our side." This was an answer unexpected by the committee and probably by the women. Most of them understood its intent and gave Wilson a standing ovation. Doyle then concluded: "I want to emphasize that the committee recognizes that there are many, many, many women, in fact a great, great majority of women, in this peace movement who are absolutely patriotic and absolutely adverse to everything the Communist Party stands for. We recognize that you are one of them. We compliment you on your leadership and on your helpfulness to us this morning." Wilson replied, "I do hope that you live to thank us when we have achieved our goal." Doyle responded, "Well, we will." Whereupon, at 12:28 P.M. on Thursday, 13 December 1962, the HUAC investigation of Communist influence in WSP was adjourned.

WSP had won its battle with HUAC. For the first time, HUAC was belittled with humor and bested in its bid for political guardianship. News stories and editorials critical of the committee and supportive of WSP were featured in major newspapers from coast to coast. "Peace Gals Make Red Hunters Look Silly," "Redhunters Decapitated," "Peace Ladies Tangle with Baffled Congress," and "It's Ladies Day at Capitol: Hoots, Howls and Charm" were some of the headlines that led Frank Wilkerson of the National Committee to Abolish the House Un-American Activities Committee to proclaim, "Magnificent women: you have made peace and civil liberties indivisible. You have dealt HUAC its greatest setback."[66]

A cartoon by Herblock in the *Washington Post* of 12 December set the tone for the liberal press. It showed three aging and baffled committee members seated at the hearing table. One turns to another and asks, "I Came in Late, Which Was It That Was Un-American—Women or Peace?"[67] A news story in the *Vancouver Sun* (British Columbia) of 14

December reflected the perceptions of many other journalists: "The dreaded House Un-American Activities Committee met its Waterloo this week. It tangled with 500 irate women. They laughed at it. Klieg lights glared, television cameras whirred, and 50 reporters scribbled notes while babies cried and cooed during the fantastic inquisition." Bill Galt, the author of this report, presented a detailed description of WSP civil disobedience in the Old House Office Building:

> When the first woman headed to the witness table, the crowd
> rose silently to its feet. The irritated Chairman Clyde Doyle of
> California outlawed standing. They applauded the next witness
> and Doyle outlawed clapping. Then they took to running out to
> kiss the witness. . . . Finally, each woman as she was called was
> met and handed a huge bouquet. By then Doyle was a beaten
> man. By the third day the crowd was giving standing ovations
> to the heroines with impunity.[68]

The hearings were a perfect foil for the humor of Russell Baker, syndicated columnist of the *New York Times*. Baker, who was an admirer of his mother's resourcefulness in adversity, reveled in the victory of female common sense over male abstraction. "If the House Un-American Activities Committee knew its Greek as well as it knows its Lenin, it would have left the women peace strikers alone. . . . Instead, with typical male arrogance, it has subpoenaed 15 of the ladies, . . . spent several days trying to show them that woman's place is not on the peace march route, and has come out of it covered with foolishness."[69] Baker reported that by the end of the hearing "the investigators looked less like dashing Red-hunters than like men trapped in a bargain basement on a sale day."

Mary McGrory in the *Washington Evening Star* also concluded that it was gender differences, not conflicting political ideologies, that had been contested in the Caucus Room of the Old House Office Building.

> The leader of the group kept protesting prettily that she was not
> really the leader at all. No man, of course, would ever deny
> being the leader of anything. Nor would he suggest for a split
> second that he didn't know exactly what was going on. But
> Mrs. Dagmar Wilson of Washington, when asked if she exer-
> cised control over the New York Chapter, merely giggled and
> said, "Nobody controls anybody in the Women Strike for Peace.
> We're all leaders."[70]

Long before Carol Gilligan, McGrory observed that the WSPers were speaking "in a different voice." She suggested that Nittle's "clutch question" regarding Communist membership in WSP "would bring a man to his knees with patriotic protest" but that it "didn't faze the feminine Dagmar Wilson." McGrory and others described the ways in which the women of WSP domesticated a hallowed male bastion, "their young crawled in the aisles and noisily sucked on their bottles during the whole proceedings." She implied that in so doing WSP had robbed this particular congressional committee of its ability to intimidate and inhibit dissent. James McCartney, in the *Chicago Daily News,* depicted the WSP occupation of HUAC's theater of operations in the following manner: "It was just like ladies day at the ball park. Babies bawled, women cheered. There were hoots and laughs. There was much clapping of hands. And all of this in the normally austere, marble columned hearing room where the always austere House Un-American Activities Committee was at work."[71]

Political theorist Jean Bethke Elshtain suggests that "WSP showed the grand deconstructive power of a politics of humor, irony, evasion and ridicule. The Women's Strike for Peace didn't proclaim that the Emperor had no clothes; rather they put him in a position where, to his own astonishment, he found he had disrobed himself with his own tactics and strategies."[72]

Much of the humor directed at the committee by the media was also condescending to the women of WSP and to all women. The WSPers were portrayed either as the essential female of the species fighting like a tiger for the protection of her young, or as a clever manipulator exercising female wiles. Even the *Daily Cardinal,* the University of Wisconsin's radical student newspaper, commented: "The Women Strike for Peace is not a collection of radicals, intellectuals, liberals, idealists, or anything else, officially deemed suspect. . . . This is a group that has been dubbed the 'bourgeois mothers' underground' in recognition of the suburban, respectable stratum from which this movement has been drawn."[73] The student editors of the *Daily Cardinal* could not conceive of women as both mothers and intellectuals, or idealists. But the majority of the WSP women, in their prefeminist consciousness, believed that being regarded as nonintellectual mothers who made the Red hunter look silly was a small price to pay for the lack of recognition of their political and tactical sophistication.

As was to be expected, the conservative press attempted to discredit the spontaneity and humor WSP had injected into an intimidating and tedious process and their appropriation of male controlled public space. William Buckley's *National Review* commented: "On the stand, counseled by the highfalutin Telford Taylor, the women . . . moved smoothly through the paces of committee-baiting; there were speeches, statements, denunciations, outbursts, and harangues, all swaddled in Motherhood v Strontium 90."[74] The *Newark Evening News* criticized the committee for not coping adequately with the WSPers: "The committee should have turned the hearings, if indeed they were necessary in the first place, over to some resourceful feminine colleagues in the House. The land is full of lady lawyers who, unlike the committee's male counsel, would take no nonsense from tricky witnesses."[75]

A WSP *National Information Memo* issued one week after the hearings thanked the women across the country and around the world for their "magnificent response" to the HUAC attack. The report took pride in the fact that the hearings had received bigger and better publicity than any since the days of McCarthy. To maximize the WSP's public relations victory, Eleanor Garst, one of the movement's chief image makers, put together a twenty-page pamphlet of favorable press clippings. They were so commendatory that no editorial comment was added.[76] The National Information Clearing House, reflecting the input of about seventy-five key women across the country, spread the word that the hearings had been beneficial to the movement, because they had given WSP an opportunity to state its purpose and "to show how impossible it was for any ideological grouping to exercise control over the thoughts and actions of the WSP women."[77]

Although most WSP activists were euphoric after the hearings, questions were raised by some women about the reasons for, and the ramification of, resorting to the Fifth Amendment. To satisfy those who doubted that the use of the Fifth Amendment was consistent with the WSP image and with the protection of the individual against the use of state power, Bella Abzug prepared a short paper on the constitutional rights of witnesses. Abzug explained that the committee's rules did not provide procedural safeguards or effective remedies against damaging or unwarranted charges, as they did not allow a witness to challenge accusations or cross-examine an accuser. Although Abzug was personally not a proponent of the use of the Fifth Amendment, preferring the challenge of the First, she explained that it had been developed by the framers of the Constitution as a response to the persecutions of religious and political dissenters in England and colonial America. She pointed out that the Supreme Court had upheld the right of witnesses to invoke the Fifth in response to interrogation by congressional committees but that, nevertheless, the sensationalism and publicity that had accompanied congressional investigations had implanted in the public mind the notion that the assertion of the Fifth Amendment privilege was equivalent to an admission of whatever was charged. "This distortion of the meaning of the Fifth Amendment," Abzug wrote, "has been fostered by investigators to justify their holding hearing after hearing with no legislative purpose, and which, when concluded, have resulted primarily in the denigration of individuals who have pleaded the Fifth and nothing more."[78] Abzug's explanation of the legality and moral acceptability of the use of the Fifth Amendment was an important affirmation of WSP conduct at the hearings for those who may have felt uncomfortable about the use of anything but the most scrupulously moralistic tactics on the part of WSP. As not one local group officially criticized WSP tactics in meeting the HUAC investigation or the choices the witnesses made in handling their own testimony, no changes in WSP policies, procedures, or rhetoric resulted from the investigation.

Dagmar Wilson's stand at HUAC made most of the WSPers proud. They understood it as an original, courageous action and a breakthrough in the fight against the inhibitory power of HUAC. But it did not meet with the approval of peace groups like SANE and Turn toward Peace. Homer Jack, executive director of SANE, criticized Wilson's "welcome everybody" stand because he believed it might call into question "the political sagacity" of groups like his own. He offered SANE as a model to those who might be shopping around for a respectable and responsible peace group, assuring them that his group would not allow people to be in "command" who "have a double standard, and judge American policy by one set of criteria and Russian or Chinese policies by another set."[79] Kay Hardman of Los Angeles, ever vigilant against Cold War Red baiting, replied to Jack: "You misread, misunderstand and mis-speak the philosophical basis of the women's peace movement in this country. We are directed toward re-formation of the individual and not to tinkering around with institutional forms—most of which at this particular time in world history, no longer fit individual needs anywhere in the world."[80] Hardman also pointed out, not without a bit of irony, that if one accepted the assumption that Communists want to manipulate peace groups, they would be more likely to join SANE, an organization that would give them adequate organizational machinery to manipulate, control, and tinker with than would WSP. She contended that "no rigid, authoritarian type personality could tolerate, for a single moment, the intuitive, agreement by consensus that is the *modus operandi* of women's peace groups."[81] In an article prepared for publication but never published, Eleanor Garst justified Wilson's stand at HUAC. "It was not the presence of communists, but the flight of liberals, and their fear of contamination, that led to the demise of good organizations." "The legacy of McCarthyism is the kind of paralysis which confines the average American intellectual to his armchair even in the face of nuclear annihilation. The few Strikers old enough to have been entrapped in McCarthyism say that they will not again be so easily cowed; and their conduct in the recent hearings would indicate that they mean it."[82]

Barbara Deming, the feminist-pacifist leader and writer, declared that she was thrilled by Wilson's testimony but pointed out what she perceived as a discrepancy in WSP philosophy. She noted that the women of WSP had stood their ground on the issue of communism, refusing to be intimidated, but that they were quite conservative on the issue of unilateral disarmament. According to Deming, when Lyla Hoffman, a former Communist, was asked if she had become an anti-Communist, she answered that she would be happy to reply if the committee would define that term—for there are many different views as to what a Communist or anti-Communist is. But when Arthur Schlesinger, Jr., inquired of a delegation of WSPers meeting with him during the hearings whether they were for unilateral disarmament, they hastily replied, "Oh, no! People keep trying to assign that belief to us, but certainly not." Deming was appalled that the WSPers had not demanded that Schlesinger define "unilateral disarmament." From its earliest days WSP had committed itself to multilateral disarmament under international control and was firm on that issue because it was part of WSP's evenhanded condemnation of both nuclear powers. It also reflected WSP's pragmatism. What Deming observed accurately was that the women of WSP, believing that they were not violating their moral principles, rejected any concept or tactic they thought to be too radical to be understood by the so-called average woman.[83]

On 14 December, the day after the hearings had ended, the *Washington Evening Star* reported that the committee planned no further open or closed sessions on WSP.[84] But a month later, J. Edgar Hoover issued a directive to twenty field offices of the FBI, instructing security officers to review their files and to maintain contact with "informants and established sources" in order to develop information concerning any Communist infiltration of WSP.[85] On 15 February 1963 the Washington field office submitted a memo to Hoover in response to his request for information. Washington informed the director that a "file review" showed that only one known current member of the Communist party was active in WSP in Washington, D.C. In addition, the memo stated that three informants who had furnished information in the past were contacted and that they could furnish no information indicating activity in WSP by the Communist party. The Washington security officer concluded: "It is felt that the WSP in Washington, D.C., does not meet the criteria for conducting a cominfil [Communist infiltration] investigation as set out in section 87 D of the Manual of Instructions. Accordingly, SFO will continue to cover WSP activity through established sources only, and furnish Bureau and interested offices any pertinent information received."[86] Needless to say, FBI surveillance of WSP did not end there, nor did investigations of the peace movement by HUAC. In the summer of 1964 Donna Allen and Dagmar Wilson of WSP, together with Russell Nixon, managing editor of the *National Guardian*, were sub-poenaed by HUAC to testify in closed hearings regarding a visit they had made to the State Department to request a visa for Kaoru Yasui, a Japa-nese peace leader and law school dean. The visa had been granted, and HUAC wanted to know why. Because the State Department refused to supply any information, Allen, Wilson, and Nixon were summoned to testify. The "HUAC Three," in 1960s parlance, refused to testify in closed session, making it clear that they were willing to talk only if the hear-ings were open to the press and public. HUAC, having learned its lesson in the earlier encounter with WSP, refused to open the sessions. The *Washington Post* commented on the investigation: "A subcommittee pre-ferred to do in secret what would probably have been embarrassing to do in public."[87] On 31 December 1964 Allen, Wilson, and Nixon were cited for contempt of Congress. They were arraigned on 8 January. At their trial, the three received twenty large vases of roses from WSP chapters as a token of support and a reminder of the earlier battle with HUAC. Again the press condemned the committee. The *Washington Post* headlined its editorial on the contempt citation "Star Chamber." It praised Wilson and Allen as "two women of high repute" and declared that "certainly there is nothing un-American in going to a department of the United States Government—openly and candidly—to submit a completely lawful request." "To put a damper on the right of petition is the real un-Americanism."[88] Wilson, Allen, and Nixon were convicted, but in August 1966 the courts refused to uphold the committee's con-tempt citations. The *New York Times* reported that in overturning the conviction of the HUAC Three "the court perpetuated a five-year losing streak by the Un-American Activities Committee at the hands of the Federal Courts."[89]

Writing in *Liberation* in 1966, Donna Allen pointed out that HUAC still existed, despite WSP's temporary victory against it, and was still violating the Constitution by harassing the peace movement. But, Allen insisted, fear of the committee had receded; in fact an investigation had become an opportunity for those under investigation to hold press con-ferences, to express their political views, to gain support and funds.[90] Walter Goodman asserted that HUAC investigations came infrequently after 1962, and when they did "the question had become, not what punishment the Committee would inflict on others, but what unpleas-antness the others planned for the Congressmen."[91] WSP can take credit for raising that question.

Although HUAC was abolished in 1975 when its jurisdiction was transferred to the House Judiciary Committee, the CIA continued its surveillance of WSP. Mary McGrory called it "The CIA's Most Ridiculous Waste of Money."[92] Her reason for choosing WSP as the most ridiculous waste, she explained, was Edith Villastrigo, WSP's Washington, D.C., coordinator. "When I ponder the fact that federal funds were used so that some agent could find out what Edith Villastrigo was thinking," she commented, "my mind stops." "It is virtually impossible not to know what Edith is thinking." Referring to the fact that WSP was suspected of being funded by the Soviets, McGrory noted that the constant stream of press releases issued by Villastrigo came typed in all caps on flimsy paper. Noting that WSP doesn't have a mimeograph machine, McGrory reasoned that, if WSP did have an alien sponsor, "it was one of exceptional chintziness." Edith dashed off a typical press release the moment she heard that the CIA had been watching her. It was on the usual flimsy paper, in caps. "WHAT DID THE CIA EXPECT TO FIND OUT WHEN THEY INFILTRATED OUR MEETINGS—THAT WE OPPOSED THE NUCLEAR ARMS RACE—THAT WE OPPOSED THE INDOCHINA WAR—THAT WE SUPPORTED THE YOUNG MEN WHO REFUSED IN GOOD CONSCIENCE TO FIGHT THAT WAR—THEY COULD HAVE READ OUR PUBLICITY FOR THAT KIND OF INFORMATION.[93]

6

A Not-so-funny Thing Happened on the Way to Disarmament

We were sidetracked by the war in Vietnam. Even though we knew that while the war was going on, the nuclear arms race would continue, we had to make a choice on what issue we would deal with immediately. There was no question it would be Vietnam because this was so urgent.
—Ethel Taylor

*A*fter having routed HUAC in its attempt to destroy the movement's political credibility and after attaining its first, if partial, victory, the ratification of the treaty prohibiting atmospheric nuclear testing, the key women of WSP were not only proud but astonished by their success. "Who would have believed three years ago that the leaders who were preparing us to accept nuclear war as inevitable would today be declaring nuclear war as 'unthinkable'?" Dagmar Wilson asked.

Who would have thought that the test ban treaty, which WSP worked so hard to bring about, would be heralded as a great achievement by the party in power, meriting that party's reelection? Isn't this what women were marching for three years ago? To make our political leaders see the light so that we could go back to our pots-and-pans and PTAs and all the duties and pleasures that we have since neglected?[1]

Tempting as the notion of a return to domestic duties and pleasures may have been, few WSP activists were ready to abandon the political sphere in which they had come to feel very much at home. In a second anniversary address in New York City Wilson spoke of an issue on many women's minds:

Some people are wondering if we will fall apart now that we have a Test Ban Treaty. They pity us, as though we have been deprived of our *raison d'être*. They refer to those two ghastly years, which we are so thankful to have survived, as our "better days." Naturally we don't believe what is good for the world is bad for the peace movement. We are grateful for a brief pause in the Cold War which enables us to take a deep breath of relatively uncontaminated air and organize our thoughts.[2]

In the second anniversary message to WSP, in which Wilson congratulated the movement on its successes in transforming foreign policy discourse, she also expressed her continuing anger and indignation toward the men in the State Department, the Congress, and the Pentagon who, as she put it, spoke of peace but prepared for war. "Is it to preserve the peace," she asked, "that we are stockpiling nuclear weapons? Is it to preserve the peace that we are trying to promote MLF [a NATO-controlled nuclear fleet]? Is it to preserve the peace that we are fighting a limited war in Vietnam?" Ignoring her own nostalgic reference to pleasures of domesticity, she urged the women she had brought together in 1961 to continue their struggle for complete and total disarmament under the supervision of an impartial international peace-keeping body.[3] Predicting that "when the Civil Defense Bill raises its ugly head again in the Senate, the women will be there, hats, flowers and all," Wilson concluded, "Others may be seeking new directions, but the women know where they are going and will find a way of getting there."

There was, however, little reflection in Wilson's message, WSP newsletters, or other internal communications, on the reasons for the movement's early political victories. There was no speculation regarding the president's motives in seeking a test ban, other than his fear of nuclear holocaust. Nobody asked whether Kennedy was downplaying the nuclear force in order to upgrade tactical weaponry for small wars in Latin America or Southeast Asia. In fact, there was little theoretical discussion in WSP publications about the causes of the Cold War or of war in general. WSP's strategy had been to focus on a clear and apparent danger to health and life and to attack it head on. The women were pragmatic and canny, in that they chose the most vulnerable targets in the Cold War arsenal. Atmospheric testing, HUAC, air-raid shelters, and the multilateral nuclear fleet (MLF) are good examples. Not only were these institutions and programs problematic for the Kennedy and Johnson administrations, but also they were easily recognizable symbols of patriotism and militarism gone awry—perfect marks for building female outrage and protest.

What kept WSP women on the picket lines in 1964, lobbying Congress, and issuing militant manifestoes, at a time when peace protest had fallen off as a result of the test ban treaty, were the increases in the military budget and the accelerated nuclear buildup despite the ratification of the test ban treaty. The number of underground nuclear tests per year was far greater than the number of atmospheric tests had been, the military budget had increased, and the "invisible war" in Vietnam was just becoming visible.[4] There were also more personal motives involved in the women's decision to carry on their political pressure and maintain their movement. Most of the key women were unwilling to give up the heady sense of political efficacy and personal importance they had experienced when the direct actions they alone created and carried through received local, national, and international attention. They were also loath to forgo the unexpected pleasures of sisterly collaboration they had experienced working with other passionate and determined women in a project with no less a goal than saving the planet. An article in *Harper's*, "Honeychile at the Barricades," records the emotions of a white middle-class housewife in Little Rock, Arkansas, who had become involved in public affairs in response to the school integration crisis. Her reluctance to return to the kitchen mirrored the emotions of many WSPers: "For two years I monitored our Senate Gallery, interviewed officials and talked to reporters. Don't laugh, but I truly felt I was making history. When I told my husband at the end of the day, 'So I said to the Mayor,' it was a lot more exciting than, 'so I said to the butcher.'"[5]

In 1964 WSP focused its protest—lobbying, demonstrating, and letter writing—on a fallout-shelter bill the Kennedy administration was pushing and later deferred, the increasing number of underground nuclear test that were venting radioactive isotopes into the atmosphere, and a State Department plan for a NATO-controlled fleet of twenty-five ships, each equipped with eight Polaris nuclear missiles. The ships, according to the plan, would be run by a majority of American and West German naval personnel. WSP decided to challenge the plan for an MLF because it threatened to open the door to the remilitarization of West Germany, a frightening prospect twenty years after World War II and the Nazi holocaust. WSP chose to target MLF because very few Americans recognized the danger it posed, and no other peace group was dealing with it.

To stage an effective protest against MLF, WSP had to educate its own participants on the plan and its ramifications. This required reams of fact sheets and flyers plus the publication of a well-documented pamphlet called *The German Problem: Roadblock to Disarmament.* It also had to bring MLF to the attention of the media and the general public, and to reach out to the peace-minded women of the NATO countries. This was no easy task, as the WSPers were soon to discover. While talking to non-WSP friends, distributing flyers at supermarkets, or even lobbying their congressional representatives, the women found that most Americans thought MLF were the initials of a new cigarette or an athletic league. But WSP persisted, even after being warned by professional peace lobbyists that NATO was a sacred Cold War institution and that the decision to confront it would lead to the movement's downfall. The national and international protests against MLF are described in more detail in chapter 9, which deals with WSP's international activities. Suffice it to say that the campaign against MLF resulted in another "sweet taste of victory" for WSP. For a variety of geopolitical and tactical reasons, not the least of which was the opposition to MLF by Cold Warriors such as Henry Kissinger, who was bemused to find himself in agreement with WSP, the State Department decided to drop the MLF plan, even as German naval personnel were already training on a U.S. warship.

WSP continued to oppose nuclear proliferation and pressure for disarmament throughout the 1960s, protesting the building of the antiballistic missile and lobbying against the research, stockpiling, and possible use of chemical and biological weapons. Throughout the 1960s and 1970s the Washington office continued to sell its own publications, *The Story of Disarmament, The German Problem: Roadblock to Disarmament,* and a *Disarmament Coloring Book* for children.

While WSP never joined forces with the civil rights movement officially, Barbara Bick, a Washington key woman and editor of *MEMO* for most of its years, recalled in 1969 that from the beginning there was a strong trend for WSP to be involved with "the other side of the coin of American war policies. . . , racism at home."[6] Bick remembered that in October 1964 WSP issued a call to its participants to cooperate with Malcolm X in a campaign for letters to be sent to African heads of state, asking them to bring the question of the Negro's plight in the United States before the United Nations. In March 1965 an article in *MEMO* described a march of over eight hundred WSP women in San Francisco to protest both the war in Vietnam and racial injustice in Alabama, at which Ralph Abernathy of the Southern Christian Leadership Conference (SCLC) was the principal speaker. Bick herself was one of the initial committee of one hundred invited by SCLC to present the demands of the Poor People's Campaign to Cabinet members. Washington, D.C., WSP participated in every level of the Poor People's Campaign, according to Bick, except decision making at the top. The women raised money in communities throughout the country, collected food, and came to Washington when summoned to march or lobby on the Hill. WSP later worked with welfare mothers, supported grape strikers, and, as Bick put it in a radio broadcast in 1969, "We are profoundly a part of the total movement of the American people to change our society . . .

but our major commitment and activities are still overwhelmingly dedicated to the single issue of peace."[7]

WSP had been urged to turn its attention to Vietnam as early as June 1963. A standing joke in the Washington headquarters was "a not-so-funny thing happened to us on the way to disarmament—the Vietnam war." The "secret war" in Vietnam was brought to the movement's attention at its second national conference by a group of women already knowledgeable about events in Southeast Asia, who proposed from the floor that WSP condemn U.S. intervention in Vietnam. There was a good deal of opposition to this motion, not because anyone in WSP approved of military intervention in Vietnam, but because most of the WSPers knew little about the U.S. role in Vietnam and believed that the average American woman knew even less. It should be recalled that the only information regarding the activities of the so-called American advisers to the Diem regime came through the pacifist or left press. It seemed to the majority of those present at the conference in 1963 that disarmament should remain WSP's sole focus, and that Vietnam was only one of many "hot spots" in the world that could distract the movement from its essential goal. Because WSP did not take votes on controversial issues, it took almost twenty-four hours of constant debate, punctuated by pauses for contemplation and soul searching, to reach a consensus that in the coming year it would "alert the public to the dangers and horrors of the war in Vietnam and to the specific ways in which human morality is being violated by the U.S. attack on . . . women and children."[8] By early 1964 WSP women were educating themselves on the history of the political regimes in the north and south, the French role in Vietnam, the Geneva Accords of 1954, and the origins of the Diem regime. As the war in Vietnam escalated and President Johnson ordered the bombing of the north, WSP, sensing another world crisis with possible nuclear consequences, turned its attention away from the nuclear arms race to ending "the illegal and immoral war in Vietnam." Again, as in the campaign against atomic testing, WSP appealed to the American people, Congress, and the president in the name of concerned, and often outraged, motherhood.

From 1964 until 1973 WSP conducted an intense and consistent campaign of lobbying, picketing, marching, and advertising in national and local newspapers on occasions like Mother's Day and Christmas. WSP women set up tables displaying literature and petitions at shopping centers, county fairs, and church doors. The women conducted sit-ins in congressional offices, interviewed hundreds of political candidates and incumbents on their stand regarding the war, circulated voters' peace pledges, chained themselves to the White House gate, and initiated lawsuits and consumer boycotts. WSP counseled young men on their legal rights in relationship to the Selective Service System, and aided and abetted those who refused to register or to serve. WSP women also held vigils at the homes of draft board members. As the war dragged on and the women became more frustrated and angry, WSP's earlier reluctance to engage in nonviolent resistance was abandoned, particularly in relation to the draft.

Much of WSP's antiwar activity was conducted in coalition with other peace groups, but WSP staged many dramatic mothers' protests at home and abroad in its own name. These were planned to appeal to the much sought-after average mother who was concerned about the fate of her son, whether he was in Vietnam, about to be sent there, on the verge of being drafted, or just a toddler who faced a world in which his life could be sacrificed at any time by the men in power who used warfare to solve world problems. WSP's most widely used slogan in the late 1960s was "Not Our Sons, Not Your Sons, Not Their Sons." A "voters' peace pledge" circulated by the WSP political action task force declared, "We mothers are fed up with politicians who preach peace but practice war."

In February 1965 WSP staged a mass lobby in Washington, demanding that Congress conduct open hearings on the Vietnam War. Fifteen hundred women delivered "gaily colored shopping bags" filled with thousands of proxies from women at home to the office of Senator J. W. Fulbright of Arkansas, the chairman of the Senate Foreign Relations Committee. They also held meetings with other members of the committee, arranged in advance by the New York legislative committee, headed by Bella Abzug.[9]

On 16 March 1965 a Detroit WSP founder and activist, eighty-two-year-old Alice Herz, set herself on fire in a shopping center in Detroit, Michigan, in desperate protest "against the escalation of the war in Vietnam." This was an action the American people could understand, Herz believed, because it mirrored the self-immolation of the Buddhist monks in Saigon who sacrificed their lives to gain world attention to the evils of the regime in South Vietnam that the United States was fighting to protect. In her suicide note Herz called on the American people "to take action before it is too late. Yours is the responsibility to decide if this world shall be a good place to live for all human beings. . . , or if it should blow itself up to oblivion." In a special note she left for her daughter, Herz wrote, "I'm not doing this out of despair, but out of hope for mankind."[10]

Herz, who was born in Hamburg, Germany, and had been active in the German peace movement in her youth, was a refugee from the Nazi regime. After settling in the United States in 1942, she continued to read on peace and pacifism and to speak, march, and correspond with newspapers and peace workers all over the world. Herz participated in the first peace strike in 1961, became a WSP key woman in Detroit, and was present at the founding conference in Ann Arbor. On 10 November 1961 she wrote to a Japanese friend to tell her of the birth of WSP. "We have organized a Women's Peace Campaign. November 1st was our start and we had a response beyond expectation." Herz closed her letter with the affirmation "I still believe that common sense and humanity will . . . prevail among the people of this and other Western countries, and that a better world will be born some day."[11]

A journalist researching Herz's death was referred by the Detroit Police Department to the Subversive Squad. When Hayes Jacobs asked whether she had been a Communist and why Herz was under surveillance by the Subversive Squad, a sergeant explained that the squad kept track of all picketing and other demonstrations. The police sergeant characterized Herz as a "goer" who "never missed a meeting of any of those peace organizations." "I've seen her around for years," the sergeant added; "she was just a pacifist. You know—always out on a march whenever someone—anyone—was demonstrating against war."[12]

Alice Herz was born a Jew but found herself emotionally and intellectually attracted to the teaching and life of Jesus. In her last years she joined the Unitarian-Universalist Church. Dr. Henry Hitt Crane, a nationally known Methodist minister and a longtime friend, stated in his eulogy, "She was trying to give her final witness to her abhorrence for all war."[13] Fifteen Wayne State University students, representing the Detroit Committee to End the War in Vietnam, visited Herz in the hospital where she lingered in pain for ten days. They brought flowers and a statement declaring that "Mrs. Herz has provided the most dramatic protest to date against the brutal war in Vietnam."[14] Letters of condolence came to WSP from all over the world. Members of the New Japan Women's Association referred to Herz as "one of America's sweetest grandmothers" and, in response to Herz's suicide note, pledged to Dagmar Wilson that they would stand up in the fight for peace in cooperation with members of WSP.[15] Los Angeles WSP sent the following message to Herz as she lay dying: "In your name we take an oath to oppose the morally indefensible policy of our government in Vietnam. Our voices will not still until the tragedy of Vietnam is peacefully resolved. Your courage and love of humanity is engraved in our hearts."[16] Although the Detroit peace women were deeply moved by Herz's action, they made it clear that they did not endorse it as a model for other antiwar protesters. A press release issued by Detroit WFP stated, "Detroit Women for Peace know that she [Herz] wanted to give her life, as she said, 'to call attention to this problem in Vietnam,' and that *she did it as an individual*" (emphasis added).[17] After visiting Herz in the hospital, Lillian Lerman, one of the founders of Detroit WFP, declared, "She is a rational, reasonable, well-educated woman. It is difficult to see how she could do this. Just imagine feeling so strongly."[18] Ruth Gage-Colby, WSP's international coordinator, spoke for all the younger WSP women who had encountered Herz at marches or felt her gentle, yet burning, moral passion at national meetings. "Our beloved friend gave her life in flame," Gage-Colby declared, "in the hope that she might, by her sacrifice, help to save humanity from nuclear fire."[19]

With the courage, personal initiative, and spontaneity WSP expected from its leaders, Lorraine Gordon of New York and Mary Clarke of Los Angeles undertook a daring mission in the spring of 1965. They were the first U.S. peace activists to travel to embattled Hanoi on a peace mission. While in Hanoi they arranged for a meeting of U.S. and Vietnamese women, which took place in Djakarta in July. There a friendship based on mutual respect was built between WSP and Vietnamese women leaders and ambassadors that existed throughout the war and is maintained until this day. Although WSP women are sometimes critical of Vietnam's postwar policies, most of the key women still feel a strong sense of responsibility to the people of Vietnam for the damage done by the United States.

In 1965 and throughout the war years, WSP used the occasions of Mother's Day, Graduation Week, and Christmas to appeal to women as mothers to speak out, demonstrate, and vote against the killing of their own sons, and to condemn U.S. brutality to Vietnamese women and children. Little was said of sacrifice of men in the war simply as men. They were consistently referred to as sons, brothers, husbands, or lovers. An ad published in the *New York Times* in 1965 showed a young man in cap and gown under the heading "He graduates in June of '65. Will he die in Vietnam in June of '66?" The ad called on mothers to join WSP in a march on Washington to tell the president, "We will not remain silent while our sons are sent to kill and be killed." The ad listed WSP's demands: stop the bombing, stop the escalation, negotiate with all parties including the National Liberation Front, and implement the Geneva Accords under United Nations auspices. Marching with WSP in the Mother's Day lobby of 1965 was Mrs. M. L. Thorne of South Dakota, the mother of a marine pilot killed in Vietnam. WSP requested that the president see her and a delegation of mothers of draft-age sons, who brought along camp stools and threatened to sit in front of the White House until President Johnson honored them with an interview. Johnson refused to see the mothers, who eventually folded their chairs and returned to their homes. A similar ad in 1967 showed two young men, one African-American, the other white, under the message "Will

They Still Be with You Next Mother's Day . . . and in the Years to Come? Or Will They Be Sacrificed for the Growing War in Asia?" The Mother's Day ad called on all women to "Support Our Sons, *Support All American Troops in Vietnam*, by Ending the War and Bringing Our Men Home Alive and Unharmed!" (emphasis added). While protesting the war as illegal and immoral, WSP never criticized the soldiers fighting in Vietnam. It did suggest, however, that many were there against their will and that some had turned against the war after seeing it firsthand.

A Christmas card to President Lyndon Johnson signed by thousands of women in 1965 pleaded with him, "For the sake of our sons, For the sake of all children, Give us Peace in Vietnam this Christmas." The WSP peace card business was apparently brisk in 1965. New York WSP reported that sample cards sent to clergy had brought good returns, that teachers and students in high schools signed hundreds of cards, and that busy shoppers at the malls were stopping to sign. The peace cards were translated into Spanish, which indicates that WSP in New York City was attempting to reach out to the Latina community. The eastern seaboard women presented thousands of these peace cards to Lady Bird Johnson in the hope that she, as a woman, would be more sympathetic than the president to WSP's call for an end to the war. A WSP delegation including a woman whose son had been killed in Vietnam was disappointed by their meeting with Liz Carpenter, Lady Bird Johnson's secretary, because Carpenter made it clear that Mrs. Johnson supported the president all the way and that she herself thought every man asked to serve should do so.

As the war continued to escalate, WSP's Mother's Day ad in the *New York Times* in 1966 announced a "Mother's March on Capitol Hill to Stop the Killing." It called on President Johnson not to "drench the jungles of Asia with the blood of our sons. Don't force our sons to kill women and children whose only crime is to live in a country ripped by civil war."[20] Fifteen hundred women from the eastern seaboard traveled to Washington to picket the White House and then fan out to lobby on Capitol Hill. The *New York Times* reported that the WSP women wore white cardboard doves pinned to their coats and hats and carried black balloons inscribed with the slogan "End the War." The balloons were released in a photogenic cloud over the White House to express WSP's grief and mourning for the killed and the killers. The *Times* also reported that for over an hour the corridors of the Senate and House were clogged with knots of women congregated before the doors of various members. As the highlight of the demonstration/lobby, hundreds of women converged in midafternoon in the hearing room of the Senate Foreign Relations Committee to leave their cardboard doves, each inscribed with a handwritten peace message, and special thanks to Senator Fulbright for his role in questioning the escalation of U.S. involvement in Vietnam.[21] Philadelphia WSP announced that it was planning to place small notices on the obituary pages of local papers as a memorial to the dead in Vietnam.[22] In February 1966 WSP conducted a Mothers' March on Capitol Hill for a cease fire in Vietnam. An ad in the *New Republic* called on women to lobby "for the U.S. to clearly offer the National Liberation Front (led by the South Vietnamese Communists) equal negotiating status" with the north and to pledge their voice and vote only to those congressmen who would work for a peaceful settlement in Asia.[23] In a Graduation Day flyer in June 1966, WSP made much of the fact that American casualties in Vietnam had passed the twenty-five thousand mark and urged women to tell the president that "you don't want your son to die." In the summer of 1966 Chicago WSP organized a peace literature caravan that traveled to the small towns outside of Chicago. Urging women to join the caravan, the Chicago WSP newsletter stated, "As the war expands, our peace efforts must also expand. Please do your part!" A report to a New York area WSP conference held in October 1966 reported the women in California were helping to maintain a Port Chicago vigil in front of a mortuary "processing bodies from Vietnam."

In the summer of 1966 Aileen Hutchinson of Washington, D.C., and Beverly Farquharson of San Jose, California, both WSP key women, joined Joyce McLean and Lisa Kalvelage of WILPF in blocking a shipment of napalm bombs that were headed for Vietnam from the port of Santa Clara, California. The women, who immediately came to be known within the movement as the "housewife terrorists" or the "napalm ladies," modestly described their daring action in the September 1966 issue of *MEMO:* "It is a long—often hilarious—story, but we did stop murder for 63 minutes before our arrest. At our trial, we learned that we had caused the barge, from which the bombs were unloaded, to miss the tide. All operations ceased for 12 hours."[24]

The "napalm ladies," possibly because they were mothers (one had five children and another was a soon-to-be grandmother with a twenty-year-old son in the marines stationed in Vietnam), were treated with lenience. They were given a ninety-day suspended sentence; two years' informal probation, which the women refused to sign because of its possible curtailment of their civil rights; and a fine, which the judge suspended because "somehow he knew we wouldn't pay a fine either."[25] The statement by the "housewife terrorists" that they had come to the port of Santa Clara "to invoke the law, not to disobey it" became a WSP leit motif as the war dragged on.[26]

WSP was the first peace group to carry a mass protest to the steps of the Pentagon in the winter of 1967, when twenty-five hundred women carrying enlarged photos of napalmed Vietnamese children under the slogan "Children Are Not for Burning" demanded to see the Pentagon generals who were responsible for the killings. One year before the now-famous National Mobilization March, described in Norman Mailer's *Armies of the Night*, WSP women literally stormed the military citadel, having removed their shoes to bang against the Pentagon doors that were hastily locked in their faces. Front-page photos of outraged women banging on the Pentagon's doors were featured in hundreds of U.S. newspapers and in the media around the world.[27] The "Pentagon" story was so widely covered that the *Washington Post*'s list of the "top women newsmakers" of 1967 included Dagmar Wilson, described as "a Washington housewife, who visited Hanoi, and headed the Women Strike for Peace march on the Pentagon." Others on the list were entertainers, like Joan Baez, Faye Dunaway, Pearl Bailey, Twiggy, and Vanessa Redgrave, and political wives and daughters, like Lady Bird Johnson, Ethel and Jacqueline Kennedy, Sharon Percy Rockefeller, and Margaret Rusk Smith, daughter of the secretary of state.[28]

In 1967 WSP women also focused their attention on ending the draft. They testified before Congress and lobbied for repeal of the Selective Service System, urged school officials to provide information on alternatives to the draft, counseled and supported young men who refused to be drafted, and eventually created WSP's statement of complicity with draft resisters, which made the women who signed it subject to arrest and persecution.

Although WSP continued to attract new participants all over the country, particularly women with sons in the armed forces or about to be drafted, it was still subjected to Red baiting by the "hawks" in Congress and in the right-wing press. But what is most unexpected and quite shocking is to discover that liberal Daniel Patrick Moynihan dismissed the group at a White House meeting in October 1969 with the comment "They are only Jewish ladies from New York."[29]

In the fall of 1967 a number of WSP activists, including Cora Weiss and Amy Swerdlow of New York, Mary Clarke of Los Angeles, Ruth Krause and Ethel Taylor of Pennsylvania, and Dagmar Wilson of Washington, D.C., joined forces with Jeannette Rankin, the first woman elected to the U.S. Congress, and Vivian Hallinan, a dynamic San Francisco Bay area business woman and leftist community organizer, to work on an almost daily basis for close to four months to organize a new broad-based women's antiwar coalition called the Jeannette Rankin Brigade (JRB).[30] Others who gave their time as members of the East Coast steering committee to recruit sponsors and adherents, negotiate rhetoric, plan programs, define the goals, and manage the logistics of the JRB were civil rights leader Ella Baker, formerly a NAACP and SCLC organizer, a key person in the founding of the Student Nonviolent Co-ordinating Committee (SNCC), and in 1967 a consultant to SCEF; feminist lawyer Flo Kennedy; church women Anne Bennett and Eleanor French; former president of the National Congress of Jewish Women Pearl Willen; and the president of WILPF, Katherine Camp. A successful effort was made by executive board members Kennedy and Baker to recruit influential African-American women as sponsors. Among them were civil rights leaders Rosa Parks and Fanny Lou Hamer; actress Ruby Dee; labor leader Doris Turner of Local 1199 of the New York Drug and Hospital Workers' Union; Wiley McLain, community worker with the Newark antipoverty unit; Juanita J. Saddler of the YWCA; May Ely Lyman of Union Theological Seminary; Vel Phillips, black city council woman from Milwaukee; and Coretta Scott King, who had worked with WSP for many years.[31]

The inspiration and impetus for the JRB had come from Jeannette Rankin, who in two separate terms of office had voted against both world wars. Rankin, an eighty-seven-year-old Gandhian pacifist, speaking at a meeting of women peace protesters in Atlanta, Georgia, in May 1967, had declared that it was unconscionable that ten thousand "American boys" had already died in Vietnam and proposed that, if ten thousand women were willing to raise their voices against the war and were sufficiently committed to the task to go to jail, they could bring the war to an end, "because you can't have war without women." Her remarks were carried on the Associated Press wire service and read by women all over the country, who wrote to the former congresswoman in agreement and praise. Vivian Hallinan, long associated with liberal and left politics on the West Coast, decided to turn Rankin's words into action. When Hallinan began to seek out the leaders of the women's peace, civil rights, and religious groups she would need to organize a protest, she was advised by the church women to abandon the notion of "going to jail," because, they argued, a commitment to civil disobedience would fail to attract the ten thousand women envisioned by Rankin. They also made it clear that they preferred to build a broad coalition of women capable of working politically in 1968 to defeat those members of Congress who still supported the war. The church women carried the day because theirs was the largest untapped female constituency the organizers wished to attract. Thus Rankin's proposal for female civil disobedience and nonviolent resistance to the Vietnam war was turned into "just another" one-day liberal march on Washington. There was, however, one difference. The JRB announced that it would convene a Congress of American Women on the afternoon of 15 January to develop programs to meet the crisis in America that would "express the political power, reason, and conscience of American women." "This is Woman Power," JRB publicity declared.

A "Call to American Women," "who are outraged by the ruthless slaughter in Vietnam, and the persistent neglect of human needs at home," was issued by an initial group of sponsors—prominent women in civil rights, peace, religious, organizations, trade unions, and the arts. As was usual at that time, the partial list of sponsors included a number of wives of prominent men.[32] The call urged women "to come to Washington on January 15th" dressed in black for mourning, to demand that "Congress, as its first order of business resolve to end the war in Vietnam, use its power to heal a sick society at home, make reparation for the ravaged land we leave behind in Vietnam, and refuse the insatiable demands of the military-industrial complex." What was most appealing for those key women of WSP who decided to participate in the organization of the JRB in the fall of 1967, and not all key women did, was that the JRB consciously united war and poverty as twin issues, thus reaching across race and class lines.

The fact that Jeannette Rankin was a suffragist, remembered for her feminist pacifist stand, attracted a group of young women who decided to use the event to insert feminist consciousness and demands into the struggle for peace. Thus working with the JRB afforded the WSP women their first connection with the pacifist-feminist suffrage generation, now called the first wave, and their first confrontations with the second wave. The radical women, as they called themselves, were critical of the notion of petitioning Congress once again, as that body had not only proven itself impotent to end the war but had never even had a chance to vote on it. What the radical women did not understand was that the so-called older women knew they could not stop the war machine even if they sat down, lay down, languished in jail, or immolated themselves. What they were trying to build was a mass women's movement that would have a ripple effect in local communities, turning women away from cooperation with the war machine and toward political action in support of antiwar candidates in the 1968 elections.[33] The radical women tended to dismiss the WSP women with a good deal of disdain, presumably because they identified them with their own mothers, whom they thought of as abysmally backward in gender consciousness and timid in defense of their own and their daughters' rights. The conflicts with the women's liberation front, another name used by the young feminists, were provoking, frustrating, and even confusing, but for some WSP women they were also a transformative experience, one that changed our lives.

On 15 January 1968, the opening day of the Ninetieth Congress, five thousand women from all over the country, most of them clad in black, trudged silently through fresh snow to the foot of Capitol Hill, led by the spry and sassy former congresswoman.[34] In the march were mothers and aunts of men in Vietnam, and mothers and grandmothers of men already killed. Most of these were women who had never participated in antiwar protest. Two women who said that they had come because they had seen war firsthand and wanted no more of it had been "Red Cross girls" in World War II. "No one wins a war," they told the *Washington Post.* A former Army nurse, wearing a Veterans for Peace cap, commented that both she and her husband served in World War II, "but this one is immoral." Many others of the marchers had been protesting for a long time. One of them was Mabel Vernon, who said she had "worked for peace since 1917" and had been to jail on behalf of the woman suffrage movement. Another suffragist, Edith Goode, complained about the police restraints. "We used to petition for women's suffrage right inside the Rotunda."[35] Rankin, scoffing at the hundreds of police that had lined the half-mile route of the march and the hundreds more guarding the Capitol, declared indignantly, "There is no reason why old ladies shouldn't be allowed to go into the Capitol." She was referring to the fact that the JRB had been barred from the Capitol by a 1946 law, which prohibited assemblage of people on the Capitol grounds. The law, which had not been applied in recent history, was challenged prior to the march by attorneys for the JRB, but it had been upheld by the court. This decision was being appealed by fifty members of the JRB, but on 15 January 1969 the Capitol remained off limits to the protesters.[36] While most of the younger women and many indignant older radicals chafed at the JRB steering committee's decision to obey the law forbidding them access to the Capitol, not one women broke away. As the *Washington Post* reported, "There were some black separatists, student activists. . . , women with jail records for civil disobedience. But they all fell in with a large solid group of middle-class women" who stood in stony silence as Viveca Lindfors read aloud their petition for redress of grievances.[37] A small delegation, headed by Rankin, was permitted to present the petition to the Speakers of the House and Senate, while Judy Collins led the women in song.[38]

It should be noted that, despite the criticism by the radical feminists that peace protest in which women presented themselves as mothers, wives, or sisters instead of citizens in their own name was a sad manifestation of "false consciousness," the JRB petition was free of maternal rhetoric. Its opening lines were "We, United States women of all races, political, and religious faiths have gathered together to petition congress for a redress of intolerable grievance, exercising herein our fundamental right under the first amendment to Peaceably Assemble and to Petition the Government." The petition went on to demand that the pledge made by President Franklin Roosevelt following World War II, that women would sit on all the committees and commissions "to win the peace," become an immediate reality.[39]

A Congress of Women, convened after the protest at the Capitol. There had been good deal of negotiating and downright fighting regarding agenda and representation on the program. Thus it was tailored to fit the demands of all the constituencies that made up the brigade. The congress was chaired, not by one, but by three women. They were Pearl Willen, representing organized Jewish women; Mary Clarke, representing WSP; and Coretta Scott King, representing church women and black women. Vivian Hallinan spoke first on the origins of the JRB, followed by a welcome from Jeannette Rankin, by greetings and messages read by African-American actress Ruby Dee, and by a report on the brigade's court action by one of its attorneys, Harriet Van Tassell. Cynthia Wedell of the National Council of Churches also addressed the group, as did Dagmar Wilson; sociologist Elise Boulding, who was both a WSP and a WILPF activist; Ella Baker; and Charlotte Bunch, of the University Christian movement, who spoke for the radical young women's anti-imperialist group of which she was a part. The program concluded with a speech by the great civil rights leader and orator Fanny Lou Hamer. The issues addressed were the brutality of the war, the persistent neglect of human needs at home, and future plans to mobilize women in all communities and on all levels of activity "dedicated to reshaping American society and restoring our country to a position of honor in the community of nations."[40]

If a woman did not pay strict attention to all the proceedings and the many interventions from the floor, she could have missed a historic bit of guerrilla theater staged by the radical women from New York. While chanting a liturgy,

> Oh women of Chalcis and Argos
> Of Manhattan and Chicago
> For three thousand years of western wars
> In submission
> We have sinned,

they carried a female dummy representing traditional womanhood across the stage, announcing that it would be buried formally that evening at Arlington Cemetery. The women's liberation front then issued a call to all radical women present to leave the official congress and follow them to a separate room for a rump session they chose to call a countercongress.[41] In a classic example of liberal mother-daughter conflict, the room for the countersession was paid for, reluctantly, by the official steering committee of the JRB. Thinking of myself as a radical woman, I followed along with many other older women, all of us in our early or midforties, some still angry that the JRB had not been more militant in resisting the government's efforts to keep it off the Capitol grounds. What we expected were more radical and militant strategies for ending the war. What we found, however, were young women rushing to the mike to speak passionately, but often incoherently, about the way in which the traditional women's peace movement condoned and even enforced the gender hierarchy in which men made war and women wept. The Chicago women contended that, "until women go beyond justifying themselves in terms of their wombs and breasts and housekeeping abilities, they will never be able to exert any political power." We had come as mourners and supplicants, they contended, "we had failed to challenge the power of men and the seeming weakness of women, and, if we didn't change our ways, women would remain powerless and wars would go on forever." The radical women's meeting was so chaotic that most "traditional" women who had always thought of themselves as radical in terms of left-right politics came away more confused than enlightened, but definitely shaken.[42] Charlotte Bunch, already a radical feminist, remembers the countercongress and the entire experience of the JRB as "one of the early confrontations between feminists and peace women about women's priorities, relationships with men, and feminism."[43] Although much of what we heard was new to us, as hard as that may be to believe today, and although some WSPers were impatient with what they perceived as self-serving and strident demands for women's equality at a time of national and international crisis, it left many of us with a great deal to think about. The trains and buses returning the JRB women to New York hummed, not with the usual reports from the congressmen visited, but with heated debates about traditional sex roles, the meaning of woman power and women's liberation, and whether or not affluent young radical women had the right to push their demands forward when our sisters were dying in Vietnam. What I believe was one of the most effective feminist consciousness raisers for the WSP cadre in the JRB was the article in the slick trendy left magazine *Ramparts* that carried a front-page photograph of a JRB protester, identified by her button, but all that was shown was her torso, with half-exposed breasts protruding. Face and head were missing, as was any serious political description of the JRB or its purpose. As Alice Echols points out, the JRB story in *Ramparts* went to great pains to distinguish the brigade women from the "narrow-minded bitches of the suffrage movement."[44] This article did much to make the women in WSP aware of how blatantly they and their younger comrades were put down and sexually objectified by the young men of the new Left, and how much WSP had in common with "the narrow-minded bitches" they now recognized as feminist, pacifist suffragists about which they knew so little. However, not all the older women were moved to question their own role and tactics. In a post-march speech at the Terra Linda Rotary Club, Vivian Hallinan defended the traditional woman, who, she asserted, can play a tremendous role in the peace movement. "We don't believe in locking the bedroom door or presenting aggression to males. We want to act politically as American patriots."[45]

By 1970 the WSP women had come to recognize that the United States would not turn away from war if foreign policy remained the exclusive game of male elites. WSP took up the JRB demand that women be included in all decision-making bodies concerned with issues of war and peace. Influenced by the rhetoric of the women's liberation movement, WSP issued a "Declaration of Liberation from Military Domination," which stated: "We women will no longer tolerate the domination of our lives and the lives of our families by the war-makers in the Pentagon and their spokesmen in Congress and the White House." It concluded: "We demand the birthright that our forefathers pledged to all Americans in 1776. We women declare our liberation from military domination which deprives us and our loved ones of life, liberty and the pursuit of happiness."[46]

But motherist consciousness continued to dominate WSP's direct actions. In the spring of 1971 a group of women in Newton, Massachusetts, desperate and frustrated with the war, conceived of a campaign they called Save Our Sons. The Newton women contacted the WSP affiliate in Boston, and through its efforts Save Our Sons became a national WSP action. A letter to President Nixon was drafted as a sample to be used by women around the country. It read: "Dear President Nixon, You will be surprised to hear from us because up to now many of have been rather quiet. . . . We think the time has come to tell you that we are not buying the war anymore . . . and we are not going to pay for it with our sons." A card with a space to affix a picture of the writer's son declared: "Mr. President: Please do not use this boy . . . or any boy anywhere for war." According to WSP's *MEMO*, tens of thousands of women new to peace action signed these letters or wrote their own messages, affixing photos of their sons. The letters came from families of POWs, Gold Star Mothers, mothers with sons in Vietnam, mothers with sons in VA hospitals, and mothers of boys in college, grade school, and kindergarten. One woman wrote:

Dear Mr. Nixon: I am sending you pictures of three of my four sons. One is a freshman at the State College of Forestry, majoring in conservation of natural resources. Certainly he's more valuable to his country practicing in his field than fighting in Vietnam. The others are young, but they have a way of becoming older. These sons are the reason I am no longer being silent about my hatred of this war. Take a look at my sons! Respectfully Frances Bourget, Manhasset, N.Y.[47]

Mrs. Joseph Wappel of Norwood, Massachusetts, wrote: "We are a Christian family, and one that prays together and we hope to God we can stay together. . . . I am tired because of continuous sleepless nights in horror of what could happen to my boys and what is happening to other mothers' boys."[48] WSP collected these letters in the office of Congresswoman Bella Abzug, who attempted with congresswomen Patsy Mink of Hawaii, Shirley Chisholm of New York, and Ella Grasso of Connecticut to make a presentation to the president, but he refused to accept them. WSP then mounted hundreds of the letters and pictures on red, white, and blue bunting that was unfurled and carried by hundreds of women in front of the White House. The President remained unmoved.

In April 1972 approximately one hundred women conducted a "die-in" at the headquarters of ITT, the makers of Wonder Bread as well as military equipment for the bombing of Cambodia. Later that year WSP women staged a sit-in outside congressional offices, demanding action from Congress to cut off the funds for the war. In June of that year more than two thousand women formed a human Ring around the Congress, demanding an end to the war. The Ring Around the Congress was conceived by Joan Baez, Coretta King (who later withdrew her support), and WSP, as a symbolic action, or stand-in, for the women and children of Vietnam.

The most original and womanly WSP projects in the period from 1962 until the end of the Vietnam War in 1973 were in the areas of electoral politics, draft resistance, and international cooperation among women for peaceful solutions to world conflicts. The following three chapters deal with these three areas of WSP activity.

7

"The Women's Vote Is the Peace Vote"

> We have a powerful force—our vote. Women of courage and persistence won us this precious right. . . . Now we must use it courageously in our own special interests, the interests of family, children, a peaceful and fruitful life.
>
> —Bella Abzug, "A Call To Women—To End the War in 1968"

From the days of the first strike through its first years, the WSP leadership was convinced that the movement's greatest appeal lay in its creative reconstruction of notions of moral motherhood and its dissociation from male political culture—both of the Right and the Left. An unsigned memo found among the national office papers expresses an opinion regarding party politics that was heard often at WSP meetings: "We can't beat the devil at his own game, and we really shouldn't be in there trying. Politics is dirty, immoral, corrupt from one end to another. I just don't see decent women sitting 'round and deciding which layer of filth to work in."[1] Bella Abzug, who was national legislative chairwoman of WSP almost from its inception, recalls that in the early days the WSP leadership acted as if politics "would taint them by taking away the purity of their goal." Abzug, on the other hand, represented a group of women who believed that the electoral process was an ideal arena for exerting meaningful peace pressure on the Congress and the president.[2] She recalls that she found WSP's major concentration on direct action and moral witness "terribly frustrating," but she was undaunted in her determination to turn WSP into an influential force in the political arena. Ultimately she succeeded.

Abzug had become a key woman in the movement's second month, when she arrived at a New York planning meeting to urge that the first East Coast march on Washington include a lobby in the halls of Congress. She argued that, if WSP were to be effective, the women would have to go to Washington with a specific proposal or resolution for congressional endorsement. As she put it, "just a call to end the arms race is not good enough." Abzug recalled in a 1980 interview that she had admonished the leaders of the new peace movement, "You just can't say that you are *against*. You have to have a plan, a specific piece of legislation." "I was always deeply an issue person," she explained.

Abzug managed to convince New York WSP to adopt a demonstration/lobby format for the 15 January 1962 march on the White House, which became a WSP hallmark throughout the 1960s and early 1970s. Abzug's keen grasp of legislative issues and congressional procedures, along with her passionate and persuasive rhetoric, identified her immediately as the logical choice for New York's legislative chairperson. As WSP required no formal elections by representative bodies, Abzug was appointed to the post on the spot. Soon afterward, she took on the role of political action coordinator for national WSP and continued to direct the movement's legislative and political campaigns until she entered Congress in 1971.

In 1962, when Abzug became a key woman in WSP, she was a forty-one-year-old practicing attorney who commuted daily to her office in New York City from Mount Vernon, New York, where she lived with her husband Martin and their two daughters, Eve and Isabelle. Martin had become interested in Westchester County SANE in the late 1950s, but Bella's political interests were elsewhere. She was deeply involved in civil rights activism, working to save her integrated neighborhood from a campaign to drive out white homeowners.[3] Bella had made a particular effort to reside in an integrated neighborhood. As she put it, she wanted her children to see the world in full color and perceive its diversity. Her opposition to racism went back more than a decade, as did her political activism, which had begun when she was still in her teens. Bella Savitsky had been a prominent student leader at Hunter College. As president of her class and president of student government, she was a controversial but greatly admired student leader, already identified with issues of peace and social justice. After graduation from Columbia Law School in 1945, where she had been an editor of the *Columbia Law Review,* Abzug became involved in the legal defense of Willie McGee, an African-American resident of Mississippi who had been sentenced to death for allegedly raping a white woman. Abzug was convinced that McGee had been framed in the same way black men had always been, since the days of slavery, for any kind of relationship with white women. "The system would not just punish them, it would destroy them," she explained with rekindled anger. "So I became . . . interested in the case."

While still in her twenties, Abzug spent two years as chief counsel for McGee. She traveled back and forth to Mississippi, challenging the exclusion of African-Americans from the jury and charging that southern judges and juries applied the death penalty for rape only to blacks. She argued the McGee case on appeal in the district and federal courts and won two stays of execution by the Supreme Court. Eventually McGee was executed, despite the protests of thousands of civil rights advocates who had supported his defense. Abzug learned a great deal from the case, not only about institutional racism but also about her own intellectual and legal abilities and her power to act courageously and persistently in the face of frustration, insults, and threats to her well-being and even to her life.

During the time she was defending McGee, Abzug also worked on a civil rights project for the National Lawyers Guild, a left-oriented lawyers' group that played a leading role in fighting civil rights cases, particularly the implementation of the Supreme Court ruling on *Brown vs. Board of Education*. She was assigned the task of drawing up viable legislative bills for introduction into the House and the Senate by members of Congress. Abzug never came to know the people who used her bills, but she loved the work because, as she explains, "this was sort of my *raison d'être* for being involved in the law." "I always believed that law could be a social instrumentality for change. My main interest for a long time as a lawyer was to preserve the Constitution by defending the rights of individuals, and to expand the protection of the Constitution particularly to those who were outside of it, like blacks." Abzug has always seen her law practice as "creating a broader horizon for people by extending rights to all oppressed." She defended a number of victims of the congressional subversive activities committees in the 1950s, people in the arts, such as Pete Seeger, Elliot Sullivan, and Jay Gorney. She even considered defending the Communist party in the Smith Act trials, but finally decided not to because the New York party line would not agree to the "Bella line," which required that the CPUSA base its defense entirely on the First Amendment to the Bill of Rights.

Bella Abzug was a feminist long before the second wave emerged in the late 1960s. Unlike the majority of her cohorts, in and outside of WSP, she had been conscious of sexual discrimination since childhood and had opposed it whenever she could. At the age of nine, she succeeded in saying *kaddish* for her father in her local synagogue although the Jewish religion allows only men to recite the prayer for the dead. When asked how she managed it, she answered, "I just stood in the corner and prayed, and the rabbi looked away." She astounds many young women today when she tells them that she was rejected from Harvard Law School in 1942 because Harvard would not admit women, and contends that even after she graduated from Columbia Law School at the top of her class, she "took a lot of crap" from male colleagues, clients, judges, and the leftist National Lawyers Guild. "I was the victim of chauvinism every inch of the way," she asserts with undiminished frustration and anger.

I remember drafting a WSP flyer with Abzug in her law office in Manhattan in the early 1960s, a process that took longer than I had expected. When I told her that I had to rush off to pick my children up from school and suggested that she finish typing the text, she replied in what I heard as a curt and lofty tone, "I don't type!" I was outraged that she considered typing to be an occupation beneath her and told her in my own curt and lofty tone that it was time she learned to do her own menial work. She then explained to me that as a young lawyer she had refused to learn to type because she feared that the male senior partners in her law firm would have her typing briefs all day long instead of composing them. With that explanation, she won me over, as she has been doing for over thirty years.

Abzug traced the origins of her deep concern for the survival of the planet to the late 1950s. She remembers urging the National Lawyers Guild to take a stand and do something about the atomic threat, but found the lawyers apathetic. In early 1960, when she turned toward SANE to express her opposition to the nuclear arms race, she found SANE's internal Red hunt as distasteful as had the founders of WSP. When Abzug heard of WSP, she was ready to be part of it, although WSP's "simple housewife" image was hardly her political or personal style. Abzug recalls that she felt somewhat out of place because she suspected that some of the WSP women were pretending to know less about politics than they actually did. She attributes this tactic to the political and sexual repression of women in the 1950s, particularly to what she calls "self-Red-baiting." She was also affronted because she believed that WSP viewed her professional status and her political accomplishments "as a problem rather than an asset." She resented the fact that the so-called housewives, with whom she had chosen to work full-time, did not recognize that *her* volunteer hours possessed a money value, while she believed that theirs did not. Twenty years later she still complained: "Nothing was too much for me to do. I made inroads into my earning capacity, and gave up my work in the Lawyers Guild. I spent all my extracurricular time as a volunteer like everybody else, but for me it was a sacrifice." Abzug is still perplexed and angry because WSP did not accept her as one of its spokespersons in the early years. She attributes this not only to her professional standing and her outspoken independence, which did not fit the image WSP sought to project, but also to her direct and insistent bid for leadership. She now understands that she frightened the women. "They could not accept real leadership," she charges. "But I refused to accept that. I am a leader and I'm not afraid to be a leader. Any movement that is afraid to have leadership is, I think, a weak movement." Despite her reservations regarding WSP's devotion to the housewife image, she was impressed with its energy, its creativity, and the opportunity it provided for her to organize women as a political force. Abzug's passionate belief in the gender gap long before it was named and recognized and her compelling oratory at the first national conference persuaded a substantial number of key women to turn to electoral politics. Elsa Knight Thompson of California was typical of those who responded to Abzug's pleas for political action: "More and more as I listened and thought. . . , it was driven home to me that willy-nilly we are a political factor, and that no amount of study or demonstrating will achieve our ends unless we can force the issues on to the floor of the House and Senate."[4]

In 1962, when WSP was one year old, peace was already becoming an issue in electoral politics. Approximately twenty candidates in a dozen states decided to run for Congress on peace platforms, whereas in 1960 there were only two.[5] This presented a problem to WSP chapters, as they had to decide whether to support the self-declared peace candidates or to remain nonpartisan. In addition, Abzug warned that endorsing independent candidates, those who were running without the support of the Democratic or Republican party, would reveal the weakness of the peace movement. Thus the women in the Riverdale, New York, WSP group chose to endorse Forrest Johnson, running as a reformer in the Democratic primary, and the women in Cambridge, Massachusetts, endorsed Elizabeth Boardman, a member of Pax, a cogender peace group, who ran as a pacifist in the Republican primary.[6] At the same time that Riverdale WSP was endorsing a male candidate in the primary, Ruth Gage-Colby, WSP's international coordinator, advised Frederic C. Smedley, who contemplated a race in the Seventeenth Congressional District against John Lindsay, a WSP favorite, that WSP would endorse only women. According to Gage-Colby, only in the event that no women succeeded in being nominated would WSP "consider supporting men who stand for office on a real peace platform."[7] Los Angeles WSP urged its participants to serve as precinct workers for three official Democratic candidates, George Brown, Jerry Pacht, and Edward Roybal, while it disavowed any affiliation with the Democratic party.[8] *La Wisp*, the Los Angeles WSP newsletter, assured its readers that its support for the three candidates who "happen to be Democrats" was mere coincidence. "We would welcome a Republican Peace candidate just as heartily."[9]

To build a unified political strategy, maximize WSP's political energy, and demonstrate women's political potential, the WSP political action committee devised a voter's peace ballot for the 1962 election. A WSP guide to the use of the peace ballot advised: "Keep in Mind: We are not a political party . . . we are a movement. We strongly recommend that the political activity of WSP be confined to supporting the peace *issues*, as a pressure group appealing to *all* voters, *all* candidates, *all* political leaders, and *all political parties*" (emphasis in original).[10] Mary Grooms, a Rochester, New York, key woman, explained the peace ballot strategy to the readers of the *Nation:* "The women realize their power is in the 'swing' vote. They point out that Mr. Kennedy won . . . by only 168,000 votes. Some election districts are won regularly by less than 100 votes. In a close contest, the women and their petition-signers could hold the balance of power."[11]

Although WSP continued to view itself as a political force influencing both parties and all candidates, by 1964 the movement's issue-oriented, nonpartisan stand gradually gave way to a policy calling for pressure on the Democratic party from *within* its ranks. A memo from the New York Legislative Committee urged all WSP women to maximize their influence on the nomination and election of local county, state, and national party leaders as well as on candidates for Congress by enrolling in a political party and joining a local political club.[12] As few WSPers were likely to feel comfortable in the Republican party, even on the liberal fringe, it was clear that the WSP political action committee was pushing the women to become a force in the Democratic party, a tactic now being used successfully by the Right in the Republican party.

In 1964 as in 1962, WSP used a peace ballot to identify opposition to Barry Goldwater, the Republican candidate for the presidency, a self-proclaimed hawk who promised to escalate the Vietnam War. This time the peace ballot was to be signed only by women. Its purpose was to identify women as a peace constituency, and the woman's vote as a peace vote. Remembering that female support for the presidential candidacy of Dwight D. Eisenhower increased substantially when he announced that he would go to Korea to negotiate an end to the war, Abzug and the political action proponents within WSP urged that WSP make every effort to demonstrate women's preference for candidates who offered nonmilitary solutions to international tensions.

WSP women spent the summer of 1964 gathering signatures on the Women's Peace Ballot and presenting them to local politicians and candidates with mixed results. In Los Angeles, for instance, the women found the responses to their ballots so disheartening that they refused to endorse any candidate.[13] But some liberal candidates in other parts of the country, particularly those who were running for the first time, were grateful for the petitions and the positive publicity they engendered for the peace issue.

WSP made its appearance in Atlantic City on the second day of the

1964 Democratic convention to exert pressure on the party for a strong peace program and "a courageous campaign dedicated to peace issues." Carrying thousands of signed ballots for peace, four hundred women from the eastern seaboard, none of them official delegates to the convention, attempted to catch the attention of the media and to impress the delegates with their electoral potential. Wearing brightly colored paper flowers and toting shopping bags decorated with peace slogans, the women marched on the boardwalk. Collecting signatures as they walked, they accumulated fifteen hundred in one hour. *MEMO* reported, "We were well received by the public, the delegates and all the TV channels. However, the pressing news of the day kept us off the news."[14] The pressing news was, of course, the struggle of the Mississippi Freedom Democratic party delegation to be admitted to the conference as the official delegation from that state. The only known WSPer who was a delegate to the convention was Anne Eaton of Ohio, the wife of millionaire industrialist Cyrus Eaton. She and Bella Abzug both spoke at the platform committee hearing, urging in the summer of 1964 that the Democrats make peace a political issue. A call to a vigil against the Vietnam War, which was to take place outside the convention and which was endorsed by the *Catholic Worker*, CNVA, FOR, the Greenwich Village Peace Center, the Student Peace Union, and the War Resisters League, stated that the vigil did not conflict with other peace and civil rights activities planned for the convention. It announced that "the Women's Strike for Peace will conduct a lobby earlier on the 25th." It is clear from this communication that WSP had decided not to confront the Democrats outside the convention, but to try to pressure from within.[15]

In the fall of 1964 WSP campaigned actively for the defeat of Goldwater and for the election of President Lyndon Johnson, who had promised no wider war. The women were gratified by the Democrats' landslide victory, but by 1965 they, along with other peace advocates, felt thoroughly betrayed by Johnson's bombing of Vietnam and ashamed that they had been taken in by his promise of peace. Fifteen hundred women joined a mass lobby in Washington in January 1966, carrying placards that read, "Mr. President, We Voted for Peace. . . . You Gave Us War!" *MEMO* reported that the impressive thing about this lobby was the number of women who participated for the first time as a result of advertisements in the *New York Times,* the *Nation,* and the *New Republic.* Interviews with new women indicated that they joined the peace marchers because they felt isolated, with no place to turn to register their frustration and anger. Mary Benson, a "pretty, young woman from Oklahoma City," said she had seen a New York WSP ad in the *New Republic.* "I have been passive, although I do feel strongly about peace," she said. "When I read the ad I knew it was time to do more than sit and argue with people." Jane Shapiro from Columbus, Ohio, stated: "I've gotten so mad—so sick of not being able to do anything. My husband and I have written thousands of letters. . . . I was glad to read about an action I could take." WSP recruited many new women through this lobby. Nan Prendergast from Atlanta, who was a Quaker active in the peace committee of the Society of Friends and was later to spark the JRB by inviting Jeannette Rankin to speak to her peace group in Atlanta, had never before lobbied Congress. It was an empowering experience for her, and she vowed that when she came back to lobby again she would bring scores with her—"and they'll be part of Women Strike for Peace."[16] Frustration with the Johnson betrayal brought over one thousand women onto the Hill, delivering proxies from those back home and attempting to speak directly to members of Congress. Late in the afternoon the women converged on the Senate Foreign Relations Committee room to leave messages and cardboard doves for their representatives. Praising the demonstration lobby format, *MEMO* announced that WSP would support such men as Republican John Lindsay, who had called the Vietnam conflict the most unwanted war in American history, and Senator Abraham Ribicoff, who urged the president to meet with the National Liberation Front of South Vietnam.

A proposal was presented at the fourth national conference that WSPers resign from the Democratic party or refuse to do precinct work as a protest against Johnson's escalation of the Vietnam War. The proposal was countered by Bella Abzug's exhortation that even more WSPers join local clubs to establish stronger influence at the precinct level; "You cannot withdraw from work which you have not done," she insisted.[17] During the years between 1965 and 1970 thousands of WSPers worked actively in the Democratic party, supporting peace candidates in the primaries and taking leadership roles in the "Dump Johnson" movement and in the Eugene McCarthy and Robert Kennedy campaigns for the presidential nomination. A report from Detroit WFP, a WSP affiliate, stated that in the 1966 Democratic primary "we lost but won." The WSP candidate in the Seventeenth Congressional District lost to another woman. But WSP felt it had won new friends and raised the war issue through "125,000 pieces of literature distributed, the door to door contact of thousands of people and the new recruits both for WSP and the student movement" that resulted from and intense campaign.[18] WSPers also interviewed hundreds of candidates and party officials, threatening them with dire consequences if they failed to act for peace when elected. An example of this kind of pressure is cited in a report in *MEMO* that in Iowa City twenty WSPers who had been active workers in Representative Schmidhauser's election campaign challenged his highly vocal support of punitive legislation against draft card burners and his support of U.S. intervention in Vietnam and the Dominican Republic. *MEMO* commented that, possibly as a result of WSP pressure, Representative Schmidhauser turned out to be the only congressman from Iowa to sign a letter to Johnson urging extension of the bombing moratorium.[19] The same issue of *MEMO* carried the reprint of an article about a forty-two-year-old mother of four children, a WSP participant who was running in the Democratic primary in Indiana. Elizabeth Savich, in true WSP fashion, stated that she had chosen to run for Congress "because my conscience would not allow me to sit at home, cozy and well fed, while our loved ones are being sacrificed in a needless war."[20]

In 1966 WSP initiated a third Voter's Peace Pledge campaign in the New York area, which elicited tens of thousands of signatures. Advertisements in the *New York Times* and the *New Republic* brought in names from small towns and counties that were very useful in pressuring Democratic party district leaders, clubs, new candidates, and incumbents. That Abzug had long-range political goals for WSP within the Democratic party is made clear by her insistence that WSP not support peace candidates who lost in the primaries and planned to run as independents. "We should not divert ourselves into narrow, limited, sectarian activity which can only serve to . . . weaken our broad support," Abzug argued. "We must be realistic if we regard our program of political action as an on-going, long-range responsibility through which we, with the support of the American people, can secure a change in the foreign policy of the United States."[21]

The WSP political strategy was clearly focused on building an anti-Johnson movement within his own party. The women were instructed to query each incumbent on whether he had supported any moves to reduce military appropriations, whether he had urged that the National Liberation Front be a party to peace negotiations and given a role in the future government, and whether or not he saw the need for a basic overhaul of U.S. foreign policy to prevent military intervention around the globe. The women were also instructed by the New York office to define the WSP's position and program to all candidates and ask them to endorse it.[22] WSP women were urged to appear in large numbers at the state and national political conventions, to testify before platform committees, and to organize mass demonstrations inside and outside state party conventions.[23] Bella Abzug testified at the national Democratic Platform Committee hearings, stating flatly that under no circumstances would WSP support the nomination or candidacy of Hubert Humphrey, because of his identification with President Johnson's policies in Vietnam.

MEMO urged WSPers involved in the McCarthy campaign to continue to circulate the WSP peace ballots, explaining that thousands of signed pledges would be interpreted by candidates as the promise of more door-bell ringers, campaign workers, and new sources of funds. Southern California WSP supported a campaign to collect 330,000 signatures to nominate forty presidential electors pledged to vote for Eugene McCarthy. WSP coordinator Mary Clarke was one of the electors and went on to became one of WSP's few delegates to the 1968 Democratic party national convention. WSP in Newton, Massachusetts, reported that it was virtually running its own McCarthy headquarters. Fifteen hundred volunteers turned out a 65 percent McCarthy vote in the primary. In the style and energy typical of WSP, there was not one paid worker in this electoral operation.

WSP women planned a peaceful picket outside the Conrad Hilton Hotel in Chicago, where the platform hearings of the Democratic national convention were to take place. WSP urged its participants to contact all women delegates and delegates' wives, asking them to join the peace forces at the convention. But the WSP initiative was overshadowed by the violence in the streets, the brutal police attack on the new left demonstrators, which made headlines across the nation and the world.

The key slogan of the WSP electoral campaign of 1968 was "Doves in Washington: Sons at Home." While that slogan reinforced WSP's maternalist politics, the 1968 peace petition also exhibited a rising awareness of the century-old struggle for women's rights when it referred to the women's vote as "a precious right won for us by women of courage and persistence." At the national WSP convention the previous year, Abzug, who was one of the first to raise feminist issues and women's history, proposed that WSP build on the "heritage of our ancestors, the suffragists." She pointed out that "they did everything we have done, but more, and on a larger and more sophisticated scale. They marched, picketed the White House, demonstrated, leafletted. . . . Several times they collected more than a million signatures on petitions for the women's vote."[24] But Abzug's invocations of the suffragists' political campaigns and her exhortations to WSPers to read Eleanor Flexner's *Century of Struggle* had little effect at the time. She recalls: "Every time I tried to show the historical perspective of the women's rights movement and the going from abolition to suffrage to peace, as well as to labor, they thought I was irrelevant. They never understood their historic role as women, and the link historically of the peace issue with the feminist issue."

Abzug never wavered in her determination to build a women's political peace force and was often bitter that WSP was insufficiently enthusiastic in its response to her electoral projects: "I left those dopey lawyers because they treated me like *shit* and they didn't understand the issues as I understood them. Now here I was with a bunch of women, and because I'm political, because I'm professional, somehow or other I can't equal them." "They put me down a lot," she recalled with rekindled rage. It is true that Abzug's attempts to establish links with feminist history did not lead to an immediate transformation of consciousness. No women's history study groups or consciousness-raising groups were established within WSP, but many women were becoming aware that their own experiences had historical roots. It took the JRB in 1968 and the Women's March for Equality in 1970 to move a number of WSPers into the feminist ranks. Bella Abzug, however, can be credited with making the first attempts, or sermons and harangues, to lead WSP beyond the politics of moral motherhood.

By the late 1960s, certain WSP women in key metropolitan areas, particularly New York, Los Angeles, San Francisco, and Chicago, came to be recognized as "pols" with influence. New York WSP was instrumental in developing peace action committees that functioned like Democratic caucuses in the boroughs and counties of the metropolitan area. Abzug recalls that in the Seventeenth Congressional District "you couldn't run for office unless you came before a peace committee of 1,000 people. Women Strike for Peace was the key factor in these caucuses and we turned around each club's vote. We did it openly, as Democrats."

WSP's most extraordinary achievement in the political arena was electing its own legislative and political action chairperson, Bella Abzug, to the U.S. House of Representatives. This accomplishment was duplicated by no other peace or women's group of the 1960s. Abzug's upset victory in the Democratic primary in the Nineteenth Congressional District in June 1970 unnerved professional politicians, but it did not surprise WSP's electoral activists, the true believers in Abzug's political action program. Peace women across the country sensed in her victory a reward for years of hard work, and a mandate for increasing their electoral efforts to end the war.

Two hundred thirty-five WSPers worked in Abzug's headquarters throughout her campaign, dozens walked the streets with her each day, and hundreds canvassed door to door. WSP women raised tens of thousands of dollars at fund-raising parties from coast to coast, distributed handbills, typed, and stuffed envelopes. These were tasks the WSP women had been performing for male peace candidates since 1962 and earlier, but never with the same pride and conviction. Abzug could not have won if she had not received the support of youth activists, women's liberation groups, neighborhood organizations, prominent journalists, trade union leaders, and theatrical celebrities as well as ordinary black, Jewish, Italian, Chinese, and Latina women. Directly after her election in 1970 she acknowledged the importance of WSP in her election: "The fact that I am legislative chairman of WSP contributed greatly to my credibility with the voters, and made them believe in my leadership. My role in WSP was an important aspect of my campaign and was prominently featured in all my materials. . . . WSP played the major role in my victory."[25] Abzug saw her electoral victory as a model for radical change in Congress. She was certain that dozens of other women would follow. "The women do the work, the women vote," she insisted; "the women maintain the political structure. The potential political power of women can turn the country around." Her prophecy has not yet been fulfilled, but it is coming closer in 1992, "the year of the woman." Many women now running for office credit Abzug with creating the political climate that makes it possible for them to run and win.

Bella Abzug entered Congress not only as a politician and legislative strategist, but as a leader in WSP's continuous efforts to insert a human, caring, and emotional dimension into the male political establishment. Her first day in Congress was choreographed by WSP. The *Washington Evening Star* reported, "With the subtle touch of an avalanche, freshman congresswoman Bella Abzug, D-N.Y., made her presence felt on Capitol Hill, as for openers, she went through two swearing-in ceremonies."[26] The first and official swearing-in took place in the House of Representatives, the second on the Capitol steps. As *MEMO* put it, "For the first time in history, a representative was inaugurated by her constituents. Five hundred WSPers chanting 'two, four, six, eight—tell 'em Bella set the date' took over the Capitol steps to launch Bella Abzug into Congress and start the national 'Set the Date' campaign for total withdrawal of all U.S. Forces from Indochina." The cheering women had come to Washington in response to a call from the New York and Washington offices. "January 21st is a historic day!" it read; "it's the day the angry women who banged their shoes on the door of the Pentagon send their first woman to the floor of the Congress. It's the day Bella Abzug goes to Washington—She calls upon all of us to go with her. . . . Bella Is Your Voice in Congress. . . . Stand with Her to Give It Force."[27]

Abzug had not come to Washington unprepared. She had asked the women to join her to support her first piece of congressional business she would introduce on her first day in office, a "Resolution to Set the Date" (HR 54), which called for the withdrawal of all U.S. forces from Indochina no later than 4 July 1971. The resolution, which had thirty-one congressional cosponsors, many of them voicing opposition to the war for the first time, was obviously prepared far in advance of the opening of the Ninety-second Congress.[28] It demonstrated Abzug's capacity for activist leadership inside the political establishment as well as outside. On her first day she also introduced HR 53, a bill to abolish the Senate Internal Security Subcommittee, successor to HUAC, cosponsored a bill to open the records of government agencies to the public, cosponsored a bill to repeal the Emergency Detention Act, and joined in sponsorship of all bills and resolutions for withdrawal from Vietnam. After she was "sworn in" by Representative Shirley Chisholm, the first black woman elected to Congress, Abzug pledged "to the women in the peace movement, from which I come, to devote my time, my energy, and my abilities in and out of Congress to help end the war in Indochina, and to bring all of our men home."[29] To make the fullest use of their day in the nation's capital, hundreds of WSP women proceeded from Abzug's swearing-in ceremony to the White House and then to the Capitol to fasten "A Proclamation to Set the Date" on the office doors of all members of the House and Senate.

Inspired by Abzug, who never gave up her role as political action whip in WSP, the Los Angeles group took the leadership in establishing a coalition effort to pressure southern California congressional representatives to cut off funds for the war. Under the slogan "Out of Asia or Out of Office," the women warned their elected representatives that thousands of voters, who could make the difference in their reelection, would no longer tolerate inaction regarding the most unpopular war in U.S. history.[30] When the New York State Democratic Committee met in New York City on 28 December 1971, WSP was mobilized to bring its protest against the resumption of the bombing of North Vietnam to the Democratic party leadership. The women picketed outside the Americana Hotel, leafletting and urging passersby to join them. As the state committee convened, they marched onto the ballroom floor to demand that the first order of business be suspended until action was taken on Vietnam, and succeeded in having a resolution passed against the bombing.

I interviewed Abzug for *MEMO* in March 1971 after she had been in Congress for three months. I asked her then if she believed that her presence in Congress was making a real difference. I reported that "Bella's usual brash, self-confident manner was shaken for a moment. She thought hard . . . and replied, 'I haven't ended the war, and that's bad—but I think my presence has exerted pressure on other congressmen and women to be more outspoken on the war issue. Because of me there are many who feel they must move.'" Never letting up her pressure on WSP, Bella added, "I can only do so much in Congress, the rest is up to you people."

In January 1972, long before Watergate, Abzug and WSP called for the impeachment of President Richard Nixon for his failure to heed a congressional mandate to end the war. On 18 January, the opening day of the Ninety-fourth Congress, Abzug planned to introduce a resolution to censure the president for "flouting the will of the American people and the mandate of Congress." Once again Abzug asked the WSP women to join her at the Capitol because "it is most urgent that you be visible in the gallery on that date."[31] Responding to Abzug's appeal, a group of women from New York and Washington undertook an action beyond her plan and expectation. Over one hundred women hid posters under their clothing, which they uncovered and raised aloft just as Abzug reached the podium and began her speech. The posters all read, "Impeach Nixon, the Mad Bomber." This action defied a legal restriction against demonstrations inside the House of Representatives. As the WSPers rose from their seats in the gallery to wave their banners, Speaker of the House Carl Albert ordered the galleries cleared. The women were hustled out, but there were no arrests. Although several of Abzug's colleagues predicted that she would be reprimanded by the congressional leadership, Abzug could not be implicated in the illegal protest, as the women had been careful not to inform her about their planned action.

In 1972 WSP gave its official backing to a presidential candidate for the first time. The National Consultative Committee called on "every woman in the peace movement to work actively for the election of George McGovern" because he was pledged to end the Vietnam War. But this did not mean that WSP was willing to give up its independent role as issue gadfly for the causes of peace and social justice. "While we work in the campaign for McGovern, for President," the New York political action committee cautioned, "WSP must continue its independent role in maintaining pressure on all candidates for better and stronger positions on the war, for amnesty, for welfare rights, for racial and social justice—and for the inclusion of women in the highest policy-making positions in the political arena and government."[32]

In July 1971 the National Women's Political Caucus (NWPC) was founded in Washington, D.C., as a nonpartisan organization to strengthen women's role in the Democratic and Republican parties, to elect substantial numbers of women delegates to both parties' national conventions, to influence party platforms, to designate candidates, and to increase the numbers of women in local, state, and federal office. Although the guidelines for candidates seeking NWPC support focused on women's rights issues, they did include such peace demands as "immediate withdrawal" from Indochina and an end to the arms race. WSP played an important role in the founding of NWPC. It was represented by Ruth Meyers and Amy Swerdlow, who attended all the planning meetings. Four WSPers were listed as conveners, and Mary Clarke of California was elected to the twenty-one-woman planning council. The WSP women, along with Abzug, tried hard to convince the NWPC that peace is a feminist issue.[33] Nobody in the caucus, not even the Republicans, endorsed the war, but not everyone agreed that peace demands should be central to the caucus program.

Working with the NWPC was an important step in the transformation of WSP consciousness. Discussions such as one that led to the resolution against the use of violence as a "traditionally masculine way of resolving conflicts" offered a new insight into war and peace issues for most of us. I was so impressed by the feminist discourse at the founding meeting of NWPC that I reprinted in the WSP *MEMO* a speech by Paula Page, the director of the Woman's Center of the National Student Association, in which she called for the creation of a women's party. "The most common objection to this idea," she argued, "is that a third party could not gain enough strength and support to win in '72." Page called this argument specious in that it rested on an unexamined conception of what winning constitutes.

> Does integration into the masculine political world, as it exists, constitute women's liberation? A real victory lies in the education which women would receive from setting up and carrying out their own program and actions, the experience they would accumulate by working with their sisters, and for their sisters, without direction from men, the insights they would gain from presenting a real challenge to the macho-power structure of our society.[34]

There was no response within WSP to this challenge, although WSP had rejected male political culture from its first days. WSP never became a force in NWPC because working for bipartisan female representation in public office did not seem as central an issue to the women as ending the war. But contact between WSP and NWPC continued through Bella Abzug and Judy Lerner of Westchester County, N.Y., who was to be an influential member of the caucus for many years.

Abzug's election to Congress and her new leadership role within the Democratic party actually served to diminish WSP's electoral role because it moved the locus of female peace pressure from the women's peace movement to the left liberal forces within the Democratic party. Abzug continued to be thought of by the women of WSP as their political voice, but her agenda for political action expanded far beyond the peace issue to the fight for women's political power within all the structures of the Democratic party.

With the withdrawal of U.S. troops from Vietnam in 1973, the WSP women moved on from day-to-day crisis-oriented political action to personal concerns, to local community problems such as the threat to the environment posed by nuclear energy, and to the growing feminist movement. For WSP women the questions raised by the women's movement regarding the sexual division of reproductive labor and political power coincided with a new stage in their life cycles. As their grown children left home, they sought to build on the skills and confidence they had gained in WSP to find paid employment in political and social service organizations. Many became the "reentry" women of the 1970s who sought advanced degrees and professional training. Of dubious value was one of the doctrines of the second wave that the women of WSP took most seriously, the denigration of volunteerism as female exploitation. This was a profound loss for WSP, because without volunteers a movement lacking a fixed structure, a paid staff, and professional organizers cannot function visibly and effectively in the political arena.

This does not mean that the women who had spent years organizing female peace pressure on the Democratic party quietly disappeared. Those who had become "pols"—precinct workers, party officials, campaign staffers, and political appointees in Democratic strongholds— have continued to work within the Democratic party for peace, for the protection of the environment, and for women's rights. Even today, they continue to call on the WSP constituency when they need their numbers and their labor, and the WSP women continue to respond.

New York City WSP women picket local draft board, October 1971. Photo by Dorothy Marder

Helen Boston of Brooklyn WSP protesting the war. Washington, D.C., 20 January 1973. Photo by Dorothy Marder

WSP March to Roll Back Prices, 7 April 1973. Photo by Dorothy Marder

WSP Pentagon protest. Photo by Dorothy Marder

Unidentified woman at WSP march. Records of Women Strike for Peace, Swarthmore College Peace Collection

WSP children protest war toys in New York City. 26 February 1973. Photo by Dorothy Marder

Plain Rapper, 10 January 1969.

Edith Villestrego, Washington, D.C. WSP coordinator in the 1970s and 1980s. Photo by Ray Pinkson

Anci Kopell (right) Seattle WSP Coordinator. Records of Women Strike for Peace, Swarthmore College Peace Collection

Irma Zigas (left) Coordinator of Antidraft Clearing House. Photo by Dorothy Marder

Hazel Grossman, San Francisco
WSP. Photo by Dorothy Marder

THE NUCLEAR ARMS RACE
CAN MAKE US
THE LAST GENERATION

STOP IT! SPEAK OUT!

WOMEN
strike for
PEACE

Photo by Dorothy Marder

8

Not Our Sons, Not Your Sons, Not Their Sons: Hell No, We Won't Let Them Go!

You boys fighting in Vietnam have heard all sorts of things about the peace marchers here at home. Now it's time you heard from us directly. We want you to know that we women who march to stop the war respect your bravery. Many of you are our own sons, and never for a minute can we forget your suffering. We march to stop the war because:

We don't want you to die for a corrupt Saigon regime whose own people do not support it.

We do not want you to kill women and children whose only crime is to live in a country ripped by civil war.
—"A Message to Our Boys in Vietnam, from Mothers Who March for Peace," New York WSP, November 1967

*H*undreds of the women in WSP who, on grounds of moral or political purity, could not or would not find a place for themselves in the partisan electoral system turned their energies, passions, and organizing skills into building a political pressure movement against the draft for Vietnam. This is not to say that hundreds of women who were working in the electoral arena did not also protest and resist the draft, and vice versa. But there was a division of labor within WSP. Those who worked on a daily basis in electoral politics and those who devoted themselves to full-time antidraft activity could not give equal attention to both these time-consuming yet essential and compelling aspects of the antiwar movement.

The key antidraft organizers, many of whom were mothers of draft-age sons and in touch with thousands of other mothers in the same predicament, sensed that conscription was the weakest link in the interventionist chain and that undermining the draft would undermine the war. They were also convinced that antidraft activity, particularly draft counseling, would be an ideal vehicle for attracting the much sought-after "ordinary woman," whose concern for the welfare of her sons might open her ears and her heart to the deeper moral and political arguments against the war. WSP already knew from experience that its message would reach all kinds of women, political or apolitical, who were concerned for the lives of their sons. As early as December 1962, a letter came to Dagmar Wilson from the mother of Lieutenant Viggo Brix, a bomber pilot who had been killed in Italy in World War II, accompanied by a check that represented one-half of his life insurance. "I can't think of a better way to use this money and I am sure Viggo would say so too. . . . I have been following the news on various peace organizations for some time and Women Strike for Peace makes sense, and as a woman I am particularly proud of you." Sixty-year-old Martha Brix explained that her son, who served with the Fifteenth Air Force in Italy, was only twenty when he was killed. She described Viggo as "a kind and gentle boy who would not willingly hurt anybody." It was letters like this one, and many more from mothers of young men killed in Vietnam, that constantly reinvigorated the WSP women who gave every free moment they had to fighting the draft.[1]

Yet for WSP to work successfully against the draft was not an easy task, as the draft was a male institution in which only men were called upon to serve, or to brave the risks and punishments of refusal. To understand WSP's role in the antidraft movement it is important to recognize that both the draft and the draft resistance, a movement composed of radical pacifists and left-wing anti-imperialists, were built on traditional gender roles: men as planners and actors, women as enablers and supporters. According to sociologist Barrie Thorne, who studied two Boston-area draft resistance groups in 1968–69, the young female cohorts of the draft-age men, who had joined the resistance to fight the war, found that they could not be principal or even significant players because the male resisters reserved for themselves the right to plan strategies, speak in public, and be interviewed by the media.[2] Leslie Cagan, an activist in the 1960s and a peace leader today, recalls a discussion of a "We Won't Go" petition drive, in which women in the room were told that they would not be allowed to speak because women did not face conscription and therefore had no right to decide the tactics of resistance.[3] Because women were permitted only to "educate, encourage, and support," their role in the movement came to be symbolized by the slogan "Gals Say Yes to Guys Who Say No." Experiences of trivialization and denigration so angered a group of young women in the Boston area that they decided to withdraw from draft resistance work to form their own resistance—to sexism.

For the key women of WSP, antidraft activity was a more positive experience. Despite frustrations based on generational, gender, and cultural conflict, the WSPers stayed in the antidraft struggle until conscription was abolished and subsequently launched a campaign for total and unconditional amnesty for all those who had refused to fight in Vietnam.

What was it about the WSP women that made it possible for them to achieve a sense of personal and social purpose in a movement defined and led by young men? One answer is that the WSPers had been socialized to identify the needs of their sons as their own and to view self-sacrifice as a positive social value. It was enough for them to know they were playing a unique and important role by providing valuable economic and political resources that neither the resisters nor their female cohorts could command.

Unlike the young women who worked in the draft resistance movement, the WSP women were viewed by the young men, not as potential sexual partners, but as political parents, a role in which the WSP women felt comfortable and effective. A letter to WSP from Gary Rader, a former marine who had become an antidraft organizer, communicated a message the women found compelling. Describing himself as "a 23-year-old facing eleven or so years in prison, working in my first movement ever, being trailed by the FBI and harassed by the police," Rader explained that the people "putting their lives on the line" by resisting the draft were "woefully young and powerless." He called on WSP to provide bail and legal defense resources. The *Sacramento Women for Peace Newsletter* urged its readers to "get behind this fine group of young idealists, working not for themselves, but for the future of the race."[4]

A call to the women in Oakland, California, to swell the ranks of a weekly WSP picket line at the local induction center, aimed at convincing young men not to step forward for induction, stated: "We know that we are effective because we can see it; we often escort young men directly from the busses to Draft Help to be counseled before they enter the induction center—this in spite of the attempt by induction officials to herd them quickly into the building. We are often thanked for being there. We are even told we are beautiful."[5] There was little overt sexual vanity here. To the WSPers the word *beautiful,* in this context, meant moral, brave, selfless, politically on-the-ball. The Los Angeles Civil Liberties Defense Committee, thanking the women for financial contributions and the provision of office space for GI resistance work, wrote to WSP: "The help that each of you has offered, and given us in our day-to-day work has been beyond what anyone could really expect."[6] And Francis Rocks, a draft resister supported by New York WSP, wrote: "I find it very difficult to express in words what I feel, although the feeling is beautiful beyond description. Brought about not by the material factor involved, but by the beauty that radiates within your organization. . . . Beyond doubt you are the best people I ever associated with."[7]

What WSP gave the draft resisters—money, space, time, and emotional support—was typically parental. While the WSPers felt comfortable and righteous providing hot food, clothing, legal defense, and friendship to the young resisters and deserters awaiting arrest by federal marshals, neither they nor the young men would have expected the middle-aged men in the antiwar movement to provide this kind of support. From men like Dave Dellinger, Dave McReynolds, or Sidney Lens they expected only political wisdom, advice, and leadership.

In return for their generous support, the women of WSP were treated by the radical young men who led the resistance with the kind of gratitude reserved for accepting mothers or doting aunts. Accordingly, WSP was rarely consulted when national policies or tactics were determined, and the women were treated with condescension when they disagreed with movement decisions. The disdain often frustrated and angered the WSPers, but it did not drive them away. The staying power of the WSP women lay, in large measure, in their political independence. They never sought to be integrated into the draft resistance movement as individuals. Instead they came to antidraft work from their separatist women's group, which shaped its own policies and decided on its own terms which issues, which groups, and which tactics it would initiate or support. A report published by the Philadelphia Committee to Support Draft Resistance, a WSP offshoot, sheds light on how WSPers perceived their relationship to the male-led movement. The Philadelphia group reported that it had "adopted" a number of young antidraft organizers and resisters and was providing them with funds for housing and office expenses, while *criticizing*, encouraging, and listening to them.[8] Criticizing and influencing dependent sons, ambiguous privileges of motherhood, mollified those who were frustrated by cultural and tactical conflicts and disguised the women's distance from decision-making power in the resistance and the larger peace movement.

In 1969, when Los Angles WSP learned that there were too few antiwar attorneys skilled in military law to deal with the growing number of desertions that year, WSP persuaded its participants to raise money for the training of military counselors and to hire a full-time lawyer to travel to military bases to protect the rights of the "in-service kids who so desperately need help."[9] The Los Angeles group was also able to raise sufficient funds to place a billboard on a well-traveled corner in Los Angeles with the message "Uptight with the Draft—Free Draft Information," followed by four telephone numbers for counseling. The ad was signed "Women Strike for Peace."[10] The WSP women knew from their experiences as mothers of draft-age sons that this was the kind of help all families, regardless of race, class, or ethnicity, needed, and they were willing, able, and proud to provide it.

The first call for mothers' involvement in draft refusal came in 1965, not from WSP but from the Mississippi Freedom Democratic party in McCombs, Mississippi. Two young African-American activists, Joe Martin and Clint Hopson, declared that "no Mississippi Negroes should be fighting in Vietnam for the white man's freedom, until all Negro people are free in Mississippi. Negro boys should not honor the draft here in Mississippi and *mothers should encourage their sons not to do so*" (emphasis added).[11] In 1965 the WSP attitude toward draft resistance was ambiguous. The sons of some WSP women were already refusing to be inducted, and individual women and chapters decided for themselves how and if to react, but the movement had no official or even nonofficial position on avoidance or resistance. Neither did SDS, the most radical student group in the country.

In late 1966, when WSP realized that renewal of the draft law was soon to be debated in Congress, it assigned itself the task of building a massive mothers' voice for abolition. This involved demonstrating, lobbying, petitioning, and testifying for abolition before Congress and at party platform hearings. An antidraft resolution based on WSP's original policy statement was agreed upon at the movement's fifth national conference. It declared:

We are opposed to U.S. policy of military intervention all over the world, and the reliance on military means for solving problems that are essentially social and political. Therefore we oppose the drafting of young men for destruction and killing in Vietnam and anywhere else in the world to further this policy of military intervention.

We also oppose universal conscription because we do not want a conscripted society. We want a free society dedicated to the pursuit of human rights.[12]

One month after WSP's antidraft resolution, the National Council of SDS, also building on its previously declared principles, asserted in the first paragraph of its antidraft resolution its opposition to the U.S. government's "illegal, and genocidal war against the Vietnamese people in their struggle for self-determination." What the two statements had in common was moral outrage. But SDS went on to argue that the draft was intimately connected with the requirements of the economic system and the foreign policy of the United States.[13]

A comparison of the two statements, developed at the same time and in the same political context, reveals the extent of the gender and age divisions between the two groups. The SDS resolution, at least five times as long as that of WSP, was more ideological, radical, and combative. SDS emphasized political and economic analysis. WSP avoided anything that smacked of left ideology and chose to use the maternal and moral language the women had used in the past to reach the much talked-about average mother. It would be a mistake, however, to conclude that, with the number of ex-Communists, socialists, and anarchists in the movement, the WSPers did not consider or understand the economic or geopolitical issues at play in Vietnam. An internal memo from New York WSP stated that "the draft has provided a seemingly comfortable solution for the social and economic problems of our underprivileged by providing them with temporary answers to their immediate concerns of employment, housing, and education."[14] This rather superficial treatment of the economic issues involved in the Vietnam War can be ascribed to the reluctance of WSP to critique, discuss, or even name the economic system. Bella Abzug attributes this to anti-intellectualism, but I attribute WSP's aversion to words like *capitalism, colonialism, imperialism,* and *socialism* to political caution and the feminine image WSP sought to project. The fact is that the WSP women made a conscious decision to disassociate themselves from left political rhetoric. They sensed that highly charged ideological words closed minds instead of opening them. While the young men of SDS, who were attempting to create a new political synthesis, were capable of developing a "new" left rhetoric appropriate for its time and purpose, the women of WSP were content to put forward a maternal politics of experience, emotion, and common sense that shunned abstraction and rigid ideology. Another difference between the two antidraft statements, developed at the same time, involves concepts of leadership. National SDS offered its chapters specific instructions for organization and action. National WSP did not presume to make programmatic or tactical decisions for its local groups. Each WSP chapter was expected to decide whether to focus on the draft, whether to publicize the national antidraft statement, and what tactics to use in its own community.

In 1966 WSP began to advise its participants to "know your sons' rights" and to inform its participants that draft counseling services were available from the Central Committee for Conscientious Objectors and the War Resisters League. WSP women were also apprised that both the National Council of Churches and the Republican Ripon Society had taken a stand against the draft.[15] The provision of such information was a much-used WSP tactic. The movement continually sought to identify itself with mainstream opinion, using the declarations of antiwar congressional representatives as well as clergy and old-line pacifist groups, in an effort to give local women the courage to bring radical thought and action into their own communities. Although WSP had not yet taken a stand on draft resistance, by late 1966 it was urging its participants not to forget the courageous young men who are refusing to fight in the "dirty war." Lists of imprisoned objectors were published in *MEMO* with their addresses so that the women could write or visit them.

When Congress voted to renew the universal military training act in 1967, despite a national WSP campaign for repeal, the WSP women were enraged. They soon came to the conclusion that the only way to undermine the draft for Vietnam was to encourage and support those who chose to evade it. As draft calls escalated, the traditional pacifist groups were overwhelmed by the volume of requests for counseling. WSPers decided to meet the rapidly growing need for draft counseling by training themselves for the role.

In October 1967 Irma Zigas, who had taken on the job of WSP's national antidraft task-force coordinator, reported that Long Island women had set up a draft information and counseling service with the aid of AFSC, and that the group was already functioning on its own in the name of WSP. Zigas reported that within two months of its founding, the Long Island service had counseled five hundred young men at private and group sessions.[16]

A Boston-area WSP newsletter reported that a chapter of Voice of Women (VOW), New England, a WSP affiliate, had already plunged into draft counseling. Fifteen to eighteen of its thirty members had attended a four-session seminar on draft counseling given by the Boston Draft Resistance, and were beginning to work with young men in their community. According to a report on this project in a Boston Draft Resistance publication, the Roxbury women were considered to be the most determined, energetic, and resourceful counselors the resistance had ever trained. At the final training session an African-American man already in the army addressed the women. "I only wish you had been here last year," he said. "They told me at the Board: sign up for three years or you don't get any educational training. But I haven't gotten any yet, and I'm going to Vietnam in two weeks."[17] This is exactly the kind of inspiration the WSP women needed to work faithfully in the counseling centers. The same newsletter that reported on VOW's draft counseling stated that at a community meeting on draft resistance at which a number of ministers and draft resisters spoke, "a large sum of money was raised by selling the multi-colored paper flowers made by Voice of Women members."

By the time the war was over, the Long Island group had counseled 100,000 young men. They did this in what they called "an off-the-street facility," organized, administered, and staffed by WSP volunteers, along with doctors, lawyers, and psychiatrists who were, for the most part, the husbands and friends of the WSPers. When I questioned Zigas in 1979 regarding her claim that 100,000 men were counseled in one WSP center in Long Island, she insisted that her estimate was accurate.[18] She explained that "in the beginning" WSP provided only ten counselors, working twice a week from 7:00 P.M. until midnight, but that "in the end" there were thirty-five to forty counselors, working five days and nights a week, often staying on till one or two in the morning. She recalled that at the height of the draft in 1968–1970 the center opened at 10:00 A.M. and was staffed by as many as "fifteen reception persons." Still thinking in terms of the movement ethos of the 1960s, Zigas, who is now a business executive, recalled with pride that "not one person was paid, not even a receptionist." If one were to consider the amount of time spent in counseling each individual to be at least two hours, and if the service were given a cash value of $10 per hour, the WSP draft counselors, in Nassau County alone, would have contributed over $1 million in labor.

Not all the WSP draft counseling centers were as large as the one on Long Island. The Chelsea-area group in New York City, which was composed mainly of retired garment workers who resided in an International Ladies' Garment Workers Union housing project and who were for the most part ideologically close to the old Left, somehow made an alliance with a group of young men of the new Left to cosponsor the Chelsea Draft Counseling Center. Theirs was no easy alliance. According to reports from Chelsea WSP, the young men were "courageous and dedicated, but impatient, and given to militant, radical confrontations." This distressed the Chelsea women because they preferred patient coalition building. Their long years of struggle in dozens of failed causes had made these women, now in their sixties and seventies, leery of "left-wing extremism," which they viewed as an "infantile disorder." Nevertheless, the older women worked with the young men and provided a service to the community. On the upper West Side of Manhattan, WSP's draft counseling was housed in a storefront in a black and Puerto Rican urban renewal area, which also contained new middle-income housing projects. This center advertised its services in a Spanish-language newspaper, worked with reform Democratic clubs, and reported that it was "hoping to train some Black counselors to work in the streets."[19]

Most of the WSP-supported draft counseling services were staffed by men as well as women. Males were needed, as there were always young men who preferred talking to a man, but that was not the general rule. In the early stages of the Long Island service the majority of the counselors were men, but they were interviewed and appointed by the WSP women. According to Zigas, the men in the Long Island center were devoted and faithful, giving as many evenings and weekends as the women who, for the most part, were not in the paid work force. However, the center was not without gender conflict. One of the difficulties was that Irma Zigas, the center director, and Bernice Crane, its political mentor, insisted that no lawyers be enlisted as draft counselors because they might exploit the draftees to build their own practices. This meant that the women who ran the center had to know the draft law, which was chaotic, subject to frequent changes due to new regulations and court decisions. This posed some problems for the nonprofessional WSPers, which they met by subscribing to the *Selective Service Law Reporter* and studying it diligently. According to Zigas, the women became so well-informed on the changes in the law that they had no problem giving lawyers "the third degree" regarding their knowledge and motivations when they offered to serve as volunteer draft counselors. As can be imagined, this did not sit well with the men. Zigas recalled with a good deal of bitterness: "It was very challenging for us and for them. They felt that the women came on too strong, that they were too bossy. . . . What the men wanted was for the women to act as hostesses and secretaries, not to take charge, or rock the boat." Resentment toward the strong WSP women who ran the center came only from the male counselors, according to Zigas, not from the draft-age men. "They thought we were the greatest thing that ever happened," Zigas contends. "Many asked, 'Why don't you show my mother what you're doing?'" Zigas and Crane believe that it was the admiration and appreciation they received from the young men who came to the center that kept the WSP draft counselors and receptionists going longer, and working harder, than the typical suburban female hospital volunteer.[20]

As a result of stories in the local press, word-of-mouth recommendations, and a large sign on the headquarters announcing "Free Draft Counseling Sponsored by Women Strike for Peace," the Long Island service attracted blue-collar workers, school dropouts, and working-class apprentices, both white and African-American. By 1970 the women who ran the WSP service in Nassau County were asked to speak at County Youth Board seminars and were given a booth at a county-sponsored Festival of Life for high school dropouts and young men on parole. They were also invited to speak on the draft at High School Guidance Association seminars and frequently to address the seniors at local high schools.[21] This is an indication of how unpopular the war had become. I remember reflecting in 1971 after speaking against the war at a high school on Long Island how different the atmosphere was from the embattled days in 1967. Being against the war in my part of Nassau County in 1971 was a respected, if not universally held, position.

WSP had apparently made a sound judgment in assuming that anti-draft activity would be a springboard for recruitment. A letter to the national office from "a group of ladies in Missoula" (Montana) indicated that they had been drawn together by a desire to educate against the draft in the local high schools and were eager to start a local WSP group. The Missoula women, like thousands of WSPers, had already written letters to all the young men classified as 1A by their local draft board, advising them that counseling on alterative service was available. They had also made contact with guidance counselors to place literature on conscientious objection in the schools and were supporting a group of twenty-five high school students who had started a draft forum. The Missoula women, who were already WSPers by virtue of their activity even if they did not recognize the fact, wanted to do more. They wanted to express their opinions more publicly, to engage in demonstrations, teach-ins, and leafletting of supermarkets. They wanted to establish a WSP chapter to receive information and share experiences with other antiwar women around the country.[22]

As WSP enlarged its draft counseling programs, a conflict developed between those women who believed that draft counseling should be a semi-professional service, free of political input, and those who felt its purpose was to raise political consciousness and build opposition to the war. While the Long Island counseling service used the slogan "Don't Dodge the Draft—Oppose It," other counseling groups refrained from displaying antiwar literature because they felt it exploited the young men, instead of merely helping them. The women working with the Long Island Draft Information and Counseling Service were known within WSP for distributing thousands of pieces of antiwar literature and petitions to the men who came though their doors. The WSPers even sold peace trinkets to mothers as they waited for sons being counseled.

Another ideological debate around draft counseling touched on issues of class and race, raising questions about the political consequences of helping a middle-class young man to evade the draft. Although WSP used the slogan "Not Our Sons, Not Your Sons, Not Their Sons," movement literature was quick to point out that "our sons" were the young men benefiting from the class inequities built into the Selective Service System. These benefits included student and teacher deferments as well as conscientious objector status, granted only to those who had sufficient education to articulate their religious or ethical objections to military service in a manner acceptable to their draft boards. A statement by Veronica Sissons, reprinted in *La Wisp*, declared that counseling those who could avoid the draft was "simply a promulgation of the racism and dollar discrimination" that had caused the war. "Who takes the place of the middle class student with a 2-S deferment," Sissons asked, "or the C.O. [conscientious objector], or the emigrant to another country?" WSP literature made it clear that the deferred student or the conscientious objector would be replaced by a poor or minority youth, "who probably was totally ignorant of his rights" and who might come home in a coffin.[23] A pamphlet, *Your Draft-Age Son: A Message for Peaceful Parents*, published by Berkeley/Oakland WFP, pointed out that the draftee for Vietnam is "young, often working-class, often black: while his board, statistics show, is overwhelmingly old, middle-class and white."[24]

The recognition of class inequities in the draft prompted WSP groups across the country to organize counseling programs that would reach young men across class and race lines. WSPers used their influence as community leaders, PTA officers, and mothers of high school students to pressure the high schools to provide seniors with alternative information on conscription, because army and navy recruiters were often present in the schools, making presentations to graduating males. Los Angeles WSP filed a suit against General Lewis Hershey, director of selective service, and several California educational officers for failing to provide information about draft alternatives in the high schools in compliance with Selective Service Regulation 1606.[25] WSP also raised public objections to the spending of tax dollars on the Reserve Officer Training Corps and military assemblies in the schools, while they refused to provide peace assemblies or opportunities for antiwar education on campus.[26] The *Daily News* of Fullerton, California, carried a picture of WSP women picketing Lowell High School in La Habra, protesting the school's refusal to allow WSP to present a program on "draft alternatives." The news story under the photo reported that many students had joined the women in a demand for more draft information.[27] Washington WSP called on the Board of Education to see to it that all males graduating from Washington, D.C., high schools be informed of their right to claim conscientious objector status as an alternative form of service. A group formed by Washington WSP, the Ad Hoc Parents Committee, informed the board of the provisions of section 6 of the Universal Military Training and Service Act as amended, and of the decisions in the case of *United States vs. Seeger* that "providing fellow citizens with information about their rights under federal law is not only law, but also one of the rights most assiduously protected by our courts under our doctrine of free speech and national privileges and immunities."[28] WSP was apparently unsuccessful. The superintendent of schools recommended against informing senior high school students "in respect to religious beliefs for exemption."[29] The principal of West High School in Columbus, Ohio, responded to a WSP demand for draft counseling in the schools by stating that "as a veteran of World War II I am certainly not in favor of this action and feel that patriotism is still in style."[30]

Failing to win their battle for draft counseling in most high schools, WSP and other peace groups organized "End the Draft" Caravans that travelled to blue collar and minority neighborhoods to counsel young men who had no access to information on legal alternatives to being drafted for Vietnam.[31] The *Washington Post* in April 1967 carried a story that illustrated the difficulties the peace women sometimes had with students they were attempting to serve. The *Post* reported that a delegation of WSPers attempting to distribute antidraft pamphlets at a high school in Hyattsville, Maryland, were heckled and booed and "nearly mobbed" by the majority of the students. They were "shooed" off the campus by policemen called by the principal. According to the *Post*,

> The ladies, who are the most militant organization of females to appear on the political scene since the suffragettes, stood their ground though surrounded and jostled, and tried to reason with the students. "You're too young to have a closed mind," shouted Mrs. Aline Berman, the wife of an American University professor, at a young man arguing with her about the war. "The heck I am," he shouted back.[32]

In Missoula, Montana, several young men who received alternative draft information mailed to them by Missoula WSP were hostile. One of the young men, disgusted by WSP's intervention, complained, "Why don't they leave the job of the draft board to the draft board instead of taking matters into their hands?" His mother was pleased that her son had reacted negatively to WSP's counseling offer. WSP defended itself to the local press by stating that the organization had not attempted to discourage young men from serving in the armed forces but was only trying to indicate to them the avenues of choice.[33]

The women who worked in coalition with SANE setting up card tables with draft information on sidewalks in front of many of New York City's high schools found that "Negro and Puerto Rican youths" were more responsive to their efforts than were white students. Shirley Solarcheck, the coordinator of draft caravans for WSP in Queens, New York, noted that the students at predominantly middle-class Forest Hills High School were "uncooperative," but that there was an excellent turnout at Woodrow Wilson Vocational High School.[34] The Chicago women who covered forty schools in their draft caravan, which was sponsored jointly with AFSC, also reported a friendlier response in poor neighborhoods than in the suburbs.[35] There is no analysis of this phenomenon in the WSP literature, but it may have influenced the women to make the substantial efforts they did to work with minority youth.

Those who refused the draft after receiving counseling and exhausting all avenues of appeal usually called upon the women of WSP to support their action. Women who might have been leery of civil disobedience in WSP's early years found these appeals hard to deny. Middle-aged wives and mothers found themselves leaving home at five or six in the morning, while their husbands and children slept, to be present at induction centers with placards supporting a particular young man who was going to refuse to step forward that day. The Nashville newsletter urged women to go to induction refusal demonstrations "because an adult on a picket line does wonders for young people as well as for the 'press image.'" The Nashville WSPers were also urged to call the parents of a draft refuser. They suggested that "a friendly call is a big help not only to their morale, but it usually affects the way the parents treat their sons."[36]

The next step for WSP was to sit in at the arraignments and trials of those who refused induction, in order to create a climate of sympathy and understanding for the resisters by showing that respectable mothers thought of these young men as exemplary citizens in the best traditions of the nation. The WSP communications network provided long lists of prisoners of conscience in jails and stockades all over the country, urging the women to write them, especially during holiday seasons. Some WSPers took long, lonely trips to visit jailed draft resisters and GIs who were incarcerated because they refused to fight. These women reported that they returned home saddened, but strengthened in their commitment to the young men who resisted. One Los Angeles WSPer made weekly visits to fifteen young men in the federal prison at Lompoc. She reported to *La Wisp:* "We talk, drink coffee, read things I bring up, and laugh a lot for three hours. Then they go back to be stripped naked for searching, and I drive back to my family in Santa Monica." Miriam Cason explained that it had taken her one year to become an accredited visitor, a right she cherished. She claimed never to have missed one visiting day, though it meant a long trip, getting sitters for her children, and "an emotional hangover" after each visit. Through WSP funding Cason was able to buy books and subscriptions to periodicals for the prisoners.[37]

WSP also picketed draft boards and the homes of board members, where the women read aloud the names of the war dead in an attempt to dramatize the human cost of the war, and thus prick the conscience of draft board members. In Oakland during a national antidraft day in 1970, East Bay WSPers, dressed completely in black and wearing skeleton masks, conducted a death watch inside the headquarters of their local draft board. The women announced to the draft board's astonished employees, "It is because we cherish life that we are here today. . . . We remind you that you are a constant and very personal Death Watch as you process young men to die in Viet Nam and Cambodia."[38] Some groups held "ask-ins," which meant going to the local draft board as a group, calling upon the press to cover the meeting, then asking questions of the board regarding its policies and procedures. A frequent question was "Have you ever classified a CO or given a hardship deferment?"[39] In Westchester and Nassau, suburban counties in New York, a project was organized in which local women walked into local draft board headquarters, copied the names of those classified 1A, looked them up in the telephone book, and called to inform them of WSP's draft counseling service. There was a sufficient number of takers for the practice to be used in other places.

The national leadership of WSP was convinced that it was inappropriate for women to take on the role of urging young men to resist the draft. This reluctance was based not only on the realization that it was the sons who had to pay the price of resistance, but also on the fact that WSP, as a movement, was intimidated by the anti-"momism" of the 1940s and 1950s that blamed assertive mothers for "sissy" sons and attacked assertive women as castrating neurotics. Thus, the WSPers were loath to speak for the sons or to seem in any way to lead or control them.

Accordingly, when Charlotte Keyes, a WSP activist from Champaign/Urbana, wrote an article published in *McCall's* in October 1966 under the title "Suppose They Gave a War and No One Came," she made it clear that her son's draft resistance was his idea, not hers. Keyes, the mother of three children, was a former social worker who had published a biography of Ralph Waldo Emerson for teenage readers and had just finished a biography of Herman Melville. But for *McCall's* she expressed herself only as a mother, praising her son's decision to resist the draft, despite the fact that he had been sentenced to three years in the federal penitentiary. She explained that her son Gene's decision not to serve was based on his belief that "there is no moral validity to any part of any law whose purpose is to train people to kill one another." Keyes expressed the doubts about Gene's action and its consequences that she believed her *McCall's* readers would recognize as their own: "Is he a nut? Doesn't he think about his parents at all? How must we feel to have such a rebel for a son? Doesn't it humiliate us in our community—a university town, where my husband teaches?" But she defended Gene and made it clear that she supported his decision. Speaking as an ordinary middle-class mother, Keyes admitted the ambivalence she and her husband felt about Gene's action, which ran the gamut from shock, disagreement, and anger to pride and finally to learning from him and changing their own lives. In trying to find the seeds of her son's action, Keyes explained, she realized that she and her husband had planted some of them. But she was careful to disavow any direct influence. "Well, we parents don't realize—do we," she reflected, "that when we inculcate our moral standards, that the children may really live by them." Charlotte Keyes concluded, "We stand by our son, and we learn from him."[40] This was true of hundreds of other WSP women whose children engaged in civil disobedience and other militant actions that made their parents fearful for their safety or their future but, nevertheless, proud. The Philadelphia women took a position similar to that of Charlotte Keyes when they endorsed and published a statement by Anne and Dane Hardy, parents of a draft refuser: "Our son refuses to accept military service. We have not advised him to take this step. Neither have we advised him to reconsider his decision. Having arrived at this difficult position because of his own conviction, our son has our full and proud approval, and we thereby share with him the responsibility for this principled act."[41]

Despite a cultural prohibition against mothers guiding or directing adult sons, a number of women in and around WSP believed that they had to seize the opportunity provided by the 1950 celebration of motherhood to refuse permission for their sons to be drafted. These women were resourceful enough to create their own legal arguments in support of the rights of mothers over the rights of the state. In 1967 a Los Angeles WSPer refused to give her son permission to report for his physical examination for the army. In a voluble and militant letter to her son's draft board, Mrs. A., as WSP called her, stated, "I feel it is my right, my privilege, and my honorable duty as a mother of three underage sons to resist and contest . . . my sons being used to aid and abet an immoral, illegal, and unjustified . . . quagmire of human misery in Vietnam." She avowed that she was a loyal and patriotic American, "imbued with a deep respect and concern for the welfare, safety, and honor of my country." "To defend America, as an American, for America and the welfare and protection of America YES!" she declared, "but to send them as aggressors upon and within the internal affairs of another country, NO! NEVER!"[42] Mrs. A. argued that a parent is responsible for her child's actions, for any debts he might incur, for any damages he might inflict, and for any contracts he might sign. She informed the draft board that she had consulted an attorney "of great authority and knowledge of civil laws, draft laws, and national and international laws," who offered to take her case to the Supreme Court. Should her efforts fail, Mrs. A. promised, she would willingly pay the penalty of imprisonment like a proper mother making a sacrifice of her freedom for her child's welfare. Promoting this new avenue of protest, Los Angeles WSP assured its followers that, "since this is the parents' action, the boys will have no black marks against their records that may affect their future lives."[43]

Mrs. A.'s son happened to have a minor skin ailment that was believed by his doctor to be too minor to defer him from military service. Yet, much to Mrs. A.'s amazement, her son was exempted from the draft on medical grounds. Los Angeles WSP gave Mrs. A. credit for the deferment, insinuating that she had created a case any draft board would hesitate to confront. Other women were urged to follow her example by signing a petition stating that they too would refuse to allow their sons to be drafted. How many other women signed the petition cannot be assessed from the WSP files because signed petitions were passed on to the agencies they addressed. It is clear, however, that mothers' draft resistance never became widespread in WSP.

One WSP-supported challenge to the Selective Service System, initiated by a mother on behalf of her son, did reach the courts in 1969. The challenge came from Evelyn Whitehorn of Palo Alto, California, who was described by the press as a middle-class, graying, forty-seven-year-old devoted mother of four boys who had never belonged to anything more controversial than the PTA and the Committee to Save Walden Pond. Whitehorn, who decided to seek a restraining order preventing the induction of her eighteen-year-old son Erik, contended that his pacifist convictions were due in large part to her efforts to bring him up with a "good moral character." East Bay WFP saw the Whitehorn case as a conflict between the rights of mothers and the power of the military state, but, as it turned out, it was not much of a contest. Erik was arrested, indicted, convicted, and imprisoned for refusing to register. At the trial, the judge belittled Evelyn Whitehorn, suggesting that she was somehow deviant because her husband, from whom she was divorced, was a number of years younger than she. The "Young World" section of *This Week* magazine reported that Whitehorn had received hundreds of letters supporting her stand, including "many from servicemen who wanted to borrow her for a while." An air force reserve officer sent Erik his reserve paycheck, and a young boy taped his allowance of five pennies to a letter, "to help because of my older brother." A grandmother in Long Island sent five dollar bills, one for each of her grandsons. According to *Plain Rapper*, the publication of the Palo Alto resistance, the Whitehorn mail was running about five hundred to fourteen in favor of their action.[44]

However, *Plain Rapper* noted growing tension between mother and son brought about by governmental pressure. "It is tough for an 18-year-old male to let his mother stand up for him, even if that is the best legal strategy available." "To make matters worse," according to the judgment of *Plain Rapper,* "mother and son are extremely articulate and sometimes find themselves competing."[45]

By the end of the summer of 1969 the Whitehorns had lost their case, their confidence in their action, and their family unity. Erik eventually went into the army to get out of jail. In a statement to the press, which was filled with regret and anger, Evelyn Whitehorn wound up her legal case. Stating that "it was hard to let all those tremendous and caring people know that their hopes would not materialize through the Whitehorns," Whitehorn decided not to appeal her son's imprisonment because "the draft law doesn't give any consideration to the . . . earnest desire of parents to interpose themselves between their offspring and injustice." She concluded that in the future "whatever I can do, or contribute, will be done only as 'me,' not with the use of any member of my family."[46] Whitehorn had been defeated not only by the Selective Service Act, but by a gender ideology that found her too presumptuous as a woman and mother.[47]

San Francisco WFP, convinced in the early stages of the Whitehorn case that parents can play an active public role against the drafting of their sons, prepared a mothers' pledge in support of Evelyn Whitehorn. It stated: "I am the mother of —— son(s) under eighteen. I will exert my legal right and duty as a parent to guide, cherish, and protect my son(s), and will refuse to allow him (them) to register for the draft."[48] Hazel Grossman, one of the key women in San Francisco WFP and the wife of Aubrey Grossman, a noted radical attorney who took on the Whitehorn case, recalled in 1981 that "there was little or no response among the WSP women to the Whitehorn case. Few signatures were gathered on the Whitehorn pledge, even in San Francisco." Grossman remembered that she could whip up no enthusiasm at the national WSP conference in 1969. She explained in a 1981 letter to me: "Our women at the time were not ready to get involved in urging, or rather encouraging 18-year-olds not to register. Perhaps their attitude had some basis. As you might know, [Erik] Whitehorn collapsed under pressure and changed his mind."[49]

Although WSP was not ready to become involved in a white middle-class mother's legal battle with the draft, the notion that mothers should use their social role to oppose the draft was occurring to women all over the country. A Mothers' Draft Resistance Movement was organized in Frederick, Maryland, by Helen Alexander, a WSP participant who used the same rhetoric and legal arguments advanced by Becky Hillman, Mrs. A. in Los Angeles, and Evelyn Whitehorn of Palo Alto. Mothers' Draft Resistance Movement called upon women, black and white, to "fill the courts with cases of mothers refusing to give up their sons to illegitimate authority, and our jails with mothers if need be."[50] Mothers' Draft Resistance Movement also distributed a badge with the slogan "The Hand That Rocks the Cradle—Should Rock the Boat." On the reverse side of the badge was the World War I song "I didn't raise my boy to be a soldier / I raised him to be my pride and joy / There would be no war today / If mothers would say / I didn't raise my boy to be a soldier." WSP publicized the Mothers' Draft Resistance Movement, but no group took it up as a major WSP action.

Because WSP was reluctant to act for the sons, it was important to the women that they find ways to act in their own names and on their own terms. The question of civil disobedience had always been difficult for WSP, not because the women opposed it in principle or were too timid to take risks, but because they saw themselves as representing the average women in middle America who might not understand or sympathize with unlawful behavior. However, as the war escalated and the women became convinced that the president was indifferent to legally sanctioned opposition, civil disobedience became an accepted vehicle of WSP antiwar protest. The question for WSP became, not should we do it, but where and how would it be most effective.

WSP had opposed the inclusion of mass draft card burning as part of the official program of one of the large antiwar mobilizations in New York in April 1967 because civil disobedience had not been part of the original call. The WSP representatives to the planning meetings for the mobilization argued that featuring draft card burning in the march would constitute a breach of faith with moderate "doves" who would be joining a peace action for the first time, only to express their demand for negotiations to end the war. The WSP stand, which was ridiculed by the young resisters, did not mean that the women were opposed to draft resistance, or even to card burning. The fact is that the WSP women were already deeply involved in support of dozens of young men who refused induction.

Only two months after WSP had stated its objection to public draft card burning at a peace march, the National Consultative Committee began to compose a women's statement of conscience and complicity with draft resisters, and to solicit signers who would vow to aid and abet resisters in defiance of the Selective Service Act. The decision to confront the Pentagon on the draft issue and provoke retaliation stemmed from the WSPers' desire to act in their own names, to take risks, and to write their own scenario. What the women hoped was that they would provoke the government to take legal action against hundreds of middle-class mothers instead of long-haired youth, and thus to tie up the courts, intensify the debate over the war, and escalate the struggle to end it. This was a different tactic from that of Mrs. A. or Evelyn Whitehorn, as it was aimed at aiding young resisters in general, not necessarily one's own son. It would be perceived by the public, WSP believed, as less self-serving or controlling than a mother pressuring her own son to evade the draft. WSP stated clearly:

> Increasing numbers of young Americans are finding that the Vietnam war so outrages their deepest moral and religious sense that they cannot serve in the Armed Forces while it continues.
>
> As Americans they have been taught respect for the rights of others and to stand up for their belief in justice.
>
> They now refuse to violate these principles. They refuse to be sent to Vietnam to kill men, women and children who have never harmed them and who have never threatened our country.
>
> As mothers, sisters, sweethearts, wives, we feel it is our moral responsibility to assist these brave young men who refuse to participate in the Vietnam war because they believe it to be immoral, unjust and brutal.
>
> Too many men have died. Too many more will die, unless they have the courage to say "No!" We can help give them that courage by giving them our support.
>
> We believe that support of those who resist the war and the draft is both moral and legal. We believe that it is not we, but those who send our sons to kill and be killed, who are committing crimes. We do, however, recognize that there may be legal risks involved, but because we believe that these young men are courageous and morally justified in rejecting the war regardless of consequences, we can do no less.[51]

To publicize the Women's Statement of Conscience and gain signatures, WSP organized the first "adult" and the only women's demonstration in complicity with draft refusal. It was planned as a triple header: a rally "to Launch a Women's Resistance"; a march to the office of General Lewis Hershey, director of selective service, to deliver the statement of conscience; and a picket line at the White House to demand that President Johnson quit listening to the generals and begin hearing the mothers of America.[52]

After WSP had issued its call for the 20 September action, the Department of the Interior announced a new ruling that limited to one hundred the number of persons permitted to picket at the White House gate. The WSP organizers felt that they could not accept this new restriction on peaceful antiwar protest. Thus they refused to cancel the march on the White House. The women appealed to sympathetic members of Congress, the American Civil Liberties Union, and the Washington police in the hope of persuading the president to waive the restriction, but it was not revoked. New York WSP bought space in the *New York Times* to publish an open letter to Lyndon Johnson asking "What Must We Mothers Do to Reach the Ear, To Reach the Heart of Our President?" "We women gave you our sons," the letter declared, "lovingly raised to live, to learn, and to create a better world. . . . you used them to kill and you returned 12,269 caskets and 74,818 casualties to heartbroken mothers." Using the stereotypical image of the "natural mother," a lioness and her cubs, the letter from WSP concluded: "We will walk where you can see us. We will walk where you can hear us. . . . a mother in defense of her family is not easily turned aside."[53]

The rally and march to challenge the draft calls, as WSP named it, drew approximately one thousand women from the eastern seaboard. It opened with an emotional outdoor rally addressed by two young male resisters and two women: Doris Turner, an African-American leader of Local 1199 of the Hospital and Health Care Workers Union; and Dagmar Wilson, who had returned the previous evening from Hanoi. Wilson told the assembled women what it was like to hide from American bombs. The bombings, she explained, made her see the realities of modern war, in which the civilian population, especially women and children, were the victims. The sympathy inspired by the resisters and the rage evoked by Wilson's description of the physical misery being inflicted on Vietnam by U.S. military forces, strengthened the women's resolve to reach the White House, come what may.

From the rally the women marched to the office of General Hershey in a casual and "straggly line," carrying a wooden coffin covered with a black shawl bearing the inscription "Not My Son, Not Your Son, Not Their Sons—Support Those Who Say No." The coffin was deposited at Hershey's door, along with hundreds of signed copies of the Women's Statement of Conscience. A delegation including Vivian Williams of Philadelphia, the mother of Private First Class Ronald Lockman, a young black man who had refused to embark for Vietnam and was under arrest as a resister, was left behind to await a meeting with the general.[54]

There had been no difficulties on the march to selective service headquarters. In fact the police allowed the women to march in the road, although the organizers had applied only for a sidewalk permit. As they reached the White House, the atmosphere changed. The women were met by a solid line of park police, standing shoulder to shoulder across Pennsylvania Avenue at Seventeenth Street, behind a green fence that blocked them from crossing the street to the White House. Incensed at the denial of their rights as mothers and citizens, the women tore down the fence, trampled on it, pushed through or crawled under the police line, withstanding clubs, shoves, and blows, to dash into the road directly in front of the White House gate. There they were stopped by another solid wall of policemen brandishing clubs. This line was too tight and fierce to overcome, so the women sat down in the road, blocking traffic and refusing to move despite threats of arrest. As they sang and chanted, Bella Abzug and Dagmar Wilson conferred with each other and the police and came to the conclusion that WSP had made its point, at least with the press and television, if not with the White House, and that they should avoid jail, especially because a national WSP conference was scheduled to convene on the following day. The sitting women refused to move until a compromise was reached with the park police, which allowed them all to march in a continuous line, but only one hundred at a time could be moving directly in front of the White House. The women reluctantly surrendered the space they had conquered, moved behind the barricades, and proceeded to do what they had intended to do, march in front of the president's door. The police pretended that they were counting, but actually looked away, as more than one hundred at a time were permitted to walk on the sidewalk outside the White House.

A front-page United Press International story in the *New York Times* with the headline "Women Fight Police near White House" reported that "police turned back women antiwar demonstrators . . . when they crashed through a wooden fence keeping them across the street from the White House." "At the height of the fracas," according to the *Times*, "about ten women were seen lying on the ground, and one had blood on her head."[55] The *Baltimore Sun* carried a photo of a bedraggled but determined woman pushing her head through a solid wall of policemen standing with arms locked. Her body was still behind the line. This wire-service picture was published across the country over the caption "Coming Through—A Women Strike for Peace demonstrator maneuvers a blockade." The *Sun* reported that there were more police on the scene than women, but that the women were not intimidated. In fact they shouted and jeered when the police announced that the WSP demonstration permit had been revoked because the women were sitting down in the road.[56] The two young male resisters, who had spoken at the rally and who had joined the women in the march, were treated much more severely than were the WSP women. They were dragged on the pavement, beaten, and arrested. This only confirmed the women in their belief that middle-aged, middle-class mothers could get away with more militancy than young men and that WSP had to do even more to aid the resistance.[57] The publicity surrounding the WSP confrontation with the police forced Secretary of the Interior Udall to announce, a few days later, that he had decided to take another look at the regulation limiting the number of demonstrators at the White House.[58] WSP instituted a legal suit to overturn the regulation and won in the courts.

The unladylike confrontation with the police at the White House contradicted the image WSP had nurtured carefully for close to six years. The District of Columbia media were outraged. The *Washington Post,* which had been kind, if condescending, to WSP in the past, became irate. An editorial in the *Post* titled "Strike Three" charged that the women's attempt to break through the police barricade by force "diminishes any influence the group might have."[59] Radio station WWDC accused the "impatient women" of breaking the rules: "All the kicking and pushing was an outgrowth of this decision to defy the police and push through their barricades. Under the circumstances, WWDC rejects the tiresome cries of police brutality."[60] WSP was not contrite. The sixth national conference, which met on the day after the confrontation, applauded "the spirit of determination displayed by the hundreds of women who challenged the arbitrary restriction of their right to demonstrate." A press release from the conference declared: "The women broke through the police lines, strengthened by their conviction that they were fighting for the lives of their sons, the survival of the people of Vietnam, and the right to petition the President. Neither billy clubs nor bruises will deter us. We will not be stopped."[61]

The FBI records on WSP reveal that one of the WSPers who signed the statement of conscience and complicity was slated for prosecution by the Justice Department, and many more might have been jailed if the convictions of Benjamin Spock, William Sloane Coffin, and Michael Ferber for conspiracy to violate the Selective Service Act had not been overturned.

While WSP had been uncomfortable about draft card burning at a mass rally in New York's Central Park in the spring of 1967, by October of that year, the movement found itself working with the young men, and Ethel Taylor, WSP's coordinator in Philadelphia, was holding the canister in which the ashes of draft cards were tossed. Taylor, a founder of Philadelphia WSP, was one of the most admired women in the movement. She was deeply committed, well read on peace history and current issues, witty, eloquent, and, what counted most with the WSP women, unassuming. Taylor was not a newcomer to peace activities when she initiated the strike action in Philadelphia in November 1961. She recalls that her mother was a member of WILPF and that she would return from school to find WILPF meetings in her home. But she was not interested in politics until the bombing of Hiroshima and Nagasaki. At that time, she was sufficiently horrified to join WILPF. In 1957, four years before the founding of WSP, Taylor was part of a delegation to the

White House to deliver ten thousand signatures in opposition to nuclear testing. She was also familiar with the indifference of public officials to polite lobbying. Congresswoman Edith Green of Oregon, who eventually met with the WILPF delegation to accept their antitesting petition, wrote in the bulletin she sent to her constituents:

> When women representing seven states came to Washington recently with 10,000 names on a petition requesting the cessation of H-Bomb tests, they were refused an audience with *anyone,* even staff members at the White House. Yet Ike had the time to personally receive representatives who wished to present the President with a sterling silver replica of the millionth baseball manufactured! A sad commentary could be written.[62]

But Taylor was not easily put off. She helped to found the Philadelphia chapter of SANE and was a member of its national board when the WSP founders issued their call to strike. Because WSP's militancy and spontaneity appealed to her, Taylor helped to organize a public hearing with Senator Hugh Scott on 1 November and stayed on to become one of the most effective of WSP's leaders and spokespersons. She became national coordinator in the late 1970s and held that position through the 1980s.

"Sometimes I wonder how a middle-aged Main Line matron got into all this," Taylor commented wryly in an interview by Lynn Litterine of the *Philadelphia Inquirer* in 1978.[63] "There was indeed something paradoxical in Ethel Taylor's manner. Her looks and demeanor read, 'ordinary,' respectable, middle-class, middle-aged. Her speech, her wit, her determination, her militancy, and her sparkle cried out, 'This woman is special.'" Taylor laughs at the memory of herself "in white gloves and hat, poised daintily at the back of a paddy wagon, expecting the policemen to help her down." After I interviewed Taylor in June 1980, she wrote to me that during the Vietnam War, whenever a difficult question came up—for instance, Tonkin Bay or prisoners of war—the press generally contacted three people—Mayor Rizzo, Senator Schweiker, and Ethel Taylor. "It was always two against one," she noted. "I was once asked by a reporter, 'Is there any circumstance under which you might agree with the Mayor and the Senator?' Fresh mouth that I am I answered, 'When their position is the same as mine.'"[64]

According to an FBI transcript of Taylor's speech on 16 October 1967, she praised the men who refused to serve in Vietnam. "We in Women Strike for Peace, we women and mothers, feel it is imperative that we project to the American people the fact that these young men are men of conscience," Taylor proclaimed. "These are heroic young men, these are patriots and they need our support." Taylor then proceeded to read the WSP statement of conscience.[65] FBI records reveal that an investigation of Taylor was undertaken "predicated upon activities . . . to conspire to violate the Selective Service Act." The FBI sought further records of Taylor's statements on the draft from three local television stations and three radio stations, but according to the FBI, none of them had any "tape recorded interviews or speeches that have not already been reported." An FBI report on the period from 10 October 1967 to 26 January 1969 indicates that the FBI was reviewing records of the Philadelphia Police Department and the Philadelphia Credit Bureau, "in an attempt to develop additional background data on Ethel Taylor." At the bottom of the page in the FBI record of its investigation of Taylor, there is the sentence "ACCOMPLISHMENT CLAIMED: NONE." Apparently Taylor was to be indicted after the government won its case against Benjamin Spock, William Sloane Coffin, and Michael Ferber. But when the government lost its case, Merna B. Marshall, U.S. attorney for the Eastern District of Pennsylvania, declined to prosecute.[66]

WSP continued to focus much of its attention on draft counseling and support for resisters, GI deserters, and emigrants to Canada until 1970. In 1970 the movement added a legislative campaign for draft repeal to its program because a number of bills before the Congress called either for reform or for total repeal. The debates over reform or repeal of the draft created what the WSP women thought of as "strange alliances." Among those who urged reform rather than repeal were such "doves" as Senators Edward Kennedy, Jacob Javits, and Edmund Muskie, and among those for repeal were such "hawks" as Robert Dole and Barry Goldwater. There were also divisions in WSP along these lines.

In 1966 Barbara Bick of Washington, D.C., had presented a paper for discussion at the annual conference, in which she argued that "in a most unfair scheme of things an army-by-choice seems to be the best solution." At that time most WSPers agreed.[67] In 1970, when repeal of the draft seemed possible due to the strength of the antiwar sentiment in the country, many WSPers could not bring themselves to support abolition. They feared that the alternative to the draft, a professional army made up of minority youth recruited because of their limited options in civilian life and led by a military elite, would be a danger to a democratic society.[68] WSP's antidraft task force supported repeal. It tried to minimize fears of a volunteer army by pointing out that militarism and conscription had always gone hand in hand.

In the fall of 1971, when the draft law expired, the WSP antidraft activists were jubilant. The antidraft task force turned its attention to the issue of amnesty for war resisters. As early as 1969 the women had decided to develop a policy on amnesty and had assigned Charity Hirsch of East Bay, California, to write it. The statement she drafted declared that the men in civilian and military jails and those in exile "had suffered enough for the mistakes of others which they had sacrificed so much to correct." WSP proposed that "every prisoner, military or civilian, jailed for trying to stop the war in Vietnam should be freed immediately. In addition everyone who had fled the country to avoid fighting in the war should be free to return home without punishment."[69] This became the WSP position. Unlike many liberal groups, WSP insisted that amnesty had to include all soldiers who refused to fight the war, though the crime charged might be refusing to obey a direct order, refusing to train soldiers, going AWOL, or deserting.

In the spring of 1972 Bella Abzug, who acted as WSP's voice in Congress, introduced the War Resisters Exoneration Act, HR 14175. Abzug's legal argument was simple. "If the duty to fight was not legitimate, then we cannot punish anyone who failed to fight regardless of the motives of his failure." At the same time that Abzug introduced her amnesty bill, congressman Edward Koch, who was later to become mayor of New York City, also introduced an amnesty bill, but his called for conditional amnesty to allow the administration to impose some form of punishment on "rebels." A central provision of the Abzug bill and of the WSP policy was to make no distinction between draft resisters and military deserters. In contrast to Koch, Abzug and WSP were careful to avoid creating a gap between the articulate middle-class conscientious objectors and the largely working-class and minority deserters who had not resisted until they found themselves on the battlefield.

In 1972 Irma Zigas, who had been the volunteer national coordinator of the WSP antidraft task force and had led the WSP campaign for amnesty, became the paid coordinator of the National Council for Unconditional Amnesty, a coalition of pacifist and anti–Vietnam War organizations. This was a huge step for Zigas, both personally and politically. No longer a suburban-housewife volunteer, she had become the leader of a mixed-gender organization and its national spokesperson. In an interview, Zigas spoke of her personal development in the "incredible Long Island anti-draft operation." She had been attracted to WSP in the early 1960s because she was concerned about nuclear fallout and the contamination of milk. She could not become active then, she explained, because her children were babies and her husband was mortally ill. By the late 1960s Zigas was a remarried widow with a combined family of five children. Finding herself with free time because the children were no longer babies and because there was no pressure to work for pay, she began to participate in WSP demonstrations and attend New York Coordinating Committee meetings, which were open to all. She volunteered for difficult assignments, exhibited a flair for community organizing and for public relations, and with these qualities and endless energy became a key woman. Zigas was ideally suited to be a WSP activist. She possessed a combative spirit, courage, persistence, and a comfortable middle-class income that allowed her the free time, discretionary funds, and occasional domestic help required to attend long meetings and conferences. As one of the "insiders" when Zigas became involved in WSP, I thought of her as just the kind of young, politically unsophisticated housewife we were always looking for. Many years later I discovered that Zigas's father had been, to use her words, "an old Eugene Debs socialist who used to go out on street corners making speeches." In an interview in San Francisco, where she now lives, she informed me that she had taken part in the Henry Wallace campaign in 1948 and that her father had been appalled to find her at a Wallace convention in Philadelphia, when she was supposed to be at the University of Chicago studying drama.[70] He apparently had no idea that she was interested in politics and that, as she sees it, "a lot of what I heard from him had rubbed off." Zigas mother was also a model for her of female independence and strength. She was a nonpolitical businesswoman who supported her daughters' antiwar activism, even if she did not always understand or agree with it.

Although Zigas's interest in politics went back to 1948, she, like many of the other WSPers, had never been a political leader and had lost interest in politics in the 1950s. In those years she had been the prima ballerina of the New Youth Yiddish Arts Theater, an offshoot of the celebrated Maurice Schwartz Jewish Theater. Later she began to act, learning to speak Yiddish phonetically. She performed in *The Merchant of Venice*, which Schwartz called *Shylock's Daughters,* and played the wife of a Haganah leader in a work called *Land of Israel.* Zigas did not follow Schwartz to Hollywood because, as she explained, "I didn't have the drive to really climb over a lot of people." She eventually became a dance therapist and worked with schizophrenics for a number of years.

Zigas attributes her attraction to WSP to her admiration for the strength and "brilliance" of the women in the local leadership. Working with women had a strong appeal for her because of the mutual support and admiration they gave each other. Beset with domestic problems and responsibilities that would have engulfed most women, Zigas nevertheless carved out a role as national coordinator of all of WSP's antidraft activities. She set up headquarters in the "finished basement" of her home in Merrick, Long Island. With a mimeograph machine, a peace-item boutique, a library, and a literature distribution service, she turned her home into a WSP office and an early and primitive draft counseling center. Zigas's antidraft activity was so visible, so militant, and so committed that she was invited to run for the presidency of the

War Resisters League and was elected. This new role did not diminish her work in WSP, nor did her appointment as coordinator of the National Council for Unconditional Amnesty. Zigas, self-deprecating about her lack of "political education," attributes her rapid rise to national leadership in the antidraft movement to the guidance of women like Bernice Crane, who helped her develop the political insights and historical, rather than emotional, understanding of the Vietnam War that made it possible for her to become an effective speaker against the draft and the war. The more Zigas gained political confidence, the more obstacles—personal and political—she was able to overcome. "In the beginning of the antidraft movement," Zigas remembered, "we [WSP] were vilified. . . . The phone would ring day and night with crank calls. We were called Communists and traitors. It was a very difficult time. But we felt committed and we had to persevere." In many instances in the early days of antidraft activity, husbands were worried for their wives' safety or angry about the number of hours spent away from home, but most of the women resisted pressures to quit because they were committed to the young men whose lives were at stake and because draft counseling was a real, practical, and effective form of protest. Asked about her husband's and children's reactions to her nonstop WSP activities and the fact that in the earliest stages of draft counseling the center was located in her own home, Zigas responded, "They couldn't wait until it was all over."

She did not understand then what she now realizes, that at the height of her activity her children resented the lack of attention and her preoccupation with people and events outside the home. But as they grew into their teens and understood what kept Zigas from home, they became very supportive. She explained that her husband was at once extraordinarily admiring of her courage and perseverance and "extremely resentful of the fact that dinner was not ready."

The same ambivalence existed in other families. In most of the WSP homes that I knew, husbands and wives shared political outlooks. Because the men were too busy with their careers or feared the economic consequences of political dissent, they viewed their activist wives as their political surrogates, much as the rising class of businessmen in the early nineteenth century encouraged their wives to stand in for them in the church and in benevolent activities. The family conflicts engendered by WSP activities were usually not over political differences but about the division of childcare and domestic labor. Neglect of the household was not accepted by the husbands or even by the WSP women themselves, except in times of world-threatening emergency such as the Cuban missile crisis. Some women did drop out of full-time WSP activity because of husbands' frustration over tasks undone and deprivation of companionship. Although the movement's spokesperson Dagmar Wilson was one whose husband insisted that she "give up" her role as a WSP leader, pressure from husbands was not an issue addressed within WSP. In the days before the personal was identified as political, familial or marital conflict was considered an individual problem a woman had to handle on her own or live with.

Despite their frustration over being dragged to meetings and demonstrations when they were hungry and tired, Zigas believes in retrospect that her children received a meaningful political education by following her around and trying to understand what she was doing. Her stepson, Barry Zigas, shocked her when at the age of seventeen he left for Sweden to sign onto a ship preparing to run the Haiphong Harbor blockade. Zigas was irate when she learned that he had decided to risk his life without consulting his parents. He, on the other hand, argued that he had learned from her that to resist the war, and to act courageously and independently, was the highest good.

WSP's role in the resistance to the draft for Vietnam exemplifies women's age-old ability to carve out political space and power for themselves in a man's world by acting in the service of others. It also demonstrates that when women carry out a militant struggle against a patriarchal institution, such as the military state, they deepen their understanding of the many ways in which they are barred from political and personal power, and begin to question the cultural assumptions on which they had previously based their claim to political influence.

9

We Have Met the Enemy—and They Are Our Sisters!

We go to show the world that women are capable
of meeting together in spite of their country's killing each other in the field of battle. . . . Women
may be able to do what no government's can do,
pave the way to peace through the love and protection of their children.
—"The Toronto Pledge"

The founders of WSP had made clear in their first call to action that they were not interested in founding a new organization of any kind, but the national response convinced them that they had to keep the peace strike idea going. If they had so much as thought of it, they would have insisted that an international association was so far beyond their dreams, their capabilities, and their resources as to be out of the question. But again, the overwhelming and enthusiastic response from women abroad was so great and so gratifying that the founders were persuaded that the new WSP movement would have to act globally from time to time.[1] Pacifist women in Great Britain, who thought of the United States as the fortress of Cold War militarism and nuclear brinkmanship, were elated to learn that ordinary American women were challenging their government's foreign policy. Typical was a congratulatory telegram from writer Vera Brittain, scientist Dame Kathleen Lonsdale, and Committee for Nuclear Disarmament leader Diana Collins, wife of Canon Collins, the dean of St. Paul's Cathedral. "Your thrilling words," the three women proclaimed, "backed by more thrilling action leaves us breathless. Be assured that women in England support you."[2] From Frankfurt, Germany, came a letter from Olga, Prinzessin zur Lippe, sister of King Bernhard of the Netherlands. She wrote: "The example of the American . . . women gives us hope that our endeavor also would be successful in some way. We would welcome very much to hear your opinion about the way we are acting, and what we could do else."[3] From Asia Dr. M. Toma, president of the Japan

Woman's Union, which was affiliated with the pro-Soviet Women's International Democratic Federation (WIDF), expressed a political ethos similar to that of WSP. "We women of the world," she wrote, "should cooperate in securing a lasting peace regardless of political views. Without peace no prospect for the future."[4] The United Women's League of Burma wrote of its fear of a third world war and offered full support to WSP's "demonstration against war preparation."[5] This group was also affiliated with WIDF, but that does not seem to have concerned the WSP founders. Eleanor Garst explained that WSP refused to "join the anticommunist clamor" because it was "an unthinking hate chorus," which would "solve nothing."[6] Judith Cook, a young mother of four who was to become a great friend and ally of WSP, announced from her home in Cornwall that she agreed with every word of WSP's "Declaration on Disarmament" and that the motto of her new mothers' organization was "Let Women Join Hands around the World against This Monstrous Thing Which Is Poisoning Our Lives." Cook informed WSP that she had already begun to contact women in other countries, "particularly those behind the Iron Curtain," in an effort to "break down the barriers of fear and suspicion caused by our mutual ignorance and mistrust."[7]

Dagmar Wilson was also convinced that, if WSP were to succeed in a campaign to reverse the nuclear arms race, it would require the cooperation of women in the Soviet bloc, who would have to oppose their governments' nuclear policies. She was optimistic that women in the East would join with WSP because "women understand compromise and the need to learn to live together." In fact, all the founders hoped interaction between women of differing national interests and political ideologies, particularly in what was then called "the East and the West," would set an example for men, pointing the way to conflict resolution, not through shows of strength, but through mediation.[8]

At the end of WSP's first month Frances Herring, who was not only a key organizer in the Berkeley area but also a great influence on Wilson and the other Washington founders, sent a personal memorandum to all WSP contacts, announcing that the new movement was "going international" and that Ruth Gage-Colby, a WILPF leader and a member of the United Nations press corps, would coordinate international initiatives. This announcement, coming from California, raised no suspicions or objections among WSP women, probably because each group felt that it could chose to accept or ignore international proposals as it saw fit. Shortly afterward Gage-Colby issued a rhapsodic communication, proclaiming that WSP had become "WISP," Women's International Strike for Peace. "Spoken aloud it sounds like the wind, and like the wind it is spreading."[9] There was little enthusiasm in the new movement for a new name, and most groups chose to continue to call them-

selves WSP or WFP (Women for Peace). Only Los Angeles and the national office in Washington adopted the WISP appellation.

Gage-Colby had apparently been chosen by Wilson and Herring to
act as coordinator because she had been active in international peace
circles for many years and worked at the United Nations as an accredited correspondent. As a result she was well acquainted with political
leaders and international bureaucrats all over the world. Her affiliation
with the United Nations went back to its founding meeting in 1948, to
which she was invited as an observer by the State Department. She
explained in an interview in 1980 that the invitation had come to her
because of her expertise on child welfare and health delivery systems.
Her competence in these areas was developed in the 1920s when she
and her pediatrician husband were responsible for establishing well-
baby clinics all over the Midwest. After the founding of the United Nations, Gage-Colby was employed by UNICEF in Cairo and other parts of
the Middle East. In the 1950s she worked in Indochina and the People's
Republic of China. "I was in Hanoi and in Saigon, and then I was even
in Shanghai, working in a program with . . . Mme Sun Yat Sen," she
recalled. After Gage-Colby suffered a heart attack in the 1950s and was
no longer permitted by her physician to work in the field, she decided
to become a free-lance United Nations correspondent.[10]

In 1961, when she joined forces with WSP, Gage-Colby was separated from her husband and living in New York City in a small pent-
house overlooking United Nations headquarters and the East River. She
seemed to possess enough independent income to permit her to work
without pay for the causes she endorsed and to go anywhere in the
world that her wishes, invitations, and schedule dictated. Gage-Colby
lived modestly, fasted every Friday in observance of her pacifist
Gandhian principles, and worked tirelessly as a peace orator, for which
she had a remarkable talent. She was the mother of one son, who,
ironically, was a U.S. Navy officer stationed at Annapolis. Although
mother and son differed politically, Gage-Colby visited her son and
grandchildren frequently.

Gage-Colby became associated with New York WSP at its very first
demonstration. From the window of the United Nations press room, she
saw a group of women marching outside the U.S. Mission to the United
Nations with banners calling for an end to the arms race, and as she put
it, "naturally I rushed out to join." In one week's time Gage-Colby had
become a key woman and the featured platform speaker at a rally of
five thousand women at the United Nations, which took place on 7
November 1961. Gage-Colby's declaration, "We are one people. We are
the human race. We all have the same ultimate goals," eloquently expressed the views of the founders of WSP and the New York women

who gathered outside the United Nations to demand an end to the nuclear arms race.

Gage-Colby also shared with the founders of WSP a disdain for Cold
War anticommunism. She supported cooperation and peace with the
USSR and evenhandedly condemned both nuclear powers for their
reckless endangerment of the planet. Her politics confused some
WSPers because she traveled frequently in the Soviet bloc countries and
at the same time maintained close connections with Cold Warriors such
as Herbert Hoover and Hubert Humphrey. Asked how she managed to
transcend Cold War barriers and ideological boundaries to maintain her
"establishment" connections, she replied: "I feel very much a world citizen. I have no feeling of being an American. That sounds disloyal, but
I've lived on this level of international contacts, international thinking
and programs for so long that I don't think of myself as an American
woman."

Gage-Colby was born in Olivia, Minnesota, a rural county seat,
where her father was a federal judge and a "rabid Republican." Her
mother was a high school teacher in her youth but took on the full-time
role of housewife and mother after marriage, and "she didn't go in for
movements at all." When I asked what brought Gage-Colby into antiwar activism when it was clearly something her family disdained, she
answered: "I was a born pacifist. I came from a family where there had
been service in the . . . Confederate Army and the Union Army, so I
knew the story of the Civil War from both sides, and I grew up hating
war, the terrible things it had done to my ancestors." One of the important events in Gage-Colby's life, of which she was most proud, was her
role in organizing a 1915 protest by the girls in her high school in western Minnesota against the sending of a group of male classmates on a
"military excursion in Mexico." "Several of the young men who were
sent were never seen again," she recalled, because they went on to join
the American Expeditionary Force in France and were killed there, or
died on the way back of the wartime influenza. A young man in whom
Gage-Colby was "very much interested" died on Armistice Day in the
Ardennes Forest, and she said the memory stayed with her.

Gage-Colby recalled that she joined WILPF in 1920 in Vienna, where
she was living with her husband, who was completing his medical training. WILPF had been founded in 1919 and did not yet have a U.S. section when Gage-Colby joined. Until the end of her life, she remained an
active member of WILPF. In 1928 she decided to break with her family's
ties to the Republican party and voted for Al Smith for president. She
did this because she valued Smith's social programs "for the people." "I
always had this feeling for protecting the weak," she recalled. "If a horse

was being beaten, I would just walk right up to the man who beat the horse, and tell him that I would beat him if he didn't stop."

In 1929 Gage-Colby ran for the state senate in Minnesota on a program that called for a better deal for women, more women in politics, and more women in public office. She lost by what she asserts was "only a very few votes, perhaps five." According to her recollection, her backers urged a recount, but she decided against it. She told me that it was because a recount would have been too expensive and might have ended in a victory for her opponent, as the difference was so small. She never considered running for political office again, "because you have to listen to a lot of people who want you to do things for them." Being controlled by a party or an organization was impossible for her. When I met Gage-Colby in late 1961 she was a free spirit, a passionate and poetic orator, a pacifist preacher, willing to work with any group that appealed to her conscience and used her talents, but very much her own person, resistant to organizational discipline.

Gage-Colby was an anti-Fascist long before the United States declared war on Hitler's Germany. Her opposition to the Nazi persecution of the Jews was manifested in her efforts, along with those of her husband, to bring the distinguished Jewish pediatrician Bela Schick out of Fascist Austria. Through the influence of her husband, who was by then a member of the faculty of the University of Minnesota Medical School, she was able to procure an appointment for Schick, who subsequently made a distinguished career in the United States. Despite her opposition to nazism, she worked with WILPF in 1940 "trying to keep America out of war" and helping to save victims of the war in Europe. She brought the two children of pacifist author Vera Brittain from London to live with her family in Minnesota to protect them from the Blitz.

Gage-Colby opposed the internment of Japanese-Americans during the war, an infringement on civil liberties and human decency that WILPF opposed, but one that many liberals and old-left radicals failed to address at the time. She recognized it as "a manifestation of racism, something I abhorred." "I went to Washington," she reminisced, "to talk it over with my friend Hubert Humphrey." After he acknowledged that her assessment of the situation was "absolutely right," she asked him to help her to found a program to get Japanese women out of the camps. Men could be freed if they were willing to join the U.S. Army, but women could be released only if they had jobs to go to, and at that time jobs were hard to come by for people of Japanese descent. According to Gage-Colby's recollection, Hubert Humphrey helped her to open a government-sponsored employment service for Japanese women in Minneapolis and St. Paul. Even in the anti-Japanese climate of World War II,

Gage-Colby and her colleagues managed to find employment for Japanese women, not only as domestics, but as nurses and office workers. Through this service Gage-Colby made so many Japanese friends that she was invited to Japan after the war and became a frequent guest of the Japanese peace movement until the end of her life.

It was her energetic and optimistic internationalism, her personal contacts, her freedom to travel at will, but most of all her eloquence that made Ruth Gage-Colby an ideal WSP leader in the early years. However, her inclination to make political and tactical decisions based only on her own religious and moral convictions, without prior consultation with the other key women in WSP, later brought the criticism that eventually drove her out of the front ranks of WSP. She viewed her departure from WSP without rancor. "I just had too much to do at the United Nations. I'm not especially an organization person. I felt I . . . gave it what I could at the beginning. . . . I'm not a joiner. . . . I like to be an independent person."

Working with the New York and Washington WSP chapters, Gage-Colby organized WSP's first international action, only six weeks after the national strike. It was a coordinated series of peace marches, rallies, visitations to public officials, and press conferences held on 15 January 1962 in the United States and in cities all over the world that was organized in the same informal manner as the 1 November peace strike. Women from various parts of the United States who had participated in the strike undertook to make contacts abroad as individuals and as part of a task force working out of the national office. Some of the women they contacted in Europe, Africa, and Asia responded by organizing meetings and marches in their own communities. The largest demonstration in this new international network, and the most visible in terms of press coverage, took place in the United States. It consisted of a picket line of three thousand women, who marched outside the White House gate. At a time when peace protest was rarely seen or heard in the United States, this gathering, which called for an end to atomic testing and the nuclear arms race, was recognized by the media as a major outburst of female concern and opposition to U.S. military policies. Journalist I. F. Stone described it as a "most moving experience to march with the women in a fierce and chilly rainstorm," and to follow them to a rally where "cables were read from similar meetings in London, Paris, Brussels, Rome, Vienna, Sydney, Calcutta, Stockholm, Montreal, both Berlins, Sofia, Budapest, Tokyo, and a woman's group in the Soviet Union."[11]

This international demonstration, which amazed its organizers by its size and impact, was acknowledged by President John Kennedy, who told the nation at a press conference that day, "I saw the ladies myself.

I recognized why they were here. There were a great number of them, it was in the rain. I understand what they were attempting to say. Therefore I consider their message received."[12]

Suspecting that the forthcoming negotiations to end nuclear testing were something the media would ignore unless they were dramatized and cast in human terms, the New York group conceived the idea that WSP move its point of pressure from Washington to Geneva, from the White House to the Palais des Nations, where the Conference of the Seventeen-Nation Committee on Disarmament was to commence its deliberations two months later, in March 1962.[13] WSP demanded that women be appointed to the U.S. negotiating team, hoping that this innovation would draw world attention to the deliberations. When the proposal was ignored by Kennedy and Khrushchev, WSP determined that, if women could not participate inside the bargaining sessions, they would make their presence felt outside.[14] In less than two months the new movement organized a delegation of fifty women, who flew to Geneva to lobby the disarmament conference.

Even conservative journalist Midge Decter grudgingly admitted that WSP had displayed a high level of initiative and competence in carrying out its first venture abroad. "For an organization so new, even though so enthusiastic, to have sparked the local raising of fifty times $350.00 fare was no mean feat," Decter acknowledged in an article on WSP in *Harper's*. It should be noted, however, that the movement's ability to raise so much money in so short a short time and to locate fifty eloquent and well-informed "housewife" leaders, ready and able to make the trip to Geneva, was due not only to the energy, passion, and competence of the organizers but also to their affluence. Hundreds of women in the WSP leadership possessed the discretionary funds for the phone calls, the plane and train fares, and the childcare, without which this volunteer organization could not have executed its spontaneous and dashing direct actions. Supportive husbands also helped to make the Geneva delegation a reality. Two young housewives with small children, Joan Mendelssohn and Ellen Polshek of New York City, devoted approximately twenty hours a day to making travel arrangements for the Geneva delegation. They gave up everything else in their lives for three weeks, while their husbands and parents cared for their children. With no previous experience in this area, they managed in a professional manner to handle passport problems, plane and hotel reservations, and the collection of briefing materials for the fifty women from different parts of the United States who made up the delegation. That these women were possessed of exceptional talent is also true. Ellen Polshek is now an attorney and her husband, James, the baby-sitter, is a world-renowned architect.

The fifty women who flew to Geneva came from the states where WSP had taken hold. New York, California, and Washington, D.C., had the highest representation. But there were also women from Connecticut, Florida, Georgia, Illinois, Louisiana, Massachusetts, Michigan, New Hampshire, New Jersey, Pennsylvania, Vermont, and Wisconsin. Included in the WSP delegation to Geneva were two African-American women: Coretta Scott King, who was joining WSP for the first time, and Clarie Harvey, a churchwoman from Louisiana. Almost all the delegates identified themselves as mothers, a few as working mothers. Several were grandmothers. A press release from New York stated that the delegation included a "ballet dancer, a photographer, a secretary, a fashion merchandiser, a painter, a psychiatric researcher, a teacher, a Ph.D. candidate, a radio broadcaster, a nurse, and many housewives." Whether intentionally or not, the medical doctor and the lawyer in the group were unmentioned. Also included in the delegation were two survivors of the major tragedies of their time: Katherine Massey, a Japanese-American from Brooklyn who lived near Hiroshima at the time of the atom bombing, died of leukemia shortly after the Geneva lobby; Frieda Aaron of the Bronx lived through the Warsaw ghetto uprising and was incarcerated in a Nazi concentration camp. One delegate was Anne Eaton, the wife of industrialist Cyrus Eaton, a proponent of East-West détente and trade. Her international contacts were invaluable to WSP.

A carefully staged send-off for the Geneva delegates was calculated to attract the press, and it did. WSP succeeded in having its mission to Geneva on behalf of a nuclear test ban treaty covered in newspapers across the country with circulations totaling millions. Feature stories about the individual women in the delegation appeared in their hometown papers, along with their statements on the nuclear emergency and the sense of urgency that moved them to action. Many newspapers reprinted the text of the petition the women were taking to Geneva. At a time when the public knew little about the dangers of nuclear testing or of the possibility of a treaty with the Russians, the women were elated that they were getting their message heard.

WSP was a visible and audible presence in Geneva in March 1962, in the streets, in the hotels, and at the Palais des Nations, which I. F. Stone described as "a den of plain and fancy prevaricators, playing games Geneva has come to know so well over the years." According to Stone, "there descended, a delegation of 50 American women on a Quixotical mission, somehow to reach the hearts and minds of the diplomats of the great powers. The U.S. government should have paid their fares, for they gave the outside world a glimpse of America not often discernible in our official representatives, and more to our country's credit."[15]

The WSPers flew into Geneva without a single confirmed appointment with any diplomat or arms negotiator. Yet in four days, largely through the efforts of Lorraine Gordon of New York, who spent most of her time in Geneva on the telephone, the women managed to talk with each of the eighteen participating delegations at least once, and several times with Arthur Dean of the United States and Valerian Zorin of the Soviet Union, the cochairmen of the conference. As they began to lobby the diplomats, the women found that most of the ambassadors from the "nonaligned" nations believed that the main obstacle to a reversal of the nuclear arms race was the mutual suspicion and tension between the nuclear powers. Some of the WSPers wept with frustration and discouragement as they came face to face with the actuality of U.S. and Russian intransigence. They began to refer to Zorin's and Dean's defense of their own country's positions as "the Cold War broken record." After a session with Ambassador Dean, Dagmar Wilson told a *New York Times* reporter that Dean's insistence that "it was all a matter of security," was a form of reasoning, "we women find it very hard to understand." The situation was similar with Zorin.

At a meeting with Zorin in which he blamed the United States for the nuclear impasse and refused to budge, I recall that I stood up and, pointing to my bulging abdomen (I was pregnant with my fourth child), demanded to know if the political stalemate was sufficient cause to endanger the health and possibly the life of the baby I was carrying, and the countless children yet to be born. I don't remember his answer, but he seemed to be visibly shaken. I realize that it was not only the proliferation of strontium 90 and the contamination of milk by iodine 131 that I was challenging, but also the immorality and carelessness of the so-called socialist leaders, who claimed to rule not for profits but for the well-being of ordinary citizens. I remember that particular confrontation with a representative Soviet power as one of the most significant moments of my life, not because I influenced Zorin—I certainly did not—but because in speaking truth to power, I experienced a moment of freedom from my own feelings of powerlessness as a woman and a citizen. I suspect that the other WSPers had similar experiences as they each had an opportunity to voice their fears and anger to Dean and Zorin.

The interaction of the WSP women, many of whom had never met each other before, was the most extraordinary aspect of the Geneva protest. The WSP delegation came from different parts of the country and from different political orientations. As representatives of their local groups they were not committed to any mutually agreed-upon set of principles, as the four-month-old movement had not yet had time to formulate them. Operating far from home, under the glare of klieg lights and cameras, in an international arena in which diplomats and journalists were seeking any excuse to dismiss them as hysterical women, the delegation pondered long and hard on each of its public actions. Some of the WSPers argued that an international setting required extreme caution, subtlety, and as much professionalism as could be mustered, while others thought of Geneva as the perfect site for guerrilla theater. What prevented the development of serious disagreements, distrust, and disgruntled minorities was the decision by the Washington leadership to arrive at all decisions by consensus. This meant that no votes were taken and no actions were agreed upon unless every woman present could live with the decision. Achieving consensus involved hours and hours of discussion, relieved by periods of silence for soul searching and meditation. Eleanor Garst, employing Quaker meeting techniques, was a masterful, nondirective chairperson. She allowed every woman's opinion and feelings to be heard. Each person felt validated in a way that magnified the energy and creativity of all. The New York women, most of whom had never experienced a Quaker meeting, were euphoric. We were learning to listen in a nonoppositional fashion and for the first time those of us who had been ignored by the liberal or old-left organizations to which we had belonged felt that we were heard and appreciated. The consensus method was used in the preparation of a joint statement with the women who had come to Geneva join WSP from Austria, Canada, France, Great Britain, Norway, Sweden, Switzerland, the USSR, and West Germany.

An example of the optimism, creativity, and naïveté characteristic of WSP at this time was the decision made by American women to ask President Kennedy to disarm a U.S. military base near the Soviet Union and transform it into a center for cultural exchange.[16] The proposal came from Mary Grooms of Rochester, New York. After hearing Arthur Dean tell the women repeatedly that the major obstacle to a test ban agreement was Soviet suspicion of the United States, she decided that WSP should make an effort to diminish Russian distrust.[17] Grooms then cornered Semyon K. Tsarapkin of the Soviet delegation to ask him why the Russians were so fearful, and he replied that it was because the Soviet Union was surrounded by American military bases in thirty-three countries. Grooms asked, "Tell me, if we women could talk our government into closing down some of those bases, would that help?" According to Grooms, Tsarapkin answered with alacrity, "One. Just one would give us faith."

Although Kennedy refused a request for a meeting with WSP representatives to discuss the Geneva mission, even after a week-long round-the-clock vigil at the White House, he was eventually forced to face the missile base proposal. A reporter asked Kennedy at his 18 April press conference: "A Soviet delegate to the disarmament conference at Geneva told representatives of Women Strike for Peace that Russia would negotiate a nuclear test ban treaty if the United States would close down just one of its missile bases overseas as a gesture of good faith. When the women reported this to Ambassador Dean, he suggested they refer the proposal to you. Would you give us your view, sir?" "I never heard that proposal made by the Soviet Union," Kennedy replied. "In other words they would agree—" he sputtered, "as suggested—well, now I don't think you can read the letter of the Chairman Premier Khrushchev to the Prime Minister Macmillan and get that impression." For once, Kennedy stammered. "There's no—we have never heard that they would agree to an effective test ban—an inspection system—if we would close down one base, in my judgement there's no evidence for believing they would." But the reporter insisted that Tsarapkin had suggested it to "these private people." Kennedy then promised that Dean would be glad to ask if this is so but that, in his judgment, based on all previous negotiations, there was no evidence that the Russians would be moved by the dismantling of a base.[18] This exchange was considered a triumph by the powerless women of WSP, because it had brought the negotiations in Geneva to international public attention, showing that ordinary women could make themselves heard in foreign policy debates.

As the days went by in Geneva, the WSP delegates, as they called themselves, grew tired, depressed, and frustrated by the slow pace of the negotiations and their own lack of impact. Shortly before their departure the WSPers debated how to inject some drama and a sense of urgency into the lackluster proceedings. They decided to stage a silent, illegal, two-mile march of women from the center of the city to the Palais des Nations. WSP had been warned by the peace bureaucrats in Geneva that protest demonstrations were illegal and that marchers would be stopped and arrested. The women decided to take the risk, and as it turned out, nobody barred their way. Upon reaching the Palais, they stood in silent vigil, expecting to remain there all day. However, after fifteen minutes at the gate they were invited inside in what the *New York Herald Tribune* called "an unprecedented breach of United Nations regulations."[19] The women, whose ranks had swelled to 103, including not only Americans and the women from Europe and the USSR who had come to meet them but also Swiss women, for whom this protest was most risky, continued their silent, disciplined vigil for another hour and a half in a conference room of the Palais. Finally, in another breach of the regulations, the cochairmen, Dean and Zorin, agreed to interrupt their proceedings to meet with the delegation. As Arthur Dean and Valerian Zorin entered the conference room where the women awaited them, Honey Knopp, a Quaker activist from Connecticut and the chief organizer of the march to the Palais, reminded the diplomats of the human consequences of their deliberations by addressing them not as ambassadors, but as "Fathers Dean and Zorin," and introducing the protesters as the "grandmothers and mothers of the world."[20] The women presented their petitions, which were accepted with the promise of serious consideration.[21] Dagmar Wilson scolded the negotiators: "You are constantly concerned with national security, national sovereignty, national prestige. All these outmoded ideas must be abandoned. . . . In your hands lies the fate of the human race. We have one great concern—our children."[22]

The Geneva delegation stopped in London on its way home, to receive an enthusiastic welcome from the British peace movement. The WSPers spoke at a public meeting in Conway Hall and at a reception at the House of Commons. A British woman who attended the reception for WSP wrote to the Washington office,

> I left the House of Commons, [where Dagmar Wilson had been the speaker] and made my way home humming the "Star Spangled Banner." I swear that you were the best ambassadors of goodwill your country has ever sent here, and your message did a tremendous lot to help eradicate the inherent antagonism which has grown up in this country to all things American since 1945.[23]

Diana Collins, who had joined the WSP women in Geneva, wrote to Dagmar Wilson: "I think that the week at Geneva was one of the most worthwhile and encouraging efforts I have ever taken part in. I can't tell you how grateful we are to you all for having initiated it. . . . Women Strike for Peace and Geneva have given us all a tremendous new boost of encouragement and hope."[24]

After the Geneva action, WSP's reputation for international activism brought it invitations to peace conferences both in the nonaligned countries and in the Soviet bloc. Whether or not to participate in these meetings, in which the WSPers would have little influence or control, was hotly debated. An invitation to the Accra Assembly for the World without a Bomb in July 1962 was accepted without any dissent by the first national conference in June, but an invitation from the Soviet Women's Committee to an international peace conference in Moscow provoked a different response. Although Dagmar Wilson and Margaret Russell, two of the Washington founders, had accepted the invitation without question, there were many women in WSP who believed that accepting Russian hospitality was inappropriate for a nonaligned peace group, because it would subject WSP to Red baiting and undermine its credibility.

Helen Klein and Helen Wurf of the Bronx spoke for those who rejected cooperation with the Russians because of their repressive domestic and foreign policies.

> Although peace and universal disarmament . . . are part of our concern, "peaceful coexistence" is not. To believe so is to misunderstand the tyranny and suppression that lie behind the phrase, to forget the brutal Soviet suppression of Hungary's fight for national liberation, to forget the gruesome conditions of life in the Siberian camps, and to fall, wittingly or not, into the role of supporting Soviet policy.[25]

Shirley Lens, a key women in Chicago who along with her husband, the pacifist socialist trade unionist Sidney Lens, was an outspoken critic of Soviet policies from a left perspective and cautioned that the movement take care "not to become partisan either in the Cold War or in the arms race." But Lens did not object to meetings with Russian women if it could lead toward disarmament. A proponent of unilateral actions by the United States to halt the arms race, Lens urged, not without a touch of irony, that WSP suggest a series of unilateral initiatives to the Soviet Union, including the renunciation of all future nuclear tests, and the opening of Soviet newspaper columns to American writers.[26] Replying to a letter from Mary Sharmat of the Women's Direct Action Project in New York City, who was firmly opposed to a WSP visit to Moscow, Wilson acknowledged that there was so much opposition to participation in a Russian conference that she had withdrawn her early acceptance and would await the decision of the forthcoming national conference.[27]

Wilson was apparently so pressured regarding the decision to accept the Russians' invitation that she consulted the U.S. National Security Council regarding the wisdom of accepting Soviet hospitality: specifically, whether such an acceptance would limit the women's free expression of their own opinions and ideas. Samuel E. Belk of the Special Staff replied that he had sounded out all those in the government "who would be intelligently responsive" to her questions and concluded that "exchange visits are a good thing—definitely." Belk pointed out, however, that the Soviet Women's Committee was an "instrumentality of the Soviet state," and if that group was paying WSP expenses, there would be an obligation to follow its program. Belk advised that WSP should be especially cautious not to be in Moscow during 8–15 July, "since a Communist-led World Congress on General Disarmament and Peace will be meeting." This was the very conference to which WSP had been invited. He urged that Wilson discuss the subject further with Sophia Jacobs, president of the National Council of Women. Somebody in Washington WSP, not Wilson, penciled the following remark on the letter next to the suggestions that WSP contact the NCW: "Is not this an instrumentality of the U.S. State?"[28]

Wilson replied that WSP was not about to sign documents "with which we do not agree." She cited the statement of Madame Khimatch, cultural attaché at the Soviet embassy in Washington, D.C., to the effect that the Soviet Women's Committee was a nongovernmental voluntary organization, supported by its 309,000 members through their unions, and that additional support came from the sale of the magazine *Soviet Woman.* This was naïve, as the Soviet Woman's Committee, which called itself a nongovernmental organization, admitted quite openly that it "works in active cooperation with the standing commissions of the USSR Supreme Soviet." It also claimed in a prospectus to have the right to initiate legislation. In fact, in the post-*perestroika* period, it readily admitted that it received its money for exchange visits from the state through the Soviet Peace Committee and that these funds were in short supply. Wilson concluded her letter agreeing to heed the State Department's warnings but asserting that the women were "determined to approach the international situation without prejudice, and with the conviction that a means of communicating with socialist countries must be found."[29]

The first national WSP conference in June 1962 agreed to send a delegation to Moscow, but only after heated debate could a consensus be achieved. Eventually the women agreed to a resolution proposed by the Los Angeles women, stating, "If fear, distrust, and hatred are ever to be lessened, it will be by courageous individuals who do not hate and fear, and can get together to make tolerable compromises. This is a role women should be particularly equipped to play."

WSP women were now encouraged to attend any and all international meetings of peace groups, on the grounds that "one can only influence policy and decisions by taking part in them."[30] Elise Boulding of Ann Arbor added another dimension to the discussion on interaction and cooperation with women in the East. "We go as ourselves," she wrote, "and we come back something more than ourselves, for we, and our counterparts in whatever land we visit, will have experienced mutual growth."[31]

Sharmat, Klein, Wurf, and the women with whom they worked were so put off by the decision to go to Moscow that they left the ranks of WSP. There were probably many others who left over the decision to work on a nonoppositional basis with the Russians. There were no lists of defections, however, as there was no official WSP organization from which one could resign.[32]

The decisions regarding who among the WSP women should represent WSP on its first Russian visit were also fraught with conflict. Hazy recollections of the demise of the Congress of American Women in 1950 may have contributed to the fears expressed by some that WSPers might make innocent statements that could be construed as pro-Soviet or anti-American and thus injure the entire movement. Wilson, basing her opinion on notions of female superiority, assured the doubters that WSP's woman's intuition would save it from ideological partisanship or other blunders. "Although some of you may be looking at us askance we have confidence in ourselves. We represent a variety of occupations, come from different racial backgrounds and from the North, South, East, and West. Whatever we do and wherever we go we will let our instincts guide us to the right actions as circumstances indicate."[33] There were pitfalls, nevertheless. According to a report in the *New York Post,* Wilson stirred up an "official ruckus" in Moscow by stating, at a joint news conference with the Soviet Women's Committee, that Nina Khrushchev had assured her that Soviet women were opposed to nuclear tests.[34] She was forced to withdraw this statement when Khrushchev's translator jumped to her feet to insist that Khrushchev had never uttered such words. Wilson conceded politely that she might have been in error, but she maintained that Khrushchev had declared that "women everywhere" were against nuclear tests. The WSPers considered it a triumph that they succeeded in drafting a joint statement with the Soviet women calling for "an agreement on the part of our own governments, and the governments of all countries, for general and complete disarmament under strict international control as proclaimed by the United Nations."[35] The joint statement, which followed neither the Soviet nor the U.S. official position, promised that the women of both countries would make every effort to educate their children and youth in the spirit of humanism and friendship.

The tension that threatened to split the movement abated as the women realized that the mission to Moscow had not destroyed their movement. Eleanor Garst, who had been skeptical about the Soviet visit, was prompted to comment: "Past criticism of foreign visitations was based on an assumption that America's innocent and naive women are going to swallow every piece of Soviet propaganda unwittingly, and promote the interests of the Soviet Union, while the wily Soviet women know exactly what they are doing, and use the Americans as tools to gain a communist world."[36] "It is conceivable," she suggested, "that communist women are learning something quite new from WSP." Although the WSP women never wavered in their opposition to Soviet nuclear policies, they were very favorably impressed by the quality of life in the Soviet Union, never recognizing in their written reports that they spoke only with trusted party people and traveled only where invited. In a report of the visit to Moscow, Wilson expressed what she called her "first impressions": "I believe that the Soviet citizen is just as satisfied with his form of Government as we are with ours. The Soviet economy is sound and expanding: luxury consumer goods are becoming more available each year. Russians are optimistic about their future—as long as there is peace."[37] WSPers continued to visit Moscow, choosing to act as observers, not delegates to international conferences, so that they would not be held responsible for resolutions over which they could have no influence. Nevertheless, Associated Press reported that the WSPers present at an international women's conference in Moscow in June 1963 had failed to walk out of the conference as right-thinking Americans should have done, in response to anti-American speeches by Cuban and Japanese delegates. The *New York Post* criticized WSP sharply in an editorial called "Ladies' Days in Moscow." Referring to the militant demonstrations at the conference by Chinese women who disagreed with the Soviet party line, the *Post* commented: "We wish the American delegation had displayed comparable valor and spirit in pressing unorthodox views that might have challenged both the Soviet and Chinese girls."[38] The fact is that the majority of the women in WSP were evenhanded in their moral condemnation of military policies in the East as well as the West. Although most WSPers, in an unconscious form of national arrogance or of left imperialism, saw the United States as the most powerful military power in the world, and thus the greatest threat to peace. WSP did, however, protest military decisions and interventions by Vietnam and the Soviet Union as well as the United States. The New York group demonstrated at the United Nations in protest against the Soviet intervention in Czechoslovakia in 1968. They carried placards that compared the Soviet action in Prague with that of the United States in Vietnam. A press statement issued by the Washington office declared, "It is too late for people on this small planet to impose the rule of force upon each other . . . as our military leaders have in Vietnam; people power is stronger than guns, tanks or bombs." An indignant letter was dispatched to the Soviet Women's Committee stating,

> Your condemnation of the United States involvement in Vietnam has always implied to us your condemnation of all attempts by military powers to use that power to control or to repress attempts of other countries to determine their own future. We have consistently opposed our government's aggression in Vietnam. . . . So, for the same reasons, we must condemn the military intervention in Czechoslovakia by your government's troops.[39]

This letter was signed by Dagmar Wilson of Washington, Ethel Taylor of Philadelphia, Mary Clarke of Los Angeles, and Cora Weiss of New York.

While there is no evidence of the reaction of the Soviet Women's Committee to the condemnation of their government's action, it was very much appreciated by the Committee of Czechoslovak Women, who wrote to WSP: "We have been very pleased by your expression of solidarity. . . . we hope that the situation in our country will be settled so that we can live here according to our imaginations and with all our forces to support the strengthening of peace and understanding among nations."[40] Not every woman in WSP agreed with the condemnation of the Soviet Union. Gertrude Leavin, who was a strong supporter of all Soviet policies and of the American Communist party, issued a statement that asserted:

> There are many of us in New York City WSP who find ourselves completely out of sympathy with both the statement re: Czech-Soviet Affairs, content of statement, haste with which it was drawn up, character of demonstration at UN. We may not accord to anyone who so chooses the privilege of speaking for the entire group with authority, inadequate information, political ignorance, etc. and must ask that steps be taken to see that such a situation is not repeated.[41]

Leavin was one of the New York women who had advocated tight organizational structure. It is my impression, although I cannot prove it, that those women who were still active in the Communist party were the most avid proponents of structure, with which they were all too familiar. They found it hard to live with WSP's undisciplined spontaneity and their lack of control over WSP's pronouncements regarding the USSR.

One of the ongoing internal disputes concerning international operations was caused, not by Cold War considerations, but by what some women perceived as the unfair and unequal way foreign delegations were organized. Women from Washington, New York, and California monopolized international assignments because they had more opportunities to meet international diplomats and bureaucrats, at embassy receptions and cultural events, who then extended personal invitations to them. To insure more inclusive participation by all areas and all women, the second national conference created an International Clearing House in Evanston, Illinois, close to a university where translators would be available. The ICH was to receive and transmit all international invitations to regional groups. The groups were asked to chose suitable local women to become part of a pool of potential international representatives. The actual representatives for a particular occasion would then be chosen by lottery. This idea conformed to the WSP notion that all WSP women were potential leaders and that a "true WSPer could be counted on to express herself in the appropriate WSP manner and language at any time and in any place."

In April 1963, one year after the Geneva lobby and demonstration, WSP organized a pilgrimage to Rome in support of Pope John XXIII's encyclical *Pacem in Terris*. The notion of a pilgrimage to Pope John appealed not only to the Catholic women in WSP, but also to the Protestants and agnostics, who were moved by the pope's sincerity, leadership, and spiritual energy and who wanted to associate themselves with his moral authority.

The Rome pilgrimage was organized and coordinated by two New England WSPers, Virginia Naeve of Vermont and Alice Pollard of New Hampshire. Both women had been part of the Geneva delegation and had seen the potential of international demonstrations for raising peace consciousness at home as well as abroad. Hedwig Turkenkopf, a key woman from New Jersey, also helped organize the pilgrimage. Turkenkopf had a long career in public service on behalf of women. During World War II she had established a personnel department at Grumman Aircraft, through which eight thousand women were hired for war work in eight plants. Turkenkopf had also served as the first woman mayor of Cedar Grove, New Jersey. She, too, had been with the WSPers in Geneva, as had Clarie Harvey from Louisiana, who joined the pilgrimage to Rome. These women were accomplished organizers and effective lobbyists, and had a flair for public relations.[42] Among the non-WSPers who participated in the Rome pilgrimage were the well-known lay Catholic leader Dorothy Day, editor of the *Catholic Worker;* Katherine Camp, who was later to become international president of WILPF; Theresa Casgrain of Montreal, president of Voice of Women (VOW) of Canada; and Lucille Rubio de Laverde, president of the Latin American section of WILPF, who described herself as "one of the first Columbian women to work for equal rights." A Japanese woman who was both a survivor of Hiroshima and a Catholic also joined the pilgrimage, as did Bea Herrick, a pacifist activist who had participated in the peace walk from San Francisco to Moscow in 1960. WSP made little of Day's presence in the delegation, possibly because the organizers were not Catholic and knew little of her work or stature as a Catholic leader, or possibly because they thought she was too radical and might be not be in favor at the Vatican. Day reported in the *Catholic Worker:* "It is . . . a true pilgrimage, to the Holy City of Rome, to the head of the Church, and for us Catholics, to the representative of Christ on Earth, to present ourselves as though a first fruit of his great encyclical *Pacem in Terris,* to thank him, to pledge ourselves to work for peace, and to ask too, a more radical condemnation of the instruments of modern warfare."[43] *Madre per la Pace,* the journal put together after the pilgrimage, reported that the pilgrims to Rome, like the Geneva lobbyists, received a good deal of publicity and a warm response from like-minded European women. Although the group did not succeed in arranging a private audience with the pope, they were heartened by his recognition of their presence in a general audience and by his appeal to all the pilgrims to work for peace. The women staged a march in Rome, as they had in Geneva, which according to peace press reports was "the first-ever pacifist march in the city."[44] At the end of their stay in Rome the peace pilgrims were pleased to see their words "Madre per la Pace" painted across many public buildings. They traveled to Geneva for an all-night vigil at the Palais des Nations and a short meeting with secretary general U Thant. Their most important work in influencing U.S. women was accomplished on their return, when they were interviewed by local newspapers and television and addressed thousands of women at community meetings.

Typical of the pilgrims to Rome was Dorothy Weedon of Concord, New Hampshire, who told the *Concord Daily Monitor* that all the U.S. pilgrims to Rome were mothers and that their "Madre" badges, which they all wore, had attracted a sympathetic response from people of all walks of life, from taxi drivers to government officials in both Italy and Switzerland. She expressed the gratitude of "all" the pilgrims to their husbands, who had demonstrated their support by their willingness to look after their families while their wives were abroad.[45] Whether this was true of all the husbands and wives did not matter. Weedon had projected the image favored by WSP of a responsible and proper, yet politically radical and militant, mother and wife.

In 1964 WSP organized a massive multinational women's rally and conference in the Hague in opposition to a NATO plan for a multilateral nuclear fleet (MLF). I remember being present at a meeting of the New York CCC when Helen Frumin of Scarsdale, New York, the WSP representative to the nongovernmental organizations (NGOs) at the United Nations, informed us that leading representatives of the "nonaligned" nations were deeply concerned about a NATO proposal for a nuclear fleet. The NATO proposal, conceived by the United States, had already received enthusiastic support from West Germany, Italy, Belgium, Britain, Greece, Turkey, and the Netherlands, according to Frumin's informants. When the WSP women looked into the matter, they learned that plans for MLF mandated that each of the NATO powers, including West Germany and Turkey, share information and decision making regarding the use of the Polaris missiles with which the fleet was to be equipped. The WSPers, upon hearing that German fingers might come near the nuclear button, jumped into action.[46] The New York and Washington leadership proposed that women of all the NATO powers unite to forestall this new proliferation of nuclear weapons. WSP issued an invitation to the women of all the NATO nations to join them in organizing a multilateral women's counterforce, which would conduct a conference and protest march at the site of a NATO ministerial council scheduled to meet at the Hague in May 1964. It was at this meeting, WSP had been informed, that MLF was to become a reality.

This campaign against the proliferation of nuclear weapons was the most ambitious project the movement had undertaken to date. Its goal was to demonstrate that military weapons did not lead to security, but rather to greater dangers for the security of the women and children of the NATO nations. In an attempt to ridicule and deconstruct military language, WSP appropriated the grandiose rhetoric of the Pentagon, calling its protest against MLF the Women's Peace "Force," announcing that the women would be heading for the Hague from their own "launching pads," promising that the British contingent would arrive by "air-lift" and that the protesting women would be "armed" with flowers.[47]

Planning the Hague action was more difficult for WSP than previous international undertakings because the MLF proposal was complex and little known or understood by the general public. In addition WSP had been warned by congressional representatives and Washington lobbyists that NATO was untouchable and that those individuals and groups who set themselves against NATO did not survive the confrontation. WSP decided to go ahead anyway. Its first step was a program of self-education and public education on the history NATO, on the question of German prewar militarism and the forces in postwar Germany seeking a return to militarism, and on the dangers of the Polaris-equipped submarines. To build support for the MLF protest, New York WSP distributed tens of thousands of copies of a fact sheet, and Washington WSP published a pamphlet on resurgent Germany, *The German Problem: Roadblock to Disarmament,* which the women sold for $1.00 a copy. H. D. Fleming called it "the most effective research booklet I have ever seen in a long research life." Bertrand Russell described it as "a scrupulously documented account of the resurgence of militarism and the new power of the old Nazism."[48]

The second step was to convince peace women in the NATO countries, who also lived under the Cold War constraints of Communist baiting, to join forces with a relatively new women's peace group that had already come under attack for alleged subversive activities. To establish the legitimacy of WSP and the MLF project, it was necessary to find politically respectable sponsors all over the United States and Europe. Building on contacts made with European women in Geneva and Rome and through WILPF, and using the talents and reputations of Ruth

Gage-Colby, Ava Helen Pauling, Frances Herring, Mary Clarke, Kay Cole, and Dagmar Wilson, who were well known in world peace circles, WSP secured endorsements from "peace personalities" in Europe as well as North America. Prestigious Nobel laureates Otto Hahn, Max Born, Linus Pauling, C. J. F. Heymans, J. D. Bernal, Lord Boyd Orr, and Bertrand Russell endorsed the NATO Women's Peace Force. Statements of support came from Thor Heyderdahl, Norman Thomas, Sean O'Casey, and Simone de Beauvoir. O'Casey sent a short message to WSP, which was reprinted for years:

> To hell with all arms,
> Excepting those
>
> Grandly grafted
> To our human bodies,
> These arms are all we need
> To give glory to God
> And all honor to man.

Simone de Beauvoir wrote: "I wish to assure the women of Strike For Peace of my solidarity. . . . I align myself with all those who are campaigning against the American project of establishing a multilateral force within NATO." Queen Mother Elizabeth of Belgium offered her strong approval but advised that she herself was not allowed to take part in political activity.[49]

The WSP organizers of the NATO Women's Peace Force made it clear that each of the women who traveled to the Hague to demonstrate her opposition to MLF represented tens of thousands of others at home. To make that projection a reality meant that dozens of meetings had to be organized on the local level, national publicity had to be arranged, and tens of thousands of signatures had to be gathered on petitions. Similar preparations for the Hague manifestation were undertaken in Great Britain, France, Belgium, and Germany.

Ruth Meyers and I were sent by WSP to Tyringe, Sweden, to the inaugural meeting of the International Confederation for Peace and Disarmament (ICPD), a new group called together to coordinate the work of antinuclear pacifist groups in the West. Our purpose in attending this meeting was to enlist support for the NATO Women's Peace Force from women already organized in the European peace movement. With no address in hand we arrived late, because our plane had been delayed, in an unlit Swedish town to hear civil rights leader Bayard Rustin's strong and beautiful voice rising in the night. We heard the words "we shall overcome," and we knew that we were not lost. We followed the song to a basement, where through a small window we could see that a meeting was already under way. We were gratified to find that the conferees were willing to receive us, although we had been warned by Ruth Gage-Colby that we might not be admitted. She based this assumption on the fact that at an earlier planning meeting of the ICPD Colin Sweet, a British representative of the World Peace Council, had been barred on the grounds that his organization was under the control of the Soviets. We had reason to believe that the ICPD, which excluded those it deemed too friendly to the Soviet Union, might be suspicious of WSP because of our decision not to exclude those with Communist leanings. Instead the European women, particularly, seemed delighted to see us, and Homer Jack of SANE, usually disapproving of WSP, made every effort to help us make our way. He suggested that Meyers and I use the entire time allotted to the U.S. delegates to explain our anti-MLF proposal. The idea of a NATO Women's Peace Force was met with enthusiasm by the middle-aged female delegates, who represented traditional cogender organizations in which they rarely played a leadership role. In fact only one woman, Peggy Duff, seemed to have any power at the meeting. And her power came from the fact that she had organized the conference.

Meyers and I called a women's meeting at teatime on the last day, which caused a stir of excitement. It was the only moment in the conference in which the European women could discuss peace issues as women in their own forum. They thanked us for providing a setting in which they could express their concerns without male input, and expressed their desire to organize women as women. Our decision to call a women's meeting was not a consciously feminist act at the time, but rather a practical move to touch base with women we wanted to enlist in the day-to-day business of organizing the Hague action. But this meeting encouraged the women who had previously been silent to speak and released a flood of energy that would carry the action along in the months to come.

At the invitation of several Danish women, whom we met at the ICPD conference, we went on to Copenhagen to enlist support for the NATO protest. In their enthusiasm our Danish friends organized a chapter of WSP, which didn't last long. We went on to the Netherlands to make arrangements for housing and conference rooms for the NATO Women's Peace Force. Finding space was difficult in a city expecting to be filled to capacity with NATO officials and their entourages, and because hotelkeepers were nervous about a peace group that might make trouble. We had the distinct feeling that we were being watched as we visited hotels and that hotel managers had already been warned against us. We finally found an inexpensive conference hotel in Scheveningen, a beach resort on the outskirts of the Hague. Meyers and I then made a

stop in London to establish a working relationship with the British Liaison Peace Committee, an umbrella group of women's organizations we
enlisted to organize the anti-MLF campaign in Britain.

As WSP began its preparations to battle the proposal for MLF, the
Pentagon disclosed that the fleet had already become a reality. From
Bonn came an announcement that in April a group of forty-nine sailors
would report to the Bremerhaven Naval Base in West Germany to begin
their training, and that they would go on to the U.S. destroyer *Biddle* in
Norfolk, Virginia, in July. WSP then released the information that its
NATO Women's Peace Force would protest the formation of the nuclear
fleet at the forthcoming NATO ministerial council meeting. A press release from WSP stated that British women would be coming to the
Hague for the NATO meeting by chartered plane, that bus loads of
women from fifty-four cities in Belgium would join the protest, and
that train loads of German women from the Rhineland and Westphalia
were planning to cross the border into the Netherlands on 13 April.

An advance party of WSPers consisting of Mary Clarke, Eleanor
Garst, Lorraine Gordon, and Amy Swerdlow arrived at the Hague well
in advance of the conference, to deal with logistics, public relations, and
possible emergencies. Gordon and I met with the chief inspector of the
police and with the press to brief them on WSP and on the purpose of
the women's conference at the small hotel Op Gouden Weiden and the
demonstration scheduled to be held outside the military barracks,
where the NATO ministers would be meeting. We thought we acted in
a businesslike, ladylike fashion, in the best WSP manner, and were met
with the cordiality we had learned to expect from most public officials.
We left assured that all would go well. But twenty-four hours before the
U.S. delegation of women was to fly out of New York for the Hague, we
realized that we were dealing with much tougher police control than
we had ever before encountered. We were informed by the border police that Ava Helen Pauling of WSP and WILPF and Katharine MacPherson of VOW in Canada had been turned back at the Schiphol Airport.
They were forbidden to enter the Netherlands, with no reason given.
The WSP advance party, along with a number of Dutch women peace
leaders, immediately initiated efforts to rescind the ban. The press was
informed, and the U.S. embassy was asked to intervene on WSP's behalf. Robert Manning, assistant secretary of state, who was at the Hague
for the NATO meeting, told Gordon and me that the U.S. embassy could
do nothing about the Dutch decision, as "our government never inter-
feres in the affairs of another country." We learned later that U.S. embassy officials had known for three days that the Dutch authorities intended to turn the women back, but had not informed WSP.

A new round of negotiations with the Dutch authorities was the only hope for a reversal. It went on nonstop with lower officials who came to our hotel, with no results. Finally, at midnight Gordon and I were summoned to the palace of the Minister of Justice—a dark, cavernous building where we waited in a series of antechambers for what seemed like hours. The minister appeared at 1:00 A.M. in a frock coat and striped trousers. He was either coming from a public function, or always dressed that way when dealing with official matters. He told us that if we abandoned the plan for a demonstration at NATO headquarters, our conference would be permitted to take place. Failing in his attempt to convince us, he left for further consultations and returned with the proposal that the demonstration would be permitted if all the women from all the countries who were coming to the Hague for the anti-MLF action would be willing to sign a statement pledging to obey all police rules. He was particularly concerned, he told us, that the women did not "sit down" outside the army barracks and refuse to move. This would precipitate a street battle with the women, which was bad for the Dutch image, and would distract from the serious high-level discussion that would be taking place inside. When we explained that we were a law-abiding and respectable group of women, including a British candidate for Parliament, he became agitated, informing us that the British pacifists were just the people he feared most. They always "sit down," he told us. Gordon and I rejected the conditions offered as long as we could, but when we were convinced that acceptance was the only way to secure the conference and the demonstration, we capitulated and agreed to the pledge not to sit down outside the army barracks.

Our decision was later challenged by a number of the WSPers who were shocked to be informed at Kennedy Airport that they could not embark for the Netherlands unless they pledged to obey all Dutch police regulations. All forty-one of the women signed the pledge, but after arriving at the Hague a number of them argued that it would have been wiser to refuse and to be forbidden to enter the Netherlands; it would have made a more interesting story, and drawn greater attention to the plan for MLF and greater sympathy for WSP. Perhaps they were right. An indication of the kind of response the NATO Women's Peace Force might have gotten had it been turned back in New York is indicated by the action of a member of the Dutch parliament who rose to demand an explanation of the decision by the minister of justice to bar peace-loving women such as Mrs. Linus Pauling from the Netherlands, while welcoming the German general who had issued the orders for the massive bombing of Rotterdam in World War II. The minister of justice responded that the women, who were foreigners on Dutch soil, were probably going to "sit down" and disturb the peace. The M.P. shot back, if foreigners were to be prevented from engaging in politics on Dutch soil, "what was NATO doing here?" The Norwegian liberal newspaper *Dagbladet* of Oslo commented: "In our opinion, the Dutch authorities have made big fools of themselves. . . . Here, suddenly an army of 800 women of different nationalities turns up." "They want to discuss something as threatening as peace, while NATO has its ministerial meeting in the Hague. . . . Maybe even sit down in front of the place of the meeting to demonstrate against a common nuclear force for NATO. . . . Such things may make a bad impression—lower the nuclear weapon-morale, so to speak."[50]

Forty-one women from the United States did get to the Netherlands to participate in the NATO Women's Peace Force, along with women from all the other NATO countries except Turkey. WSP was aware that it could not claim to represent a cross-section of American female opinion if its delegation did not include black and working-class women. But it had to go outside its own constituency to recruit women who were not white and middle-class. The Detroit women enlisted Lorraine Thomas, an African-American woman active in her local NAACP housing committee, who was also a member of the Democratic State Committee. She told the *Detroit News* that she had become interested in WSP because she loved people and didn't want any of them to die in a nuclear war. She was so concerned about nuclear proliferation, she explained, that she was using her two-week vacation as a senior insurance clerk at Detroit Metropolitan Hospital to make the trip to the Netherlands. "This is no sacrifice on my part. I plan to stay as close to the group as I can and learn. It is important for the women of the world to get to know each other and their common interests. Racial peace as well as nuclear peace depends on learning about other people."[51] Lavinia Franklin of Washington, D.C., a leader of the National Baptist Women's Convention and past president of the National Association of Ministers' Wives, also attended the Hague protest. She described herself, in the short biography each delegate was asked to provide, as "a contralto soloist, church organist, and speaker." Franklin was a widow and had three children and three grandchildren. Blanche Calloway Jones identified herself as Cab Calloway's sister, but she was much more than that. Jones was a radio commentator with her own program, a Democratic committeewoman, a member of the National Board of the Urban League, and of the NAACP and CORE. Another African-American delegate, Dora Wilson, was a sophomore at Tougaloo College, majoring in music education. Only eighteen years old, she was an honor student, secretary of the Student Council, and a member of Clarie Harvey's organization, Womanpower Unlimited, as well as a leader in the YWCA. Sonia P. Kaross added trade union representation to the delegation. She had been business manager of the Bay Area Joint Board of the Textile

Workers of America for twenty years, and vice president of the San Francisco Labor Council. Although her press biography indicated that she had participated in a World Congress against War in 1932, little attention was paid to this piece of history.

One hundred thirty women from Britain, including five from Scotland, joined WSP at the Hague. Thirty-five women came from Belgium, fifteen from France, twelve from Canada, eleven from Norway, and two each from Portugal, Italy, Denmark, and Luxembourg. Greece and Iceland were each represented by one woman. Two hundred Dutch women also participated in the conference. Eight hundred women from all walks of life arrived by bus from West Germany. It was a stirring moment for the American women, particularly those of Jewish descent, when their West German sisters came across the Dutch border, debarking from their buses into the arms of waiting WSPers. Each American woman understood fully that the German women had been adult citizens during the Nazi years. The question on the minds of all the Americans was, Where were you then? Why didn't you protest? The German women, sensing our discomfort, spoke of the Holocaust, admitting that they knew about the gas chambers, had opposed both the Nazis and the war, but had been helpless to do anything. They expressed shame and remorse, asserting that they had come to the Hague to meet us, despite opposition and possible persecution from their government, because they wanted to take a political stand against another world atrocity.

On Wednesday, 13 May, an estimated fifteen hundred women from fourteen of the NATO nations marched outside the Princess Juliana Kazerna, the military barracks where the NATO council was meeting. They walked silently in a cold drizzle in single file, each woman wearing an armband designating her home country and carrying a tulip to symbolize the fragility of life. A delegation presented itself at the barracks' gate to deliver a statement in opposition to MLF. British delegate Judith Cook reported her impressions: "The sight of the serried ranks of soldiers, military police, civil police, mounted police, and police with dogs set against 14 women in summer dresses, their arms filled with tulips, was one I shall not forget."[52] A joint message was delivered to the NATO ministers by fourteen women from the NATO nations. It called for a complete test ban treaty, military cutbacks, a nonaggression pact, and a nuclear-free zone for central Europe. An Associated Press story published in the *Denver Post* commented that two of the women's three demands actually coincided with stated U.S. government policy. Implying that the women's pressure on NATO was unnecessary, the AP story stated that "Washington is against the spreading of nuclear weapons and has long sought general and complete disarmament . . . only to run into a persistent Soviet road block on the inspection issue."[53]

After the march the women returned to their conference to plan future action to halt MLF, and to lobby the NATO ministers. An international clearing house, WSP-style, was set up in London to coordinate ongoing efforts against MLF. Fifteen women from the United States presented approximately one and one-half feet of petitions to the public affairs representative of the American embassy, who assured them that Secretary of State Dean Rusk would be informed. The U.S. delegation then went on to Frankfurt to meet with a branch of the World Organization of Mothers of All Nations (WOMAN), founded by Dorothy Thompson in 1946. Ethel Taylor, Philadelphia coordinator, wrote that to her and many other women in the U.S. delegation "the visit to West Germany was our most important step." The peace groups there, she explained, felt a need not to be isolated from peace groups in other countries.[54] Mary Lou Schneider of San Francisco, who was an active member of the Council of Democratic Clubs (CDC), told the Communist party publication *People's World* that the NATO Feminine Force" had "opened a dialogue among women of the NATO countries that would lead to future joint activities. She announced that the next action being planned was a protest against the launching of the USS *Biddle,* a 4,500-ton guided-missile destroyer at Norfolk, Virginia, on 15 July." The *Biddle* was to be manned by 336 men from seven NATO countries, including West Germany. This demonstration did take place, along with another in New York City when the *Biddle* was docked there. In Los Angeles a model of the *Biddle* was carried through the streets, then christened the "Biddle-Riddle" as a WSPer broke a bottle of vinegar over it and wished it a short life and an abrupt end. One of the placards carried by the middle-aged WSPers read, "Beatles—Yes, Biddles—No." In Whittier City, California, the launching and sinking of paper *Biddle*s in a local park was covered on television. Thus a project to share nuclear know-how and management with West Germany was brought to public scrutiny, something that would not have happened if WSP had not decided to oppose MLF.

On 15 December 1964 Donna Allen of Washington, D.C., and Mary Clarke of Los Angeles were among fifteen women arrested and jailed in Paris while attempting, once again, to deliver a protest against MLF to NATO headquarters. They were informed that demonstrations at NATO offices were prohibited by a special mandate against manifestations during NATO ministerial council meetings, a mandate that was apparently conceived and put in place after the NATO Women's Peace Force march at the Hague. Clarke and Allen were told that if they repeated the offense they would be put over the border, and if they repeated it again they would be forbidden ever to enter France. Clarke, Allen, and Madeline Duckles of Berkeley also represented WSP at a gathering of fifteen hundred women and men from ninety national and international peace groups who gathered in Paris to lobby against MLF.[55] When Allen and Clarke complained to the U.S. embassy about their treatment in Paris, they were surprised to be greeted with sympathy. The embassy officials told the women that they were impressed with WSP's knowledge and information on MLF and gave them the impression that the MLF plan was being reconsidered.

In 1965 WSP women traveled to Europe again to join men and women representing fifty organizations from the United States, West Germany, Belgium, France, the Netherlands, Norway, and Great Britain to lobby the NATO council against MLF. At this meeting, where the WSP representatives were recognized for their leadership on this issue, Cora Weiss was one of three keynote speakers, with Colin Jackson and Konni Zilliacus. The secretary's report of the meeting described Weiss as a housewife from New York, "whose delivery was brilliant and forthright as she spoke of the need to keep reminding our foreign ministers to keep the German finger off the nuclear trigger."

It is difficult to determine the extent of WSP influence on the decision by the Pentagon not to deploy MLF, but it is clear that WSP was the only peace group in the United States to campaign actively and dramatically against a NATO nuclear fleet. Again, as in the case of the test ban treaty, WSP strengthened the position of those forces in the administration that favored nuclear reduction or, as in the case of Henry Kissinger, believed that making West Germany a nuclear partner would be a catastrophic error. WSP chalked up the MLF campaign as another victory for the housewife brigade.

Without any doubt, the most remarkable and daring international gathering of women organized by WSP was the meeting in Djakarta between ten American women and nine Vietnamese women: six from the North Vietnam Women's Union and three from the South Vietnam Women's Liberation Union. Until this meeting in July 1965, WSP's international actions had been totally within the law and safe in political terms. But WSP women began to feel that the escalation of the Vietnam war called for more militant action than had been undertaken heretofore.

In the spring of 1965, after the bombing of North Vietnam had begun, Mary Clarke and Lorraine Gordon became the first representatives of the U.S. peace movement to visit Hanoi. The two had been invited to Moscow, as WSP representatives, for a celebration of the twentieth anniversary of the end of World War II. In Moscow they decided, on their own initiative, to contact representatives of Vietnam to discuss the war and hear firsthand the Vietnamese point of view. After making a favorable impression on the Vietnamese representatives in

Moscow, they were invited to go to Hanoi to view the devastation caused by U.S. bombing and to meet with the leaders of the North Vietnam Women's Union. It took a good deal of courage for two American women to go to a city subject to frequent bombings, in a country considered enemy territory by their own government, in a part of the world neither had ever visited. It was particularly difficult because there was no time or appropriate way to consult family and WSP colleagues at home. Nevertheless, Clarke and Gordon decided to make the trip because they wanted to find out, in those early days of the war, if there was some way they, as women, could smooth the path to peaceful negotiations. Although this was the first trip by American peace leaders since the bombing had begun, it was not reported in the press because the women, both experts in public relations, decided that it would be irresponsible for them to implicate WSP in a meeting that it had not endorsed.

While in Vietnam, Clarke and Gordon spoke with male and female leaders of North Vietnam and the National Liberation Front (NLF); witnessed the building of bomb shelters in Hanoi, which they interpreted to mean that the Vietnamese were making preparations to withstand years of bombing; and took steps to plan a joint public conference of U.S and Vietnamese women, tentatively scheduled to take place in Djakarta in July. When they returned to the United States, the two women found a good deal of interest in their visit but also objections and hesitations regarding a conference with the Communist forces in Vietnam. A number of women believed it would jeopardize WSP's credibility as an independent peace group by placing it squarely in the pro-Communist camp. As WSP did not take votes on issues of this sort, preparations went forward to send ten WSPers to meet with the Vietnamese. The women chosen were Nancy Gitlin of Ann Arbor, an SDS activist; Beverly Axelrod of San Francisco; Aline Berman, Margaret Russell, and Bernice Steele of Washington, D.C.; Shirley Lens of Chicago; and Esther Jackson, Phyllis Schmidt, Frances Herring, and Mary Clarke of California.[56] In a statement issued on the departure of the WSP representatives to Djakarta that is strikingly similar to those issued by the women from the warring nations who gathered at the Hague in 1915 to seek a way to end World War I, Southern California WSP declared: "We go to show the world that women are capable of meeting together in spite of their countries' killing each other in the field of battle. . . . Women may be able to do what no governments can do, pave the way to peace through the love and protection of their children."

With the cooperation of the Indonesian government, the WSP women spent five days conferring with six women from North Vietnam and three from NLF of the south. The group from North Vietnam consisted of a professor, a lawyer, a doctor, a news editor, and two cadres from the North Vietnam Women's Union. The women from NLF included a representative of the South Vietnam Women's Liberation Union, a leader of the Teachers' Patriotic Union, and a member of an organization called Students for Liberation. The teacher from Saigon who had traveled a good portion of the way to the conference by foot was Nguyen Thi Binh who had literally walked out of South Vietnam to come to Hanoi to meet the plane that took her to the meeting with the U.S. women in Djakarta. She was to become the foreign minister of the Provisional Revolutionary Government of South Vietnam and its chief negotiator at the Paris peace talks. WSP never expressed any discomfort that its representatives at international meetings were nonprofessional housewives, while the women who represented North or South Vietnam presented themselves as workers, students, professionals, and artists.

The Vietnamese and U.S. women, coming from different cultures, regions, and political and economic systems, spent sixteen hours each day talking to each other in what Aline Berman, a Chinese-American WSP, characterized as "a friendly manner, with no hostile attitude . . . exhibited by anyone."[57] The Americans received a detailed briefing on the Geneva Accords, which the Vietnamese wanted to see implemented at that time. The Americans were told in graphic detail about the physical devastation of Vietnam, "the cruel and barbarous bombing and killing," and many personal tragedies caused by the war. After five days living together in Djakarta in an informal atmosphere of women sharing information about the war and their lives, speaking together and sharing photos of children and family, strong bonds were forged. The WSPers came away reinforced in their commitment to campaign for U.S. withdrawal from Vietnam. This was the outcome that the Vietnamese anticipated when they expended a sizable amount of their sparse resources on meetings with American peace activists. They believed that showing their human face to Americans would be rewarded with the kind of understanding, concern, and guilt that those who returned from meetings with the Vietnamese invariably transmitted to the American people. The WSP women accepted, approved, and passed on to their sisters in WSP, and to their communities, the Vietnamese charge that the United States was interceding in a civil war in Vietnam and that, unlike the situation in Korea after World War II, the "red" Chinese were not combatants in Vietnam. Both these assumptions contradicted notions held by most Americans, who received their information on Southeast Asia from the mainstream press.

When the WSPers returned from Djakarta, the *Washington Evening Star* reported that WSP was passing on charges by the Vietnamese that

U.S. bombing raids in North Vietnam had come as close as ten miles to Hanoi, that toxic chemicals were being used against the civilian population, and that "the so-called strategic villages in South Vietnam were nothing more than concentration camps."[58] The *New York Times* characterized the WSP charge that the United States had violated the Geneva Accords of 1954 as a mere echo of Hanoi's propaganda line.[59] On the other hand, WSP found a sympathetic audience among those already skeptical or critical of the U.S. role in Vietnam. The Djakarta delegation gathered large and enthusiastic audiences for firsthand reports, which the publication *Peace Action* described as "transforming impersonal headlines into a moving story of the suffering and aspirations of the Vietnamese people, caught up in a cruel and needless war."[60]

WSP was the first American women's peace group to establish person-to-person relations with the Vietnamese. Vietnamese leaders concerned with external relations began to think of the WSP women as very dear, old friends. A number of the wartime generation of Vietnamese women leaders have since died—notably Phan Thi Ann and Vo Thi Te—but others remain personal friends of a number of WSP women. We write to each other, meet at gatherings such as the International Conference for the United Nations Decade on Women in Copenhagen in 1980 and in Nairobi in 1985. In Nairobi Cora Weiss, Barbara Bick, Judy Lerner, and I shared a moving lunch meeting with Nguyen Thi Binh and Ngo Ba Than, a lawyer and former non-Communist leader of the opposition forces in Saigon, whose arrest WSP had protested by picketing the South Vietnamese embassy in New York. Ngo Ba Than was one of the first postwar officials in Ho Chi Minh City, but she now plays a much diminished role. We mourned the death of Phan Thi Ann, a member of the Vietnamese parliament and a wise leader of the women's union. She was a political pro, but we found her to be nondoctrinaire and pragmatic, a motherly figure to her comrades and even to us. Together, we recalled Ethel Taylor's comment on her return from Hanoi: "We traveled half way around the world to enemy country, and to me it felt like coming home to family and friends." We also deplored the loss in status of these wartime Vietnamese women leaders, now reduced to lesser roles; Binh, for instance, who acted as the foreign minister of the Provisional Revolutionary Government of the south and chief negotiator for NLF at the Paris peace talks, had by 1985 been reduced in power and status to vice minister of education. She now is a member of the parliamentary committee on external affairs, but in a meeting this past summer at the home of Cora Weiss, we realized how limited are her power and knowledge of inside events such as civil liberties violations in Vietnam to which we (Cora Weiss, Judy Lerner, Lorraine Gordon, and I) raised objections regarding which she had little or no authority. She defended her country and was hurt that we were critical. We attempted to explain that it was our zealous regard for the rule of law and human freedom that had persuaded us to oppose our country's war on Vietnam and that we had not changed, but we could see that Binh and her translators felt that our friendship and loyalty were in question. Some of us speculate today that the postwar government of Vietnam would have been more humane and more peaceful had it not removed women like Nguyen Thi Binh from the first ranks of leadership. We have no evidence or understanding yet as to why this happened. Perhaps it is because the victorious military leaders now control Vietnam. This is an important subject for further research and discussion by feminist peace theorists.

After the Djakarta meeting the North Vietnam Women's Union invited Dagmar Wilson, Mary Clarke, and Ruth Krause to visit their country in 1967. While the United States officially barred travel to North Vietnam, the Supreme Court had decided in earlier cases that travel to proscribed nations was legally permissible if one's passport was not stamped. So the three women flew to France to pick up North Vietnamese visas, then to Cambodia, where they boarded an International Controls Commission plane, which took them to Vientiane, Laos, and Hanoi, where the border control, in deference to their request, did not stamp their passports. In Vientiane the WSP group inspected the bombed areas and visited hospitals where victims of the bombings were being treated. Like subsequent visitors they were given fragments of the deadly CBU bomb, which contains steel pellets that spread throughout the bodies of its victim, to show Americans at home. We were also presented finger rings made from parts of downed U.S. airplanes. So outraged were visiting peace activists by the brutalities inflicted on Vietnam that many of those who received these gruesome souvenirs wore them proudly as a symbol of their solidarity with the Vietnamese. When Wilson witnessed American bombers flying over Hanoi, she felt so passionately angry that she stated at a public rally held a day after her return, "I wanted to take up a gun and shoot back. I never thought I'd want to do that in my life. . . . All one's normal feelings of national unity go out the window," Wilson explained to a *Washington Post* reporter. "You have no idea of who the enemy is—the enemy is war and violence."[61] Wilson fell in love with the Vietnamese, as did most of the other peace movement visitors. What she saw was "the grace of life in the villages, and the unity of the people." "Everyone suffers together and they understand each other's suffering," she observed. She was particularly moved by the fact that children whose parents were killed "became everybody's children."

The WSP delegates were treated as important visitors by the Vietnamese. They met with the prime minister twice and with the heads of various governmental bureaus, particularly those dealing with health, education, and culture. The WSPers were not prone to ask questions about internal politics or the right of dissent in Vietnam, something they cherished at home, because the standpoint of the peace movement was that the Vietnamese people had a right to determine their own destiny and that it was our government that was already interfering too much.

Wilson, Krause, and Clarke were taken, at their own request, to visit U.S. prisoners of war and were permitted to bring back letters to the families of those they had seen. In July 1966 WSP had sent a telegram to Hanoi, urging restraint in the treatment of captured pilots, because the Vietnamese had threatened to try them as war criminals.[62] In 1967, Wilson, Krause, and Clarke were apparently satisfied that the prisoners were being treated humanely, although the three pilots they visited were too groggy to talk to them. The Vietnamese apologized, stating that the prisoners had just been awakened. In retrospect it seems hard to believe that U.S. prisoners would not have awakened instantly for a meeting with women from home, had they not been sedated or threatened. But none of us questioned the WSP delegation's assessment. In 1969, two years after Wilson's visit to Vietnam, the *Baltimore Evening Sun* quoted her to the effect that the prisoners were surprised at how well they were treated.[63] We took on faith the Vietnamese assertion that the prisoners were fed better than their own people because Americans could not survive on the Vietnamese people's limited wartime rations. Questions regarding possible mistreatment of prisoners were never raised with the Vietnamese hosts, because the WSP women felt deeply that the American flyers were the transgressors and the Vietnamese were the victims. As Marilyn Young has pointed out, the Vietnam War was, in the view of Americans, even those of the Left, an American war. We were the principle actors, the subject, and Vietnam was the other, the object. We were concerned mainly with our actions, not with theirs.[64]

In 1973 WSP rejected the returning POWs' charge that the peace movement had lengthened the war. Daring to challenge the judgment of the POWs, who had become national heros, WSP argued they had been out of the country and in isolation and therefore could not be aware of the terrible division in the country and the growing repugnance against the war. WSP stated: "To say that the Vietnamese were encouraged to continue the war because of our activity is to fail to understand the driving force on the part of the Vietnamese to rid their country of foreign intervention for hundreds of years."WSP argued that the Pentagon Papers revealed that there had been many opportunities to end the war, but that successive administrations had rejected them because their policy was to seek an unattainable victory.[65]

While in Hanoi Wilson, Clarke, and Krause, along with leaders of the North Vietnam Women's Union, agreed to organize a conference for women of the five countries sending supplies and/or men to fight in Vietnam. The stated purpose of the conference was to strengthen communications and cooperation among all forces fighting against the American presence in Vietnam. To implement the plan, WSP sent two representatives to Prague in February 1968 to meet with representatives of the women's organizations of Vietnam to plan and organize the conference. Prague was chosen as the site of the planning meeting because Czechoslovakia was a country friendly to North Vietnam and willing, through its women's union, to pay all the expenses of the planning meeting. It was agreed that the conference would be small and that it should be cosponsored by WSP and the North Vietnam Women's Union. France was chosen as the site of the conference because there were several Vietnamese women already in residence there as part of the negotiating team at the Paris peace talks, and because the Union des Femmes Françaises agreed to provide room and board in a children's camp, simultaneous translation in French and English, and a technical staff.

The Paris Conference of Women to End the War in Vietnam took place during 3–6 April 1968. Present, as planned, were women from North and South Vietnam, the United States, Australia, Canada, Great Britain, Japan, New Zealand, and West Germany. It was agreed that invitations should not be extended to women in South Korea, Thailand, or the Philippines, as it would be too dangerous for those living under such oppressive regimes to participate.

The Vietnamese women who had planned the conference with WSP representatives had made it clear that they wanted a varied U.S. delegation representing a broad spectrum of female peace activists, including representatives of antidraft organizations, the black community, theatrical celebrities, and churchwomen. Accordingly, WSP pulled together a multifaceted delegation of women leaders prepared to bring the message from the Vietnamese to their constituencies.[66]

This meeting, like all others between U.S. and Vietnamese women, was an intense emotional, as well as political, experience. Anne Bennett reported: "With our Vietnamese friends, we reached an immediate understanding. Each and every one of us shared the same concern for the future of all people and particularly for the children."[67] The women of South Vietnam told agonizing tales of life and death under Diem repression and of the bombing of civilians. One of the Vietnamese stated, as the American women fought back tears, that she could not imagine that the Americans could be so cruel. It was an undeclared decision by all of WSP women who visited Vietnam or met with Vietnamese women not to cry, as that form of emotional relief seemed too easy a way out. "They put poisonous snakes in the trousers of girls and tied the ends to force them to give information on where the Vietcong were hiding." "The snakes wriggled into the internal organs of the girls," the Vietnamese reporter explained, as the horrified WSPers held their ears and clenched their teeth. It was almost unbearable for the U.S. women to hear of American troops thrusting bayonets into the bellies of pregnant women. "The woman died very quickly," the WSPers were told by a woman from the south. "I happened to see this with my own eyes."[68]

The reports of atrocities made it clear to the WSPers that, if the Vietnamese women were subject to a greater burden in the war because of their sex, the female sex in America bore a greater responsibility to end the war. This conference went beyond previous meetings of U.S. and Vietnamese women in endorsing the position that "the National Liberation Front of South Vietnam represents the fundamental aspirations of the South Vietnamese people." The conference demanded that the U.S. government recognize the NLF in negotiations to end the war. A joint statement of those present at the conference, "members of Parliament, artists, lawyers, housewives, physicians, teachers, women of different colors, religious and political backgrounds," called upon all women throughout the world to join in a "strong movement to support the people of Vietnam, in order to contribute to a safe and happy future for Vietnamese children and children everywhere." It was also pledged that the women's peace movements in the nations sending troops to Vietnam would make every effort to help young men resisting military service. As a result, WSP of New York volunteered to prepare a list of the names and addresses of sympathetic people in Canada and Europe willing to help immigrating resisters to establish themselves in the countries of their choice.

On 4 July 1969 another delegation of three WSPers, Ethel Taylor of Philadelphia, Madeline Duckles of Berkeley, and Cora Weiss of New York, were invited to visit Hanoi. As in the case of previous and subsequent delegations, WSP did not choose its representatives; it merely responded to invitations made by the Vietnamese to specific North American women who had come to their attention as WSP leaders. They chose women they had met at international conferences, through newspaper reports, or on the advice of American friends they had come to trust.

Ethel Taylor was a capable organizer, with a talent for public relations, an eloquent, if not bombastic, public speaker, known for her integrity and wit. At the time of her invitation to Vietnam in 1969, Taylor was the mother of two adult children. One was a draft-age son about whom she was very much concerned.

Madeline Duckles was a leading member of East Bay, California, WFP and an active leader of the Committee of Responsibility that had brought napalmed Vietnamese children to the United States for medical treatment. The wife of a music professor at University of California, Berkeley, she was living in Italy in the late 1960s and was often asked to act as a WSP representative at peace conferences in Europe. There she met women from Vietnam, who found her to be the kind of empathic person they could work with. *Soviet Woman,* the organ of the Union of Soviet Women, in paying tribute to U.S. women for their "courageous" opposition to the Vietnam War, noted "the agitated words" of WSP representative Duckles, who had declared, "I don't want my five sons to be killed in Vietnam. But even more, I don't want my five sons to turn into beasts and kill Vietnamese children and women."[69] As it turned out, none of Duckles's sons had to serve in the armed forces, because they were too tall to meet army regulations.

In addition to being a key woman in WSP, Cora Weiss was a leader in the various antiwar "mobilizations," as the coalitions that organized the mass demonstrations against the war were called. She had become active in WSP, as others had, because of her concern about nuclear contamination. At the time, she was a young mother of two, with another child on the way. She had just moved to Riverdale, a suburban area within New York City, when one of the founders of the local WSP group, Leona Grant, came by to invite her to join a group of about fifty or sixty women who, as Cora put it, "would get on the train to Washington."[70] Weiss had not been actively involved in the peace movement until then, although her parents, Sam and Vera Rubin, had been involved in humanitarian and radical causes since she was a child. Cora's father was well known for his philanthropy in Africa and Israel, and her mother was an activist anthropologist, whose research and educational projects brought her to the Caribbean, where she supported anticolonialist scholars. Home was always "an active place," but she says that she never felt pressure from her parents to become politically active. "I was just an alive, alert, interested person" is her explanation for her involvement in radical peace politics. She remembers that she cut her political teeth during the McCarthy days, while she was at the University of Wisconsin in the senator's home state. She became involved in a campaign called "Joe Must Go," organizing the collection of almost 400,000 signatures for recall of the senator. In the late 1950s and early 1960s Weiss devoted her time to the African liberation movement and later served as executive director of the African-American Student Foundation. The foundation brought African students from the newly liberated nations in East Africa to be educated in the United States to take on administration and leadership posts in their respective countries after the British left. Asked why she turned toward WSP from such important work on behalf of African independence, she replied, "I had young children. There was no way I could stay out of it [the peace movement] then, just as there's no way I can stay out of it now."

Weiss started at the grass roots level in Riverdale but soon became a representative to the CCC in Manhattan. She went on to become a frequent WSP representative at international meetings and demonstrations. This came naturally to Weiss, as she was an enthusiastic and articulate public speaker, an excellent organizer with a flair for public relations, a consistent activist, and able to pay her own way to Europe and Asia. "I was always an internationalist," she points out. "I came from that kind of background, I guess." She takes pride in the fact that she helped to put together the first African student association in the United States, which was founded at the University of Wisconsin. She recalls that she was head of the international speakers bureau for the student government at the University of Wisconsin, where she consistently tried to get speaking jobs for African and Indian students because "that was how they could make some money."

Weiss's interest in international cooperation, solidarity, and support for people struggling for independence eventually made her one of the Americans closest to the Vietnamese on both a personal and political level. She maintains that she understood early that contact with the Vietnamese people was going to be a key element in fighting for peace. "If governments couldn't talk to each other, I sensed that the people could."

On her first trip to Vietnam in 1969, Weiss represented WSP. She remembers 1969 as the year of the October Moratorium and the November Mobilization, two of the largest demonstrations staged by the antiwar movement. Weiss, who represented WSP in the leadership of the November Mobilization, which brought half a million people to Washington, went directly from the platform of the mobilization rally to Hanoi. Weiss argues that WSP played an "extremely important" role in building the broad coalitions against the war, "because we were the reasonable voice . . . that insisted on opening the movement to the wider spectrum." She was referring to WSP's rejection of extremist actions and opposition to civil disobedience at mass demonstrations, because the key women were afraid that the "average woman" would be repulsed. Weiss was eventually asked to be one of the cochairpersons of the umbrella organization, the Mobilization against the War in Vietnam. "There were five chairpeople, one of them had to be a woman, and it was me. It's called tokenism," she explained. But this response does not explain why Weiss was the woman chosen. Undoubtedly her high energy, superb organizational skills, and broad contacts made her an ideal program director. She, also like most of the other WSPers, was not yet a feminist and could manage to deal with the young and old men who ran the "Mobe," in a spirit of deference and service characteristic of WSP.

The Weiss, Taylor, and Duckles delegation to Vietnam, like the Wilson delegation, requested permission to see and talk with American prisoners. The Vietnamese responded by arranging a visit to the detention camp that was named Hanoi Hilton by the American pilots. Weiss remembers that the camp was clean and neat, with guinea pigs and chickens on the lawn, shade trees, a cabbage patch, and barbells for exercise. "Rooms opened for us," according to Weiss, "included a shower room, two dorms with eight or ten beds in each. Mattresses, blankets, mosquito netting, chess sets, and playing cards were all visible." She told me that she wondered what was going on behind the many closed doors and felt some anxiety because the camp was heavily guarded. She could get no answer to her questions because the commander was "not very talkative," nor were the responsible people in Hanoi willing to give any details about the prisoners. Though she abhorred what the pilots had done, Weiss recalls that she wished she could take all of them home.

Three pilots, Mark Gartley of Greenville, Maine, Paul Gordon Brown of Newton, Massachusetts, and Bill Mayhew of New Manchester, West Virginia, were brought to a private building in Hanoi for a short talk with Weiss and Duckles. (Taylor had become ill and returned home). The three looked well, according to Weiss, voiced no complaints, and proceeded to give the American women messages to relay to their families. Weiss stated in a 1981 interview that the pilots went out of their way to tell the WSPers that they were grateful to the Vietnamese for protecting their lives, as they could easily have been killed by the local peasants who found them on the ground after they were shot down. Weiss could not forget something that struck her at the time for their optimism and belief in the American economic system. One of the pilots asked her to remind his folks to keep his profit-sharing fund current. He also told the women what they wanted to hear, that he had been a fool to go from graduation into the marines. Although he stated clearly that the Vietnamese were "really not friendly" to the American soldiers, Weiss and Duckles also did not express any suspicion of mistreatment, something most of the POWs reported on their return home.

On their departure from Vietnam Weiss and Duckles were presented with over three hundred letters from prisoners to take back to the United States and a memorandum from the Vietnamese indicating that American prisoners would be permitted to receive letters and packages from home. Ethel Taylor had brought to Vietnam over one hundred letters from American families with the hope that she could persuade the Vietnamese to distribute them. One was from a neighbor who had not heard from her son since he was shot down in November 1965. Taylor made a determined effort to find out if he was alive. She appealed to the leaders of the North Vietnam Women's Union, who, just as she was boarding a plane at the Hanoi airport for her journey home, informed her that Jon Reynolds was alive and well and that his parents would receive a letter soon. As soon as Taylor returned from Hanoi she wired Jon's parents who were abroad, "North Vietnamese women state Jon alive and well." After receiving her first letter from Jon, Mrs. Reynolds told the *Philedelphia Inquirer* that her son gave "The women who visited Hanoi all the credit for opening up the channel of communication." Not all wives and mothers were happy to hear from their husbands and sons through WSP. In the FBI files on WSP is an article from the *Ledger Star* of Norfolk, Virginia, printed sometime in April 1970 that stated "two prisoners of war wives of Virginia Beach announced . . . they will refuse to accept any more letters from their husbands forwarded from Vietnam by the Women's Strike for Peace Committee. These women do not want their personal hardships to be used as propaganda to undermine the war effort."[71]

The Weiss, Taylor, and Duckles visit initiated a program of communication between the POWs and their families. Although the role of intermediary between the families of the prisoners and the government of Vietnam was a fitting one for a mothers' peace movement, it must be made clear that it was not WSP per se but the Committee of Liaison with Servicemen Detained in North Vietnam that became the official conduit for the letters back and forth. At the time of Weiss's journey to Vietnam as a WSP representative, she had already undertaken a role that would catapult her beyond WSP and the mobilization into a full-time job as cochairperson of the Committee of Liaison with Servicemen Detained in North Vietnam. She was to become one of the chief organizers and director of delegations and visitations to Hanoi. It all happened, she explained, because attorney William Kunstler, while on a trip to meet the Vietnamese at the Paris peace talks, was informed by them that Hanoi was ready to initiate some systematic communication about the POWs. The lack of communication was being used by the U.S. administration to incite anger toward the North Vietnamese. He passed this information to noted pacifist Dave Dellinger, editor of *Liberation* magazine; Cora Weiss of WSP; and Stewart Meacham of AFSC. They responded by writing a memo to the Vietnamese stating that they and several other peace leaders were prepared to act as liaison with American families of POWs by transmitting information and mail to and from Hanoi, so that the families of the pilots could know finally which men were actually prisoners of the Vietnamese. The State Department understood that only representatives of the peace movement could act in this capacity, as the Vietnamese would not deal with the U.S. government until what they referred to as "genuine peace talks" were under way. According to Weiss, some families had not heard from their sons or husbands since they had been downed, which could have been as far back as August 1965. Weiss carried with her to Hanoi the letter that she, Dellinger, and Meacham had written, which she presented to members of the Committee for Solidarity with the American People in Hanoi. They in turn indicated that they were ready to respond. Even in our interview in 1981, eight years after the war had ended, Weiss was careful to point out that she never negotiated officially with the government of Vietnam, but rather with the various peace committees.

Weiss is convinced that the peace movement's concern for the prisoners and their families made it more difficult for the Vietnamese to harm them. In 1980 she asserted, with the intense passion and conviction she had felt a decade earlier: "We were doing a humanitarian job, and I had do it because as a woman I really felt for those families. . . . Even though they were families that represented everything that I opposed . . . they were mothers and children, and if I could make their life a little better, and if it was a move towards ending that most outrageous war, then I had to do it." Despite her personal courage in traveling back and forth to a country under siege, her exceptional energy and organizational skill, and the fact that she represented the Committee of Liaison, not WSP, Weiss believes that the Vietnamese always considered her merely a housewife. "To them I was not a professional," she asserted. When I reminded her that *housewife* was the term we in WSP celebrated, Weiss acknowledged that the Vietnamese admired the WSP housewives as a powerful force and held the movement in great esteem. "We demonstrated to the Vietnamese that we were not fearful women, that we were determined women, we were committed women, we were disciplined women, and we were politically responsible, and I guess they saw this." She suggested something with which I concur, that the Vietnamese held WSP and the WSP women they worked with in greater regard than did the larger U.S. peace movement. Weiss thinks it is important to note that the Vietnamese understood that WSP was outside the Communist party, and suspects that working closely with WSP was one of their first experiences with the non-Communist left outside of their country.

Weiss, like the other key women of WSP whom I have interviewed, was proud of WSP's effectiveness, which she attributed to its utilization of a mother's way of political organizing—"your kids get sick and you make them better."

This maternal metaphor in many ways described the relationship that Weiss built with the Vietnamese top leadership. She devoted herself to Vietnam, the country, and its representatives, not only politically but personally. When representatives of the Democratic Republic of Vietnam assumed observer status at the United Nations, Weiss helped them to set up their office and residences in New York City, including assistance with the purchase of furniture and appliances. She still has close ties with Vietnam and entertains members of their United Nations delegation at her home frequently, although she is now more critical of their policies than she was during the war. Weiss asserts that her commitment to Vietnam comes from her sense of responsibility to "clean up the part of the mess our government made there."

The women of WSP who traveled to Vietnam during the war learned much about effective female leadership in time of revolutions and war, and dedication to community above family and self from the Vietnamese women. What made a particular impression was their strength, courage, quiet dignity, self-reliance, and self-sacrifice. The WSPers had never met revolutionary leaders nor a woman such as Nguyen Thi Binh, who was playing a high-level role in her country's foreign affairs and who was gentle, humble, unassuming, yet unshakable in her patriotism and revolutionary fervor. Particularly poignant for the WSPers was her separation from children and family, a condition that most of the Vietnamese female leadership endured.

It seemed to those of us who had the opportunity to meet the Vietnamese in their own country that, if thousands of American women could also see them face to face and hear their stories, the women's antiwar movement would grow in size and deepen in conviction and commitment. The only way this could be done was by bringing Vietnamese women to Canada, as their enemy status barred them from visiting the United States. A plan was conceived by WSP and VOW of Canada to hold a conference of Vietnamese women in Toronto, and to several other parts of Canada where U.S. women could come across the border to meet them.

It soon became clear that WSP and VOW were not alone in their desire to strengthen female solidarity with the Vietnamese. A group of radical young women in and around Washington, D.C., who were working in a group called the Women's Anti-imperialism Collective and were already part of the emerging women's liberation movement, also wanted to share experiences and strategies with the Vietnamese. Charlotte Bunch, who had just come back from a visit to Vietnam as a representative of the Women's Anti-imperialism Collective, recalled in a 1990 interview that her interest in a meeting between the leadership of the North Vietnam Women's Union and the U.S. women's liberation movement was to focus, not solely on the war, but on the fight for women's emancipation and how it could be integrated into the anti-imperialist struggle in the United States and Southeast Asia. This was obviously not the agenda to which WSP subscribed, and this difference in standpoint created a deep tension between WSP and the younger radical women. The young women were openly critical and disdainful of the older WSPers, whom they scorned as politically and culturally regressive and totally lacking in feminist consciousness. To iron out tensions and difficulties between the two groups and because the Vietnamese were genuinely interested in learning more about the women's liberation movement, which they recognized as an important new political tendency on the Left, they invited WSP and representatives of the radical women in Washington to meet them in Budapest at a meeting of WIDF to set up an agenda and make final preparations for the meetings with North American women in Canada.

Mary Clarke and I were sent to this meeting by WSP. The Women's Anti-imperialism Collective of Washington, D.C., also sent two representatives. It was not easy for the Vietnamese to work with both groups. There was a great deal of disagreement concerning the agenda, with WSP pushing only to develop empathy and understanding of the Vietnamese predicament, and the representatives of the radical women insisting that there be a thorough discussion of the relationship of patriarchy to militarism and an investigation of the role and status of women in Vietnam, including their attitude toward lesbianism.

That the Vietnamese were experienced coalition builders and negotiators of factional struggles is illustrated by the way they handled both women's groups. They were very careful in Budapest and later in Toronto not to take sides in the internal factional politics of the U.S. women's movement, cooperating with all groups and individuals who opposed the war. Their solution at the planning meetings in Budapest was to refer to WSP as "our old friends" and to honor their long relationship with WSP, while they referred lovingly to the radical young women as their "new friends." They insisted that the Americans resolved the agenda dispute among themselves, a request none of us guilty Americans could refuse. Alice Wolfson, one of the representatives of the Women's Anti-imperialism Collective at the Budapest meeting, reported in *off our backs*, a women's liberation journal published in Washington, D.C., that she was moved by the warmth of the Vietnamese women: "They kiss you on both cheeks and they hug you a real, true, warm hug. . . . if you're sitting next to one of them she will take your hand or put her arm around you. . . . No amount of Marxist theorizing can possibly be as meaningful in terms of dedication, as five minutes spent with a Vietnamese woman."[72]

While the Vietnamese seemed to be in greater sympathy with WSP's agenda for the conference, they were also very open to the young women's questions and went out of their way to show their respect and admiration for them. Wolfson concluded: "Because the Vietnamese were so sensitive to us, and because their example was one of love and kindness, we are able to work collectively with love for each other." In the months before the conference in Canada the women's liberation movement debated whether the meeting with the Vietnamese was an activity that furthered women's liberation or that diverted women from the struggle against patriarchy, of which militarism was only one off-shoot. The debate was never resolved.

All through the early spring WSP negotiated with various radical women's groups and minority women's organizations, and finally a coalition was achieved to sponsor a conference in Toronto and a sub-sequent meeting in Vancouver, for which nearly one thousand American women crossed the border. Madeline Duckles described the preparatory meeting for Vancouver as "grim, ghastly." "The Red guard revolutionaries acted like imperialists, Women's Liberation acted like arrogant men, and WSP-VOW—all six of us from WISP, my god, my god, acted like, I quote, 'fuckin' rich-bitch liberals.'"[73] Duckles recognized, however, that any representative body of U.S. women would suffer from tensions that difference and unequal power relations create. Women's liberation people returning to Washington from Toronto reported to *off our backs* that the conference was marked by "tensions, alienation, anxiety, and confusion coming out of factionalism, racism, liberalism, and other movement maladies. There were devastating problems between women's liberation and black, Puerto Rican, and Chicana women." Women of color demanded separate workshops to deal with what they perceived as their separate reality and to focus on racism. Although the conference was marred by dissension, WSP women were thrilled to meet with the Vietnamese and gratified because their meetings received front-page and prime-time coverage in Canada.

For WSP, the tone of the conference in Toronto was set on the first day, when Helen Boston, an African-American woman active in a Brooklyn chapter, greeted the guests from Vietnam with the statement "My only wish is that my son didn't hurt nobody before they got him." Weeping Vietnamese women embraced this African-American mother who declared that her oldest son had died in vain.[74] Cora Weiss reported in *MEMO* that the women from both countries wept, kissed, ate, talked, and laughed together. "An outpouring of gifts and money made vivid the simple message, 'we are sisters together; we will help each other; we wish neither Vietnamese nor American loss.' . . . It was instant love."[75] As the Vietnamese women leaders came from the middle class and had been educated in French schools, it was not difficult for them to communicate with WSPers. One Vietnamese woman exemplified the commonality of consciousness between the Vietnamese and the women of WSP when she spoke of the way in which normal life was disrupted by war: "It is normal for a man and a woman to fall in love, to marry and bear children. We must maintain family life. We have learned to live underground, to educate our children there, and to maintain as normal a life as possible." Although the WSPers were more than sympathetic to the Vietnamese women's struggle to keep their families together, the Vietnamese view of "normal life" did not go unquestioned by the radical feminists. I and other middle-aged WSPers listened carefully after a group of women who identified themselves as representatives of the women's liberation movement asked a question regarding attitudes toward lesbianism in Vietnam. The male interpreters, who had been sent, we felt, to supervise the women, did not seem to understand the term *lesbian.* They did not appear to be any more enlightened when the American women explained that lesbianism meant "women loving women." Finally, after whispered consultations with each other, the men acknowledged that "yes, adolescent women sometimes fall in love in boarding school, but when they grow up they marry men and lead a normal life." A number of the WSPers considered the question on lesbianism frivolous and diversionary, but others were beginning to recognize that issues such as sexual choice are as essential to the self-determination of women as national independence is to the self-determination of all the people of Vietnam.

Some of us in WSP were, after ten years of militant antiwar struggles, just beginning to make a connection between war and male violence against women. I was one of those. As editor of *MEMO* I decided to reprint the comments of Renee Blackhann, a reporter for the radical left publication *National Guardian* that identified the war as a feminist issue:

> Contrary to previous beliefs of many women, the war is a feminist issue. The visitors' tales of women brought to hospitals with their breasts sliced off by bayonets of GIs; with a beer bottle brutally inserted into the vagina; women refused permission in jail to wear clothes or bathe, even during menstruation; . . . leaves no doubt that the struggle against the Indochina war is intimately related to the struggle by women everywhere for dignity and equality.[76]

After the Canadian meetings, I was invited, in my capacity as editor of *MEMO,* to join a WSP delegation to Hanoi in September. The other members of the delegation were Irma Zigas of Nassau County, New York, WSP and the War Resisters League, and the Reverend Willie Barrow of SCLC and Operation PUSH in Chicago. In a letter to the National Consultative Committee of WSP, Zigas and I explained that we had been invited because the North Vietnam Women's Union had worked with us previously in Paris, Stockholm, Budapest, and Toronto, and that Willie Barrow was asked because the Vietnamese were "very anxious to make contact with Black women in the United States and that Willie had impressed them greatly at the Toronto meeting in April." We explained that we had decided to respond to the invitation only because Vietnam had been downgraded as a news story by the U.S. media, and that even peace people were beginning to waver in their interest in ending the war. Zigas and I paid our own way to Vietnam, as many of the other WSPers who visited Vietnam had done, and the New York WSPers raised the money for Willie Barrow's airfare. We were not the first WSPers to visit Vietnam, but our experience was nevertheless overwhelming.

Unlike previous WSP delegations, we determined to investigate the status of women in Vietnam and to learn how and why certain women had become national leaders. It was clear that women had made great strides in achieving decision-making power in a country recently liberated from colonial rule, where polygamy had not been abolished until 1960. We were impressed with the fact that women were running factories, cooperative farms, and militia units, and that there were 125 women in the national assembly. We praised the Vietnamese women as a gentle force and the Vietnamese people for their efforts to integrate women into all aspects of national life. We understood that it was not an easy task to overcome a national culture that held women in low esteem, but we were thrilled to learn that Ho Chi Minh considered it an essential goal for the new Vietnam. Only a few years later we were dismayed to learn that the wartime women deputies and ministers were being pushed out of the front ranks of national leadership and that the Communist party was exhorting women to make up for the losses of the war by taking on the triple duty of working in social production and caring for their children and for their aging parents. We remembered, with pain, the radical feminist slogan "Mme Binh: Live Like Her!" Some of us wondered if we should have paid more attention to the warnings of lesbian feminist Rita Mae Brown, who had asked, "Why travel to Hanoi when you can go to Hoboken and see the same show?" Cassandra-like she predicted, "When the Vietnamese sisters throw out the invader they will have yet another war on their hands, the war against sexism in their own society."[77]

Sad to say, the Vietnamese women leaders we admired so much are not fighting that war against sexism because they have been set back by the economic deprivation and political uncertainty that besets their country due to the devastating war, our country's continued refusal to offer economic or humanitarian aid, and the demise of their "socialist" allies in Europe.

Most of the WSP women who traveled to Hanoi to meet the revolutionary women of Vietnam are engaged today in some aspect of the struggle for women's rights. For many, their feminist consciousness was advanced by their meetings with women from Vietnam. The political status of the Vietnamese women leaders, their courage and capacity to carry on the fight for liberation or act as ministers of state with grace and civility despite tragic personal losses, gave us confidence in our own powers. Their ability to hold high office with strength and confidence accompanied by humility and concern for others, even Americans, awakened our sense of our own possibilities and gave us role models. In working with the women of Vietnam to end American intervention, we recognized our own potential powers for leadership in political and public life.

Conclusion

I could dance, dance, dance and be fresher after,
I could dance away numberless suns,
To no weariness let my knees bend.
Earth I could brave with laughter,
Having such wonderful girls here to friend
Oh the darling, the gracious, the beautiful ones!
Their courage unswerving and witty
    Will rescue our city.
—Aristophanes, *Lysistrata*

WSP entered the political arena in what was to become a decade of political, racial, cultural, and sexual ferment. Unlike the civil rights or the women's movement, WSP seemed to have arrived from nowhere, with no political or organizational roots, no ideology or social theory. The movement's only demand was to save the children from nuclear holocaust. Its chief slogan was "End the Arms Race—Not the Human Race."

But the women who founded WSP, appearances to the contrary, were not political neophytes. All the Washington founders had met as members of SANE, and many of the local organizers knew each other from WILPF. Still others had been involved in Quaker pacifism or Communist popular front groups in the late 1930s and 1940s. What these women shared, in addition to social concerns, was the role of mother and homemaker, middle-class affluence, and moral indignation.

Although WSP arrived on the political scene with energy, creativity, passion, and determination, it also carried with it the heavy baggage of the political repression, cultural conformity, and antifeminism that marked the Cold War consensus of the 1950s. The women of WSP, like millions of their cohorts in the period after World War II, had given up jobs, careers, professional training, and dreams of personal achievement to become full-time mothers and consenting members of the culture of domesticity. Possessing little awareness of their contribution to sex-role stereotyping and female oppression, they were not aware in their early years that they were fighting a battle of the sexes, a woman's battle against the male elites who decided issues of life and death for all of

233

humanity. They had no notion that they were also challenging the gendered division of labor and power in the political culture of the Left as well as the Right. In years of struggle, planning strategies, and making programmatic and tactical decisions, they began to feel their power, enjoy their victories, and savor their political acuity. They also began to perceive the forces that held them back personally as well as politically. Most of the women of WSP were prepared, if resistant at first, to hear, understand, and even embrace their daughters' critique of the sex-role system that emerged at the end of the decade. Thus this evaluation of WSP, which I situate in current debates among feminist scholars and activists regarding the relationship of traditional female culture to radical social change and to feminism, is in the spirit of WSP as it was transformed in the early 1970s.

The question that WSP asks of women's history is, Can an organization that builds on traditional female culture, even when effective in achieving some reforms, actually contribute to world peace if, in stressing mothers' role and rights, it reinforces female marginality? In using the term "women's culture," I am referring not only to the consciousness, moral values, relationships, and networks of support among women that grow out of their maternal and domestic practice, but also to what Gerda Lerner has described as "the ground upon which women stand in their resistance to patriarchy and their assertion of their own creativity in shaping society, in other words, the ways in which women, as a group, have historically re-defined and recast male-imposed roles and tasks on their own terms and from their own vantage point."[1]

The story of WSP is the story of white, middle-class women who built on the post–World War II celebration of domesticity and motherhood to challenge militarist definitions of national interest and male control of foreign policy and the atom bomb. By exposing the way in which male world leaders were recklessly threatening the health and life of future generations, thus preventing conscientious mothers from carrying out their prescribed roles of nurturance and life preservation, the organizers of WSP were able to break through the Cold War consensus that had silenced foreign policy dissent in the United States for over a decade. WSP warned that the health of future generations would be damaged by the contamination of children's milk with radioactive fallout from atomic testing. The women insisted that there was no such thing as a safe dose of strontium 90 or iodine 131 at a time when the dangers of atomic radiation were hidden from the public. As Jean Bethke Elshtain and Sheila Tobias suggest in the introduction to their collection of essays on women and militarism, "WSP made the most of a particular historic construction of women as mothers, and demonstrated the latent political power of that role."[2]

WSP rhetoric and tactics forwarded a maternalist "standpoint," in the sense used by feminist political theorist Nancy Hartsock and philosopher Sara Ruddick, who identify a "standpoint" as an engaged vision of the world that is opposed and holds itself superior to dominant ways of thinking.[3] WSP's standpoint, its challenge to male militarism, was based on the conviction that the preservation of life on earth is of greater value to the human race than the promotion and defense of abstract and outmoded notions of national advantage. While the political and moral standpoint WSP projected grew out of what Ruddick has called "maternal practice," it was based on more than the knowledge, experience, and convictions derived from years devoted to "caring labor" in the home. Most of the women who participated in the WSP campaign against the bomb and the Vietnam War had been politically concerned citizens, with a strong internationalist bent and a concern for issues of peace and social justice, before they became mothers. They were the kind of women who, in the years before World War II, might have called themselves "antiwar," "anti-imperialist," or "anti-Fascist." They believed that conflicts between nations could be mediated without military force and that ordinary citizens should demand of their governments a higher moral standard than military blackmail. In fact, one of the first stated principles of WSP was support for and strengthening of the United Nations.

In stressing maternal outrage at the threat to the health and welfare of their children, the WSPers were not only expressing their own sense of male betrayal of the agreement they, as women, had made with society to sacrifice their own personal interests and career goals in favor of raising the next generation, they were also trying to speak to the American people in a language they believed would be understood and accepted. Other motivations for privileging the maternal viewpoint were the perceived need to circumvent the Red baiting and the political isolation that had greeted all foreign policy dissent in the 1950s, and to avert the misogynous attacks on intellectual and political women they had experienced in the late 1940s and 1950s; the years of the "feminine mystique." WSP never claimed that women were more peaceful, more nurturant, more "connected" than men, only that the male militarists, particularly those who were escalating the nuclear arms race, had run amok. Eleanor Garst writing in *MEMO* in 1966 advised: "Let us not blame the men; let's just improve our communication. Let's tell them we don't mean that they should kill other women's children to protect our security; that essentially other women's children are like our own. And whatever the color of their eyes, we want them all to live and laugh, to fulfill their dreams."[4] WSP sensed that attacking men was, in 1961, unacceptable as a political tactic. In addition, many of the women who came out of the Left believed that class conflict and racial oppression were the primary causes of war and that individual men, many of whom were as powerless as women, were actually potential allies. In the early days of WSP, before the women "came on strong" and made the movement the center of their lives, husbands were often willing and needed allies.

Pam Block, a student at Hampshire College, brings a young, fresh, yet incisive eye to WSP's gender consciousness. In commenting that WSP leaders often denied the relationship of the peace strike to the battle of sexes as portrayed in Aristophanes' play *Lysistrata*, she draws attention to the ways in which the WSP women denied the pleasures of their new women-centered lives.[5] The joys of sisterhood were hidden in WSP rhetoric because the women were conditioned to self-sacrifice rather than self-fulfillment. Yet the image WSP projected of concerned, understandably emotional, middle-class matrons was not merely a ruse perpetrated by the women to disguise deeper political motives. I recall that I stressed my maternal interests, rather than my radical politics, when I spoke and wrote for WSP, because I believed that my genuine motherly concerns would be received and understood by nonpolitical women, the media, and public officials. I was certain, on the other hand, that my radical ideas regarding economic and social justice would turn them away and place me outside credible political discourse. Most WSPers did not have to make special efforts to talk and act like "ordinary mothers," because that is the way they had been talking and acting for many years. Maternal thought and language, local community concerns, and the consumerist suburban culture had made a profound impact on their consciousness and dictated to a large degree the way we had come to observe the world. The Los Angeles newsletter, *La Wisp*, on the occasion of the movement's second anniversary did not present a theoretical or even a political analysis of the movement's accomplishments and its future goals. Instead it proclaimed: "We all know what two-year-olds are like—loveable, busy, noisy, not easy to get along with. WSP is a typical two-year-old. So we've gotten some of what we wanted but we want more. A partial test ban treaty is not enough."[6] Carol Urner, a deeply political person sent by WSP to Hiroshima to participate in an international conference, could not transcend her maternal guilt. "Attendance at this conference was a rare privilege and opportunity," she wrote to Wilson. "Now I'll have to work twice as hard when I return to the United States and my family. (I do wish we didn't have to leave the children for so long for trips like this! But it is for them— and all the children—that we do it.)"[7] Although most of the WSPers were familiar with left and pacifist discourse, as well as the rhetoric of the State Department, the women refused to speak in terms of "capitalism" "imperialism," "containment," deterrence," or even of "truth to power," because they believed that ideological language obliterated the felt experiences of ordinary mothers.

This does not means that the WSP leadership was anti-intellectual. Most of the key women read voraciously on the scientific aspects of the nuclear threat, the status of disarmament negotiations, and foreign relations, not only to understand issues they believed to be matters of life and death but also to prepare materials for public education and persuasion.[8] They knew by the time the movement was six months old that they possessed more knowledge and understanding of the components and the dangers of radioactive fallout than did most of the men in Congress, and at least as much as the members of the Atomic Energy Commission, who pursued a policy of "hear no evil and see no evil" in regard to the dangers of nuclear testing. Later in the 1960s the WSPers mastered the draft laws, keeping up with their frequent revisions, in order to council young men on their rights to evade military service. When they spoke of disarmament treaties or strontium 90 or the Geneva Accords of 1954, which divided Vietnam into two separate countries, WSPers deliberately used the language they believed the women they met every day in the supermarket, the pediatrician's office, the PTA, the cooperative nursery school, or the League of Women Voters would accept.

For WSP, as for the other political movements of the 1960s, the Nazi holocaust and the creation of the atom bomb had made the search for historical models seem futile. The sense that Marxism, liberal theory, and Christian pacifism all had failed to retard the planetary drift to self-destruction pervaded WSP. The women were given to paraphrasing Albert Einstein's statement that the atom bomb had changed everything but the way we think. WSP shared with SDS and SNCC the belief that only "a new insurgency" and a new participatory political format could address the problems of the nuclear age.[9]

However, the women of WSP, unlike the young men in SDS, gloried in their "outsider" standing. Their attitude was similar to that of Virginia Woolf, who observed in *Three Guineas* that "we can best help you to prevent war not by joining your society but by remaining outside your society."[10]

Given its double vantage point of radical politics and female powerlessness, why did WSP find it so hard in the early 1960s to perceive the connection between sexual inequality in foreign policy decision making and the entire gender system? A Pentagon officer, commenting on a paper about WSP and foreign policy dissent that I presented at a meeting of the Society of Historians of Foreign Relations, refused to believe that women in WSP who had been associated with left and liberal groups were not automatically feminists. He did not understand that it was precisely because so many WSPers came out of the Left of the 1930s and 1940s that they had not been exposed to feminism. In reviewing the history of WSP, I noted that, for the most part, the women who had been close to the Communist party had even less historical memory of the women's rights and suffrage movements than did those with Quaker, Unitarian, liberal, or anarchist background. For people on the Left in the 1930s and 1940s, the pressing issues of the Depression and the rise of fascism led to a focus on genderless working-class unity and international collective security, pushing the history of the fight for women's rights into the background. Communists and their sympathizers believed that female equality was an essential aspect of social justice but that the fight for socialism was the only appropriate fight for female emancipation, and that insistence on women's rights was a politically incorrect vestige of nineteenth-century bourgeois feminism.

Having no feminist history and theory to build on, WSP was unable to offer a gendered critique of the nuclear arms race and the Vietnam War. The woman of WSP, and I include myself, had neither the language nor the analytical tools to make a connection from woman's secondary status in the family and in the economy to her political powerlessness, or to understand the relationship between military aggression and domestic violence. All WSP could do in the early 1960s was to forward women into the political arena to cry out against male abuse of power and nuclear brinkmanship. This was no easy task at a time when peace protest and strong political women were anathema.

Out of WSP's struggle for the test ban treaty of 1963 came its first gender demand, that women be represented on disarmament negotiating teams and all governmental bodies dealing with the issues of health, life, and death. Equal rights and power for women in all areas of life was not even a dream until WSP encountered the second wave of feminism. It was not until the early 1970s that WSP women were able to move from begging and cajoling the men in Congress to heed their demands for peace to promoting the candidacy of one of their own leaders. WSP supported Abzug's candidacy under the slogan "This Woman's Place Is in the House—the House of Representatives."

Feminist critics of maternalist peace politics argue that those women's movements that stress female identification with nurturance and moral guardianship as the basis for peace activism project an essentialist view of women that reinforces the myth that biology is destiny, and inhibits the struggle for female equality and empowerment. They contend that the notion that women are the peaceful sex allows men to make war as they have throughout recorded history. Simone de Beauvoir was adamant on this issue. "Women should desire peace as human beings, not as women," she declared in a 1983 interview. "And if they're being encouraged to be pacifists in the name of motherhood, that's just a ruse by men who are trying to lead women back to the womb." "Women," she declared, "should absolutely let go of that baggage."[11] Anthropologist Micaela di Leonardo argued, in an article on antimilitarism and feminist theory, that "the moral mother argument is a poor organizing tool: it does not challenge us to think in complex ways about the sources of military threat, nor about women's consciousness and social activity. We must retire moral mothers from the field."[12] Di Leonardo is correct in her observation that a political movement based solely on maternal thinking is hampered in its ability to offer an adequate analysis of the role of the economic, political, and gender factors in the militarization of contemporary society. But her assertion that the moral-mother argument is a poor organizing tool is historically inaccurate and leads her to a simplistic, undialectical view of women's movements for social transformation. Di Leonardo fails to account for the ways in which nineteenth-century women's movements based on traditional female culture moved their participants from moral reform to the abolition of slavery and to women's rights, and from temperance to peace and socialism. She also ignores WSP's energy, creativity, playfulness, and organizational brilliance, as well as its impact on the campaign for the test ban treaty of 1963. Di Leonardo also fails to perceive the sense of personal empowerment that women develop in years of political struggle and to understand the transformations in consciousness that can take place in women who have functioned primarily as mothers and housekeepers, when they find themselves in a separatist movement, relying for the first time on themselves and their sisters for political analysis and tactical decisions—counting on their own courage and ingenuity in their confrontations with world leaders, hostile congressional committees, and intransigent police.

It is important to note that throughout the 1960s the key women of WSP maintained that they had left their homes only to save the children and that when the political emergencies, such as the nuclear threat and the Vietnam War, were resolved they would return to full-time homemaking. Yet most of the women of WSP never did go home, because when the Vietnam War was over they no longer perceived the home as the center of their lives or responsibilities. As Joan Kelly suggested in her essay "The Doubled Vision of Feminist Theory," while women build their understanding of the world on received definitions and ideology, they also develop a consciousness from experience, particularly from struggle, that can be oppositional to received notions of self and society.[13] Frances Fox Piven states in an article on women and the state:

> I think the public articulation and politicization of formerly insular female values may even be comparable to such historic developments as the emergence of the idea of personal freedom among a bonded European peasantry, or the spread of the idea of democratic rights among the small farmers of the American colonies. . . . Each of these ideological developments reflected the interplay of traditional and transforming influences. And each brought enormous political consequences in its wake.[14]

The phenomenal growth of WSP in 1961 and 1962, a period of relative quiet in terms of foreign policy dissent and peace protest, reveals that maternal rhetoric can be an inspirational organizing tool, a source of energy, commitment, and passion for traditional middle-class white women. It can mobilize a deeply felt woman's critique, and project an alternative vision of international relations and social interaction, along with fresh forms of dissent and direct action. It can also, in the case of WSP, have a powerful effect on the media and on liberal politicians.

Because WSP was an intentionally separatist organization, it was free to reject male political culture. Jeanne Bagby, a WSP founder, expressed the joy many of us felt working only with women. She wrote to *Liberation* magazine in 1966: "It was great working without men! Organizations invariably suffered from the hierarchical formalistic impediments we so briskly ignored. Our naïve disorganized methods seem to annoy men of all ages."[15] In over a decade of successful political campaigning, first for a test ban treaty, then for U.S. withdrawal from Vietnam, the women of WSP transformed themselves from "ordinary housewives" and mothers into leaders, public speakers, writers, organizers, political tacticians, and analysts. WSP had, without intending to, created a female community in which reasoning ability, organizational skills, and rhetorical talents were valued above maternal competence. WSP women also set an example of female courage, political responsibility, and leadership for their own children, male and female, and for their husbands. A postcard from Washington WSP, dated 8 January 1963, a month after the HUAC investigation, announced: "Another Daring Move: Women Strike for Peace invites men to a night out to meet the ladies . . . and hear their interpretation of how to make history."[16] In fact, WSP succeeded, occasionally, in reversing traditional sex roles on the family level. In 1962 Philadelphia WSP organized a men's auxiliary and tried to promote the concept nationally. A Mr. Max Millman was listed in the national women's peace movement bulletin as someone who could give advice to other men wishing to start a similar group.[17]

Tired of the "democratic centralism" of the old Left and the top-down leadership of liberal peace groups, in which women's ideas, values, and feelings had been ignored, WSP insisted on collective leadership and local autonomy. WSP developed a nonhierarchical, loosely structured communications network and a consensus form of decision making that stressed process and inclusion, active listening instead of debating, and conscious efforts to share responsibility and skill development. Long meetings and long speeches were frowned upon, creativity, laughter, and playfulness were prized. This movement format, it has been argued, is most consistent with the feminist concepts of freedom and interdependence based on self-realization and support for others.[18] WSP's organizational style foreshadowed the emotional, poetic, and self-empowering guerrilla theater of the Women's Pentagon Action, in which a number of leading WSPers participated.

Mickey Flacks, a member of SDS in the sixties, believes that WSP's "unorganizational" format, developed in 1961 and 1962, played a key role in shaping the later antiwar movement and the women's liberation movement. "It was never given enough credit for this," she stated in a 1980 interview. Flacks recalled that she, Casey Hayden, and Sharon Jeffry were involved with WSP in Ann Arbor, Michigan, in 1962. "There was a community of the Left around the mimeograph machine in Ann Arbor," Flacks reflected, "and women like Hayden and Jeffry were in contact with WSP, and were inspired by what they saw in WSP of how it was possible to have much less of a gap between leadership and membership than in the new Left and how leadership could be shared."[19] Flacks contends that the WSPers in Ann Arbor, who were making their own ideological and tactical decisions, were the role models for Hayden and Jeffry, who were later to become the leading critics of SDS for the way in which it used women to do traditional female work and kept them from leadership. Flacks regrets that WSP's feminist organizational format was not fully recognized in the late 1960s and during the 1970s. She believes, and I agree, that it was because it was never consciously articulated and "because most of the young feminists never gave the movement the attention it deserved." Discussions with young women who were involved in radical feminist groups in the late 1960s and early 1970s reveal that WSP's middle-class, middle-aged "lady" image offended young women rebelling against their mothers, whom they perceived as politically and culturally backward.

WSP, on the other hand, found itself being influenced by the insights of the radical feminists. The older women not only understood but "felt" the younger women's critique of the male Left. It was a little more difficult, however, and took a little more time and exposure to consciousness raising and study, for the WSPers to accept and internalize the analysis of women's secondary status in the family and the economy offered by the second wave of feminism. Particularly difficult for the maternalist WSPers was the notion of putting women's rights on a par with social issues such as war, poverty, and racism.

Nevertheless, feminist consciousness and rhetoric rose markedly within WSP in the early 1970s. The women of East Bay WFP wrote to WSP's national office that they would like to propose that the next national conference discuss the relationship of WSP to the women's liberation movement. The East Bay group urged that WSP welcome the development of the new movement and approve and support its demand for equal opportunity, equal pay, the right to abortion, and the need for childcare centers. But the East Bay women were at odds with the women's liberation movement for "its narrowness of approach," specifically, its failure to take a stand on war and racism.[20] WSP's primary motive in joining the Women's Strike for Equality in 1970 was to add to the women's rights agenda a call for the immediate withdrawal of all U.S. forces from Southeast Asia. Bella Abzug spoke for WSP at the strike rally, declaring,

> We know that equality and liberation cannot be achieved by American women while our sisters in Vietnam and elsewhere are bombed, burned, murdered and raped. It is hard to talk about free abortions on demand when our hospitals are being closed down because funds are spent on the war, not for health needs: We know that women cannot get meaningful equality in jobs and education while [the] education program is being drastically cut back and unemployment is on the rise due to misdirected national priorities. . . . On this anniversary of Women's Suffrage, we feel very strongly that we must raise the demand for . . . an end to military domination of our lives.[21]

Any evaluation of WSP as a women's movement must acknowledge that, without setting out to do so, WSP's militant struggle against militarism in the 1960s helped to give dignity to the denigrated term *housewife* and to change the image of the good mother from passive to militant, from silent to eloquent, from private to public. In proclaiming that the men in power could no longer be counted on for protection, WSP exposed one of the most powerful myths of male militarists—that wars are waged by men to protect women and children. In a time when the prevailing family ideology confined mothers to family service, WSP stressed the social, communal, and global obligations of motherhood, thus challenging the feminine mystique under which the WSPers had lived most of their adult lives. By making a recognized contribution to the achievement of a test ban, the demise of MLF, the withdrawal of

U.S. troops from Vietnam, and the end of the draft for Vietnam, WSP also raised its participants' sense of political efficacy and self-esteem as women. WSP's greatest achievement in the 1960s was to make nuclear arms a women's issue. It politicized maternal values and made clear to its participants and supporters that the personal is political and that the private and public spheres are one.

The story of WSP makes it clear that female difference and gender equality are not polar opposites doomed never to merge. The history of WSP shows that women who build on traditional female consciousness to enter the political arena do not have to be trapped in that culture or bound forever to stereotypical notions of maternal rights and responsibilities. A separatist women's peace movement engaged in militant conflict with the patriarchal militarist state can develop a cadre of women who find themselves increasingly oppositional to the gendered division of political power in the nation and in the peace movement. WSP's legacy to the ongoing feminist peace movement is a history of intelligent, courageous, and resourceful struggle, and the message that political engagement leads to personal growth and empowerment as well as social transformation.

Notes

Introduction

1. Of the millions of women remaining in the work force after the war, most were unmarried or over thirty-five. See William Henry Chafe, *The Paradox of Change: American Women in the 20th Century* (New York: Oxford University Press, 1991), 154–72.

2. For an excellent discussion of women's labor-force participation during and after the war and the postwar push to domesticity for mothers of young children, see ibid., 121–93.

3. Ferdinand Lundberg and Marynia Farnham, *Modern Woman: The Lost Sex* (New York: Harper and Row, 1947); Agnes Meyer, "Women Aren't Men," *Atlantic Monthly,* August 1950, 32.

4. Ashley Montagu, "The Natural Superiority of Women," *Saturday Review,* 27 September 1958, 13–14; Adlai Stevenson, "Commencement Address at Smith College," *Women's Home Companion,* September 1955, cited in Betty Friedan, *The Feminine Mystique* (New York: Dell Publishing Co., 1963), 54; Benjamin Spock, *The Common Sense Book of Baby and Child Care* (New York: Duel, Sloan, and Pearce, 1945), 484.

5. See Eileen Eagan, *Class, Culture, and the Classroom: The Student Peace Movement of the 1930s* (Philadelphia: Temple University Press, 1981), 184–232.

6. Irving Howe, a young socialist and student at the City College of New York in the 1930s, described the ASU as his "home and passion," "a school in both politics and life." It provided a sense of belonging and meaning, and its Marxist perspective gave him a way of looking at the world that was in tune with his own experiences (*Steady Work* [New York: Harcourt, Brace, and World, 1966], 350, cited in Eagan, *Class, Culture, and the Classroom,* 137).

7. Eagan, *Class, Culture, and the Classroom,* 230.

8. See Gertrude Bussey and Margaret Tims, *Women's International League for Peace and Freedom, 1915–1965* (London: George Allen and Unwin, 1965), for the story of Gertrude Baer's work for peace through two world wars.

9. Amy Swerdlow, "The New York Ladies' Anti-Slavery Society, 1834–1840: Organization, Leadership, Tactics," master's essay, Sarah Lawrence College, 1973.

10. Amy Swerdlow, "The Politics of Motherhood: The Case of Women Strike for Peace and the Test Ban Treaty," Ph.D. diss., Rutgers University, 1984. Here are some examples of the misrepresentation of WSP in historical accounts: Fred Halsted in his reminiscence of the antiwar movement of the 1960s and early 1970s states, "Common in the early years of the 1960s were demonstrations of women, often organized by Women Strike for Peace. These were small

demonstrations, usually numbering only a few dozen participants" (*Out Now! A Participant's Account of the American Movement against the Vietnam War* [New York: Monad Press, 1978], 8). This is totally incorrect, as the earliest demonstrations in 1961 and 1962 involved tens of thousands of women. Charles DeBenedetti in *The Peace Reform in American History* (Bloomington: Indiana University Press, 1980), which praised WSP for its stand against HUAC, characterizes the actions of WSP in 1964 as feminist. This is completely inaccurate as WSP was a movement that built on women's traditional role as mothers. Dave Dellinger in *More Power Than We Know: The People's Movement toward Democracy* (Garden City, N.Y.: Doubleday, 1975) is dismissive and condescending regarding the role of WSP in the planning meetings of the mass antiwar demonstrations of the 1960s.

11. Sara Evans, *Personal Politics: The Roots of Women's Liberation in the Civil Rights Movement and the New Left* (New York: Knopf, 1979), x.

12. I have been fortunate to have access to a full run of the national publications, including a series of communications memoranda called "Issues for Discussion"; the national publication, *MEMO;* and the Los Angeles newsletter, *La Wisp.* In the files of the (national) Washington, D.C., office, which I acquired just before they were to be destroyed, I found many local newsletters in addition to hundreds of flyers, newspaper clippings sent in by local groups, correspondence, and individual women's scrapbooks. Dagmar Wilson was very generous in opening up her own papers to me without restrictions. These included correspondence, letters to and from political contacts and friends in the United States and abroad, and drafts of talks. Included are a letter from Eleanor Roosevelt and from Jacqueline Kennedy. Lorraine Gordon of New York presented me with her scrapbooks, and I have also been able to read the scrapbook of Alice Herz, a founder of Detroit WSP (now in Women Strike for Peace Papers, Swarthmore College Peace Collection [hereafter WSP Papers]). In addition I have had access to forty-nine volumes of FBI reports on WSP, in the possession of Barbara Bick, and the newspaper and magazine articles relating to WSP collected by the Department of Justice. The Los Angeles WSP and San Francisco Women for Peace (WFP) papers are in the Swarthmore College Peace Collection (SCPC). Those papers that I have collected over the last twenty years have been deposited at the Swarthmore College Peace Collection. Hundreds of other WSP activists kept scrapbooks of the movement, as they did of their own family mementos. I would like to encourage any of the WSPers who read this book to deposit their souvenirs of WSP in the Swarthmore College Peace Collection for future historians of women and peace.

13. I. F. Stone to National Office of WSP, Washington, D.C., reprinted in *MEMO,* April 1970, 14.

14. Jerome Weisner, quoted in Andrew Hamilton, "MIT: March 4 Revisited amid Political Turmoil," *Science,* 13 March 1970, 1476.

15. Eric Bentley, *Thirty Years of Treason: Excerpts from Hearings before the House Committee on Un-American Activities, 1938–1968* (New York: Viking Press, 1971), 951; Walter Goodman, *The Committee: The Extraordinary Career of the House Committee on Un-American Activities* (New York: Farrar, Strauss, and Giroux, 1964), 435, 437.

16. Even Mercedes Randall, an intellectual pacifist who wrote the biogra-

phy of the WILPF leader and Nobel Prize winner Emily Balch, assumed that the women who founded the Women's Peace Party "were the first in 1914 and 1915 to think *internationally*" (*Improper Bostonian* [New York: Twayne Publishers, 1964], 7, emphasis in original).

Chapter One

1. The number fifty thousand became part of the founding legend of WSP. It was an estimate, according to the organizers, based on reports from the sixty cities where strike actions were staged. In order to verify this figure I tallied the highest numbers I could find reported by the strike organizers or local papers for each city, and even with this generous method of estimation I could arrive at a total no higher than twelve thousand strikers. Strike actions took place in Yuma, Ariz.; Albany, Berkeley, Carmichael, Claremont, Covina, El Centro, Inglewood, La Jolla, Los Angeles, Menlo Park, Mill Valley, Oakland, Orinda, Richmond, Sacramento, San Diego, San Francisco, San Jose, Santa Barbara, Santa Cruz, and Walnut Creek, Calif.; Denver, Colo.; New Haven, Conn.; District of Columbia; Miami Beach, Fla.; Champagne/Urbana, Chicago, and Winnetka, Ill.; Ankeny and Iowa City, Iowa; Baltimore, Md.; Acton, Boston, Cambridge, Martha's Vineyard, and Watertown, Mass.; Ann Arbor and Detroit, Mich.; Minneapolis and St. Paul, Minn.; Kansas City and St. Louis, Mo.; Camden, Elizabeth, Newark, Paterson, and Trenton, N.J.; Albany, Auburn, Ithaca, Mount Vernon, New York City, Rochester, Schenectady, Syracuse, and Westchester County, N.Y.; Cincinnati, Cleveland, Columbus, and Dayton, Ohio; Portland, Oreg.; Bethlehem, Easton, Erie, and Philadelphia, Pa.; Seattle, Wash.; and Madison, Wis. ("Report to Women around the United States of America on the Women's Strike for Peace, November 1961," Washington, D.C., mimeographed flyer, WSP Papers).

2. *Sacramento Union,* 2 November 1961; *Washington Post* 2 November 1961.

3. *San Francisco Chronicle,* 2 November 1961.

4. The *Los Angeles Times* on 1 November 1961 stated that there were four thousand marchers. On 2 November 1961 it revised the figure to two thousand.

5. *Newsweek,* 13 November 1961, 21–22.

6. Sophia Wyatt, "One Day's Strike for Peace," *Manchester Guardian,* 12 April 1962, 2.

7. Interview with Dagmar Wilson, Leesburg, Va., November 1976.

8. Dagmar Wilson, introduction to *Journal of Women Strike for Peace: Commemorating Eighteen Years of Conscientious Concern for the Future of the World's Children* (New York: Women Strike for Peace, 1979), 2.

9. Also present at the exploratory meeting were Ralph Russell, Anne Bloom, Mary Chandler, and Lawrence Scott. Several of the founders believe that Jeanne Bagby was there, but the minutes do not show her name (notes for the planning meeting, 21 September 1961, typescript, WSP Papers). For a complete list of those involved in planning the strike, see Swerdlow, "Politics of Motherhood," 34.

10. Wilson, introduction to *Journal of Women Strike for Peace,* 2. WSP Papers.

11. Eleanor Garst, draft of letter, Washington, D.C., 22 September 1961, mimeo, WSP Papers. Groups of women throughout the country, joining together on an ad hoc basis, quickly reprinted the letter and an accompanying

248 NOTES TO PAGES 18–21

flyer with only minor changes to meet local needs. The Philadelphia reprint stated: "This project was initiated by a group of Washington, D.C., housewives and developed in Philadelphia by a group of concerned women." In Cleveland ten thousand copies were printed with an additional heading, "We Want Our Children to Live." A postscript explained that the letter was being circulated by a group of Cleveland housewives. On the North Shore of Chicago the word *strike* was rejected. The heading "Women: Participate in Your Government" was substituted. At least one man was involved in spreading the word of the strike, as a telegram to Eleanor Garst from Sol Lunde indicates: "Campaign for Telegrams for Peace November 1st in full swing. Good luck" (St. Louis, 29 October 1961, WSP Papers).

12. Wyatt, "One Day's Strike for Peace."

13. The decline in women's political role in the postwar period can be appreciated by comparing the groups that organized the women's strike in 1961 with the Women's Peace Parade Committee of 1914, which formed hastily at the outbreak of World War I. Fanny Garrison Villard, a nationally known philanthropist, suffragist, pacifist, and descendent of a distinguished reform family, was the parade leader. Well-known suffragists on the committee who were also public figures included Harriet Stanton Blatch and Carrie Chapman Catt. Leading figures in the field of social work, such as Lillian Wald, Lavinia Dock, and Mary K. Simkovitch, were also on the committee, along with labor activists Mary Drier, Leonora O'Reilly, and Rose Schneiderman. Other notable women involved were Mary Beard, Charlotte Perkins Gilman, and Henrietta Rodman. Among the organizers of WSP none had a national leadership role in any political or women's organization, nor were any of them known for their professional achievements. Dagmar Wilson was a successful children's book illustrator, but not a person of national prominence.

14. See Milton Steven Katz, "Peace, Politics, and Protest: SANE and the American Peace Movement, 1957–1972," Ph.D. diss., St. Louis University, 1973, 109–30; Barbara Deming, "The Ordeal of SANE," *Nation,* 11 March 1961, 200–205; A. J. Muste, "The Crisis in SANE," *Liberation,* July–August 1960, 10–13; A. J. Muste, "The Crisis in SANE, Act II," *Liberation,* November 1960, 5–8; Nathan Glazer, "The Peace Movement in America," *Commentary,* April 1961, 288–96; Linus Pauling, *No More War!* (New York: Dodd, Mead, and Co., 1958), 160–78.

15. "Who Are These Women?—You Ask," Washington, D.C., n.d., WSP Papers. The other organizers were Jeanne Bagby, Martha Dudley, Althea N. Dobson, Eleanor Garst, Folly Fodor, Miriam Levin, Janice Holland, E. Pauline Meyers, Janet Neuman, Margaret Russell, and Nancy P. Strauss.

16. Wilson probably used the term *suffragettes,* not as a derogation, but because she was brought up in England where the term was used widely. In the United States the term used for the women who fought for the vote is *suffragist.*

17. Dagmar Wilson to Eleanor Roosevelt, Washington, D.C., 12 October 1961, WSP Papers.

18. The *London Times* of 2 November 1961 reported that "Faye Emerson, the actress" recited Tennyson's "Locksley Hall" at a rally on 1 November. A letter from Dagmar Wilson to Emerson (Washington, D.C., 28 October 1961, WSP

Papers) indicates it was Wilson who suggested the poem. "Locksley Hall" is a nineteenth-century utopian vision of a moral, just, prosperous, and peaceful world, a vision that was part of WSP's political heritage.

19. Todd Gitlin, a former Students for a Democratic Society (SDS) activist, in a study of the relationship of SDS to the media, argues that in contemporary society for a movement to "matter," to communicate its goals and intention, it has no choice but to rely on the mass media to spread and legitimize its message (*The Whole World Is Watching: Mass Media in the Making and the Unmaking of the New Left* [Berkeley: University of California Press, 1980], 3).

20. The letter to Jacqueline Kennedy produced one of her very rare political comments. After thanking WSP for presenting her with the appeal, she declared: "I agree that as women, we should exert our great influence in the cause of world peace. As mothers we cannot help but be concerned about the health and welfare of our husbands and children." She then went on to repeat the official Cold War line: "I know that you will agree with me that the only route to peace for us is strength, and therefore join in support of the policies of this administration which are dedicated toward that end" (Jacqueline Kennedy to Dagmar Wilson, The White House, Washington, D.C., 13 November 1961; *Washington Post*, 15 November 1961).

21. Dagmar Wilson, "For Immediate Release, Women Strike for Peace," Washington, D.C., n.d., mimeo, WSP Papers.

22. *Baltimore Sun*, 29 October 1961.

23. Mary McGrory, "A Hue and Cry Is Raised," *Washington Evening Star*, 26 October 1961.

24. Gaye Tuchman, "The Symbolic Annihilation of Women by the Mass Media," in *Hearth and Home: Images of Women in the Mass Media*, ed. Gaye Tuchman, Arlene Kaplan Daniels, and James Benet (New York: Oxford University Press, 1978), 5.

25. *Baltimore Sun*, 29 October 1961.

26. *Washington Evening Star*, 26 October 1961.

27. See Dorothy Dinnerstein, *The Mermaid and the Minotaur: Sexual Arrangements and Human Malaise* (New York: Harper Colophon Books, 1976); Carol Gilligan, *In a Different Voice: Psychological Theory and Women's Development* (Cambridge: Harvard University Press, 1982); Sara Ruddick, *Maternal Thinking: Toward a Politics of Peace* (Boston: Beacon Press, 1989).

28. Carol Cohn, "Emasculating America's Linguistic Deterrent," in *Rocking the Ship of State*, ed. Adrienne Harris and Ynestra King (Boulder, Colo.: Westview Press, 1989), 165.

29. *Los Angeles Mirror*, 27 October 1961; *Los Angeles Times*, 2 November 1961.

30. *Washington Post*, 2 November 1961. See also *Sacramento Union*, 2 November 1961.

31. *Washington Post*, 2 November 1961.

32. *San Francisco Chronicle*, 3 November 1961.

33. *Los Angeles Mirror*, 1 November 1961.

34. *Los Angeles Express*, 11 November 1961.

35. *Philadelphia Inquirer*, 2 November 1961.

36. *Washington Post*, 17 November 1961.

37. These questions were posed by sociologist Elise Boulding when she decided to undertake a study of the women who made up the new movement, WSP (*Who Are These Women? A Progress Report on a Study of Women Strike for Peace* [Ann Arbor, Mich.: Center for Research on Conflict Resolution, 1963]).

38. *Los Angeles Mirror,* 2 November 1961.

Chapter Two

1. "Report on the Women's Strike for Peace," 1.

2. See Harriet Hyman Alonso, *The Woman's Peace Union and the Outlawry of War, 1921–1942* (Knoxville: University of Tennessee Press, 1989); Charles Chatfield, ed., *Peace Movements in America* (New York: Schocken Books, 1972); Blanche Wiesen Cook, "The Woman's Peace Party," *Peace and Change* 1 (Fall 1972): 36–42; Blanche Wiesen Cook, ed., *Crystal Eastman on Women and Revolution* (New York: Oxford University Press, 1978); Lela B. Costin, "Feminism, Pacifism, Internationalism, and the 1915 International Congress of Women," *Women's Studies International Forum* 5 (1982): 301–15; DeBenedetti, *Peace Reform in American History;* Marie Louise Degen, *The History of the Women's Peace Party* (New York: Garland Publishing, 1972); Frances Early, "Feminism, Peace and Civil Liberties," *Women's Studies* 18:95–115; Linda Schott, "The Woman's Peace Party and the Moral Basis for Women's Pacifism," *Frontiers* 3 (1985): 18–24; Barbara Jean Steinson, "The Mother Half of Humanity: American Women in the Peace and Preparedness Movements in World War I," in *Women, War, and Revolution,* ed. Carol Berkin and Clara Lovett (New York: Holmes and Meier Publishers, 1980), 259–84.

3. See William Ladd [Philanthropos], *On the Duty of Females to Promote the Cause of Peace* (Boston: American Peace Society, 1836).

4. See Rosemary Radford Ruether, "Feminism and Peace," *Christian Century,* 31 August–7 September 1983, 771; Blanche Glassman Hersh, *The Slavery of Sex* (Urbana: University of Illinois Press, 1978), 6–38.

5. Julia Ward Howe, *Reminiscences, 1819–1899* (Boston: Houghton Mifflin and Co., 1899), 163. In her eighties Howe wrote a hymn of peace much less well known than her hymn of battle: "For the glory that we saw / In the battle flag unfurled, / Let us read Christ's better law, / Fellowship for all the World."

6. "Exposition of Sentiments of the Women's Festival for Universal Peace," in *The Women's Peace Festival, June 2, 1873* (Boston: W. F. Brown and Co., 1874), 20–21. A WSP definition of peace was provided by the *Women's Peace Movement Bulletin* of 20 February 1964. To the question, "What do we mean by world peace?" the bulletin replied, "A condition of harmonious activity and inter-relationships which find expression at all levels, starting with the individual unit and extending to interpersonal relations in family, community, the state and nation, and ultimately in international affairs on a worldwide scale. In this definition, peace is not merely an absence of war, hot or cold. It is a deliberately created and sustained attitude of cooperation for the common good or the good of the whole." The WSP definition omits social injustices caused by class, race, or sex as a cause of war.

7. Historian Judith Papachristou points out that female peace activists at the turn of the century saw no contradiction between the celebration of female cul-

ture and the struggle for sexual equality, as their goal was to integrate female values into the body politic ("American Women and Foreign Policy, 1898–1905: Exploring Gender in Diplomatic History," *Diplomatic History* 14 [1990]: 493–509).

8. *Woman's Journal,* 18 January 1886, 20, cited in ibid., 498.

9. Papachristou, "American Women and Foreign Policy," 503.

10. Merle Curti, *Peace or War: The American Struggle, 1636–1936* (New York: W. W. Norton and Co., 1936), 117.

11. Carrie Chapman Catt, *Addresses Given at the Organizational Conference of the Women's Peace Party, Washington, D.C., January 10, 1915,* 4, cited in Marie Louise Degen, *History of the Women's Peace Party* (New York: Garland Publishing, 1972), 51.

12. Dagmar Wilson's statement in October 1961 ("Women spend years of their lives bringing up children to be healthy individuals and good citizens. Now in the nuclear age all women—not only mothers—have an equal duty . . . an even clearer and more urgent duty . . . to work for peace in order that our children may have a future") is based on the same belief that women have a special connection to and responsibility for maintaining international peace ("For Immediate Release," Washington, D.C., n.d., mimeo, WSP Papers, 2).

13. Degen, *History of the Women's Peace Party,* 40–41.

14. Coralie Franklin Cook, "Votes for Mothers," in "Votes for Women: A Symposium by Leading Thinkers of Colored America," *Crisis,* 10 August 1915, 184–85.

15. In 1950 the distinguished political journalist Dorothy Thompson was arguing in her column in the *Ladies' Home Journal* (November 1951, 11, 137) that women were a powerful and natural political force for peace, an "untapped source of spiritual power, which if . . . released might contribute to a reconsideration of policies based entirely on force." Only one year later the powerful Senator J. W. Fulbright, also writing in the *Ladies' Home Journal* (November 1951, 11, 137), urged women to participate in the political process but only on the local level, to "get better men elected." By 1955 Adlai Stevenson saw women's political role merely as providing a vision in her home of the meaning of life and freedom ("Commencement Address at Smith College," cited in Friedan, *Feminine Mystique,* 54).

16. Crystal Eastman to Jane Addams, 28 June 1917, Women's Peace Party Papers, DC43, Correspondence box 9, SCPC, cited in Joan Jensen, "All Pink Sisters: The War Department and the Feminist Movement in the 1920s," in *Decades of Discontent: The Women's Movement, 1920–1940,* ed. Lois Scharf and Joan Jensen (Boston: Northeastern University Press, 1983), 202.

17. C. Roland Marchand, *The American Peace Movement and Social Reform, 1898–1918* (Princeton: Princeton University Press, 1972), 183.

18. *Report of the International Congress of Women, 1915, The Hague,* 35, cited in Degen, *History of the Women's Peace Party,* 84. For details of the plan for mediation conceived by Julia Grace Wales, see Walter I. Trattner, "Julia Grace Wales and the Wisconsin Plan for Peace," *Wisconsin Magazine of History* 44 (Spring 1961): 203–13.

19. Former president Theodore Roosevelt denounced the women as "hysterical pacifists" and compared them with the "copperheads of the Civil War,

who did all they could to break up the Union and to ensure the triumph of slavery, because they put peace as the highest of all good" (Allen F. Davis, *American Heroine: The Life and Legend of Jane Addams* [New York: Oxford University Press, 1973], 233).

20. See Arthur S. Link, *Wilson: Confusion and Crisis* (Princeton: Princeton University Press, 1964), 314–18; Lillian Wald, *Window on Henry Street* (Boston: Little, Brown, 1934), 289–98.

21. William L. O'Neill, *Everyone Was Brave* (Chicago: Quadrangle Books, 1969), 182.

22. See Joan Hoff-Wilson, "'Peace Is a Woman's Job. . .': Jeannette Rankin and Her Lifework," *Montana: The Magazine of Western History* 30 (Spring 1980): 38–53; Ted Carlton Harris, *Jeannette Rankin: Suffragist, First Woman Elected to Congress, and Pacifist* (New York: Arno Press, 1982).

23. Alice Paul, "Conversations with Alice Paul: Woman Suffrage and the Equal Rights Amendment: An Interview Conducted by Amelia Fry in 1972," Bancroft Library, University of California, Berkeley, 175ff., cited in Barbara Miller Solomon, "Dilemmas of Pacifist Women, Quakers, and Others in World Wars I and II," in *Witnesses for Change: Quaker Women over Three Centuries,* ed. Elisabeth Potts Brown and Susan Mosher Scuard (New Brunswick, N.J.: Rutgers University Press, 1989).

24. Jacqueline Van Voris, *Carrie Chapman Catt: A Public Life* (New York: Feminist Press at the City University of New York, 1987), 186.

25. Emily Balch's *Out of Haiti,* which examined the economic, political, health, sanitation, education, and judicial situation in this small island recently occupied by U.S. Marines, was the result of one such fact-finding mission. See Florence Brewer Boekel, "Women in International Affairs," *Annals of American Academy of Political and Social Science* (May 1929): 230–48; Randall, *Improper Bostonian,* 303–4.

26. Alonso, "To Make War Legally Impossible," 61.

27. See ibid.

28. The organizations involved in NCCCW were the American Association of University Women, the Council of Women for Home Missions, the Committee on Women's Work of the Foreign Missions Conference of North America, the General Federation of Women's Clubs, the National Board of the Young Women's Christian Association, the National Council of Jewish Women, the National League of Women Voters, the Women's Christian Temperance Union, the Women's Trade Union League, the National Federation of Business and Professional Women's Clubs, and the National Conference of the American Ethical Union. See Van Voris, *Carrie Chapman Catt,* 198–210; Curti, *Peace or War,* 272.

29. I base this assumption on the fact that the names of Catt and NCCCW never appeared in WSP documents of any kind. I also base it on my personal acquaintance with the key women, who used everything they knew and thought to develop WSP policies. If they had known of NCCCW, they would have referred to it as an organization to be emulated or criticized.

30. Brenda J. Marston, "'We Want Our Vote to Count': Women's Peace Activism, 1914–1934," master's thesis, University of Wisconsin, Madison, 1985.

31. This information comes from folders 15, 17, 33, and 36 in the Elizabeth

Tilton Collection in the Arthur and Elizabeth Schlesinger Library on the History of Women in America, Radcliff College, Cambridge, Mass., cited in Nancy Cott, *The Grounding of Modern Feminism* (New Haven, Conn.: Yale University Press, 1987), 94.

32. That the use of the term Spider Web Chart was no random choice was suggested to me by Asian scholar Marilyn Young, who points out that the use of spider imagery plays to male fear and loathing of the mythic female power to entrap and destroy its innocent male victims—as the female black widow spider is known to do.

33. Catt also published an open letter to the Daughters of the American Revolution, in which she took the organization to task for lumping together communism, Bolshevism, socialism, liberalism, and ultrapacifism (Van Voris, *Carrie Chapman Catt,* 194–95).

34. Ibid, 195. See also John M. Craig, "Redbaiting, Pacifism, and Free Speech: Lucia Ames Mead and Her 1926 Lecture Tour in Atlanta and the Southeast," *Georgia Historical Review* 71 (Winter 1987): 601–22.

35. Van Voris, *Carrie Chapman Catt,* 83.

36. Ibid., 93–94. Bella Abzug recalls that WSPers talked of dropping flyers from airplanes, but by the 1960s it was illegal.

37. Dorothy Detzer, *Appointment on the Hill* (New York: Henry Holt and Co., 1948), 151–71.

38. Barbara Melosh, "'Peace in Demand': Anti-war Drama in the 1930S," *History Workshop* 22 (Autumn 1986): 72.

39. The popular front, which involved building large coalitions of liberal to left-leaning citizens opposed to the rise of fascism in Europe and Asia, grew out of a strategy or line of action developed by the Communist party. It was adopted by the Communist International in 1935 in response to left disunity in the face of Hitler's fateful victory in Germany. For the CPUSA it meant turning away from class struggle; working with all progressive forces, even the middle class; entering electoral politics; and identifying itself with the democratic political and cultural traditions in America. See Malcolm Sylvers, "Popular Front," in *Encyclopedia of the Left* (New York: Garland Publishing, 1990), 591–95; Robert Shaffer, "Women and the Communist Party, USA, 1930–1940," *Socialist Review* 9 (May 1979): 73–118.

40. See Amy Swerdlow, "Congress of American Women," in *Encyclopedia of the American Left*, ed. Mari Jo Buhle, Paul Buhle, and Dan Georgakas (New York: Garland Publishing, 1990), 161–62.

41. Congress of American Women, *American Women in Pictures*, souvenir journal (New York: Congress of American Women, n.d.), 5.

42. "Preamble, Constitution," *Congress of American Women* (New York: Congress of American Women, n.d.), 3. It is interesting to note that the two pioneers of U.S. women's history who were particularly aware of issues of race and class, Eleanor Flexner and Gerda Lerner, were both active members of CAW. See Gerda Lerner, "The Lady and the Mill Girl: Changes in the Status of Women in the Age of Jackson," *American Studies Quarterly* 10 (Spring 1969): 5–15; Eleanor Flexner, *Century of Struggle* (Cambridge: Harvard University Press, 1959).

43. "Manifesto for the Defense of Peace," in Congress of American Women, *American Women in Pictures* (New York: Congress of American Women, n.d.), 9.

44. *Herald Tribune* (Paris), 7 December 1948. The *New York Times* reported that at a meeting of the WIDF Council held in Moscow in November 1949 Muriel Draper, vice president of CAW, attacked the United States, charging that "because of the absence of social legislation for women the children of some millions of working mothers in the U.S. roam the streets, and fatal accidents to them are multiplying. She said U.S. industrialists are discharging married workers and apparently 'it is a crime to work if you love'" (*New York Times*, 20 November 1949).

45. *Christian Science Monitor*, 26 January 1949.

46. House Un-American Activities Committee, *Report on the Congress of American Women*, 81st Cong., 1st sess., 23 October 1949, 1 (Washington, D.C.: Government Printing Office, 1949).

47. Anthony has refused to discuss these charges with me, stating in a telephone conversation in 1977 that she was subject to incredibly unjust persecution, but that she is writing her own book in which she will detail all the false charges.

48. House Un-American Activities Committee, *Report on the Congress of American Women*, 100. The HUAC investigation of Susan B. Anthony II drove her out of politics and out of the country. She reappeared on the national political scene twenty-seven years later to a thunderous ovation at the National Women's Conference in Houston in 1977, where she rose to speak in favor of the Equal Rights Amendment, which she and CAW had opposed in the late 1940s (*The Spirit of Houston: The First National Women's Conference: An Official Report to the President, the Congress, and the People of the United States* [Washington, D.C.: National Commission on the Observance of International Women's Year, 1978], 148).

49. Susan B. Anthony II, "Is It True What They Say about Women?" *Women's Home Companion*, June 1945, 2.

50. House Un-American Activities Committee, *Report on the Congress of American Women*, 102.

51. Elaine Tyler May, *Homeward Bound: American Families in the Cold War Era* (New York: Basic Books, 1988), 159.

52. Ibid., 160.

53. Lawrence K. Frank and Mary Frank, *How to Be a Woman* (New York: Bobbs-Merrill Co., 1954), 69.

54. Alice K. Leopold, "The Family Woman's Expanding Role," *Marriage and Family Living*, August 1958, 278.

55. Norman Cousins, "Modern Man Is Obsolete," *Saturday Review*, 18 August 1945, 5.

56. Paul Boyer, *By the Bomb's Early Light: American Thought and Culture at the Dawn of the Atomic Age* (New York: Pantheon Books, 1985), 22.

57. W. Sterling Cole to President Dwight D. Eisenhower, 5 April 1954, Dwight D. Eisenhower Papers, cited in Robert A. Divine, *Blowing on the Wind: The Nuclear Test Ban Debate, 1954–1960* (New York: Oxford University Press, 1978), 23.

58. Pauling, *No More War!* 158–59, cited in Katz, "Peace, Politics, and Pro-

test," 58. Katz points out that as a result of this appeal a series of scientific conferences from both Cold War blocs began to meet in Pugwash, Nova Scotia, encouraging those inclined to optimism to believe that there might be some accommodation between the nuclear powers in the near future.

59. Katz, "Peace, Politics, and Protest," 87.

60. *Newsweek,* 6 May 1957, 51.

61. "The Milk All of Us Drink—and Fallout," *Consumer Reports,* March 1959, 103.

62. Steven M. Spencer, "Fallout: The Silent Killer," *Saturday Evening Post,* 29 August 1959, 86.

63. See Paul Boyer, "From Activism to Apathy: The American People and Nuclear Weapons, 1963–1980," *Journal of American History* 70 (March 1984): 821–44.

64. Eugene J. Rosi, "Mass and Attentive Opinion on Nuclear Weapons Tests and Fallout, 1954–1963," *Public Opinion Quarterly* 29 (Summer 1965): 280–97. Rosi did not record differences between male and female attitudes. A number of social scientists have observed the greater reluctance of women to endorse the use of military force. Alfred Hero, who analyzed data from Gallup, Roper, *Fortune,* the National Opinion Research Council, and the Survey Research Center revealed that "a pattern stands clear that for over 25 years women have been more opposed to the use of force than men" ("Public Reaction to Government Policy," in *Measures of Political Attitudes,* ed. John P. Robinson et al. [Ann Arbor, Mich.: Institute for Social Research, 1968], 52–54).

65. Otto Nathan and Heinz Norden, *Einstein on Peace* (New York: Simon and Schuster, 1960), 640–41.

66. Catherine Cory to Norman Cousins and Clarence Pickett, 20 September 1957, SANE Papers, Series B, SCPC, cited in Divine, *Blowing on the Wind,* 166. Other founders of SANE wanted a broader attack on militarism. It was eventually agreed that SANE would call for a cessation of testing as a first step toward disarmament.

67. For information on Lenore G. Marshall see *The Personal Record of a Life: Lenore Marshall,* ed. Janice Thaddeus (New York: Horizon Press, 1980). Josephine Pomerance was a member of WILPF and founded the Committee for World Development and World Disarmament, a service organization providing information and speakers on disarmament and economic development. She was also a former head of the Disarmament Information Committee of the American Association for the United Nations and cochairperson of the Task Force for a Nuclear Test Ban.

68. Katz, "Peace, Politics, and Protest," 87, 106.

69. Deming, "Ordeal of SANE," 201.

70. See Katz, "Peace, Politics, and Protest," chapter 3, "Communist Infiltration in the Nuclear Testing Movement?" 142–45.

71. Deming, "Ordeal of SANE," 202.

72. Muste, "Crisis in SANE," 11.

73. Washington Executive Board to National Committee, Washington, D.C., n.d., SANE Papers, box 20, SCPC, cited in Katz, "Peace, Politics, and Protest," 148.

74. Wilson's recollection of her reaction to the decision of SANE's National Board to exclude alleged Communists from membership is that "you had to shut up or get out. . . . I didn't officially withdraw, but I was to respond to national with a letter which I never wrote. I sort of lost heart." Wilson apparently did not remember the official protest from the Washington chapter (interview, Leesburg, Va., November 1976).

75. A. J. Muste, "A Time to Weep?" *Liberation,* October 1961, 5.

76. *I. F. Stone's Weekly,* 11–18 September 1961, 1.

77. *Ladies' Home Journal,* April 1961, 43.

Chapter Three

1. "Report on the Women's Strike for Peace," 1. WSP Papers.

2. Ibid., 3.

3. Interview with Ethel Taylor, Bala-cynwood, Pa., June 1980; interview with Hazel Grossman, San Francisco, January 1977.

4. Ethel Taylor, "A Personal Reaction to the Urbana Conference," *Issues for Discussion* 1 (July 1963), WSP Papers.

5. Evelyn Alloy to Executive Committee, WILPF, Philadelphia, 27 March 1962, WILPF Papers, SCPC.

6. Minutes of the National Executive Committee of WILPF, 27 March 1962, WILPF Papers, SCPC.

7. "Cooperation with Other Organizations," n.d., WILPF Papers, SCPC.

8. Interview with Ruth Gage-Colby, New York City, April 1980. Barbara Bick, a key woman in Washington, D.C., also remembers this meeting between the two groups as "very cordial" and "noncompetitive" (interview, Washington, D.C., November 1976).

9. Interview with Mickey Flacks, Amagansett, N.Y., September 1980.

10. Marjorie Hunter, "Women's Peace Campaign Gaining Support." *New York Times,* 22 November 1961. Twenty-two years later the *New York Times* (27 June 1983) reported that the commander of the army depot at Seneca, where women were holding an encampment to protest the presence of nuclear weapons, stated that he felt frustrated "because the women maintain they have no leader and are sometimes vague in describing what they plan to do."

11. *North Shore Women for Peace,* Chicago, 6 February 1963, WSP Papers, 1.

12. Kay Hardman to Dagmar Wilson, Sherman Oaks, Calif., 20 June 1962, WSP Papers.

13. *New York Post,* 6 May 1963.

14. Valerie Delacorte to Dagmar Wilson, New York City, 10 December 1961, WSP Papers.

15. This information is based on interviews with Dagmar and Christopher Wilson, Leesburg, Va., November 1976.

16. *Washington Post,* 29 October 1961.

17. This is a question Betty Friedan asked in *The Feminine Mystique:* "Why does the professional illustrator who heads the movement say she is 'just a housewife,' and her followers insist that once testing stops, they will stay happily at home with their children?" (361).

18. Interview with Dagmar Wilson, Leesburg, Va., November 1976.

19. Speech by Dagmar Wilson, Hotel Roosevelt, New York City, November 1979.

20. Dagmar Wilson, "My Role in the Formation of Women Strike for Peace," n.d., WSP Papers, 1.

21. Midge Decter and other Cold Warriors found Wilson's political attitudes both vague and dangerous. In a critique of WSP, published in *Harper's*, March 1963, under the title "The Peace Ladies," Decter argued, "One of the most depressing aspects of the current situation is how much it reminds one of the almost pathological incredulity with which large segments of the liberal community greeted revelations about such things as the Moscow trials, and over a decade later, Soviet espionage in the U.S. in general, and Alger Hiss in particular" (53).

22. For Jerome Frank's message see "Breaking the Thought Barrier: Psychological Challenges of the Nuclear Age," *Psychiatry: Journal for the Study of Interpersonal Processes* 23 (August 1960): 245–66.

23. Wilson's recollection in 1977 seems to be in conflict with the record. The record reveals that the Washington, D.C., SANE chapter opposed the exclusionary membership regulations. But the other Washington women I interviewed all agreed that SANE had capitulated to Cold War reasoning. Folly Fodor, one of WSP's founders, claims that it was the "discontented ones" who formed the nucleus of WSP.

24. *I. F. Stone's Weekly,* 11–18 September 1961, 1.

25. Interview with Christopher Wilson, Leesburg, Va., November 1976.

26. This admission was made in a three-way discussion among Dagmar Wilson, Christopher Wilson, and me in an interview at the Wilsons' home in Leesburg in 1976.

27. Dagmar Wilson to Miriam Levin, penciled note attached to a letter from Wilson to Linus Pauling, Washington, D.C., 16 January 1963, WSP Papers.

28. Dagmar Wilson and Belle Schultz to the Washington, D.C., Steering Committee, 3 July 1963, WSP Papers.

29. Dagmar Wilson to Peggy Darnell, 9 May 1962, WSP Papers.

30. Dagmar Wilson and Belle Schultz to the Washington, D.C., Steering Committee, 3 July 1963, WSP Papers.

31. Interview with Eleanor Garst, Washington, D.C., 6 November 1976. Most of the following information comes from the interview and from other conversations with Garst during the years we were both active in the movement, picketing, traveling, and writing statements together.

32. In 1976 Garst found the brief that she and her husband had written and reported that she still thought it "pretty good."

33. In a 1982 letter to me Garst explained that a bill enabling the conscription of women stood enough chance of passage that church and labor leaders combined to defeat it. "Women were more united than today in their opposition to being drafted" (Washington, D.C., 11 March 1982, WSP Papers).

34. Carol Urner to Seymour Friedan, Portland, Oreg., 29 August 1961, WSP Papers.

35. This was not a new idea. The pre–World War I feminist pacifists also took the position that "our men in political life are hampered by their political affili-

258 NOTES TO PAGES 63-66

ations." See Janet E. Richards's speech in *Addresses at the Organizational Conference,* 14.

36. The background on Folly Fodor comes from an interview with her, Washington, D.C., 6 November 1976.

37. Other mothers continue to report similar motivations for engaging in antimilitarism activities. Joan Reivich recalled to a reporter for the *Germantown Courier:* "I was in a hospital bed with my [newborn] baby during the Vietnam War. I saw a picture of a mother holding a baby who had been killed in the war. It touched me in a way that nothing has." This led to her 1988 activities with a mothers' peace network called Madre, which worked to aid mothers and children in Nicaragua and opposed U.S. intervention in that country. Alison McFall, a mother of two who is also active in Madre, says she joined the group because she had a conflict between all the happiness she was having with new babies and knowing how much hardship there is in Nicaragua due to U.S. intervention. She was also concerned that her children might be forced to fight in future wars (*Germantown Courier* [Pa.], 11 May 1988).

38. This information came from Barbara Bick, who was one of the key women in the Washington, D.C., area. Fodor was obviously not successful in her feminist protest, as *Potomac,* the weekly magazine section of the *Washington Post,* carried a picture of Fodor running a mimeograph machine at the WSP office with the caption "Mrs. Robert Fodor, above with her children, runs off a WSP memo at the main office." Whether or not to use one's own name is not a new issue for traditional women involved in protest movements. In 1834, for instance, at the First Anti-slavery Convention of American Women, a discussion was held regarding whether the roll of participants should be published with the appellation of *Mrs.* or *Miss.* The New Yorkers, who were the most conservative of the antislavery women, used *Mrs.* or *Miss,* but most of the women from Philadelphia and Boston did not. The proceedings of the convention recorded that a large proportion of the members who declined the appellation of *Mrs.* or *Miss* were not even members of the Society of Friends (*Proceedings of the Anti-slavery Convention of American Women Held in the City of New York, May 10, 11, 12, 1837* [New York: William S. Dorr, 1837], 15).

39. This is the only contemporary survey of the WSP constituency that I have been able to uncover.

40. Boulding, "Who Are These Women?" Boulding, who was already involved in the peace movement, was impressed and intrigued by the spontaneity of the WSP movement but sensed that it needed better communication. Boulding was a key woman in Ann Arbor WSP, so she had no trouble enlisting the group in her survey project. She credits Jean Converse, Elizabeth Converse, Marcia Barrabee, and Philip Converse, a WSP husband working at the Survey Research Center, with helping to formulate the questionnaire at the formative stage. John Sonquist, another WSP husband, working at the center, supervised the machine tabulation.

41. The questionnaire was divided into three parts: "Participation in Women's Peace Group" explored how the respondent became involved in WSP, what activities she participated in, and how centrally she was involved with the group; "Goals and Activities of WSP" explored respondents' perceptions of the

group's goals and activities and their effectiveness; "Background Information" elicited data on age, education, occupation, and parental, family, and childhood experiences.

42. Elise Boulding was a trained sociologist and a woman of deep social conscience, but in 1962 she did not think it important to include questions on class status, ethnic, or racial background.

43. U.S. Department of Labor, *Trends in Educational Attainments of Women* (Washington, D.C.: U.S. Government Printing Office, 1968), 11.

44. Of those who were "joiners," Gail Eaby, one of the key women in Los Angeles, was not unusual. She was a member of the American Civil Liberties Union, League of Women Voters, Centinella-Bay Human Relations Committee, United World Federalists, and the Unitarian Social Action Committee.

45. Boulding, "Who Are These Women?" 6.

46. In my own experience, I found very few women in their early twenties. Most of the key women were in their midthirties to late forties. Some of the national leaders were of an earlier generation. These included Ruth Gage-Colby, Ava Helen Pauling, and Frances Herring.

47. In studying the New York Ladies' Anti-slavery Society of the 1830s I found the same thing to be true. See Swerdlow, "New York Ladies' Anti-Slavery Society."

48. *Peace Assembly,* Cedar Rapids, Iowa, Women for Peace, June 1963, newsletter, WSP Papers, 2.

49. WSP activities participated in by respondents: letter writing 80%; literature distribution 69%; demonstrations 66%; self-education 40%; economic pressure 33%; visits to officials 30%; peace research 21%; direct action 4%; civil disobedience 2%.

50. Boulding, "Who Are These Women?" 17.

Chapter Four

1. Elise Boulding, "To All Women's Peace Groups in Correspondence with the Women Strike for Peace of Washington, D.C.," Ann Arbor, Mich., n.d., WSP Papers.

2. Memo from Frances Herring to Elise Boulding, Ruth Gage-Colby, Dagmar Wilson, Lorraine Gordon, Mary Clarke, and Vera Foster, Berkeley, Calif., 28 December 1961, WSP Papers.

3. *Women's Peace Movement Bulletin,* 6 February 1963, 7.

4. *New York Times,* 2 April 1962.

5. *Women's Peace Movement Bulletin,* 20 February 1963. Barrie Thorne, writing of the male-led antidraft movement of the late 1960s, stated that "in some respects, the report of the event was the event, and the edge of reality became blurred" ("Resisting the Draft: An Ethnography of the Draft Resistance Movement," Ph.D. diss., Brandeis University, 1971, 342). Historian Daniel Boorstin argues that demonstrations, marches, and draft card turn-ins were "pseudo events" created for the convenience of the reprinting and reproducing media (*The Image: A Guide to Pseudo Events in America* [New York: Harper and Row, 1964], 11).

6. *New York Times,* 19 April 1962.

7. Ibid.

8. *La Wisp*, 7 November 1962, 9.

9. *London Times Mirror*, 4 October 1979.

10. *Labor News*, 26 April 1963.

11. *San Francisco Chronicle*, 25 March 1962.

12. Interview with Mickey Flacks, Amagansett, N.Y., September 1980.

13. Dagmar Wilson to Mrs. Harry Cooper, Washington, D.C., 26 March 1962, WSP Papers.

14. "Women Strike for Peace: Women for Peace Steering Committee Questionnaire," filled out by Dagmar Wilson, n.d., mimeo, WSP Papers.

15. "What Is an A.A.W.F.P. Anyhow?" *Ann Arbor Women for Peace Monthly Bulletin*, October 1963, WSP Papers, 1–2.

16. Eleanor Garst, "Women: Middle Class Masses," *Fellowship*, November 1962, 10–12.

17. Decter, "Peace Ladies," 50.

18. *White Plains Reporter Dispatch*, 17 January 1963.

19. Ibid.

20. Emily Greenblatt to Dagmar Wilson, Washington, D.C., 16 April 1962, WSP Papers.

21. Jo Freeman, "The Tyranny of Structurelessness," *Berkeley Journal of Sociology* 17 (1972–73): 151–64.

22. Interview with Mickey Flacks, Amagansett, N.Y., September 1980.

23. Virginia Naeve to Dagmar Wilson, South Woodstock, Vt., 30 May 1962, WSP Papers.

24. Minutes of 13 December 1962 meeting, Women Strike for Peace, held at the Woodrow Wilson Foundation, mimeo, WSP Papers.

25. Anne Cochran to "Dear Strikers," Alexandria, Va., 5 March 1962, WSP Papers.

26. Dagmar Wilson to Anne Cochran, Washington, D.C., 16 March 1962. There is no signature on the letter, but the address and telephone number supplied are Wilson's.

27. Jeanne Bagby, "Policy Paper #8: For Thought and Discussion," National Information Clearing House, Washington, D.C., 27 May 1963, mimeo, WSP Papers, 1.

28. Helen Frumin to Dagmar Wilson, Scarsdale, N.Y., 27 September 1962, WSP Papers.

29. Los Angeles WSP, Chairman, Mary Clarke, Los Angeles, n.d., mimeo, WSP Papers.

30. "Everyone Can Act in A-Bomb Movement," *Correspondence* (Detroit), January 1962, 1.

31. "Proposed Structure for Women Strike for Peace, Metropolitan New York, New Jersey, Connecticut," n.d., mimeo, WSP Papers.

32. I don't recall ever being elected to any position in WSP, but I was active in all its inner circles. I was editor of the New York area newsletter by volunteering to edit it, and editor of the national *MEMO* by the decision of a national conference. My local chapter, Great Neck, never objected; in fact it supported all my efforts although I was never elected to represent it.

33. *Women's Peace Movement Bulletin,* 18 March 1962, 8.

34. Frances Herring, transcript of radio station KPFK WSP commentary, May 1967, WSP Papers.

35. Frances Herring, "To End the Arms Race—Not the Human Race," *MEMO,* April 1970, 3–4, WSP Papers.

36. The treaty was signed in Moscow on 5 August 1963 and ratified by the Senate on 24 September. For a full history of the test ban treaty see Harold Karan Jacobson and Eric Stein, *Diplomats, Scientists, and Politicians: The United States and the Nuclear Test Ban Negotiations* (Ann Arbor: University of Michigan Press, 1966).

37. *Philadelphia Inquirer,* 20 September 1963.

38. Jerome Weisner, quoted in Hamilton, "MIT," 1476.

39. Interview with Eleanor Garst, Washington, D.C., November 1976.

40. Jeanne Bagby, "Behind the Scene: The Psychological Panorama Underlying the Beat Extravaganza," *Liberation,* May 1959, 11–13.

41. Bagby's passionate concern for the fate of the planet is revealed in a poem she wrote eight months before the women's peace strike. It was called "Oh What Farewells": "Let me begin / my goodbyes love / here in a pleasant bright good morning / where there's not a hint / of adieu or of death / let me begin beloved earth / before your lover Sun bursts wide / and all your flesh is torn. / Let me begin also / before we feed the streets / with blood, before / we become momentary messages / burnt into walls, before / our children are devoured / by the Insatiable One / we somehow failed to satisfy. / Let me begin before / love vanishes / for lack of lovers / let me begin / sweet history / before the end of man" (*Liberation,* March 1961).

42. Jeanne Bagby, "Report on Health Hazards from Fallout," Washington, D.C., WSP, 1 December 1961, WSP Papers, 1.

43. George Raine, "Expert Faults U.S. on 50s Atomic Tests: Testified at Fallout Trial That Protection against Unknown Danger Was Inadequate," *New York Times,* 10 October 1982.

44. For more information on WSP's role in disseminating information on the dangers of nuclear fallout, see Swerdlow, "Politics of Motherhood," 379–448.

45. *Washington Post,* 26 April 1962. An editorial in the *Birmingham News* (27 March 1962) accused WSP of "milking an issue dry."

46. *New York Herald Tribune,* 15 January 1962. The story was reported in the *New York Times,* the *Boston Herald,* and the *Washington Post,* 15 January 1962, and the *Washington Evening Star,* 16 January 1962. See also *I. F. Stone's Weekly,* 22 January 1962, 1.

47. *New York Post,* 17 January 1962.

48. *New York Times,* 16 January 1962.

49. The suggestion to Milton Viorst to raise a question about the women came from the New York public relations committee, which at the time consisted of Lorraine Gordon, Nancy Mamis, and Amy Swerdlow.

50. *Los Angeles Herald Examiner,* 26 January 1962.

51. Minutes of Third National Conference, Winnetka, Ill., 4–7 June 1964, mimeo, WSP Papers.

52. *Newsweek,* 15 January 1962, 51. The *New York Times* (29 January 1962) reported that aides in charge of sifting White House mail stated that few pamphlets had been returned.

53. Portland WFP had conducted dramatic first-day-of-the-month vigils for almost a year, carrying black umbrellas decorated with the slogan "Peace Is the Only Shelter." The WFP vigils received a good deal of publicity from the local media, which had been bombarded with WSP press releases and position papers. The Portland women also developed their expertise in arguing against civil defense in a long legislative battle in which they testified at hearings and debated on radio and television. Portland voters eventually refused a special levy for civilian defense, but they were overridden by the governor, who sought state and federal funds for the program. Finally, through persistent efforts by WFP, the City Council of Portland voted against funding civil defense, thus eliminating fallout shelters from the city budget entirely (memo from Phoebe L. Freedman to National Information Clearing House, Portland, Oreg., 3 November 1963, WSP Papers).

54. *National Information Memo,* 31 March 1964, WSP Papers, 2.

55. Seymour Melman, *The Peace Race* (New York: George Braziller, 1962).

56. "Policy Statement Adopted at First National Conference, Ann Arbor, Michigan," June 1962, mimeo, WSP Papers. SDS also adopted its Port Huron Statement in June 1962.

57. Mary Clarke, "Summary of Decisions at Seven WSP National Conferences," n.d., mimeo, WSP Papers.

58. Elsa Knight Thompson, "My Personal Impression of the Ann Arbor Conference," n.d., mimeo, WSP Papers, 1.

59. I recall that Dagmar Wilson came to New York to discuss with WSP leaders and other peace people the possibility of chartering a plane for a flight into the Havana airport, where presumably the presence of respectable middle-class American mothers sitting-in on the airstrip would prevent the United States from dropping bombs. Neither the plan nor the plane ever got off the ground, but when the crisis was over, the Ann Arbor women submitted a proposal to the national *MEMO* calling for the creation of a group of women willing to become hostages in international emergencies to prevent the use of atom bombs.

60. Policy Paper no. 2, December 1962, mimeo, WSP Papers, 1.

61. *National Information Memo,* 28 June 1963, WSP Papers, 4.

62. Barbara Bick, transcript of radio station KPFK WSP commentary, May–June 1969, WSP Papers.

63. Elsa Knight Thompson, "My Personal Impression."

64. Eunice Armstrong to Mary Clarke, Scarborough, N.Y., 18 June 1962, WSP Papers.

65. *National Information Memo,* 28 June 1963, WSP Papers, 5.

66. Ruth Kiesel, Los Angeles WSP, to Christopher L. Taylor, President, Los Angeles NAACP, to be read at Rally for Freedom, Wrigley Field, Sunday, 26 May 1963. The resolution was also adopted by Whittier WSP and presented to the California WSP state conference in Asilomar, 24–26 May 1963.

67. Dagmar Wilson to Barbara Deming, Washington, D.C., 15 October 1963, WSP Papers, 1, 3. Deming replied: "I wonder in this case whether, if there were

some woman who felt moved to go to Tennessee, she might not be able to do peace work simultaneously—precisely among the women in the project" (Barbara Deming to Dagmar Wilson, Wellfleet, Mass., 9 October 1963, WSP Papers).

68. Message to WSP from Mrs. Martin Luther King, reprinted in an ad by Women Strike for Peace, *California Eagle,* 23 May, 1963.

69. The Jeannette Rankin Brigade joined the issue of war and poverty, adding women's rights, which was not at that time part of the WSP agenda. The brigade is discussed in greater detail in chapter 6.

70. Chester Bowles, *Promises to Keep: My Years in Public Life, 1941–1969* (New York: Harper and Row, 1971), 526. Caroline was the president's young daughter.

71. Arthur M. Schlesinger, Jr., *A Thousand Days: John F. Kennedy in the White House* (Boston: Houghton Mifflin Company, 1965), 896.

72. *New York Times,* 11 June 1963.

73. Aileen Hutchinson, in U.S. Senate, Committee on Foreign Relations, *Hearings before the Committee on Foreign Relations on the Treaty Banning Nuclear Weapons Tests in the Atmosphere, in Outer Space, and Underwater,* 88th Cong., 1st sess., August 12–15, 19, 20, 22, 23, 26, 27, 1963, 744.

74. Ibid., 906.

75. Maurine Neuberger, 24 September 1963, quoted in newsletter, WSP of New York, New Jersey, Connecticut, October 1963, WSP Papers, 1.

76. *Washington Post,* 25 September 1963.

77. Reported in newsletter, WSP of New York, New Jersey, Connecticut, October 1963, WSP Papers, 4. I have not been able to find a copy of the Adlai Stevenson letter in the WSP archives.

78. *Woman's Day,* November 1963, 37–39, 141–42.

79. Ibid.

80. Address by Dagmar Wilson at WSP second anniversary celebration, New York City, 1 November 1963, WSP Papers, 3–4.

Chapter Five

1. Those subpoenaed in connection with the 1962 WSP hearings were (in order of their appearance before the committee) Blanche Posner, Ruth Meyers, Lyla Hoffman, Elsie Neidenberg, Sylvia Contente, Rose Clinton, Iris Freed, Anna MacKenzie, Elizabeth Moos, Ceil Gross, Jean Brancato, Miriam Chesman, Norma Spector, and Dagmar Wilson. Spector never testified. She was excused due to illness. Two men active in the peace movement were also subpoenaed. They were William Obrinsky of SANE and the Staten Island Community Peace Group and John W. Darr, Jr., of the Greenwich Village Peace Center.

HUAC was established in 1938 and abolished in 1975. For most of its lifetime, the committee was known for its sensational investigations of the Communist threat in the United States. It searched for Communist party members and Communist influence in the film industry, organized labor, the government, the clergy, the academy, and peace organizations. In 1947 the committee launched an investigation into communism in the motion picture industry, which resulted in the Hollywood blacklist, barring actors and writers suspected of Communist leanings from employment in the film industry. But it was the committee's investigation in 1948 of Alger Hiss and the subsequent conviction of Hiss for perjury that established HUAC as a major political force.

2. Bentley, *Thirty Years of Treason*, 951. Frank Wilkerson, executive director of the National Committee to Abolish the House Un-American Activities Committee, wrote to Eleanor Garst, Kay Johnson, Margaret Russell, and Dagmar Wilson on 14 December 1962, "You have dealt HUAC its greatest setback" (WSP Papers). Charles DeBenedetti in *The Peace Reform in American History* stated that "WSP activists challenged for the first time the House Un-American Activities Committee's practice of identifying citizen peace seeking with Communist subversion. . . . The open disdain of the WSP for HUAC did not end the Congress's preference for treating private peace action as subversive. But it did help break the petrified anti-Communism of Cold War American politics and gave heart to those reformers who conceived of peace as more than military preparedness" (167–78).

3. Eleanor Garst to Dagmar Wilson, Amy Swerdlow, Lorraine Gordon, and Lyla Hoffman, Washington, D.C., 30 November 1962, WSP Papers.

4. The contrast between the SANE and WSP decisions in the face of a congressional investigation was made even more acute because two of the previously non-WSP women subpoenaed were members of Henry Abrams's organization, the Conference of Greater New York Peace Groups.

5. "Ann Arbor Conference, 9–10 June 1962," Los Angeles Statement 1, mimeo, WSP Papers.

6. Women Strike for Peace, "House Un-American Activities Committee Subpoenas," n.d., WSP Papers. The anti-HUAC statement was composed by the New York and Washington leadership in the usual collaborative fashion, with no pride of authorship or desire for credit, so today it is difficult to know who wrote which part. It was distributed through official WSP channels via the national office.

7. Bentley, *Thirty Years of Treason*, 951.

8. *New York Times*, 7 December 1962.

9. *Washington Post*, 6 December 1962.

10. Jack Lotto, "On Your Guard: Mothers Pro-Red Target," *New York Journal American*, 4 April 1962.

11. Decter, "Peace Ladies," 48.

12. *San Francisco Examiner*, 21 May 1962.

13. FBI file 100-39566-8.

14. Ibid.

15. See *Los Angeles Times*, 2 November 1961.

16. Légat Berne to Director FBI, 4 April 1962, FBI file 100-39574-187.

17. To SAC, WFO 100-39566 (C) from SA F. B. Griffith, Jr., "Subject: Women Strike for Peace (WSP) Information concerning Internal Security," 28 May 1965, FBI file 100-39566-753.

18. A. E. Wessel, "The American Peace Movement: A Study of Its Themes and Political Potential," Rand Corporation, Santa Monica, Calif., 1962, mimeo, 3.

19. "HUAC Hearing Called December 11–12," Washington Committee to Abolish the House Un-American Activities Committee, Washington, D.C., 4

December 1962, WSP Papers. The committee erred in stating that WSP supported the Peace Corps. There is no evidence of this in any of WSP's published materials.

20. *Washington Post,* 6 December 1962.

21. "SANE Protests Un-American Activities," 4 December 1962, WSP Papers.

22. Decter, "Peace Ladies," 53; House Un-American Activities Committee, *Communist Activities in the Peace Movement (Women Strike for Peace and Certain Other Groups): Hearings,* 87th Cong., 2d sess., 11–13 December 1962, 20.

23. Goodman, *Committee,* 435–37.

24. Telegram from Frances Herring to Dagmar Wilson, Berkeley, 6 December 1962, WSP Papers.

25. Quoted from Amy Swerdlow, transcript of radio station KPFK WSP commentary, May–June 1967, WSP Papers.

26. The constant discussion within WSP about who was and who was not subpoenaed, and why, led one self-styled wit among the WSP husbands to remark, "Some of the ladies seem to be suffering from subpenis envy."

27. Washington, D.C., WSP to "Dear WISPs," 6 December 1962, WSP Papers.

28. Sarah Shoresman of North Shore WFP in Winnetka, Ill., wired the Washington office that she had approximately fifteen volunteers from the Chicago area ready to "speak for peace." But before sending individual wires to HUAC, Shoresman wanted to consult on wording. The Washington office suggested: "At a time when the Geneva negotiations on a test ban treaty and disarmament are currently taking place, it weakens our government's position to be attacking the group in the United States that has worked most actively for these things during the last year. It gives democracy a black eye and makes the Geneva talks seem insincere. We request permission to testify concerning Women Strike for Peace" (telegram from Sarah Shoresman, North Shore Women for Peace, to Washington, D.C., WSP, 11 December 1962; answer in undated memo attached to Winnetka telegram; both in WSP Papers).

29. Telegram from Elsa Knight Thompson and Pamela Ford to Washington WISP, 6 December 1962, WSP Papers; Greta Wolfe, Corresponding Secretary, Champaign/Urbana WFP, to Washington, D.C., WSP, 8 December 1962, WSP Papers.

30. Carol Urner to Francis Walter, House Un-American Activities Committee, Portland, Oreg., reprinted in *Women's Peace Movement Bulletin,* 20 December 1962, 5. Mary Grooms also distributed a letter to Francis Walters, offering to testify "to help the committee fully understand our deep concern for the survival of man" (Mary Grooms to Francis Walters, Rochester, N.Y., 5 December 1962, mimeo, WSP Papers).

31. Victor S. Navasky, *Naming Names* (New York: Viking Press, 1980), 351–52.

32. *Chicago Daily Tribune,* 13 December 1962.

33. Denver Women for Peace to New York WSP and Dagmar Wilson, Washington WSP, 6 December 1962, WSP Papers.

34. Untitled press clipping in WSP Papers.

NOTES TO PAGES 107–11

266   NOTES TO PAGES 107–11

35. Lyla Hoffman, typewritten statement, New York, n.d., WSP Papers.

36. Interview with Elizabeth Moos, New York City, May 1981.

37. "Statement by Mrs. Sylvia Contente concerning Her Being Subpoenaed to Appear before House Un-American Activities Committee on Tuesday, December 11, 1962," New York, mimeo, WSP Papers.

38. According to Susan B. Anthony's grandniece, Susan B. Anthony II, the statues were intended to stand with other sculptured notables on the main floor of the Capitol, but were relegated to the basement crypt.

39. It should be noted that Agnes Meyer had made the same point in a speech to WILPF on 20 June 1960. Commenting on a Senate investigation of antinuclear scientist Linus Pauling, Meyer stated: "Any woman who is intimidated by the possibility of McCarthy-like attacks should remember that Jane Addams met the same fate with serenity. Because of her call for international peace negotiations, she was called a Red, she was hounded by secret service agents, and innocent meetings at Hull House—even to hear music—were under police surveillance for subversive activities" (*I. F. Stone's Weekly,* 27 June 1960, 4).

40. *Washington Daily News,* 14 December 1962.

41. Another indication of the confusion and paranoia a summons from HUAC could generate came on the next day when a delegation of women arrived at the White House to keep a lobbying appointment with Arthur Schlesinger, Jr., aide to President Kennedy. According to a report by Robert Light in the *National Guardian,* which coincides with my memories of the occasion, there was a good deal of confusion at the White House gate as the WSP delegation began to gather. The four women who arrived first were startled by the brusque and anxious manner of the guards. After their names were checked, the guards demanded, "Where are the rest of the women?" "They're coming in another taxi and should be here momentarily," was the answer. A grilling about how many women were expected and when they would arrive, and an enforced wait for one latecomer, Amy Swerdlow, ensued. After the meeting, as the women left Schlesinger's office, a White House aide explained that they had been grilled because the White House police were on alert after being warned that WSP was planning to "storm the East Gate." Later one woman quipped, "Arthur Schlesinger should have known that we don't advocate a 'first strike' policy" (Robert Light, "Women for Peace Too Sharp for HUAC at Smear Hearings," *National Guardian,* 20 December 1962, 20).

42. House Un-American Activities Committee, *Communist Activities in the Peace Movement,* 2064–65.

43. Ibid., 2066.

44. Ibid.

45. Ibid., 2067.

46. Ibid., 2072.

47. *National Information Memo,* 21 December 1962, WSP Papers, 2; House Un-American Activities Committee, *Communist Activities in the Peace Movement,* 2072.

48. Testimony of Blanche Posner, accompanied by counsel Victor Rabinowitz, in House Un-American Activities Committee, *Communist Activities in the Peace*

Movement, 2074. Of the ten WSP witnesses in this investigation, five were college graduates, and five had only a high school education.

49. See Light, "Women for Peace," 116.

50. House Un-American Activities Committee, *Communist Activities in the Peace Movement,* 2074–75.

51. Ibid., 2085.

52. Ibid., 2092–93.

53. Testimony of Ruth Meyers, accompanied by counsel Leonard Boudin, in House Un-American Activities Committee, *Communist Activities in the Peace Movement,* 2095–2103.

54. House Un-American Activities Committee, *Communist Activities in the Peace Movement,* 2101.

55. *National Guardian,* 20 December 1962.

56. Mary McGrory, "Probers Find Peacemakers More Than a Match," *Washington Evening Star,* 12 December 1962.

57. Lyla Hoffman, typewritten statement, New York, n.d., WSP Papers.

58. Testimony of Lyla Hoffman, accompanied by counsel Telford Taylor, in House Un-American Activities Committee, *Communist Activities in the Peace Movement,* 2103–14.

59. Testimony of Anna MacKenzie, accompanied by counsel Telford Taylor, in House Un-American Activities Committee, *Communist Activities in the Peace Movement,* 2139. See *Washington Post,* 13 December 1962.

60. Testimony of Anna MacKenzie, accompanied by counsel Telford Taylor, in House Un-American Activities Committee, *Communist Activities in the Peace Movement,* 2139.

61. Ibid., 2140.

62. *National Guardian,* 20 December 1962.

63. WSP statement "At the close of the second day."

64. Testimony of Dagmar Wilson, accompanied by counsel Lawrence Speiser, House Un-American Activities Committee, *Communist Activities in the Peace Movement,* 2187–2201.

65. Dagmar Wilson to Amy Swerdlow, Leesburg, Va., 18 August 1981.

66. Frank Wilkerson to Eleanor Garst, Kay Johnson, Margaret Russell, and Dagmar Wilson, Washington, D.C., 14 December 1962, WSP Papers.

67. *Washington Post,* 12 December 1962. In a more serious vein, an editorial presented on the air by WJZ TV sounded like it had been written by a WSP activist. WJZ asked, "Since when is it un-American to be concerned about radiation poisoning and nuclear destruction? To our minds, anyone who is *not* concerned about this grisly prospect is really un-American" (transcript, Westinghouse Broadcasting Co., Baltimore, 13 December 1962, 7:25 P.M., 14 December 1962, 2:25 P.M., WSP Papers).

68. Bill Galt, "Women Make Hearing a Comedy: It's Not Un-American to Giggle," *Vancouver Sun* (British Columbia), 14 December 1962.

69. Russell Baker, "The Ladies Turn Peace Quiz into Greek Comedy," *Detroit Free Press,* 16 December 1962.

70. Mary McGrory, "Peace Strike Explained: 'Nobody Controls Anybody,'" *Washington Evening Star,* 14 December 1962. The WSP women also saw the

HUAC confrontation as a manifestation of the battle of the sexes. Mary Grooms of Rochester, N.Y., stated that after listening to two days of the questioning she became convinced that "these men don't understand how women think. Even if they should study it for 50 years they never would understand the structure of Women Strike for Peace. They're using masculine logic and we're using feminine logic. The two just don't meet" (*Rochester Democrat and Chronicle*, 13 December 1962). Kay Hardman wrote to the *New York Times*, "Alfred Nittle's problem is not unusual; the best analogy may be the husband whose wife has gone to the hospital to have a baby and who is confronted with arrangements for carpooling the older children to school, dancing lessons, Boy Scouts, and the dentist. Not understanding the art of the strategic phone call, he usually ends up in wild confusion and does all the driving himself—if he can find the street address" (*New York Times*, 31 December 1962).

71. James McCartney,"It's Ladies' Day at the Capitol: Hoots, Howls—and Charm," *Chicago Daily News*, 14 December 1962.

72. *Women, Militarism, and War: Essays in History, Politics, and Social Theory*, ed. Jean Bethke Elshtain and Sheila Tobias (Totowa, N.J.: Rowman and Littlefield, 1990), 40. Alice Herz, a Detroit WFP member, wrote to Dagmar Wilson after the hearings, "Enthusiastic congratulations. This cry of the women seemed to me like the cry of the little child in . . . Anderson's fairy-tale. . . . But the Emperor has nothing on!" (Alice Herz to Dagmar Wilson, Belle Schultz, and all the other women concerned, Detroit, n.d., WSP Papers).

73. *Daily Cardinal*, 14 December 1962.

74. *National Review*, 31 December 1962, 497.

75. *Newark Evening News*, 15 December 1962.

76. Washington, D.C., WSP, "So Many Great Things Have Happened," 1963, WSP Papers.

77. *National Information Memo*, 21 December 1962, WSP Papers, 1.

78. "Report on Constitutional Rights: Prepared by Bella Abzug, New York," *National Information Memo*, 21 December 1962, WSP Papers, 4.

79. Homer A. Jack, "The Will of the WISP versus the Humiliation of HUAC," transcript of a talk on radio station WBAI, New York, 28 December 1962, WSP Papers.

80. Kay Hardman to Homer Jack, Sherman Oaks, Calif., 5 January 1963, WSP Papers. The Los Angeles County Federation of Labor, AFL-CIO, also criticized WSP for its "include everybody stand." In a pamphlet the Labor Council charged that "there are statements by leaders of the Women's International Strike for Peace that they will accept into their movement 'women of all . . . political persuasions.' This reveals an utter failure to comprehend the nature of Communism and the role of Communists or those within its orbit" ("Totalitarian Intruders of the Left," Los Angeles, January 1963, unpaginated).

81. Kay Hardman to Homer Jack, Washington, D.C., 5 January 1963, WSP Papers.

82. Eleanor Garst, untitled typescript, Washington, D.C., n.d., first page missing, WSP Papers, 4.

83. Barbara Deming, "Letter to WISP," in *Revolution and Equilibrium* (New York: Grossman Publishers, 1971), 143–44.

84. *Washington Evening Star,* 14 December 1962.

85. Director FBI to SAC, WFO, "Women Strike for Peace, aka Women's International Strike for Peace, Info concerning Internal Security," FBI file 100-39566-33. The field offices notified were Atlanta, Baltimore, Buffalo, Chicago, Cincinnati, Cleveland, Denver, Detroit, Las Vegas, Los Angeles, Miami, Minneapolis, Newark, New Haven, New Orleans, New York, Philadelphia, San Diego, San Francisco, and Springfield, Ill.

86. To Director FBI from SAC, WFO 100-39566 (C) 0, 15 February 1963, FBI file 100-39566-345.

87. *Washington Post,* 6 December 1964.

88. Ibid.

89. *New York Times,* 3 August 1966.

90. Donna Allen, "HUAC Faces the New Spirit," *Liberation,* October 1966, 596.

91. Goodman, *Committee,* 144.

92. Mary McGrory, "The CIA's Most Ridiculous Waste of Money," *Washington Evening Star,* 29 June 1975.

93. Ibid.

Chapter Six

1. "Women Strike for Peace: A Short History of Activities during 1963 and 1964," Washington, D.C., n.d., mimeo, WSP Papers, 2.

2. Address by Dagmar Wilson, Second Anniversary Celebration, New York City, 1 November 1963, typescript, WSP Papers, 4, 6.

3. "Women Strike for Peace: A Short History of Activities during 1963 and 1964," 6.

4. For an excellent analysis of post–test ban nuclear escalation, see Lawrence S. Wittner, *Cold War America: From Hiroshima to Watergate* (New York: Praeger Publishers, 1974), chapter 8.

5. Florence B. Robin, "Honeychile at the Barricades," *Harper's,* October 1962, 173–77.

6. Bick, transcript of radio station KPFK WSP commentary, 1.

7. Ibid., 2.

8. Barbara Bick, "Women and the Vietnam War," *MEMO,* April 1970, 9.

9. "For Immediate Release, Women Strike for Peace," Washington, D.C., n.d., WSP Papers.

10. Hayes B. Jacobs, "The Martyrdom of Alice Herz," *Fact,* July–August 1965, 15.

11. Alice Herz to Mr. Shibata, Detroit, 10 November 1961, WSP Papers.

12. Jacobs, "Martyrdom of Alice Herz," 13.

13. *Detroit News,* 18 March 1965.

14. Ibid.

15. Iwanami Group, Jimbo-cho Bloc, Chiyoda Branch (New Japan Women's Association), to Dagmar Wilson, Tokyo, n.d., WSP Papers.

16. Press release, Los Angeles WSP, 18 March 1965, WSP Papers.

17. "For immediate release from Detroit Women for Peace," n.d., WSP Papers.

18. From Detroit Women for Peace, Detroit, n.d., mimeo, WSP Papers.

19. Tribute by Ruth Gage-Colby to Alice Herz at the memorial, 4 April 1965, Detroit, WSP Papers, 1.

20. *New York Times,* 2 February 1966.

21. *New York Times,* 10 February 1966.

22. "Mothers' March May 15," Philadelphia WSP, n.d., mimeo, WSP Papers.

23. *New Republic,* 5 February 1966, 23.

24. Beverly Farquharson, "The Housewife Terrorists," *MEMO,* September 1966, 12.

25. Ibid.

26. Ibid.

27. *Washington Evening Star,* 15 February 1967.

28. *Washington Post,* 1 January 1968.

29. I am indebted to Melvin Small for this information. He found it in notes from a 17 October 1969 meeting in Dwight Chapin's "handwritten scribbles" (Chapin file, box 1, Special Files, Nixon Presidential Materials Project, Alexandria, Va.).

30. The policy committee of the Jeannette Rankin Brigade included the following key women of WSP: Mary Clarke, Ruth Krause, Cora Weiss, Lorraine Gordon, Amy Swerdlow, Ethel Taylor, Dagmar Wilson, Frances Herring, and Coretta Scott King. They were nine out of twenty-five, or over one-third.

31. Women identified with WSP who were listed on the original call as organizers of the brigade were Donna Allen, Mary Clarke, Anne Eaton, Frances Herring, Coretta Scott King, Ruth Krause, Lynn Lane, Peggy Papp, Ruth Rosenwald, Amy Swerdlow, Ethel Taylor, Cora Weiss, and Dagmar Wilson.

32. "A Call to American Women," Jeannette Rankin Brigade, New York, 1967, 3, in my possession. Among the early sponsors listed in the call were, in addition to the members of the steering committee already mentioned, Kay Boyle; Niki Bridges, wife of the labor leader Harry Bridges; Eva Coffin, wife of William Sloane Coffin, then chaplain at Yale University; actress Ruby Dee; Anne Eaton, wife of millionaire businessman Cyrus Eaton; Judith Morse Eaton, daughter of antiwar senator Wayne Morse; psychologist Carolyn Goodman, mother of Andrew Goodman, one of the three young civil rights workers killed in Mississippi; Lorraine Gordon, one of the founders of New York WSP who was listed as Mrs. Max Gordon; African-American leader Anna Arnold Hedgeman; Margaret Kuhn, later to lead the Gray Panthers; Mrs. Burton Lane, wife of the composer, who under her own name, Lynn, was a WSP activist; actress Viveca Lindfors; scholar and author Helen Merrill Lynd; author Jessica Mitford; WSP activist Peggy Papp, who was listed as Mrs. Joseph Papp; old-line pacifist Mercedes Randall, who had written a biography of Nobel Peace Prize winner Emily Balch; poet Muriel Rukeyeser; Mrs. Robert Ryan; Susan Sontag; and Jane Spock, listed as Mrs. Benjamin Spock.

33. For an excellent discussion of the role of the radical women in JRB, see Alice Echols, "'Woman Power': Exploring the Relationship between the Antiwar Movement and the Women's Liberation Movement," in *Give Peace a Chance,* ed. Melvin Small and William D. Hoover (Syracuse, N.Y.: Syracuse University Press, 1992), 158–70.

34. *New York Times*, 18 January 1968.

35. Ibid.

36. The issue was later resolved in favor of the right of assembly on Capitol grounds.

37. *Washington Post*, 16 January 1968.

38. The delegation that was permitted to enter the Capitol to present the petition to Congress included the sister and niece of Rankin, Edna McKinon and Dorothy Brown of Montana; Coretta Scott King; Vivian Hallinan; Katherine Camp; Dagmar Wilson; Sister Marguerite Haffner of Chicago; Mrs. J. Preston Irwin, Republican national committeewoman of Cleveland; Vivian Williams of Philadelphia, mother of Private Ronald Lockman, an African-American war resister; Cynthia Wedell, president of the National Council of Churches; Mrs. Edgar Siskind, wife of a prominent Chicago rabbi; Linda Morse of the Student Mobilization of New York; Bobby Hodges of the Black Congress of Los Angeles; Gwen Griffin of Berea, Ky.; and Mrs. Ernest Gruening, wife of the senator from Alaska.

39. "Petition for Redress of Grievances to the President and the Congress of the United States," typescript in my possession.

40. Program of the Jeannette Rankin Brigade, Washington, D.C., 15 January 1968, in my possession.

41. "Liturgy for the Burial of Traditional Womanhood," Radical Women's Group, New York City, n.d., mimeo, in my possession.

42. Echols, "Woman Power," 176; "The Jeannette Rankin Brigade: Woman Power?" in *Notes from the First Year* (New York: New York Radical Women, 1968), 22.

43. Charlotte Bunch, *Passionate Politics: Feminist Theory in Action* (New York: St. Martin's Press, 1987), 5.

44. Echols, "Woman Power," 178.

45. *Independent Journal* (San Rafael, Calif.), 12 March 1968.

46. "Declaration of Liberation from Military Domination, Washington, 18 March 1970," *MEMO*, April 1970, inside back cover.

47. Frances Bourget to President Nixon, Manhasset, N.Y., n.d., WSP Papers.

48. Mrs. Joseph Wappel to President Nixon, Norwood, Mass., n.d., WSP Papers.

Chapter Seven

1. Typewritten note, unsigned, first page missing, WSP Papers, 2.

2. Interview with Bella Abzug, Amagansett, N.Y., September 1980, WSP Papers. All subsequent quotes are from this interview unless otherwise indicated.

3. It is interesting to note that Eleanor Garst, one of the founders, was also working full-time on this issue in Washington, D.C., in the early 1960s. See chapter 3.

4. Elsa Knight Thompson, "My Personal Impression."

5. Marquis Childs reported in the *Washington Post* (10 August 1962) that at least twenty candidates were running for Congress on platforms calling for disarmament and an end to nuclear testing. Mary Grooms, a WSP activist from Rochester, N.Y., reported in the *Nation* (28 June 1962, 27) that the peace move-

ment was forced to consider the following questions: "Should peace groups endorse or run candidates? Should the peace groups get together and form a third
party? Or should they back issues and remain nonpartisan?"

6. *Riverdale Press*, 29 March 1962; *New York Times*, 28 April 1962.

7. Ruth Gage-Colby to Frederic C. Smedley, New York City, 3 May 1962,
WSP Papers.

8. Mary Clarke, the Los Angeles coordinator, told me in 1988 that Roybal
was still grateful to WSP for crucial help in winning his congressional seat. "We
just went in and took over; straightened out the office mess, and organized the
canvassing," Clarke recalled in a telephone interview in September 1988.

9. *La Wisp*, 7 May 1962, 3.

10. "Guidelines for Use with Political Parties," n.d., mimeo, WSP Papers.

11. Mary Grooms, "Peace Takes to the Hustings," *Nation*, 28 July 1962, 27.

12. Memo from the New York Legislative Committee, 7 October 1963, WSP
Papers.

13. *Women's Peace Movement Bulletin*, June 1964, 9.

14. *MEMO*, September 1964, 3.

15. "Silent Vigil," 2-page flyer, WSP Papers.

16. *MEMO*, February 1966, 2–3.

17. Alice Hamburg, report on Political Action Workshop, Fourth Annual
Conference WSP-WFP, San Francisco, 21–24 October 1965, WSP Papers.

18. *MEMO*, July–August 1966, 4.

19. *MEMO*, February 1966, 8.

20. *Journal and Courier* (Lafayette, Ind.), 24 January 1966, reprinted in
MEMO, February 1966, 10.

21. *MEMO*, May 1966, 5.

22. WSP Political Action Committee, New York, "Issues and Methods," n.d.,
mimeo, WSP Papers.

23. Abzug told the Platform Committee of the Democratic national convention in 1968, "As a women's peace group we have participated in the American
protest movement and the political campaigns which have laid the ground work
for the present challenges for alternative policies and leadership within the Democratic party. We have sensed a great stirring among the electorate, an overwhelming desire for an end to the war in Vietnam, to racism and poverty at
home, and a searching for leaders whom they can respect and trust. . . . There
are great new resources of strength available to the Democratic party, if only it
will place people politics ahead of machine politics" (transcript of testimony on
behalf of WSP before the 1968 Platform Committee of the Democratic national
convention, 6 August 1968, WSP Papers).

24. Bella Abzug, "Summary of Report to WSP National Convention," New
York City, 21 September 1967, mimeo, WSP Papers.

25. *MEMO*, Summer 1980, 8.

26. *Washington Evening Star*, 21 January 1971.

27. "Demonstrate with Bella Abzug on the Capitol Steps in Washington,
D.C.," WSP, New York, January 1971, WSP Papers.

28. They were James Abourezk, S.D.; Joseph Addabbo, Herman Badillo,
Jonathan Bingham, Shirley Chisholm, John Dow, Seymour Halpern, Edward

Koch, Charles Rangel, Benjamin Rosenthal, William Fitts Ryan, and James
Scheuer, N.Y.; Les Aspin and Robert Kastenmeier, Wis.; Phillip Burton, Ronald
Dellums, Don Edwards, Paul N. McCloskey, Thomas Rees, Edward Roybal,
Jerome R. Waldie, Calif.; Patsy Mink, Hawaii; Abner Mikva, Ill.; Andrew Jacobs,
Jr., Ind.; Robert Drinan, Mass.; Parren Mitchell, Md.; Robert Eckhardt, Texas;
William Clay, Mo.; John Conyers, Jr., Mich.; Don Fraser, Minn.; and Ken
Hechler, W. Va.

29. Bella Abzug, "For Release on Delivery," 21 January 1971, WSP Papers.

30. *MEMO*, Spring 1972, 19.

31. Bella Abzug, Congress of the United States House of Representatives, to
"Dear WSPers," 7 January 1972, WSP Papers.

32. "Women Strike for Peace Urges Support for McGovern for President,"
New York WSP, 1972, WSP Papers.

33. The WSP conveners were Bella Abzug, Mary Clarke, Ruth Meyers, and
Amy Swerdlow. Those who worked on coordination were Judy Lerner, Bess
Berkowitz, and Barbara Bick.

34. *MEMO*, Fall 1971, 8.

Chapter Eight

1. Martha Brix to Dagmar Wilson, Chicago, 31 December 1962, copy, WSP
Papers.

2. Thorne, "Resisting the Draft," 170. See also Barrie Thorne, "Gender Imagery and Issues of War and Peace: The Case of the Draft Resistance Movement
of the 1960s," in *The Role of Women in Conflict and Peace*, ed. Dorothy McGuigon
(Ann Arbor: University of Michigan Center for Continuing Education, 1977),
55. Thorne notes that during World War I Emma Goldman believed that
women did not have as much right as men to speak out against military conscription. Goldman wrote, "I took the position that, as a woman, and therefore
myself not subject to military service, I could not advise people on that matter.
. . . But I could say to those who refuse to be coerced into military service that
I would plead their cause and stand by their act against all odds" (*Living My Life*
[Garden City, N.Y.: Doubleday, 1931], 598, cited in Thorne, "Resisting the
Draft," 192).

3. Leslie Cagan, "Women and the Anti-draft Movement," *Radical America* 14
(September–October 1980): 9.

4. Newsletter, Sacramento WFP, July–August 1969, WSP Papers, 2.

5. Ibid.

6. Leo Frumkin, Chairman, GI Civil Liberties Defense Committee, to
Women Strike for Peace, cited in *La Wisp*, September 1969, 6.

7. Thank-you letter from Francis Rocks, minutes of New York Area Central
Coordinating Committee, 25 October 1967, WSP Papers.

8. Newsletter, Philadelphia WSP, January 1968, 11, WSP Papers.

9. *La Wisp*, September 1969, 3.

10. *San Fernando Valley Times*, 17 January 1970.

11. Newsletter, Mississippi Freedom Democratic Party, 28 July 1965.

12. Irma Zigas, "Women Strike for Peace and the Draft," transcript of radio
station KPFK WSP commentary, May–June 1969, WSP Papers. See also news-

letter, WSP of New York, New Jersey, Connecticut, December 1966, 4; newsletter, San Francisco WFP, March 1971, 3.

13. Antidraft resolution adopted by the National Council, Students for a Democratic Society, Berkeley, Calif., 28 December 1966, WSP Papers.

14. "To Local and National WSPers re: Draft," New York WSP, 3 May 1967, WSP Papers.

15. Newsletter, WSP of New York, New Jersey, Connecticut, December 1966, 3.

16. Irma Zigas, "Draft Resistance Report," New York, 18 October 1967, WSP Papers.

17. "Announcements and Actions," unidentified, undated newsletter, probably VOW, 5, WSP Papers.

18. Interview with Irma Zigas, Merrick, N.Y., 26 June 1979.

19. Ibid.

20. Because of fears that records might be stolen or subpoenaed by the Justice Department, WSP kept no lists of those counseled or those who acted as counselors. The figures presented by Zigas, which are based on her assessment, confirmed by Bernice Crane, have to be recognized as estimates.

21. Irma Zigas to Trudy Young, National WSP Coordinator, Merrick, N.Y., 30 October 1970, WSP Papers.

22. Jenny Warwick to Washington, D.C., WSP, Missoula, Mont., 26 February 1968, WSP Papers.

23. Veronica Sissons, "Who Buys That Dream?" La Wisp, September 1969, 3.

24. "Your Draft-Age Son: A Message for Peaceful Parents," Berkeley/Oakland WFP, April 1968, pamphlet, WSP Papers, 8.

25. The suit named Long Beach Draft Board No. 25, Woodrow Wilson High School of Long Beach, Long Beach Unified School District, Los Angeles County Board of Education, and the State Board of Education (Los Angeles Times, 16 December 1969; Press Telegram [Long Beach, Calif.], 15 December 1969).

26. La Wisp, December 1969, 1.

27. Daily News (Fullerton, Calif.), reprinted in MEMO, 5 April 1967, 14.

28. Ad Hoc Parents Committee to Chairman, Board of Education, District of Columbia, Washington, D.C., 16 May 1967, WSP Papers.

29. Gertrude L. Williamson, Executive Secretary to the Board of Education, District of Columbia, to Molly Kanarek, Washington, D.C., 22 June 1967, WSP Papers.

30. D. P. Randall, West High School, to Doreen Wohl and Shirley Brustein, Columbus, Ohio, 1 May 1967, WSP Papers.

31. The other groups WSP worked with on high school draft actions included SANE, War Resisters League, AFSC, WILPF, SDS, CORE, and FOR.

32. Washington Post, 11 April 1967.

33. Reprint of an untitled, undated newspaper article from Missoula, Mont., in MEMO, September 1968, 9.

34. New York Times, 16 April 1967.

35. "Call for National Action on the Draft," MEMO, March 1967, 3.

36. Newsletter, Nashville Women for Peace and Social Justice, n.d., WSP Papers.

37. *La Wisp,* June 1967.

38. Newsletter, East Bay WFP, July 1970, WSP Papers, 2.

39. See newsletter, Nashville Women for Peace and Social Justice, n.d., WSP Papers.

40. Charlotte Keyes, "Suppose They Gave a War and No One Came," *McCall's,* October 1966, 26, 187–91.

41. Philadelphia WSP, "Women Strike for Peace Supports Draft Resistance," n.d., mimeo, WSP Papers.

42. Los Angeles WSP, "To Selective Service System, Local Board No. . . ," n.d., mimeo, WSP Papers.

43. Los Angeles WSP, "The Draft," n.d., mimeo, WSP Papers.

44. "Young World," *This Week,* 13 April 1969; *Plain Rapper,* 10 January 1969, 2.

45. *Plain Rapper,* 10 June 1969, 1–2.

46. Evelyn Whitehorn, statement to the press, 25 August 1969, photocopy, WSP Papers.

47. There were others who developed their own legal arguments for draft refusal. A letter from two women in Glendora, Calif., suggested a reversal of traditional sexual attributes. The letter to WSP stated naïvely that "women by law are equal to men and may go to court and win a decision on equal wages, etc." "Therefore," the two women from Glendora asked, "cannot a man claim equality to a woman and achieve a deferment from the draft, proving himself to be the equal of women in his apathy toward violence?" There is no evidence that such a case was ever taken to court (Anita Walley and Cassy Vaughan, "To Whom It May Concern," Glendora, Calif., n.d., WSP Papers).

48. San Francisco WSP, "Pledges of Support to Mrs. Whitehorn," n.d., mimeo, WSP Papers.

49. Hazel Grossman to Amy Swerdlow, San Francisco, 11 September 1981, WSP Papers. Some animosity had developed between Whitehorn and her attorney Aubrey Grossman, and she eventually changed lawyers, indicating that she was disillusioned with both Grossman and her case. "Erik as a client was getting lost not in a case, but in a 'cause.'" She complained that there was not enough law on her side and too much rhetoric (Evelyn Whitehorn, statement to the press, 25 August 1969, WSP Papers).

50. Mothers' Draft Resistance, "An Appeal to Mothers Black and White," Frederick, Md., n.d., WSP Papers.

51. "Women's Statement of Conscience to Be Presented to General Lewis Hershey, Director of Selective Service," Washington, D.C., n.d., mimeo, WSP Papers.

52. This WSP demonstration in support of draft resistance actually took place one month before a widely publicized delegation of writers, academics, and other professionals visited the attorney general to declare with more specificity than WSP that they would "counsel, aid, and abet draft resisters." See Denise Levertov, "The Intellectuals," *North American Review,* January 1968, 11.

53. *New York Times,* 15 September 1967.

54. *Philadelphia Inquirer,* 21 September 1967.

55. *New York Times,* 21 September 1967.

56. *Baltimore Sun,* 21 September 1967.

57. Another incident of militant "ladies" getting away with more radical action than men is attested to by a police sergeant who said of a group of women struggling for integrated schools in Little Rock, Ark., "These ladies would come in here and not let me get a word in edgewise. If a man had tried it I would have locked him up good and proper" (Robin, "Honeychile at the Barricades," 174).

58. *Washington Post,* 22 September 1967.

59. Ibid.

60. Perry S. Samuels, transcript of WWDC Editorial 1, 22 September 1967, WSP Papers.

61. "For Immediate Release," Washington, D.C., WSP, 22 September 1967, WSP Papers.

62. Quoted in Ethel Taylor, "WILPF Takes 10,000 Signatures to White House," *Four Lights,* October 1957, 1.

63. Lynn Litterine, "A Rebel in White Gloves," *Philadelphia Inquirer,* 14 March 1978.

64. Ethel Taylor to Amy Swerdlow, Philadelphia, 11 June 1980, WSP Papers.

65. "Resistance Day," Independence Hall, Monday, 16 October 1967, tape 1, side 1, 41–52.

66. On 7 February 1969 a memo from the Philadelphia field office noted that an investigation of Ethel Taylor had been undertaken (U.S. Department of Justice, Philadelphia office, FBI Field Office file 25-39333). The memo stated that the Philadelphia office of the FBI would maintain contact with U.S. attorney Merna B. Marshall regarding prosecution of the matter. Another memo on the same date indicates that the Philadelphia office of the FBI was attempting to develop additional background data on Taylor (FBI Field Office file 25-562936). On 2 October 1968 Marshall advised the FBI that she was "still considering prosecution in this matter" (2 October 1968, FBI Field Office file 25-39333, FBI Bureau file 25-562936). In December 1969 Marshall said she planned to take no action on the matter until specific instructions were received from the Justice Department (22 December 1969, Title Ethel Rose Taylor, FBI Field Office file 25-39333, FBI file 25-562936). Eventually on 20 November 1970, after the Spock, Coffin, and Ferber case had not held up in the First Circuit Court of Appeals of Boston, Marshall advised the FBI that upon specific instructions the Department of Justice she "declined prosecution in this matter" (FBI Field Office file 25-39333, FBI Bureau file 25-562936).

67. Barbara Bick, "Notes on the Draft," Washington, D.C., WSP Papers, 3.

68. Irma Zigas, "Draft Repeal and a Voluntary Army," Anti-draft Clearing House for Women, Merrick, N.Y., n.d., mimeo, WSP Papers, 2.

69. "Proposed Statement on Amnesty Submitted by Charity Hirsch," East Bay (Calif.) Women for Peace, Washington, D.C., n.d., WSP Papers.

70. The information and quotations that follow are from an interview with Irma Zigas, San Francisco, 26 June 1979.

Chapter Nine

1. "Report on the Women's Strike for Peace."

2. "Not before January 13th," WSP press release, n.d., WSP Papers.

3. Olga, Prinzessen zur Lippe, to Women Strike for Peace, Frankfurt, 23 November 1962, WSP Papers. Similar messages arrived from other international women's peace advocates. Klara Fassbinder, a leader of the German women's peace organization Frauen und Frieden, wrote to Dagmar Wilson from Bonn, "You are not only an example of courage, but you give us ideas, or at least you are encouraging the timid people to dare something" (WSP Papers). A cable from Belgium proclaimed, "A new star of peace appears in the west. . . . it will encourage women in the whole world" (newsletter no. 1, Washington, D.C., WSP, 1 March 1962, WSP Papers).

4. M. Toma, President, Japan Woman's Union, to Dagmar Wilson, Tokyo, 26 March 1962, WSP Papers.

5. Ma Myat Mon, General Secretary, United Women's League of Burma, to Dagmar Wilson, Rangoon, 27 January 1962, WSP Papers.

6. Typed manuscript of an article prepared for publication by Eleanor Garst, n.d., WSP Papers, 2.

7. Judith Cook to Washington, D.C., WSP, Penzance, Cornwall, England, 13 March 1962, WSP Papers. Cook, a young woman with no political experience, had become an instant leader and national personality for outspoken antinuclear declarations in the name of mothers and housewives. In April 1962 she came to the United States to deliver peace petitions collected at the Aldermarston march in London. The petitions were addressed to Ambassador Adlai Stevenson, U.S. representative at the United Nations. With her came Anne Kerr, a London County councillor, who was the leader of a group called Women against the Bomb. Their visit to Washington was timed to coincide with that of British prime minister Harold Macmillan. Together with WSP women, Kerr and Cook picketed the White House while Macmillan was meeting with President Kennedy, and attempted to stop Macmillan's car as he came through the White House gate. The two women stayed at my home in Great Neck, N.Y. We became personal friends, meeting in England and the United States at international conferences and demonstrations. Cook went on to become a reporter for the British newspaper *Guardian*. Kerr was elected to Parliament. She made headlines in the United States when she testified at the 1968 trial of the Chicago Seven that she had witnessed police brutality outside the Democratic convention. What amused the press was that she insisted upon calling the judge "my lord."

8. Dagmar Wilson to Mrs. S. H. Linden, Washington, D.C., 22 November 1961, WSP Papers.

9. Ruth Gage-Colby, "Greetings and Salutations," New York, 10 December 1961, mimeo, WSP Papers.

10. Interview with Ruth Gage-Colby, New York City, June 1980.

11. *I. F. Stone's Weekly,* 22 January 1962, 1.

12. *New York Times,* 16 January 1962.

13. Newsletter no. 1, Washington, D.C., WSP, March 1962, WSP Papers.

14. WSP had proposed for the post of U.S. negotiator the following women: Senator Edith Green; Dr. Frances Herring of Berkeley WSP; Ruth Gage-Colby, WSP international coordinator; and Dagmar Wilson, WSP founder and spokesperson.

15. *I. F. Stone's Weekly,* 16 April 1962, 3–4.

16. *New York Times*, 6 April 1962.

17. See Mary Grooms, "Give Us a Missile Base," *Nation*, 5 May 1962, 395–97.

18. *New York Times*, 19 April 1962.

19. *New York Herald Tribune*, 5 April 1962.

20. *National Guardian*, 16 April 1962.

21. The "Petition to the Seventeen-Nation Disarmament Conference" read in part: "We the undersigned believe that an arms race cannot lead to peace and that our only hope for survival lies in an international agreement for general and complete disarmament." The petition called for "a nuclear test ban treaty . . . through bold agreement by the 17 nations representing the United Nations at this conference" (Women Strike for Peace, n.d., mimeo, WSP Papers). (When the conference met, it was called the Conference of the Eighteen-Nation Committee on Disarmament.)

22. *I. F. Stone's Weekly*, 16 April 1962, 4.

23. J. L. Grunewald to Dagmar Wilson, London, 11 April 1962, WSP Papers. Dagmar Wilson to Messrs Zorin and Dean at Palais des nations, 4 April 1962. WSP Papers

24. Diana Collins to Dagmar Wilson, London, 11 April 1962, WSP Papers.

25. Policy Paper no. 7, National Information Clearing House, WSP Papers.

26. Shirley Lens, "Proposal for National Action," *National Information Memo*, 26 June 1962, WSP Papers.

27. Dagmar Wilson, draft of a letter to Mrs. Seymour Melman and Mrs. Stephen Sharmat, Washington, D.C., 26 June 1962, WSP Papers.

28. Dagmar Wilson to Samuel E. Belk, Special Staff, National Security Council, State Department, Washington, D.C., 1 June 1962, WSP Papers; "Off the Record," embassy briefing, Washington, D.C., 18 July 1962, WSP Papers.

29. Dagmar Wilson to Samuel E. Belk, Special Staff, National Security Council, State Department, Washington, D.C., 23 June 1962, WSP Papers.

30. *Women's Peace Movement Bulletin*, 17 June 1962. Emily Balch, a founder of WPP and WILPF and a winner of the Nobel Peace Prize, expressed similar sentiments in 1952 when she stated: "The Russian people is not synonymous with the government, anymore than the American people is fully expressed by what we call Washington. Let us make the most of all non-political contacts" (Philadelphia, 26 April 1952).

31. *Women's Peace Movement Bulletin*, 17 June 1962.

32. There is one official resignation on file, from Marcia Hovey of Maryland, a member of the Washington steering committee. She wrote that she believed the visit to Russia had nothing to do with the purpose for which the women had banded together and that it would impair the effectiveness of WSP as an instrument for peace (Marcia Hovey to Steering Committee, University Park, Md., 18 June 1962, WSP Papers).

33. "Message from Dagmar Wilson," Washington, D.C., 11 July 1962, mimeo, WSP Papers.

34. *New York Post*, 19 July 1962.

35. A joint resolution drafted by Soviet and American women at a meeting in Moscow, 15 July 1962, WSP Papers.

36. Eleanor Garst, typescript, WSP Papers, 8.

37. "From Mrs. Dagmar Wilson for Immediate Release," Washington, D.C., 21 September 1962, typewritten draft, WSP Papers.

38. *New York Post,* June 1963.

39. "Women Strike for Peace to Soviet Women's Committee, for Immediate Release," National Office of WSP, 11 August 1968, WSP Papers.

40. Chairman, Committee of Czechoslovak Women, to "Dear Friends," Prague, 10 September 1968, reprinted in a memo from Washington WSP, 20 September 1968, WSP Papers. WSP also criticized the Soviet Union for selling magnesium to Dow Chemical Company during the Vietnam War. This magnesium, according to WSP, was used in the manufacture of the deadly, burning napalm used by the United States in Vietnam. The Soviet Peace Committee denied the charges (Michael Katov, Secretary, Soviet Peace Committee, to Dagmar Wilson, Mary Clarke, and Dorothy Benson, Moscow, 12 April 1967, WSP Papers).

41. Gertrude Leavin's statement, n.d., typescript, WSP Papers.

42. Alice Pollard, "Women for Peace, Women Strike for Peace Leaving N.Y. April 20," press release, Hanover, N.H., 18 April 1963, mimeo; Alice Pollard, "Women for Peace Pilgrimage to Rome 24 April 1963," press release, Domus Pacis, Rome, 24 April 1963, mimeo; "Brief Biographies of Women Peace Pilgrimage to the Vatican, Leaving New York April 20," Hanover, N.H., n.d., mimeo; all in WSP Papers.

43. Dorothy Day, "On Pilgrimage," *Catholic Worker,* May 1963, reprinted in *Madre per la Pace: Rome-Geneva Pilgrimage,* August 1963, WSP Papers, 15.

44. *Peace News* (London), 10 May 1963.

45. "Concord Woman Is Peace Pilgrim," *Concord Daily Monitor,* 21 May 1963, reprinted in *Madre per la Pace,* WSP Papers, 10.

46. "Some Questions and Answers on the Multi-lateral Nuclear Force and Proliferation of Nuclear Arms through NATO," New York WSP, n.d., WSP Papers.

47. Lorraine Gordon and Amy Swerdlow, "For Immediate Release from Women Strike for Peace," New York WSP, n.d., mimeo, WSP Papers; Harriet Shapiro, Ruth Meyers, and Lorraine Gordon, "For Immediate Release, Please," New York City, 8 May 1964, WSP Papers.

48. *The German Problem: Roadblock to Disarmament* (Washington, D.C.: Women Strike for Peace, 1964).

49. All of these messages are in WSP Papers.

50. Translation of article in *Dagbladet* (Oslo), 13 May 1964, typescript, WSP Papers.

51. *Detroit News,* 5 May 1964.

52. *National Guardian,* 30 May 1964, 9.

53. *Denver Post,* 13 May 1964.

54. Ethel Taylor, "Report from the Hague," in newsletter, Philadelphia WSP, July 1964, WSP Papers, 1.

55. According to FOR, not a single line about the Paris meeting and demonstration appeared in the U.S. press, although it was probably the largest single gathering of peace groups ever to take place in Paris (*Fellowship,* February 1965, 3).

56. There were no women from New York in the delegation because New York decided to sit this one out, on the grounds that it was not the appropriate moment for such a meeting and that it would discredit WSP if not enough preparation was made to develop a representation composed of many political viewpoints.

57. *Washington Evening Star,* 19 July 1965; *Peace Action,* August–September 1965, 2.

58. *Washington Evening Star,* 22 July 1965.

59. *New York Times,* 19 July 1965.

60. *Peace Action,* August–September 1965, 2.

61. *Washington Post,* 26 September 1967.

62. *Newsday,* 21 July 1966.

63. *Baltimore Evening Sun,* 25 March 1969.

64. Marilyn B. Young, *The Vietnam Wars: 1945–1990* (New York: HarperCollins, 1991).

65. National Consultative Committee, "Press Statement on POW Charges Issued at NCC Meeting," Philadelphia, 14 March 1973, WSP Papers.

66. The delegation included Irma Zigas, a representative of both WSP and the broader antidraft movement; two church women: Anne Bennett, a Protestant church leader and peace activist, who was the wife of John Bennett, president of Union Theological Seminary; Mia Adjali, director of the Women's Division of the Methodist Mission to the United Nations; three black activists: Victoria Gray Adams, an organizer of the Mississippi Freedom Democratic party; Althea Alexander, Los Angeles social worker and community leader, active in an organization called Black Resistance against the War, a member of Mothers of Watts, and a board member of the Los Angeles Area Federation of Settlements; and Gwen Gillion, active in Wisconsin draft resistance and formerly an organizer for SNCC and the Mississippi Freedom Democratic party; Marie Peterson, the mother of a son who had been wounded in Vietnam and another who was a conscientious objector; film and stage actress Viveca Lindfors; photographer Eva Coffin, daughter of Artur Rubinstein and then wife of William Sloane Coffin, chaplain of Yale University; Lennie Zeisler, a representative of a young feminist group called Radical Women; journalist Vivian Cadden, senior editor of *McCall's;* and a number of WSPers, including Ethel Taylor and Mary Clarke. Among the Vietnamese participants were Phan Thi Ann, Bui Thi Cam, Nguyen Thi Binh, Ma Thi Chu, Nguyen Ngoc Dung, and Phan Thanh Van. From Great Britain came M.P. Anne Kerr. VOW of Canada sent its leaders Muriel Duckworth and Katharine MacPherson, old friends of WSP, as were the German representatives Countess Mira von Kuhlmann and Elly Steinmann, who had both participated in the NATO Women's Peace Force at the Hague.

67. *L'Humanité,* 27 April 1968.

68. "Torture Made in USA," *MEMO,* Fall 1971, 14–15.

69. *Soviet Woman,* 10 November 1965, 24.

70. This and subsequent quotes from Cora Weiss, unless otherwise indicated, come from an interview that took place in Bridgehampton, N.Y., 11 July 1981.

71. *The Philadelphia Inquirer,* 31 December 1969.

72. "Files on Women Strike for Peace," 7:8653-4, cited in Pam Block, "Motherhood and Power in Women Strike for Peace," a Division 3 Project, Hampshire College, December 1989. I am indebted to Pam Block for her insightful analysis of motherhood and power in WSP, written from the perspective of a thoughtful young feminist and scholar.

73. Alice Wolfson, "Budapest Journal," *off our backs*, 14 December 1970, 1–2.

74. Madeline Duckles to Trudy Young, Berkeley, 19 April 1969, 1.

75. *MEMO*, Fall 1969, cover photo.

76. Ibid., 4.

77. Ibid.

78. Rita Mae Brown, "Hanoi to Hoboken: A Round Trip Ticket," *off our backs*, 25 March 1971, 4–5.

Conclusion

1. See Ellen DuBois, Mari Jo Buhle, Temma Kaplan, Gerda Lerner, and Carol Smith-Rosenberg, "Politics and Culture in Women's History: A Symposium," *Feminist Studies* 6 (Spring 1980): 53. I am also indebted to Temma Kaplan for her insights into the ways in which "motherist" politics generate and constrain women's political culture. See Temma Kaplan, "Female Consciousness and Collective Action: The Case of Barcelona, 1910–1918," *Signs* 7 (Spring 1982): 545–66.

2. Jean Bethke Elshtain and Sheila Tobias, eds., *Women, Militarism, and War: Essays in History, Politics, and Social Theory* (Totowa, N.J.: Rowman and Littlefield, 1990), 3.

3. Ruddick, *Maternal Thinking*, 129.

4. Message from Eleanor Garst, reprinted in *MEMO*, 31 May 1966.

5. Block, "Motherhood and Power," 14.

6. *La Wisp*, 16 November 1963, 9.

7. Carol Urner to Dagmar Wilson, Hiroshima-Kyoto train, 2 August 1963, WSP Papers.

8. See Swerdlow, "Select Bibliography Suggested to WSP Participants by the Women Strike for Peace National Office, Local Groups, and Clearing Houses, 1962–1963," in "Politics of Motherhood," 527–32.

9. The term "new insurgency" was used by Tom Hayden and Richard Flacks to describe the rising grass roots activism of the early 1960s, which they hoped would transform American politics. See James Miller, *Democracy in the Streets* (New York: Simon and Schuster, 1987), 176–77.

10. Virginia Woolf, *Three Guineas* (New York: Harcourt Brace Jovanovich, 1966), 143.

11. Alice Schwartzer, "Simone de Beauvoir Talks about Sartre," *MS*, August 1983, 37.

12. Micaela di Leonardo, "Morals, Mothers, Militarism: Antimilitarism and Feminist Theory (a Review Essay)," *Feminist Studies* (Fall 1985): 612.

13. Joan Kelley, "The Doubled Vision of Feminist Theory: A Postscript to the Women and Power Conference," *Feminist Studies* (Spring 1979): 216–27.

14. Frances Fox Piven, "Women and the State: Ideology, Power, and the

Welfare State," in *Gender and the Life Course,* ed. Alice Rossi (New York: Aldine, 1984), 267.

15. Jeanne Bagby, letter to *Liberation,* December 1966, 33.

16. Washington, D.C., WSP to Folly Fodor, "Another Daring Move," 8 January 1963, postcard, WSP Papers.

17. *Women's Peace Movement Bulletin,* 19 May 1962.

18. Bruce Kokopeli and George Lakey, "Leadership for Change," *WIN,* 2 November 1978, 13.

19. Interview with Mickey Flacks, Amagansett, N.Y., 1 September 1980.

20. Evelyn Kinkaid and Judy Nakadegawa, cochairmen, East Bay WFP, to Trudy Young, National Office WSP, New York City, 1 October 1970, WSP Papers.

21. "For Immediate Release from Women Strike for Peace, National Office," n.d., WSP Papers.

Bibliography

Manuscript Collections

Women's International League for Peace and Freedom. Papers. Swarthmore College Peace Collection, Swarthmore College, Swarthmore, Pa.

Women Strike for Peace. Papers. Swarthmore College Peace Collection, Swarthmore College, Swarthmore, Pa.

——. Records, 1958–1969. State Historical Society of Wisconsin, Archives Division, Madison.

Unpublished Material

Adler, Leslie K. 1970. The Red Image: American Attitudes toward Communism in the Cold War Era. Ph.D. dissertation, University of California, Berkeley.

Alonso, Harriet Hyman. 1982. A Shared Responsibility: The Women and Men of the People's Council of America for Democracy and Peace, 1917–1919. Master's thesis, Sarah Lawrence College.

Breines, Winifred. 1979. Community and Organization: The New Left as a Social Movement, 1962–1968. Ph.D. dissertation, Brandeis University.

Buhle, Mari Jo. 1981. Feminism and Progressivism: The Women of Hull House: A Comment. Paper read at the Fifth Berkshire Conference in Women's History, 16–18 June, Vassar College.

Horne, Gerald. 1982. Black and Red: W. E. B. DuBois and the Afro-American Perspective to the Cold War, 1944–1963. Ph.D. dissertation, Columbia University.

Katz, David Howard. 1973. Carrie Chapman Catt and the Struggle for Peace. Ph.D. dissertation, Syracuse University.

Katz, Milton Steven. 1973. Peace Politics and Protest: SANE and the American Peace Movement, 1957–1972. Ph.D. dissertation, St. Louis University.

Katz, Neil H. 1974. Radical Pacifism and the Contemporary American Peace Movement: The Committee for Nonviolent Action, 1957–1967. Ph.D. dissertation, University of Maryland.

McNeal, Patricia. 1974. The American Catholic Peace Movement, 1928–1972. Ph.D. dissertation, Temple University.

Myers, Frank Earle. 1965. British Peace Politics: The Campaign for Nuclear Disarmament and the Committee of 100, 1957–1962. Ph.D. dissertation, Columbia University.

O'Brien, James Putnam. 1971. The Development of a New Left in the United States, 1960–1965. Ph.D. dissertation, University of Wisconsin.

Schaffer, Ronald. 1959. Jeannette Rankin, Progressive-Isolationist. Ph.D. dissertation, Princeton University.

Steinson, Barbara Jean. 1977. Female Activism in World I: The American Women's Peace, Suffrage, Preparedness, and Relief Movements, 1914–1919. Ph.D dissertation, University of Michigan.

Swerdlow, Amy. 1984. The Politics of Motherhood: The Case of Women Strike for Peace and the Test Ban Treaty. Ph.D. dissertation, Rutgers University.

Thorne, Barrie. 1971. Resisting the Draft: An Ethnography of the Draft Resistance Movement. Ph.D. dissertation, Brandeis University.

Tobias, Sheila. 1983. Feminism and the Arms Race. Paper read at Sarah Lawrence College, 7 May, Bronxville, N.Y.

Wessel, A. E. 1962. The American Peace Movement: A Study of Its Themes and Political Potential. Rand Corporation, Santa Monica, Calif. Mimeo.

Wittner, Lawrence S. 1967. The American Peace Movement, 1941–1960. Ph.D. dissertation, Columbia University.

Public Documents

Calkin, Homer L. 1977. *Women in American Foreign Affairs.* Washington, D.C.: U.S. Department of State.

President's Commission on the Status of Women. 1963. *American Women: Report of the President's Commission on the Status of Women.* Washington, D.C.: U.S. Government Printing Office.

U.S. Congress. House. Committee on Un-American Activities. 1949. *Report on the Congress of American Women.* 81st Congress. Washington, D.C.: U.S. Government Printing Office.

———. 1951. *Report on the Communist 'Peace' Offensive: A Campaign to Disarm and Defeat the United States.* Washington, D.C.: U.S. Government Printing Office.

———. 1963. *Communist Activities in the Peace Movement (Women Strike for Peace and Certain Other Groups): Hearings.* 87th Congress, 2d session. Washington, D.C.: U.S. Government Printing Office.

U.S. Congress. Senate. Committee on Foreign Relations. 1963. *Hearings before the Committee on Foreign Relations on the Treaty Banning Nuclear Weapons Tests in the Atmosphere, in Outer Space, and Underwater.* 88th Congress, 1st session. Washington, D.C.: U.S. Government Printing Office.

U.S. Department of Defense. 1982. *Women in America's Defense.* Washington, D.C.: U.S. Government Printing Office.

U.S. Department of Labor. 1968. *Trends in Educational Attainments of Women.* Washington, D.C.: U.S. Government Printing Office.

Books and Pamphlets

Addams, Jane. 1930. *The Second Twenty Years at Hull-House.* New York: Macmillan.

Addresses Given at the Organizational Conference of the Women's Peace Party, Washington, D.C., January 10, 1915. 1915. Chicago: Women's Peace Party.

Alonso, Harriet Hyman. 1989. *The Woman's Peace Union and the Outlawry of War, 1921–1942.* Knoxville: University of Tennessee Press.

Altbach, Philip G., and Lauter, Robert S. 1972. *The New Pilgrims: Youth Protest in Transition.* New York: David McKay Company.

Anderson, Karen. 1981. *Wartime Women: Sex Roles, Family Relations, and the Status of Women during World War II.* Westport, Conn.: Greenwood Press.

Arendt, Hannah. 1970. *On Violence*. New York: Harcourt, Brace, Jovanovich.

Aronson, James. 1970. *The Press and the Cold War*. Indianapolis: Bobbs-Merrill Company.

Ball, Howard. 1986. *Justice Downwind: America's Atomic Testing Program in the 1950s*. New York: Oxford University Press.

Banks, J. A. 1972. *The Sociology of Social Movements*. London: Macmillan.

Barth, Allen. 1955. *Government by Investigation*. New York: Viking Press.

Baxter, Sandra, and Lansing, Marjorie. 1980. *Women and Politics*. Ann Arbor: University of Michigan Press.

Bell, Daniel, ed. 1955. *The New American Right*. New York: Criterion Books.

———. 1959. *The End of Ideology*. Glencoe, Ill.: Free Press.

———. 1967. *Marxian Socialism in the United States*. Princeton, N.J.: Princeton University Press.

Bentley, Eric. 1971. *Thirty Years of Treason: Excerpts from Hearings before the House Committee on Un-American Activities, 1938–1968*. New York: Viking Press.

Berkin, Carol, and Lovett, Clara, eds. 1980. *Women, War, and Revolution*. New York: Holmes and Meier Publishers.

Berman, Ronald. 1968. *America in the Sixties: An Intellectual History*. New York: Free Press.

Blatch, Harriot Stanton. 1918. *Mobilizing Woman Power*. New York: Woman's Press.

———. 1940. *Challenging Years*. New York: G. P. Putnam's Sons.

Bloom, Lynn Z. 1972. *Doctor Spock: Biography of a Conservative Radical*. Indianapolis: Bobbs-Merrill Company.

Bontecou, Eleanor. 1953. *The Federal Loyalty Security Program*. Ithaca, N.Y.: Cornell University Press.

Booth, Paul L. 1964. *Peace Politics: A Study of the American Peace Movement and the Politics of the 1962 Congressional Election*. Ann Arbor, Mich.: Peace Research and Education Project.

Boulding, Elise. 1963. *Who Are These Women? A Progress Report on the Study of Women Strike for Peace*. Ann Arbor, Mich.: Center for Conflict Resolution.

———. 1977. *Women in the Twentieth-Century World*. New York: Sage Publications.

Boyer, Paul. 1985. *By the Bomb's Early Light: American Thought and Culture at the Dawn of the Atomic Age*. New York: Pantheon Books.

Brinker-Gabler, Gisela. 1980. *Women against War*. Frankfurt: Fisher Taschenbuch Verlag.

Brittain, Vera. 1940. *Wartime Letters to Peace Lovers*. London: Peace Book Company.

———. 1957. *Testament of Experience: An Autobiography, 1925–1950*. London: Victor Gollancz.

———. 1964. *The Rebel Passion: A Short History of Some Pioneer Peace-makers*. Nyack, N.Y.: Fellowship Publications.

Broch, Peter. 1970. *Twentieth-Century Pacifism*. New York: Van Nostrand Reinhold Company.

Brock-Utne, Birgit. 1985. *Educating for Peace: A Feminist Perspective*. New York: Pergamon Press.

Bussey, Gertrude, and Tims, Margaret. 1965. *Women's International League for*

Peace and Freedom, 1915–1965: A Record of Fifty Years' Work. London: George Allen and Unwin.

Caldicott, Helen. 1980. *Nuclear Madness.* New York: Bantam Books.

Cambridge Women's Peace Collective. 1983. *My Country Is the Whole World: An Anthology of Women's Work on Peace and War.* Boston: Pandora Press.

Carr, Robert K. 1952. *The House Committee on Un-American Activities, 1945–1950.* Ithaca, N.Y.: Cornell University Press.

Chafe, William Henry. 1972. *The American Woman: Her Changing Social, Economic, and Political Roles, 1920–1970.* New York: Oxford University Press.

———. 1991. *The Paradox of Change: American Women in the 20th Century.* New York: Oxford University Press.

Chambers, John Whiteclay II, ed. 1976. *The Eagle and the Dove: The American Peace Movement and United States Foriegn Policy, 1900–1922.* New York: Garland Publishing, Inc.

Chatfield, Charles, 1971. *For Peace and Justice: Pacifism in America, 1914–1941.* Knoxville: The University of Tennessee Press, 1971.

———, ed. 1972. *Peace Movements in America.* New York: Schocken Books.

Clarke, Ida Clyde. 1918. *American Women and the World War.* New York: D. Appleton Company.

Congress of American Women. N.d. *American Women in Pictures.* New York: Congress of American Women.

Cook, Alice, and Kirk, Gwyn. 1983. *Greenham Women Everywhere.* London: Pluto Press.

Cook, Blanche Wiesen, ed. 1978. *Crystal Eastman on Women & Revolution.* New York: Oxford University Press.

———, ed. 1971. *The Organized American Peace Movement in War Time, 1914–1919.* New York: Garland Publishing. Inc.

———. 1981. *The Declassified Eisenhower: A Divided Legacy of Peace and Political Warfare.* New York: Doubleday & Company, Inc.

———. *Eleanor Roosecelt. 1884-1933.* Volume One. New York, Viking.

———, ed. 1978. *Crystal Eastman on Women and Revolution.* New York: Oxford University Press

Cook, Blanche Wiesen, Charles Chatfield, and Sandi Cooper, eds. 1971. *The Garland Library of War and Peace: A Collection of 360 Titles.* New York: Garland Publishing, Inc.

Cook, Fred J. 1971. *The Nightmare Decade.* New York: Random House.

Cooper, Sandi. 1991. *Patriotic Pacifism: Waging War on War in Europe 1815-1914.* New York: Oxford University Press.

Coss, Clare. 1989. *Lillian Wald: Progressive Activist.* New York: Feminist Press

Cott, Nancy. 1977. *The Bonds of Womanhood.* New Haven: Yale University Press.

———. 1987. *The Grounding of Modern Feminism.* New Haven: Yale University Press.

Craypol, Edward P., ed. 1987. *Women and American Foreign Policy: Lobbyists, Critics, and Insiders.* New York: Greenwood Press.

Curti, Merle. 1936. *Peace or War: The American Struggle, 1636–1936.* New York: W. W. Norton and Company.

———. 1946. *The Roots of American Loyalty.* New York: Russell and Russell.

Davis, Allen F. 1973. *American Heroine: The Life and Legend of Jane Addams.* New York: Oxford University Press.

Dean, Arthur H. 1966. *Test Ban and Disarmament: The Path of Negotiation.* New York: Harper and Row.

DeBenedetti, Charles. 1980. *The Peace Reform in American History.* Bloomington: Indiana University Press.

Degen, Marie Louise. 1972. *The History of the Women's Peace Party.* New York: Garland Publishing.

Dellinger, Dave. 1975. *More Power Than We Know: The People's Movement toward Democracy.* Garden City, N.Y.: Doubleday.

Deming, Barbara. 1971. *Revolution and Equilibrium.* New York: Grossman Publishers.

Detzer, Dorothy. 1948. *Appointment on the Hill.* New York: Henry Holt and Company.

Dickstein, Morris. 1977. *Gates of Eden: American Culture in the Sixties.* New York: Basic Books.

Dinnerstein, Dorothy. 1976. *The Mermaid and the Minotaur: Sexual Arrangements and Human Malaise.* New York: Harper Colophon Books.

Divine, Robert A. 1978. *Blowing on the Wind: The Nuclear Test Ban Debate, 1954–1960.* New York: Oxford University Press.

Donner, Frank J. 1973. *The Un-Americans.* New York: Ballantine Books.

———. 1980. *The Age of Surveillance: The Aims and Methods of America's Political Intelligence System.* New York: Knopf.

Eagan, Eileen. 1981. *Class, Culture, and the Classroom: The Student Peace Movement of the 1930s.* Philadelphia: Temple University Press.

Earhart, Mary. 1944. *Frances Willard: From Prayers to Politics.* Chicago: University of Chicago Press.

Echols, Alice. 1989. *Daring to Be Bad: Radical Feminism in America, 1967–1975.* Minneapolis: University of Minnesota Press.

Elshtain, Jean Bethke. 1987. *Women and War.* New York: Basic Books.

Elshtain, Jean Bethke, and Tobias, Sheila. 1990. *Women, Militarism, and War: Essays in History, Politics, and Social Theory.* Totowa, N.J.: Rowman and Littlefield.

Enloe, Cynthia. 1983. *Does Khaki Become You? The Militarization of Women's Lives.* Boston: South End Press.

Epstein, Barbara Leslie. 1981. *The Politics of Domesticity.* Middletown, Conn.: Wesleyan University Press.

Etzioni, Amatai. 1962. *The Hard Way to Peace: A New Strategy.* New York: Collier Press.

Evans, Sara. 1979. *Personal Politics: The Roots of Women's Liberation in the Civil Rights Movement and the New Left.* New York: Knopf.

Feminism and Nonviolence Study Group. 1983. *Piecing It Together: Feminism and Nonviolence.* London: Calverts Press.

Ferber, Michael, and Lynd, Staughton. 1971. *The Resistance.* Boston: Beacon Press.

Ferrell, Robert H. 1952. *Peace in Their Time: The Origins of the Kellogg-Briand Pact.* New Haven: Yale University Press.

Fiedler, Leslie A. 1948. *An End to Innocence: Essays on Culture and Politics.* Boston: Beacon Press.

Finn, James. 1967. *Protest: Pacifism and Politics.* New York: Random House.

Fleming, D. F. 1961. *The Cold War and Its Origins, 1917–1960.* Garden City, N.Y.: Doubleday.

Flexner, Eleanor. 1959. *Century of Struggle.* Cambridge, Mass.: Harvard University Press.

Florence, Barbara Moench, ed. 1978. *Lella Secor: A Diary in Letters, 1915–1922.* New York: Burt Franklin and Company.

Foster, Catherine. 1989. *Women for All Seasons: The Story of the Women's International League for Peace and Freedom.* Athens: University of Georgia Press.

Frank, Lawrence K., and Frank, Mary. 1954. *How to Be a Woman.* New York: Bobbs-Merrill Company.

Freeland, Richard M. 1972. *The Truman Doctrine and the Origins of McCarthyism.* New York: Knopf.

Freeman, Jo. 1975. *The Politics of Women's Liberation.* New York: David McKay Company.

Friedan, Betty. 1963. *The Feminine Mystique.* New York: Dell Publishing Company.

Fussell, Paul. 1975. *The Great War and Modern Memory.* New York: Oxford University Press.

Gaddis, John Lewis. 1972. *The United States and the Origins of the Cold War.* New York: Columbia University Press.

Gardner, Lloyd C. 1970. *Architects of Illusion.* Chicago: Quadrangle Books.

Gilligan, Carol. 1982. *In a Different Voice: Psychological Theory and Women's Development.* Cambridge, Mass: Harvard University Press.

Gilman, Charlotte Perkins. 1923. *His Religion and Hers: A Study of the Faith of Our Fathers and the Work of Our Mothers.* New York: Century Company.

Gioseffi, Daniela, ed. 1988. *Women on War: Essential Voices for the Nuclear Age.* New York: Simon and Schuster.

Gitlin, Todd. 1980. *The Whole World Is Watching: Mass Media in the Making and the Unmaking of the New Left.* Berkeley: University of California Press.

———. 1987. *The Sixties: Years of Hope, Days of Rage.* New York: Bantam Books.

Goldman, Eric F. 1950. *The Crucial Decade and After: America, 1945–1965.* New York: Vintage Books.

Goodman, Walter. 1964. *The Committee: The Extraordinary Career of the House Committee on Un-American Activities.* New York: Farrar, Strauss, and Giroux.

Greenwald, Maurine Weiner. 1980. *Women, War, and Work: The Impact of World War I on Women Workers in the U.S.* Westport, Conn.: Greenwood Press.

Griffith, Robert, and Theoharis, Athan, eds. 1974. *The Spector: Original Essays on the Cold War and the Origins of McCarthyism.* New York: New Viewpoints.

Gusfield, Joseph R. 1970. *Protest, Reform, and Revolt.* New York: John Wiley and Sons.

Hallowes, Frances S. 1914. *Women and War: An Appeal to the Women of All Nations.* London: Headley Brothers.

Halsted, Fred. 1978. *Out Now! A Participant's Account of the American Movement against the Vietnam War.* New York: Monad Press.

Harris, Adrienne, and King, Ynestra, eds. 1989. *Rocking the Ship of State*. Boulder, Colo.: Westview Press.

Harris, Ted Carlton. 1982. *Jeannette Rankin: Suffragist, First Woman Elected to Congress, and Pacifist*. New York: Arno Press.

Hartmann, Susan M. 1982. *The Home Front and Beyond: American Women in the 1940s*. Boston: Twayne Publishers.

Hawkes, Jacquetta. 1962. *Women Ask Why: An Intelligent Woman's Guide to Nuclear Disarmament*. London: Campaign for Nuclear Disarmament.

Hellman, Lillian. 1976. *Scoundrel Time*. Boston: Little, Brown and Company.

Herman, Sondra. 1969. *Eleven against War*. Stanford, Calif.: Hoover Institution Press.

Hersh, Blanche Glassman. 1978. *The Slavery of Sex*. Urbana: University of Illinois Press.

Herzog, Arthur. 1963. *The War Peace Establishment*. New York: Harper and Row.

Higgonet, Margaret Randolph, et al., eds. 1987. *Behind the Lines: Gender and the Two World Wars*. New Haven: Yale University Press.

Hodgson, Godfrey. 1976. *America in Our Time*. New York: Vintage Books.

Hole, Judith, and Levin, Ellen. 1971. *Rebirth of Feminism*. New York: Quadrangle Books.

Honey, Maureen. 1984. *Creating Rosie the Riveter: Class, Gender, and Propaganda during World War II*. Amherst: University of Massachusetts Press.

Howe, Julia Ward. 1899. *Reminiscences, 1819–1899*. Boston: Houghton Mifflin and Company.

Hutchins, Grace. 1932. *Women and War*. New York: Central Committee of the Communist Party.

Hutson, Susan Hoffman. 1978. *McCarthy and the Anti-Communist Crusade: A Selected Bibliography*. Political Issues Series, vol. 5, no. 2. Los Angeles: Center for the Study of Armament and Disarmament.

Innes, Kathleen E. 1934. *Women and War*. London: Friends Peace Committee.

Isserman, Maurice. 1982. *Which Side Were You On? The American Communist Party during the Second World War*. Middletown, Conn.: Wesleyan University Press.

———. 1987. *If I Had a Hammer: The Death of the Old Left and the Birth of the New Left*. New York: Basic Books.

Jacobs, Paul, and Landau, Saul. 1966. *The New Radicals: A Report with Documents*. New York: Random House.

Jacobson, Harold Karan, and Stein, Eric. 1966. *Diplomats, Scientists, and Politicians: The United States and the Nuclear Test Ban Negotiations*. Ann Arbor: University of Michigan Press.

James, Edward T., ed. 1971. *Notable American Women*. Cambridge, Mass.: Harvard University Press.

Jones, Lynne, ed. 1983. *Keeping the Peace*. London: Women's Press.

Kahn, Herman. 1960. *On Thermonuclear War*. Princeton, N.J.: Princeton University Press.

Kaledin, Eugenia. 1984. *Mothers and More: American Women in the 1950s*. Boston: Twayne Publishers.

Kennan, George F. 1957. *Russia, the Atom, and the West*. New York: Harper and Brothers.

Kenniston, Kenneth. 1971. *Youth and Dissent: The Rise of the New Opposition*. New York: Harcourt Brace Jovanovich.

Key, Ellen. 1916. *War, Peace, and the Future*. New York: G. P. Putnam and Sons.

Kissinger, Henry A. 1960. *The Necessity of Choice: Prospects of American Foreign Policy*. New York: Harper and Brothers.

Kolko, Gabriel. 1962. *Wealth and Power in America: An Analysis of Social Class and Income Distribution*. New York: Praeger Publishers.

Ladd, William [Philanthropos]. 1836. *On the Duty of Females to Promote the Cause of Peace*. Boston: American Peace Society.

LaFeber, Walter. 1969. *America, Russia, and the Cold War*. New York: John Wiley and Sons.

Lait, Jack, and Mortimer, Lee. 1952. *USA: Confidential*. New York: Crown Publishers.

Lasch, Christopher. 1962. *The American Liberals and the Russian Revolution*. New York: McGraw-Hill Book Company.

————. 1966. *The Agony of the American Left*. New York: Vintage Books.

Lauter, Paul, and Howe, Florence. 1970. *The Conspiracy of the Young*. New York: World Publishing Company.

Lens, Sidney. 1982. *Radicalism in America*. Cambridge, Mass.: Schenkman Publishing Company.

Lerna, Gerda. 1993. *The Creation of Feminist Consciousness From the Middle Ages to 1870*. New York: Oxford University Press.

Levy, Gunter. 1988. *Peace and Revolution: The Moral Crisis of American Pacifism*. Grand Rapids, Mich.: William B. Erdman Publishing Company.

Lipset, Seymour Martin. 1960. *The Political Man*. Garden City, N.Y.: Doubleday and Company.

Lipset, Seymour Martin, and Raab, Earl. 1970. *The Politics of Unreason*. Chicago: University of Chicago Press.

Lomos, Charles W., and Taylor, Michael, eds. 1971. *The Rhetoric of the British Peace Movement*. New York: Random House.

Lundberg, Ferdinand, and Farnham, Marynia. 1945. *Modern Woman: The Lost Sex*. New York: Duel, Sloan, and Pearce.

Lynd, Alice. 1968. *We Won't Go: Personal Accounts of War Objectors*. Boston: Beacon Press.

Lynd, Staughton. 1973. *Nonviolence in America: A Documentary History*. New York: Bobbs-Merrill Company.

Lyttle, Bradford. N.d. *You Come with Naked Hands: The Story of the San Francisco to Moscow Walk for Peace*. Raymond, N.H.: Greenleaf Books.

MacDonald, Dwight. 1957. *Memoirs of a Revolutionist*. New York: Farrar, Strauss, and Cudahy.

McGuigon, Dorothy, ed. 1977. *The Role of Women in Conflict and Peace*. Ann Arbor: University of Michigan Center for Continuing Education.

McGuliffe, Mary Sperling. 1978. *Crisis on the Left: Cold War: Politics and American Liberals, 1947–1954*. Amherst: University of Massachusetts Press.

McLean, Scilla, et al. 1980. *The Role of Women in Peace Movements, in the Development of Peace Research, and in the Promotion of Friendly Relations between Nations*. New York: UNESCO.

Mailer, Norman. 1959. *Advertisements for Myself*. New York: G. P. Putnam's Sons.

———. 1968. *The Armies of the Night*. New York: New American Library.

Mandelbaum, Michael. 1981. *The Nuclear Revolution*. Cambridge: Cambridge University Press.

Marchand, C. Roland. 1972. *The American Peace Movement and Social Reform, 1898–1918*. Princeton, N.J.: Princeton University Press.

Markowitz, Norman D. 1973. *The Rise and Fall of the People's Century: Henry A. Wallace and American Liberalism, 1941–1948*. New York: Free Press.

May, Elaine Tyler. 1988. *Homeward Bound: American Families in the Cold War Era*. New York: Basic Books.

Mead, Lucia Ames. 1909. *A Primer of the Peace Movement*. London: International Peace Association.

Melder, Keith E. 1977. *Beginnings of Sisterhood*. New York: Schocken Books.

Menashe, Louis, and Radosh, Ronald. 1965. *Teach-Ins: USA*. New York: Frederich A. Praeger.

Millard, Betty. 1952. *Women on Guard: How the Women of the World Fight for Peace*. New York: New Century Publishers.

Miller, Douglas T., and Nowak, Marion. 1977. *The Fifties: The Way We Really Were*. Garden City, N.Y.: Doubleday and Company.

Millis, Walter, and Real, James. 1963. *The Abolition of War*. New York: Macmillan.

Mills, C. Wright. 1958. *The Causes of World War III*. New York: Ballantine Books.

Montagu, Ashley. 1953. *The Natural Superiority of Woman*. New York: Macmillan.

Moritzan, Julius. 1912. *The Peace Movement in America*. New York: G. P. Putnam's Sons.

Mumford, Lewis. 1954. *In the Name of Sanity*. New York: Harcourt, Brace, and Company.

Nathan, Otto, and Norden, Heinz. 1960. *Einstein on Peace*. New York: Simon and Schuster.

Navasky, Victor S. 1980. *Naming Names*. New York: Viking Press.

Newfield, Jack. 1966. *A Prophetic Minority*. New York: New American Library.

Novich, Sheldon. 1969. *The Careless Atom*. Boston: Houghton Mifflin Company.

O'Neill, William L. 1969. *Everyone Was Brave*. Chicago: Quadrangle Books.

———. 1971. *Coming Apart: An Informal History of America in the 1960s*. Chicago: Quadrangle Books.

———. 1982. *A Better World: The Great Schism, Stalinism, and American Intellectuals*. New York: Simon and Schuster.

Packard, Vance. 1959. *The Status Seekers*. New York: David McKay Company.

Paper, Lewis J. 1975. *The Promise and the Performance: The Leadership of John F. Kennedy*. New York: Crown Publishers.

Parkin, Frank. 1968. *Middle Class Radicalism: The Social Bases of the British Campaign for Nuclear Disarmament*. Manchester, England: Manchester University Press.

Pauling, Linus. 1958. *No More War!* New York: Dodd, Mead, and Company.

Pethick Lawrence, Emmeline. 1938. *My Part in a Changing World*. Reprint. New York: Hyperion, 1979.

Proceedings of Peace Meeting Held at Union League Hall, New York, December 23, 1870, Women's Peace Congress. 1871. Philadelphia: John Gillam and Company.

Randall, Mercedes. 1964. *Improper Bostonian*. New York: Twayne Publishers.

———. 1972. *Beyond Nationalism: Social Thought of Emily Greene Balch*. New York: Twayne Publishers.

Reardon, Betty A. 1985. *Sexism and the War System*. New York: Teacher's College, Columbia University.

Reich, Charles A. 1969. *The Greening of America*. New York: Random House.

Rich, Adrienne. 1976. *Of Woman Born: Motherhood as Experience and Institution*. New York: W. W. Norton and Company.

Richards, Laura E., and Howe, Maude Elliott. 1925. *Julia Ward Howe*. Boston: Houghton Mifflin Company.

Robinson, John P., et al. 1968. *Measures of Political Attitudes*. Ann Arbor, Mich.: Institute for Social Research.

Rogin, Michael Paul. 1967. *The Intellectuals and McCarthy: The Radical Spector*. Cambridge, Mass.: MIT Press.

Roszak, Theodore. 1969. *The Making of a Counter-culture*. Garden City, N.Y.: Doubleday and Company.

Ruddick, Sara. 1989. *Maternal Thinking: Toward a Politics of Peace*. Boston: Beacon Press.

Rupp, Leila J. 1978. *Mobilizing Women for War: German and American Propaganda, 1939–1945*. Princeton, N.J.: Princeton University Press.

Rupp, Leila J., and Taylor, Verta. 1987. *Survival in the Doldrums: The American Woman's Rights Movement, 1945 to the 1960s*. New York: Oxford University Press.

Scharf, Lois, and Jensen, Joan, eds. 1983. *Decades of Discontent: The Women's Movement, 1920–1940*. Boston: Northeastern University Press.

Schlesinger, Arthur M., Jr. 1965. *A Thousand Days: John F. Kennedy in the White House*. Boston: Houghton Mifflin Company.

Schmidt, Karl. 1960. *Henry Wallace: Quixotic Crusade*. Syracuse, N.Y.: Syracuse University Press.

Shingo Shibata, Phoenix. 1976. *Letters and Documents of Alice Herz: The Thought and Practice of a Modern-Day Martyr*. Amsterdam: B. R. Gruner.

Siegel, Frederick F. 1984. *Troubled Journey: From Pearl Harbor to Ronald Reagan*. New York: Hill and Wang.

Small, Melvin, and Hoover, William D., eds. 1992. *Give Peace a Chance*. Syracuse, N.Y.: Syracuse University Press.

Smelser, Neil. 1962. *Theory of Collective Behavior*. New York: Free Press.

Spock, Benjamin. 1945. *The Common Sense Book of Baby and Child Care*. New York: Duel, Sloan, and Pearce.

Starobin, Joseph R. 1972. *American Communism in Crisis, 1943–1957*. Cambridge, Mass.: Harvard University Press.

Stevenson, Adlai. 1953. *Major Campaign Speeches, 1952*. New York: Random House.

Stone, I. F. 1963. *The Haunted Fifties*. New York: Random House.

Stouffer, Samuel A. 1955. *Communism Conformity and Civil Liberties*. Garden City, N.Y.: Doubleday and Company.

Swados, Harvey. 1962. *A Radical's America*. New York: Little, Brown and Company.

Swerdlow, Amy, and Lessinger, Hanna, eds. 1983. *Class, Race, and Sex: The Dynamics of Control.* Boston: G. K. Hall.

Taylor, Telford. 1955. *Grand Inquest: The Story of Congressional Investigations.* New York: Simon and Schuster.

Teodori, Massimo. 1969. *The New Left: A Documentary History.* New York: Bobbs-Merrill Company.

Thaddeus, Janice, ed. 1980. *The Personal Record of a Life: Lenore Marshall.* New York: Horizon Press.

Theoharis, Athan. 1971. *Seeds of Repression: Harry S. Truman and the Origins of McCarthyism.* Chicago: Quadrangle Books.

Thompson, Dorothy, ed. 1983. *Over Our Dead Bodies: Women against the Bomb.* London: Virago Press.

Tischler, Barbara L., ed. 1992. *Sights on the Sixties.* New Brunswick, N.J.: Rutgers University Press.

Tobias, Sheila, et al. 1982. *What Kinds of Guns Are They Buying for Your Butter?* New York: William Morrow and Company.

Trebilcot, Joyce. 1984. *Mothering: Essays in Feminist Theory.* Totowa, N.J.: Rowman and Allanheld.

Trials of the Resistance. 1970. Introduction by Murray Kempton. New York: New York Review.

Tuchman, Gaye; Daniels, Arlene Kaplan; and Benet, James; eds. 1978. *Hearth and Home: Images of Women in the Mass Media.* New York: Oxford University Press.

Van Voris, Jacqueline. 1987. *Carrie Chapman Catt: A Public Life.* New York: Feminist Press at the City University of New York.

Vickers, George R. 1975. *The Formation of the New Left: Early Years.* Lexington, Mass.: D. C. Heath and Company.

Villard, Fanny Garrison. 1924. *William Lloyd Garrison on Non-resistance.* New York: National Press Printing Company.

Von Suttner, Bertha. 1894. *Lay Down Your Arms.* Reprint. New York: Garland, 1972.

————. 1910. *Memoirs of Bertha Von Suttner.* Reprint. New York: Garland, 1972.

Waggaman, Mary. 1947. *Women Workers in Wartime and Reconversion.* New York: Paulist Press.

Waskow, Arthur I. 1965. *The Worried Man's Guide to World Peace: A Peace Research Handbook.* New York: Anchor Books.

Weber, David R., ed. 1978. *Civil Disobedience in America.* Ithaca, N.Y.: Cornell University Press.

Whyte, William H., Jr. 1957. *The Organization Man.* New York: Simon and Schuster.

Williams, William Appleman. 1972. *The Tragedy of American Diplomacy.* New York: Delta/Dell Publishing.

Wilson, Elizabeth. 1980. *Only Halfway to Paradise: Women in Postwar Britain, 1945–1968.* London: Tavistock Publications.

Wilson, John. 1973. *Introduction to Social Movements.* New York: Basic Books.

Wittner, Lawrence S. 1970. *Rebels against War: The American Peace Movement, 1941–1960.* New York: Columbia University Press.

———. 1974. *Cold War America: From Hiroshima to Watergate.* New York: Praeger Publishers.

Women's International Democratic Federation. 1952. *For Their Rights as Mothers, Workers, Citizens.* Berlin: Women's International Democratic Federation.

Women Strike for Peace. 1962. *The Story of Disarmament, 1945–1962.* Washington, D.C.: Women Strike for Peace.

———. 1963. *So Many Great Things Have Been Said.* Washington, D.C.: Women Strike for Peace.

———. 1979. *Journal of Women Strike for Peace Commemorating Eighteen Years of Conscientious Concern for the Future of the World's Children.* Philadelphia, Pa.: Women Strike for Peace.

Woolf, Virginia. 1966. *Three Guineas.* New York: Harcourt Brace Jovanovich.

Yergin, Daniel. 1977. *Shattered Peace: The Origins of the Cold War and the National Security State.* Boston: Houghton Mifflin Company.

Zaroulis, Nancy, and Sullivan, Gerald. 1984. *Who Spoke Up? American Protest against the War in Vietnam, 1963–1975.* Garden City, N.Y.: Doubleday and Company.

Articles

Abrams, Irwin. 1962. Bertha Von Suttner and the Nobel Peace Prize. *Journal of Central European Affairs* 22, no. 3: 286–307.

Adams, Nina. 1992. The Women They Left Behind. In *Give Peace a Chance,* ed. Melvin Small and William D. Hoover, 182–95. Syracuse, N.Y.: University of Syracuse Press.

Addams, Jane. 1915. Women, War, and Babies. *Harper's Weekly,* 31 July, 101.

As, Berit. 1982. A Materialistic View of Men's and Women's Attitudes toward War. *Women's Studies International Forum* 5:355–64.

Beard, Mary. 1947. Women's Role in Society. *Annals of the American Academy of Political and Social Science* 251:1–9.

Beechey, Veronica. 1979. On Patriarchy. *Feminist Review* 3:66–82.

Bernstein, Barton J. 1974. Review Essay: Henry A. Wallace and the Agony of American Liberalism: A Political Pariah in the Cold War. *Peace and Change* 2 (Fall): 62–66.

Birmingham Feminist History Group. 1979. Feminism as Femininity in the Nineteen-Fifties? *Feminist Review* 3:48–65.

Boekel, Florence Brewer. 1929. Women in International Affairs. *Annals of American Academy of Political and Social Science* (May): 230–48.

Boyer, Paul. 1984. From Activism to Apathy: The American People and Nuclear Weapons, 1963–1980. *Journal of American History* 70 (March): 821–44.

Cagan, Leslie. 1980. Women and the Anti-draft Movement. *Radical America* 14 (September–October): 9–11.

Cagan, Leslie, et al. 1982. Peace at Any Price? Feminism, Anti-imperialism, and the Disarmament Movement. *Radical America* 16 (January–April): 45–56.

Cantor, Milton. 1968. The Radical Confrontation with Foreign Policy: War and Revolution, 1914–1920. In *Dissent,* ed. Alfred Young. DeKalb: Northern Illinois University Press.

Chamberlain, Mary. 1915. The Women at the Hague. *Survey,* 5 June, 219–22, 236.

Chomsky, Noam; Lauter, Paul; and Howe, Florence. 1968. Reflections on a Political Trial. *New York Review of Books,* 22 August, 23–30.

Cohn, Carol. 1989. Emasculating America's Linguistic Deterrent. In *Rocking the Ship of State,* ed. Adrienne Harris and Ynestra King. Boulder, Colo.: Westview Press.

Conway, Jill. 1971–72. Women Reformers and American Culture, 1870–1930. *Journal of Social History* 5 (Winter): 164–77.

Cook, Blanche Wiesen. 1972. The Woman's Peace Party: Collaboration and Non-cooperation in World War I. *Peace and Change* 1 (Fall): 36–42.

———. 1977. Female Support Networks and Political Activism: Lillian Wald, Crystal Eastman, and Emma Goldman. *Chrysalis,* Autumn 1977. Reprinted in Linda Kerber and Jane De Hart, eds., *Women's America: Refocusing the Past,* 306–325. New York: Oxford University Press, 1991.

Cook, Coralie Franklin. 1915. Votes for Mothers. In Votes for Women: A Symposium by Leading Thinkers of Colored America. *Crisis,* 10 August, 184–85.

Costin, Lela B. 1982. Feminism, Pacifism, Internationalism, and the 1915 International Congress of Women. *Women's Studies International Forum* 5:301–15.

Craig, John M. 1987. Redbaiting, Pacifism, and Free Speech: Lucia Ames Mead and Her 1926 Lecture Tour in Atlanta and the Southeast. *Georgia Historical Review* 71 (Winter): 601–22.

Decter, Midge. 1963. The Peace Ladies. *Harper's,* March, 48–53.

Demarth, N. J., III; Marwell, Gerald; and Aike, Michael T. 1971. Criteria and Contingencies of Success in a Radical Political Movement. *Journal of Social Issues* 27:63–80.

Deming, Barbara. 1961. The Ordeal of SANE. *Nation,* 11 March, 200–205.

Devere, Allen. 1934. The Peace Movement Moves Left. *Annals of the American Academy of Political and Social Science* 175 (September): 154–55.

Donner, Frank J. 1982. But Will They Come? The Campaign to Smear the Nuclear Freeze Movement. *Nation,* 6 November, 456–65.

DuBois, Ellen; Buhle, Mari Jo; Kaplan, Temma; Lerner, Gerda; and Smith-Rosenberg, Carrol. 1980. Politics and Culture in Women's History: A Symposium. *Feminist Studies* 6 (Spring): 26–64.

DuPlessix Gray, Francine. 1969. The Ultra Resistance. *New York Review of Books,* 25 September, 11–22.

Early, Frances. 1986. The Historic Roots of Women's Peace Movement in North America. *Canadian Woman Studies* (Winter): 43–48.

———. 1990. Feminism, Peace and Civil Liberties: Women's Role in the Origins of the World War I Peace Movement. *Women's Studies* 18:95–115.

Echols, Alice. 1992. "Women Power": Exploring the Relationship between the Antiwar Movement and the Women's Liberation Movement. In *Give Peace a Chance,* ed. Melvin Small and William D. Hoover, 159–70. Syracuse, N.Y.: Syracuse University Press.

Elshtain, Jean Bethke. 1980. Women, War, and Feminism. *Nation,* 14 June, 705, 722–24.

———. 1982. Women as Mirror and Other: Toward a Theory of Women, War, and Feminism. *Humanities in Society* 5 (Winter–Spring): 29–44.

———. 1983. On Beautiful Souls, Just Warriors, and Feminist Consciousness. *Women's Studies International Forum* 5:341–48.

Finch, Roy. 1959. The Liberation Poll. *Liberation* 4 (November): 14–17.

———. 1963. The New Peace Movement: Part I. *Dissent* 10 (Winter): 86–95.

———. 1963. The New Peace Movement: Part II. *Dissent* 10 (Spring): 138–48.

Flacks, Richard. 1967. The Liberated Generation: Roots of Student Protest. *Journal of Social Issues* 23:55–75.

———. 1971. The New Left and American Politics after Ten Years. *Journal of Social Issues* 27:21–34.

Gaddis, John L. 1977. Containment: A Reassessment. *Foreign Affairs* 55:873–87.

Gage-Colby, Ruth. 1963. Women Strike for Peace. *New World Review* 31 (June): 5–8.

Gallico, Paul. 1956. You Don't Know How Lucky You Are to Be Married. *Reader's Digest*, July, 134–36.

Garst, Eleanor. 1962. Women: Middle Class Masses. *Fellowship*, November, 10–12.

Gill, Gerald. 1992. From Maternal Pacifism to Revolutionary Solidarity: African-American Women's Opposition to the Vietnam War. In *Sights on the Sixties*, ed. Barbara L. Tischler, 177–96. New Brunswick, N.J.: Rutgers University Press.

Glazer, Nathan. 1961. The Peace Movement in America. *Commentary*, April, 288–96.

Gordon, Suzanne. 1983. From Earth Mother to Expert. *Nuclear Times* 1 (May): 13–16.

Graebner, William. 1980. The Unstable World of Benjamin Spock: Social Engineering in a Democratic Culture, 1917–1950. *Journal of American History* 67 (December): 612–29.

Harrington, Michael. 1955. The Post-McCarthy Atmosphere. *Dissent* 11 (Autumn): 291–94.

———. 1962. The New Peace Movement. *New Leader*, 20 August, 6–8.

Hartmann, Susan M. 1978. Prescriptions for Penelope: Literature on Women's Obligations to Returning World War II Veterans. *Women's Studies* 5:223–39.

Hartsock, Nancy. 1982. The Barracks Community in Western Political Thought: Prolegomena to a Feminist Critique of War and Politics. *Women's Studies International Forum* 5:283–86.

Hoff-Wilson, Joan. 1980. "Peace Is a Woman's Job": Jeannette Rankin and Her Lifework. *Montana: The Magazine of Western History* 30 (Spring): 38–53.

Houseman, Judy. 1982. Mothering, the Unconscious, and Feminism. *Radical America* 16 (November–December): 47–62.

Howe, Irving. 1955. America: The Country and the Myth. *Dissent* 3 (Summer): 241–44.

Jacobs, Hayes B. 1965. The Martyrdom of Alice Herz. *Fact*, July–August, 11–17.

Kazin, Michael. 1981. European Nuclear Disarmament: Interview with E. P. Thompson. *Socialist Review* 58 (July–August): 9–34.

Kelley, Joan. 1979. The Doubled Vision of Feminist Theory: A Postscript to the Women and Power Conference. *Feminist Studies* (Spring): 216–27.

Kennan, George F. 1947. The Sources of Soviet Conduct. *Foreign Affairs* 25:566–82.

King, Ynestra. 1981. May the Circle Be Unbroken: The Eco-feminist Imperative. *Tidings* (May): 1–3.

———. 1983. Feminism and the Revolt of Nature. *WIN*, February, 11–15.

Leopold, Alice K. 1958. The Family Woman's Expanding Role. *Marriage and Family Living*, August, 278–83.

Letter from East German Women. 1983. *Radical America* 17 (January–February): 37–41.

Luft, Joseph, and Wheeler, W. M. 1948. Reaction to John Hersey's *Hiroshima*. *Journal of Social Psychology* 28:135–40.

Lynd, Staughton. 1965. The New Radicals and Participatory Democracy. *Dissent* 12 (Summer): 324–33.

Mailer, Norman. 1968. The Battle of the Pentagon. *Commentary,* April, 33–57.

Martinson, Robert. 1960. A Black Eye for the Un-Americans. *Liberation* 5 (July–August): 15–17.

Mead, Margaret. 1955. The New Isolationism. *American Scholar* (Summer): 378–82.

Melosh, Barbara. 1986. "Peace in Demand": Anti-war Drama in the 1930s. *History Workshop* 22 (Autumn): 72–88.

Merding, Janey. 1979. Feminism and Pacifism: Doing It Our Way. In Feminism, Pacifism, and Reproductive Rights: A WIN Special Collection. New York: WIN.

Mills, C. Wright. 1954. The Conservative Mood. *Dissent* 1 (Winter): 22–31.

Mitzman, Arthur. 1959. Not SANE Enough. *Liberation* 4 (October): 16–18.

Muste, A. J. 1960. The Crisis in SANE. *Liberation* 5 (July–August): 10–13.

———. 1960. The Crisis in SANE: Act II. *Liberation* 5 (November): 5–8.

———. 1960. Pacifism Enters a New Phase. *Fellowship,* 1 July, 21–25, 34.

———. 1961. A Time to Weep? *Liberation* 6 (October): 5–8.

Nottingham, Elizabeth. 1947. Toward an Analysis of the Effects of Two World Wars on the Role and Status of Middle Class Women in the English-Speaking World. *American Sociological Review* 12 (December): 666–75.

O'Brien, James Putnam. 1972. Beyond Remembrance: The New Left in History. *Radical America* 6 (July–August): 12–48.

Osgood, Charles E. 1959. Suggestions for Winning the Real War with Communism. *Journal of Conflict Resolution* 3 (December): 296–324.

Our Country and Our Culture. 1952. *Partisan Review* 19 (September–October): 562–97.

Papachristou, Judith. 1990. American Women and Foreign Policy, 1898–1905: Exploring Gender in Diplomatic History. *Diplomatic History* 14:493–509.

Phillips, William. 1976. What Happened in the Fifties? *Partisan Review* 43:337.

Rainey, Carol. 1983. A History of Women in the Peace Movement. *Forum* 9, no. 4:5–6, 8.

Rose, Willie Lee. 1982. Reforming Women. *New York Review of Books,* 17 October, 45–49.

Rosi, Eugene J. 1965. Mass and Attentive Opinion on Nuclear Weapons Tests and Fallout, 1954–1963. *Public Opinion Quarterly* 29 (Summer): 280–97.

Roszak, Theodore. 1969. The Hard and the Soft: The Force of Feminism in Modern Times. In *Masculine/Feminine: Readings in Sexual Mythology and the Liberation of Women,* ed. Betty Roszak and Theodore Roszak, 87–104. New York: Harper Colophon Books.

Ruddick, Sara. 1980. Maternal Thinking. *Feminist Studies* 6 (Summer): 342–67.

———. 1984. Preservative Love and Military Destruction: Reflections on Mothering and Peace. In *Mothering: Essays in Feminist Theory,* ed. Joyce Trebilcot, 231–62. Totowa, N.J.: Rowman and Allanheld.

Ruether, Rosemary Radford. 1983. Feminism and Peace. *Christian Century,* 31 August–7 September, 771–75.

Schiffrin, André. 1968. The Student Movement in the 1950s: A Reminiscence. *Radical America* 2 (May–June): 26–41.

Schlesinger, Arthur M., Jr. 1967. Origins of the Cold War. *Foreign Affairs* 46 (October): 22–52.

Schott, Linda. 1985. The Woman's Peace Party and the Moral Basis for Women's Pacifism. *Frontiers* 3:18–24.

Schweitzer, Albert. 1957. A Declaration of Conscience. *Saturday Review,* May 18, 17–20.

Spiegelman, Robert. 1982. Media Manipulation of the Movement. *Social Policy* 13:9–16.

Stein, Robert, and Conners, Carolyn. 1962. Civil Defense Protests in New York. *New University Thought* 3 (Spring): 81–83.

Steinson, Barbara Jean. 1980. The Mother Half of Humanity: American Women in the Peace and Preparedness Movements in World War I. In *Women, War, and Revolution,* ed. Carol Berkin and Clara Lovett, 259–84. New York: Holmes and Meier Publishers.

Stoll, Louise. 1962. Women Strike for Peace. *New University Thought* 2 (Spring): 146–47.

Stone, I. F. 1970. Theatre of Delusion. *New York Review of Books,* 8 April, 15–24.

Suttner, Bertha Von. 1899. Universal Peace: From a Woman's Standpoint. *North American Review* 169 (July): 50–69.

Swerdlow, Amy. 1971. "Up from the Mud: Some Observations on Women's Liberation in North Vietnam." WIN 15, 6–10 December

———.1982. Ladies' Day at the Capitol: Women Strike for Peace Confronts HUAC. *Feminist Studies* 8 (Fall): 493–520.

———. 1992. "Not My Son, Not Your Son, Not Their Sons": Mothers against the Draft for Vietnam. In *Sights on the Sixties,* ed. Barbara L. Tischler, 163–76. New Brunswick, N.J.: Rutgers University Press; and in 1992. *Give Peace a Chance,* ed. Melvin Small and William D. Hoover, 171–81. Syracuse, N.Y.: University of Syracuse Press.

Theoharis, Athan. 1971. The Threat to Civil Liberties. In *Cold War Critics,* ed. Thomas G. Paterson, 266–98. Chicago: Quadrangle Books.

Thorne, Barrie. 1977. Gender Imagery and Issues of War and Peace: The Case of the Draft Resistance Movement of the 1960s. In *The Role of Women in Con-*

flict and Peace, ed. Dorothy McGuigon, 55–60. Ann Arbor: University of Michigan Center for Continuing Education.

Tischler, Barbara L. 1992. Voices of Protest: Women and the GI Antiwar Press. In *Sights on the Sixties*, ed. Barbara L. Tischler, 197–210. New Brunswick, N.J.: Rutgers University Press.

Trattner, Walter I. 1961. Julia Grace Wales and the Wisconsin Plan for Peace. *Wisconsin Magazine of History* 44 (Spring): 203–13.

Tuchman, Gaye. 1978. The Symbolic Annihilation of Women by the Mass Media. In *Hearth and Home: Images of Women in the Mass Media*, ed. Gaye Tuchman, Arlene Kaplan Daniels, and James Benet. New York: Oxford University Press.

Warnock, Donna. 1982. Feminism and Militarism: Can the Peace Movement Reach Out? *WIN*, 15 April, 7.

Whyte, William H., Jr. 1951. The Wives of Management. *Fortune*, October, 86–88.

Williams, William Appleman. 1967. The Cold War Revisionists. *Nation*, 13 November, 492–95.

Index